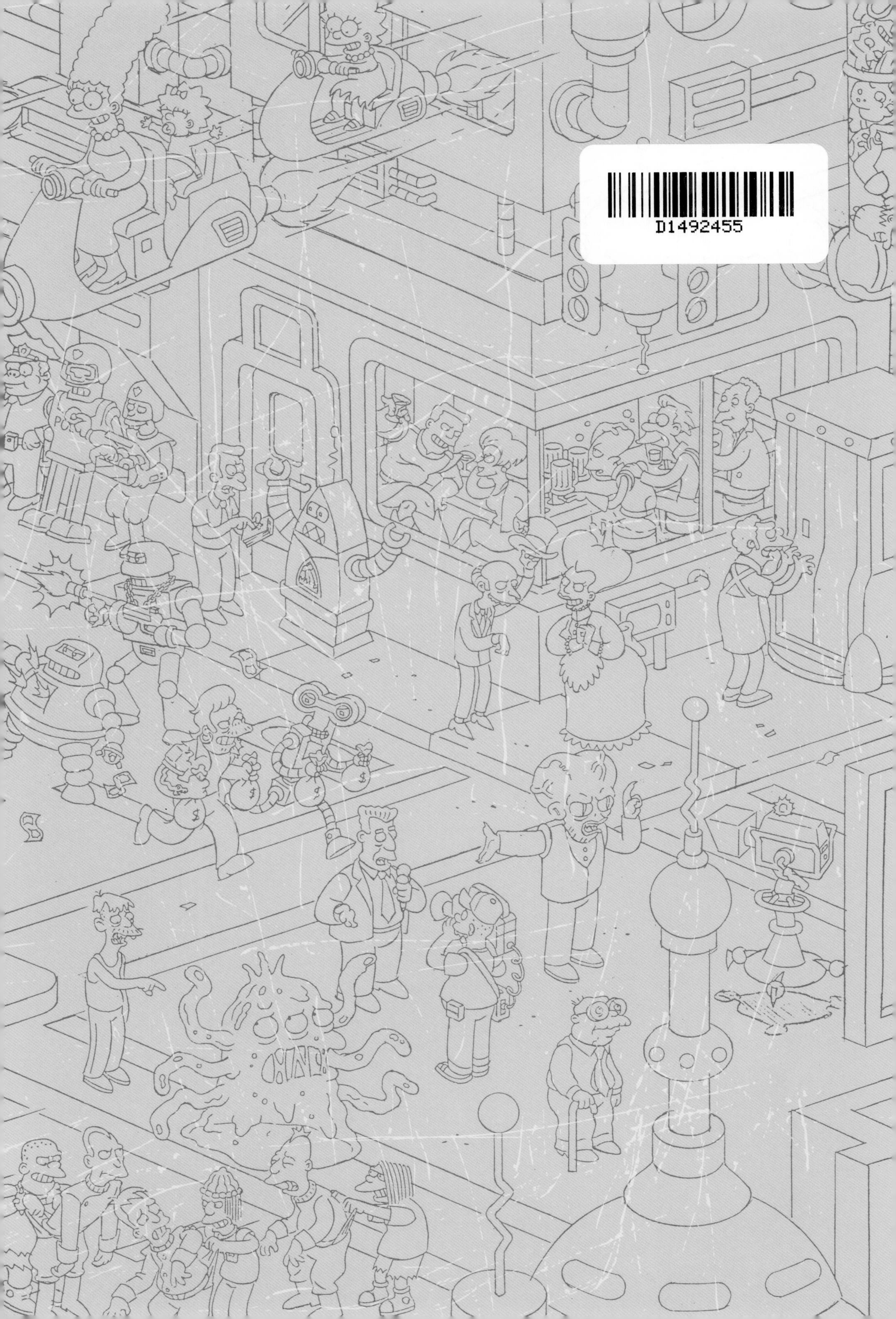

THE SIMPSONS FUTURAMA CROSSOVER CRISIS

ABRAMS COMICARTS, NEW YORK

ACKNOWLEDGMENTS

This book would not be possible without the contributions of:
Matt Groening, Susan A. Grode, Bill Morrison, Terry Delegeane, Robert Zaugh,
Nathan Kane, Serban Cristescu, Christopher Ungar, Jason Ho, Karen Bates,
Nathan Hamill, Art Villanueva, Mike Rote, Sherri Smith, Pete Benson, Mili Smythe,
Deanna MacLellan, Ursula Wendel, Vyolet N. Diaz, Ian Boothby, James Lloyd, Steve
Steere Jr., Andrew Pepoy, Rick Reese, Joey Mason, Steve Vance, Cindy Vance,
Tim Bavington, Sondra Roy, Mike Allred, Laura Allred, Sergio Aragonés, Kyle Baker,
Gene Colan, Geof Darrow, John Delaney, Evan Dorkin, Sarah Dyer, Glenn Fabry,
Ryan Brown, Peter Kuper, Tone Rodriguez, Alex Ross, Stan Sakai,
Ty Templeton, Herb Trimpe, and Bernie Wrightson.

Book Concept and Content Editor: Bill Morrison
Book Design: Serban Cristescu
Cover by: Bill Morison, Jason Ho, Steve Steere Jr.,
and Serban Cristescu

Editor: Sofia Gutiérrez
Project Manager: Charles Kochman
Design Manager: Neil Egan
Production Manager: Alison Gervais

Library of Congress Cataloging-in-Publication Data

Groening, Matt.
    The Simpsons/Futurama crossover crisis / by Matt
Groening; edited by Bill Morrison.
        p. cm.
    First published as two two-part comic book mini-series
(2002–2005), under the titles:
Futurama/Simpsons infinitely secret crossover crisis,
and, The Simpsons/Futurama crossover crisis II.
    ISBN 978-0-8109-8837-8 (Harry N. Abrams, Inc.)
    1. Graphic novels. I. Groening, Matt. II.
Futurama/Simpsons infinitely secret crossover crisis. III.
Simpsons/Futurama crossover crisis II. IV. Title.

    PN6728.S49G865 2010
    741.5'973—dc22

                2009027985

Printed and bound in China
10 9 8 7 6 5 4 3 2 1

Abrams ComicArts books are available at special
discounts when purchased in quantity for premiums and
promotions as well as fundraising or educational use.
Special editions can also be created to specification. For
details, contact specialmarkets@abramsbooks.com or the
address below.

ABRAMS
THE ART OF BOOKS SINCE 1949
115 West 18th Street
New York, NY 10011
www.abramsbooks.com

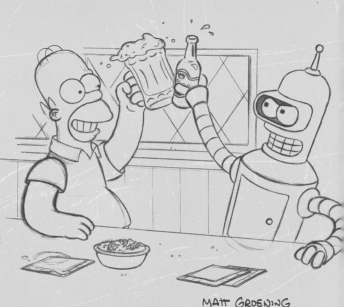

CONTENTS

WELCOME TO OUR UNIVERSES!

On one side, we give you *The Simpsons*, the garishly colored but otherwise totally realistic TV show that pokes gentle fun at our culture via the sweet, fumbling fools of Springfield. And on the other side of the time and space barrier of believability is *Futurama*, the dark matter–fueled enterprise that attempts the near-impossible mingling of science fiction and comedy in a way that might actually elicit a chuckle or two.

Pesky fans have asked if these two worlds would ever meet, and to tell you the truth, I never thought it would happen. In the *Futurama* universe, *The Simpsons* is still cranking out new episodes a thousand years from now, while in the *The Simpsons* universe I'm known only as the creator of *Futurama.* This is what mighty philosophers call a meta-fictional cosmic mind-baffler.

So how do you bring two universes together? It all started with excitable Bongo Comics creative director Bill Morrison jumping up and down over a pitch from one-man writing team Ian Boothby. Beginning with the plausible premise of Mayor Quimby in the re-election fight of his life against the Simpsons' cat, Snowball II, and reaching its climax a thousand years later in the mean (as in downright angry) streets of New New York City, this crazy epic practically wrote and drew itself. Although, to be fair, James Lloyd did provide stunning artwork, and Team Bongo did pull together this bright and shiny, slipcased, diecut edition brought to you by the fine people at Abrams ComicArts.

Just to make this book that much more splendid, art director Serban Cristescu unlocked our time vaults to bring you scads of extra art and stories that either inspired or were inspired by this multipart comic book event. We also invited our freakishly talented friends Sergio Aragonés, Alex Ross, Stan Sakai, Mike Allred, and Peter Kuper, among others, to favor us with a little *Futuro-Simps* fusion of their own.

So, as they say in Springfield, "Enjoy your book, man!" And, as they say in *Futurama,* "Enjoy your book—in pill form, man!"

Your pal,

MATT GROENING

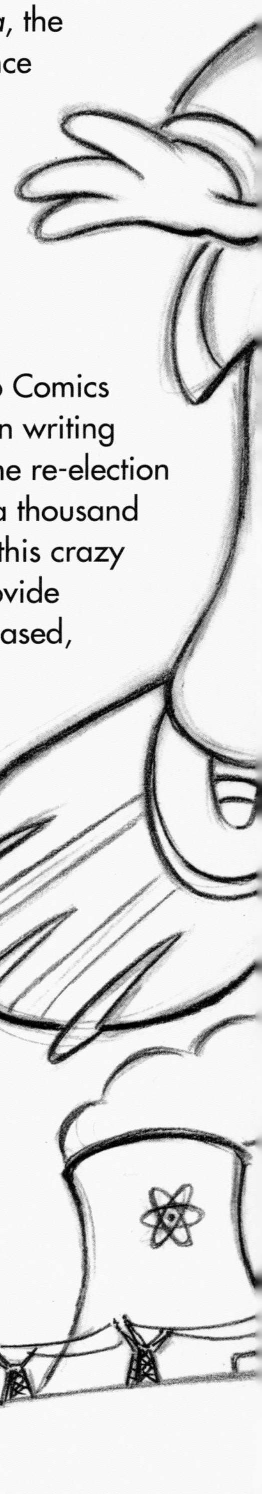

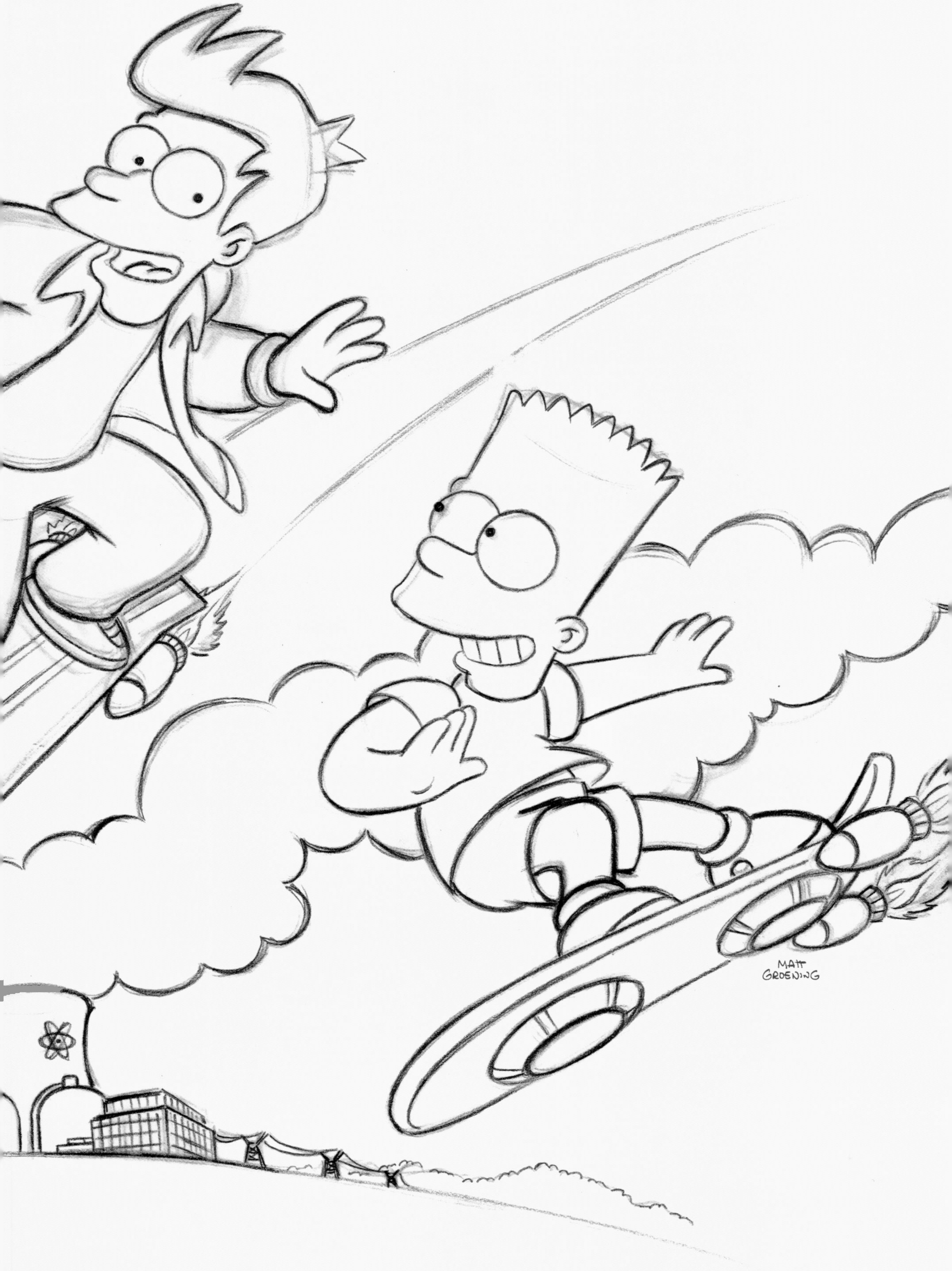
MATT
GROENING

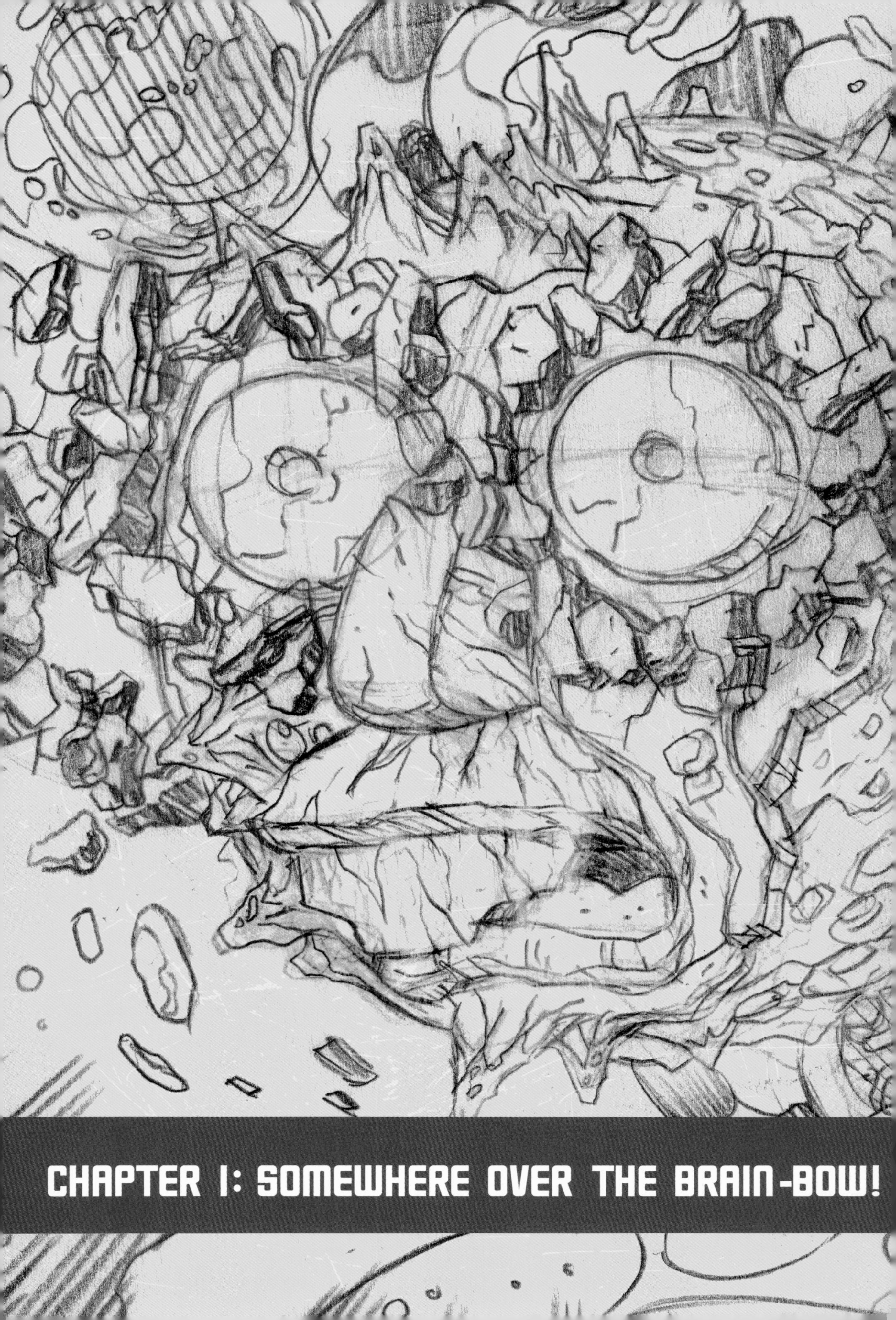

CHAPTER 1: SOMEWHERE OVER THE BRAIN-BOW!

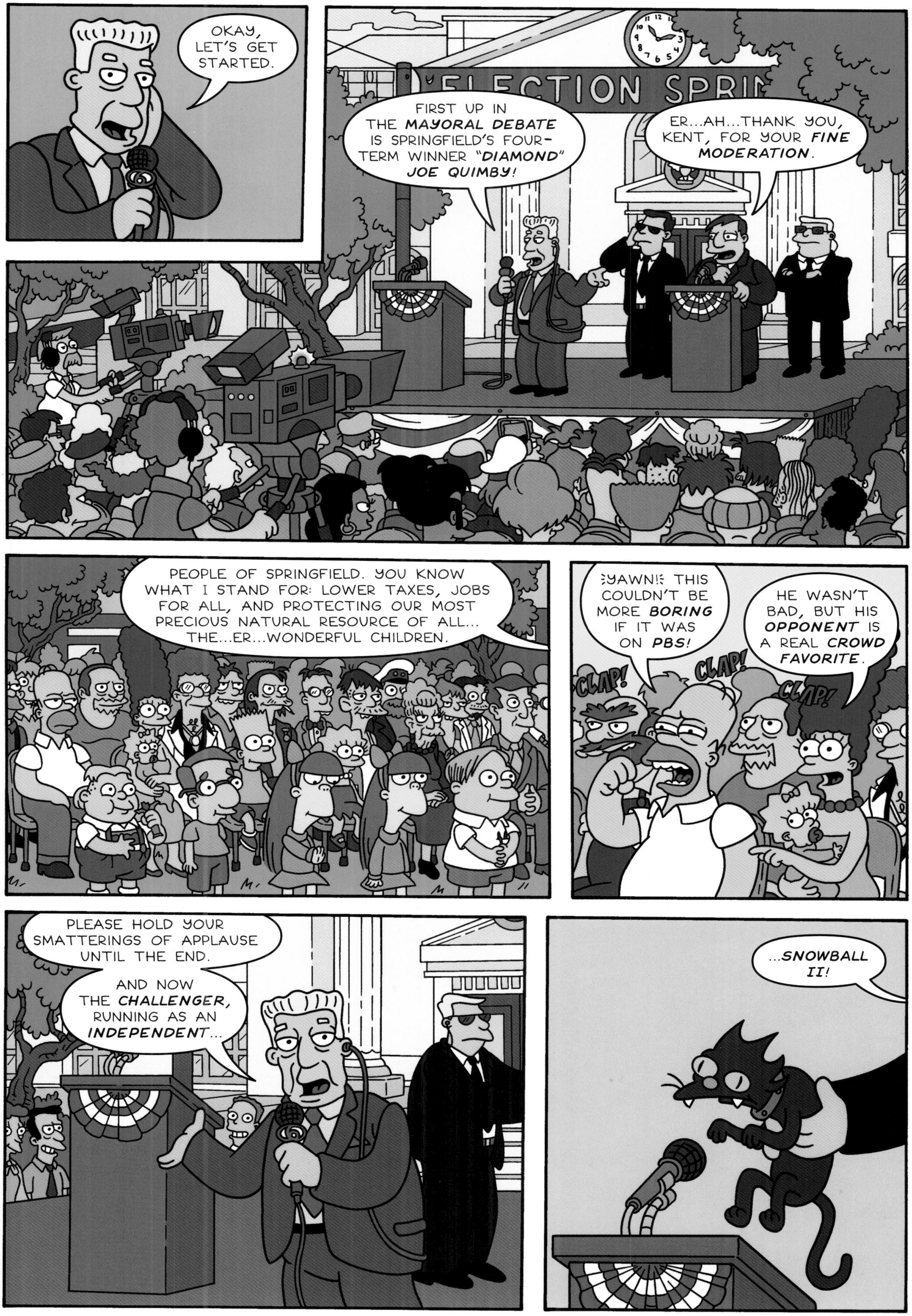
OKAY, LET'S GET STARTED.
FIRST UP IN THE *MAYORAL DEBATE* IS SPRINGFIELD'S FOUR-TERM WINNER "*DIAMOND*" *JOE QUIMBY*!
ER...AH...THANK YOU, KENT, FOR YOUR *FINE MODERATION*.
PEOPLE OF SPRINGFIELD. YOU KNOW WHAT I STAND FOR: LOWER TAXES, JOBS FOR ALL, AND PROTECTING OUR MOST PRECIOUS NATURAL RESOURCE OF ALL... THE...ER...WONDERFUL CHILDREN.
CLAP!
CLAP!
CLAP!
:YAWN!: THIS COULDN'T BE MORE *BORING* IF IT WAS ON *PBS*!
HE WASN'T BAD, BUT HIS *OPPONENT* IS A REAL *CROWD FAVORITE*.
PLEASE HOLD YOUR SMATTERINGS OF APPLAUSE UNTIL THE END.
AND NOW THE *CHALLENGER*, RUNNING AS AN *INDEPENDENT*...
...*SNOWBALL II*!

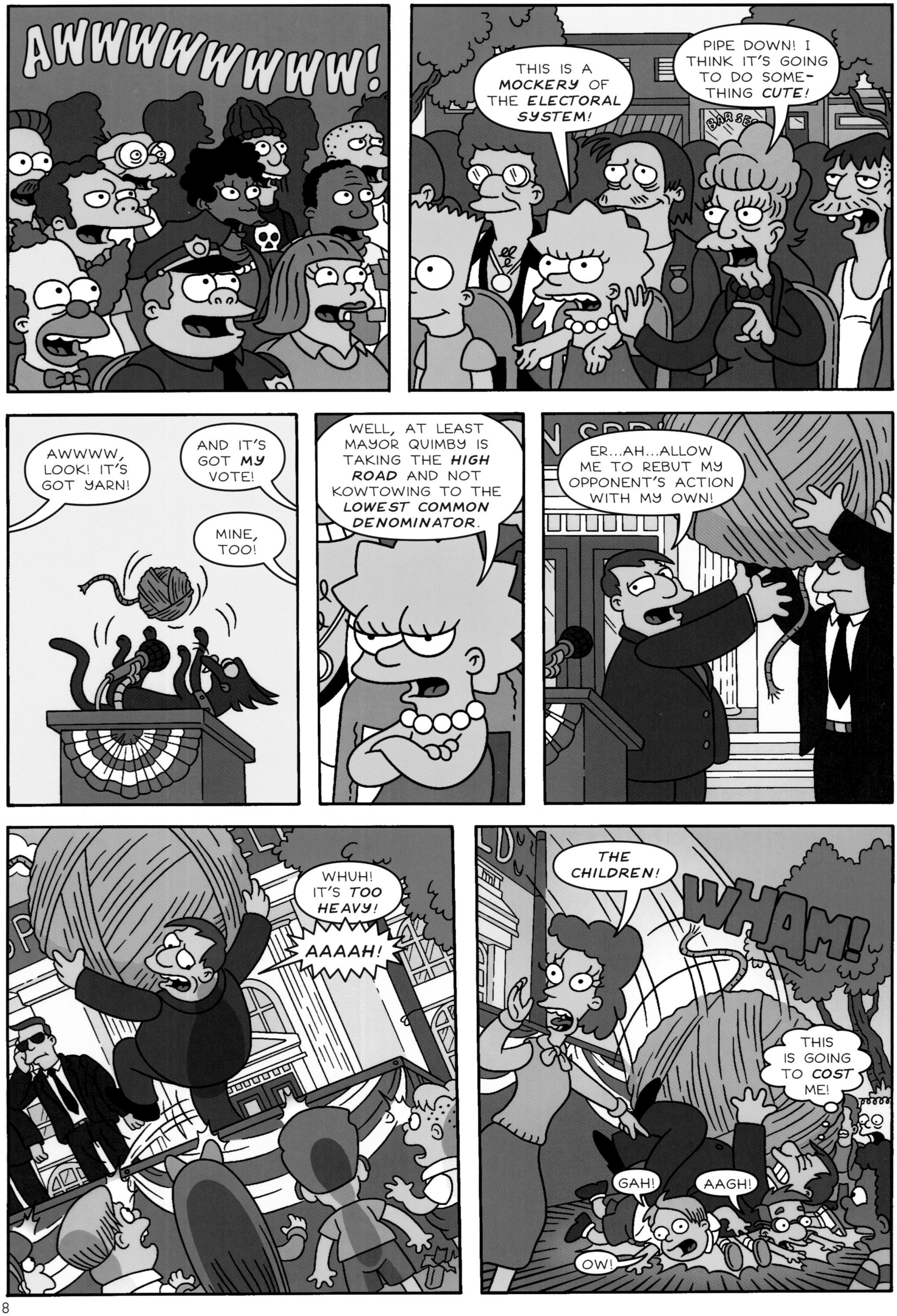
AWWWWWWWWW!
THIS IS A MOCKERY OF THE ELECTORAL SYSTEM!
PIPE DOWN! I THINK IT'S GOING TO DO SOME-THING CUTE!
AWWWW, LOOK! IT'S GOT YARN!
AND IT'S GOT MY VOTE!
MINE, TOO!
WELL, AT LEAST MAYOR QUIMBY IS TAKING THE HIGH ROAD AND NOT KOWTOWING TO THE LOWEST COMMON DENOMINATOR.
ER...AH...ALLOW ME TO REBUT MY OPPONENT'S ACTION WITH MY OWN!
WHUH! IT'S TOO HEAVY!
AAAAH!
THE CHILDREN!
WHAM!
THIS IS GOING TO COST ME!
GAH!
AAGH!
OW!

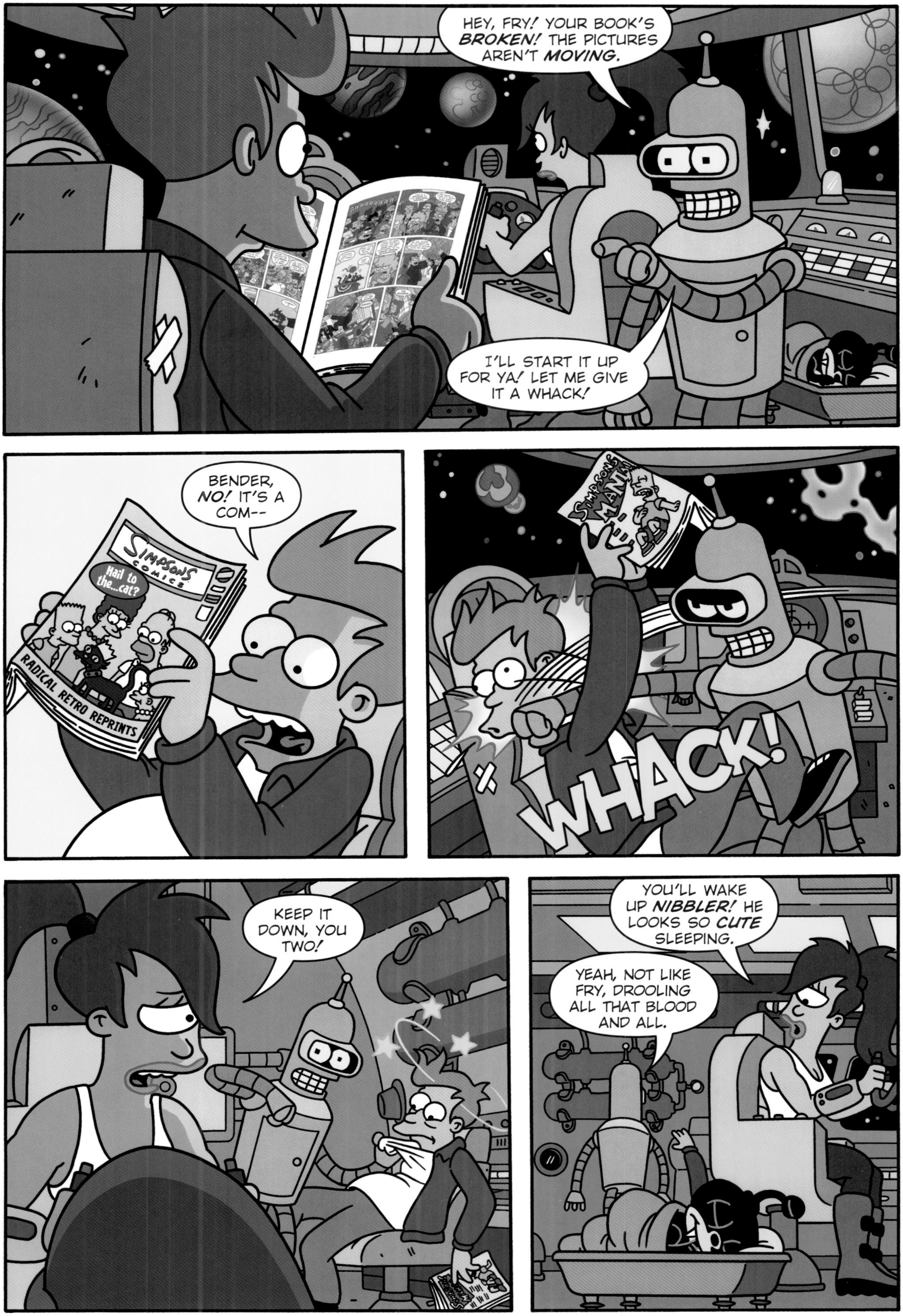
HEY, FRY! YOUR BOOK'S BROKEN! THE PICTURES AREN'T MOVING.
I'LL START IT UP FOR YA! LET ME GIVE IT A WHACK!
BENDER, NO! IT'S A COM--
SIMPSONS COMICS
Hail to the...cat?
RADICAL RETRO REPRINTS
WHACK!
KEEP IT DOWN, YOU TWO!
YOU'LL WAKE UP NIBBLER! HE LOOKS SO CUTE SLEEPING.
YEAH, NOT LIKE FRY, DROOLING ALL THAT BLOOD AND ALL.

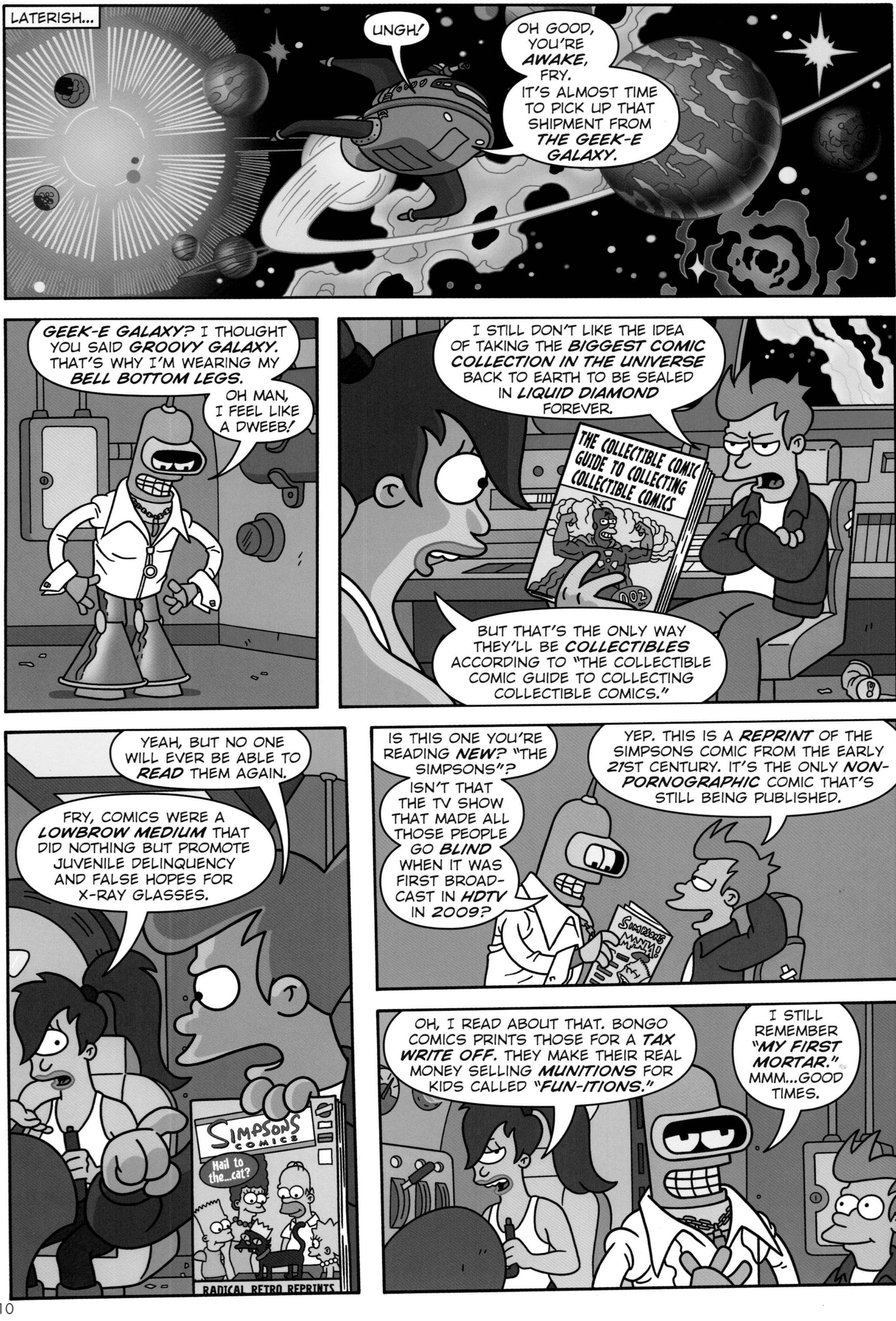

LATERISH...
UNGH!
OH GOOD, YOU'RE AWAKE, FRY. IT'S ALMOST TIME TO PICK UP THAT SHIPMENT FROM THE GEEK-E GALAXY.
GEEK-E GALAXY? I THOUGHT YOU SAID GROOVY GALAXY. THAT'S WHY I'M WEARING MY BELL BOTTOM LEGS.
OH MAN, I FEEL LIKE A DWEEB!
I STILL DON'T LIKE THE IDEA OF TAKING THE BIGGEST COMIC COLLECTION IN THE UNIVERSE BACK TO EARTH TO BE SEALED IN LIQUID DIAMOND FOREVER.
THE COLLECTIBLE COMIC GUIDE TO COLLECTING COLLECTIBLE COMICS
BUT THAT'S THE ONLY WAY THEY'LL BE COLLECTIBLES ACCORDING TO "THE COLLECTIBLE COMIC GUIDE TO COLLECTING COLLECTIBLE COMICS."
YEAH, BUT NO ONE WILL EVER BE ABLE TO READ THEM AGAIN.
FRY, COMICS WERE A LOWBROW MEDIUM THAT DID NOTHING BUT PROMOTE JUVENILE DELINQUENCY AND FALSE HOPES FOR X-RAY GLASSES.
SIMPSONS COMICS
Hail to the...cat?
RADICAL RETRO REPRINTS
IS THIS ONE YOU'RE READING NEW? "THE SIMPSONS"? ISN'T THAT THE TV SHOW THAT MADE ALL THOSE PEOPLE GO BLIND WHEN IT WAS FIRST BROADCAST IN HDTV IN 2009?
YEP. THIS IS A REPRINT OF THE SIMPSONS COMIC FROM THE EARLY 21ST CENTURY. IT'S THE ONLY NON-PORNOGRAPHIC COMIC THAT'S STILL BEING PUBLISHED.
OH, I READ ABOUT THAT. BONGO COMICS PRINTS THOSE FOR A TAX WRITE OFF. THEY MAKE THEIR REAL MONEY SELLING MUNITIONS FOR KIDS CALLED "FUN-ITIONS."
I STILL REMEMBER "MY FIRST MORTAR." MMM...GOOD TIMES.

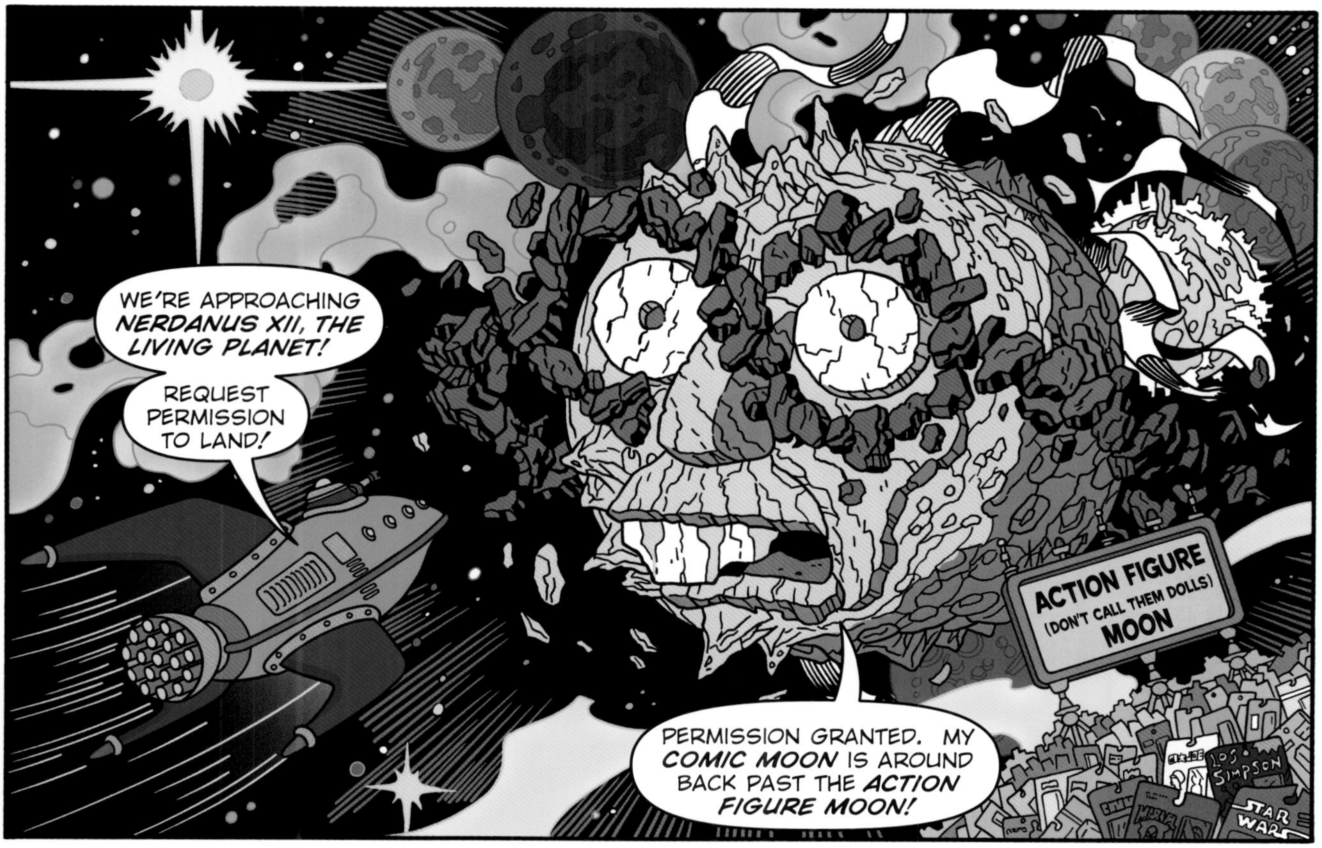
WE'RE APPROACHING NERDANUS XII, THE LIVING PLANET!
REQUEST PERMISSION TO LAND!
ACTION FIGURE (DON'T CALL THEM DOLLS) MOON
PERMISSION GRANTED. MY COMIC MOON IS AROUND BACK PAST THE ACTION FIGURE MOON!
LOS SIMPSON
STAR WARS

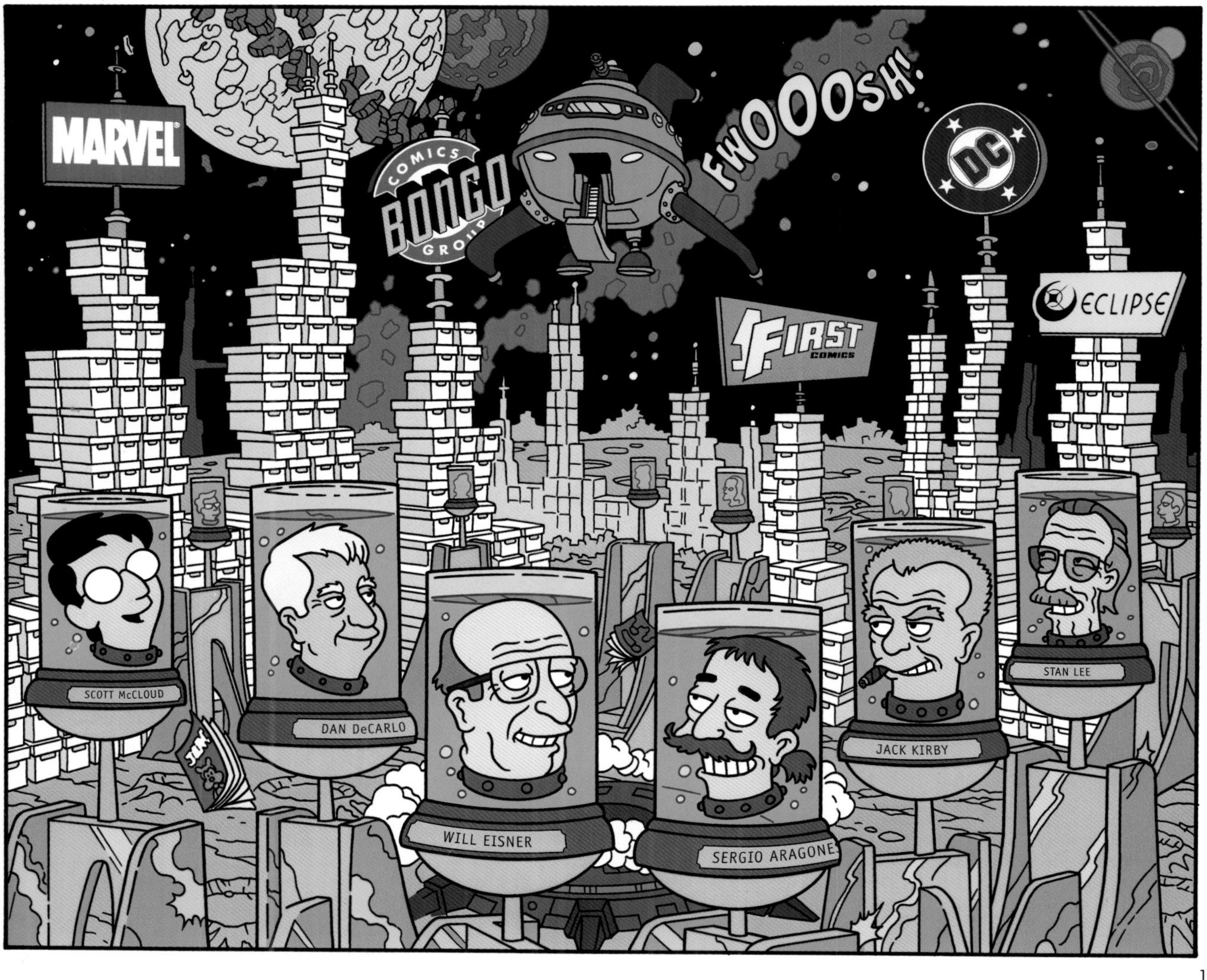
MARVEL
COMICS BONGO GROUP
FWOOOSH!
DC
ECLIPSE
FIRST COMICS
SCOTT McCLOUD
DAN DeCARLO
WILL EISNER
SERGIO ARAGONE
JACK KIRBY
STAN LEE

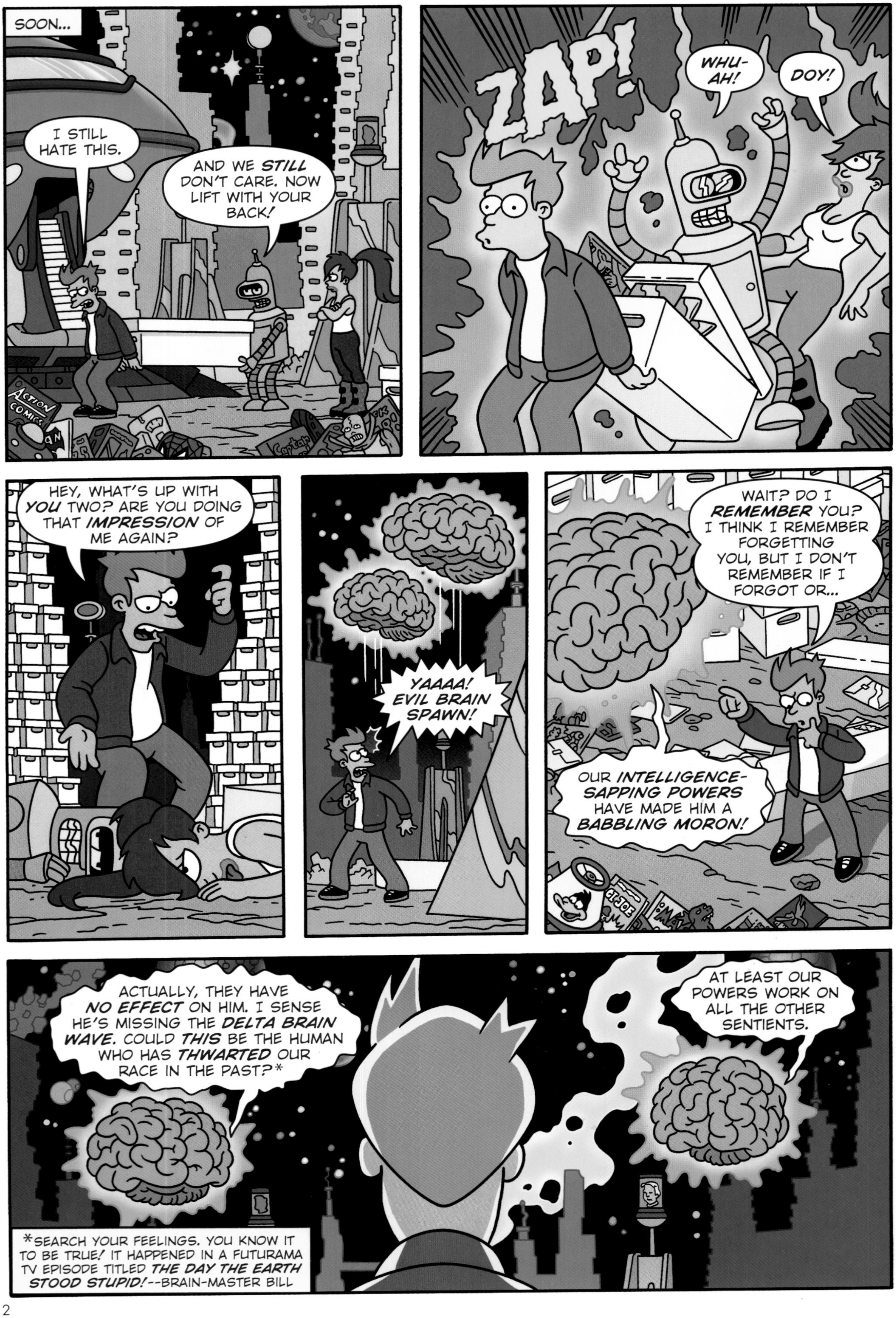
SOON...
I STILL HATE THIS.
AND WE STILL DON'T CARE. NOW LIFT WITH YOUR BACK!
ACTION COMICS
ZAP!
WHU-AH!
DOY!
HEY, WHAT'S UP WITH YOU TWO? ARE YOU DOING THAT IMPRESSION OF ME AGAIN?
YAAAA! EVIL BRAIN SPAWN!
WAIT? DO I REMEMBER YOU? I THINK I REMEMBER FORGETTING YOU, BUT I DON'T REMEMBER IF I FORGOT OR...
OUR INTELLIGENCE-SAPPING POWERS HAVE MADE HIM A BABBLING MORON!
G.I. JOE
ACTUALLY, THEY HAVE NO EFFECT ON HIM. I SENSE HE'S MISSING THE DELTA BRAIN WAVE. COULD THIS BE THE HUMAN WHO HAS THWARTED OUR RACE IN THE PAST?*
AT LEAST OUR POWERS WORK ON ALL THE OTHER SENTIENTS.
*SEARCH YOUR FEELINGS. YOU KNOW IT TO BE TRUE! IT HAPPENED IN A FUTURAMA TV EPISODE TITLED THE DAY THE EARTH STOOD STUPID!--BRAIN-MASTER BILL

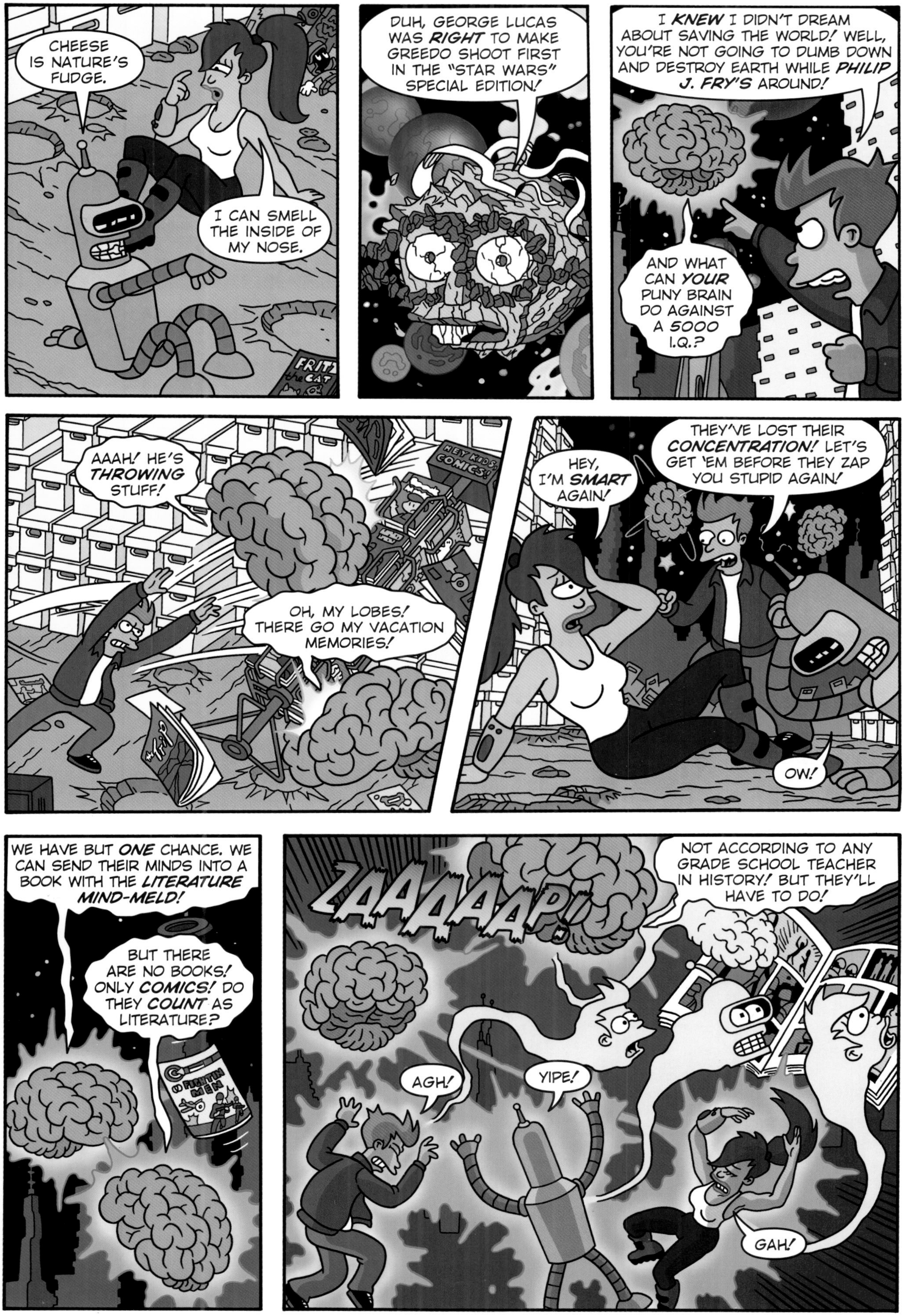
CHEESE IS NATURE'S FUDGE.
I CAN SMELL THE INSIDE OF MY NOSE.
FRITZ the CAT
DUH, GEORGE LUCAS WAS RIGHT TO MAKE GREEDO SHOOT FIRST IN THE "STAR WARS" SPECIAL EDITION!
I KNEW I DIDN'T DREAM ABOUT SAVING THE WORLD! WELL, YOU'RE NOT GOING TO DUMB DOWN AND DESTROY EARTH WHILE PHILIP J. FRY'S AROUND!
AND WHAT CAN YOUR PUNY BRAIN DO AGAINST A 5000 I.Q.?
AAAH! HE'S THROWING STUFF!
HEY KIDS, COMICS!
OH, MY LOBES! THERE GO MY VACATION MEMORIES!
HEY, I'M SMART AGAIN!
THEY'VE LOST THEIR CONCENTRATION! LET'S GET 'EM BEFORE THEY ZAP YOU STUPID AGAIN!
OW!
WE HAVE BUT ONE CHANCE. WE CAN SEND THEIR MINDS INTO A BOOK WITH THE LITERATURE MIND-MELD!
BUT THERE ARE NO BOOKS! ONLY COMICS! DO THEY COUNT AS LITERATURE?
ZAAAAAP!
NOT ACCORDING TO ANY GRADE SCHOOL TEACHER IN HISTORY! BUT THEY'LL HAVE TO DO!
AGH!
YIPE!
GAH!

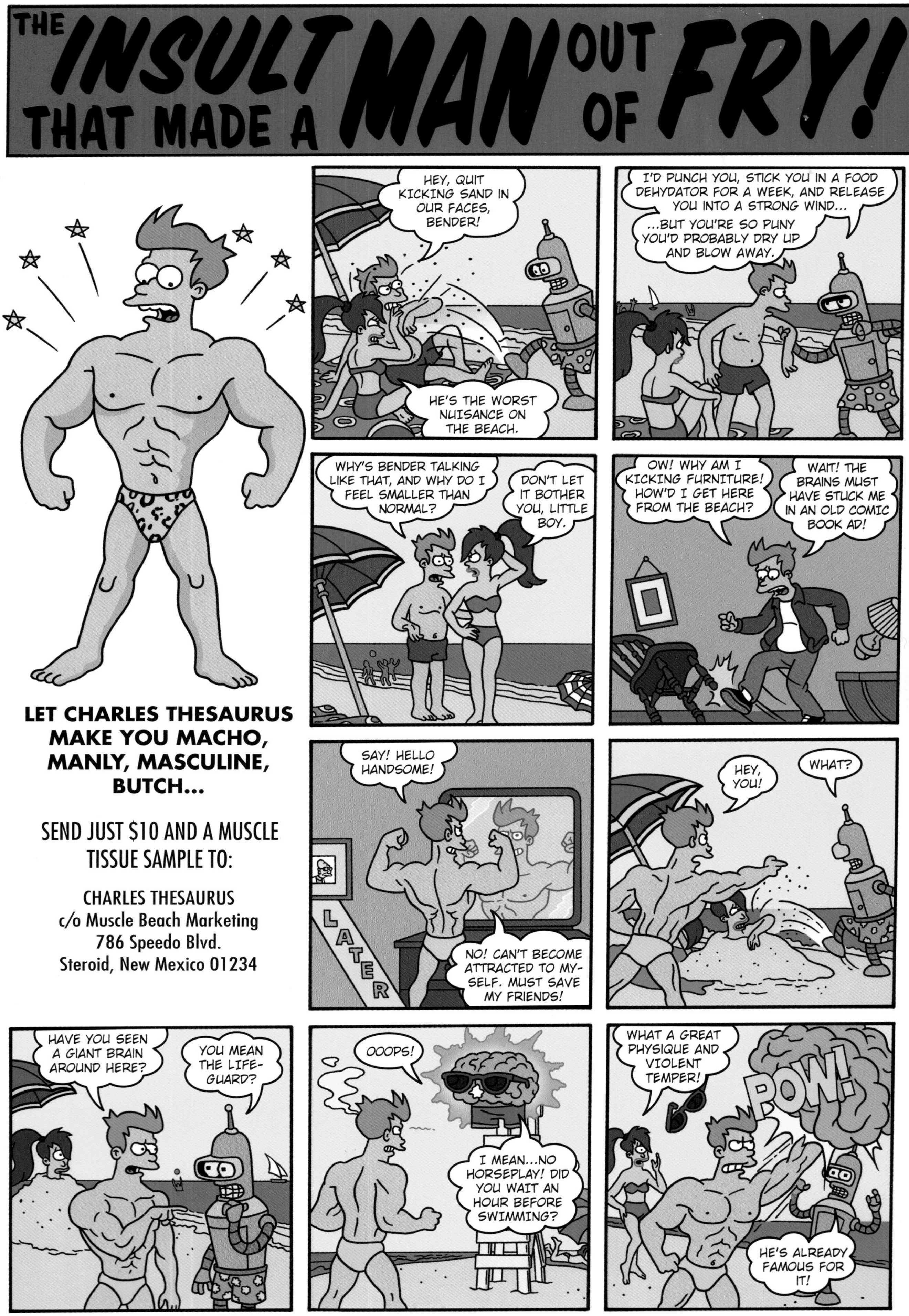
THE INSULT THAT MADE A MAN OUT OF FRY!
LET CHARLES THESAURUS MAKE YOU MACHO, MANLY, MASCULINE, BUTCH...
SEND JUST $10 AND A MUSCLE TISSUE SAMPLE TO:
CHARLES THESAURUS
c/o Muscle Beach Marketing
786 Speedo Blvd.
Steroid, New Mexico 01234
HEY, QUIT KICKING SAND IN OUR FACES, BENDER!
HE'S THE WORST NUISANCE ON THE BEACH.
I'D PUNCH YOU, STICK YOU IN A FOOD DEHYDATOR FOR A WEEK, AND RELEASE YOU INTO A STRONG WIND...
...BUT YOU'RE SO PUNY YOU'D PROBABLY DRY UP AND BLOW AWAY.
WHY'S BENDER TALKING LIKE THAT, AND WHY DO I FEEL SMALLER THAN NORMAL?
DON'T LET IT BOTHER YOU, LITTLE BOY.
OW! WHY AM I KICKING FURNITURE! HOW'D I GET HERE FROM THE BEACH?
WAIT! THE BRAINS MUST HAVE STUCK ME IN AN OLD COMIC BOOK AD!
SAY! HELLO HANDSOME!
LATER
NO! CAN'T BECOME ATTRACTED TO MY-SELF. MUST SAVE MY FRIENDS!
HEY, YOU!
WHAT?
HAVE YOU SEEN A GIANT BRAIN AROUND HERE?
YOU MEAN THE LIFE-GUARD?
OOOPS!
I MEAN...NO HORSEPLAY! DID YOU WAIT AN HOUR BEFORE SWIMMING?
WHAT A GREAT PHYSIQUE AND VIOLENT TEMPER!
POW!
HE'S ALREADY FAMOUS FOR IT!

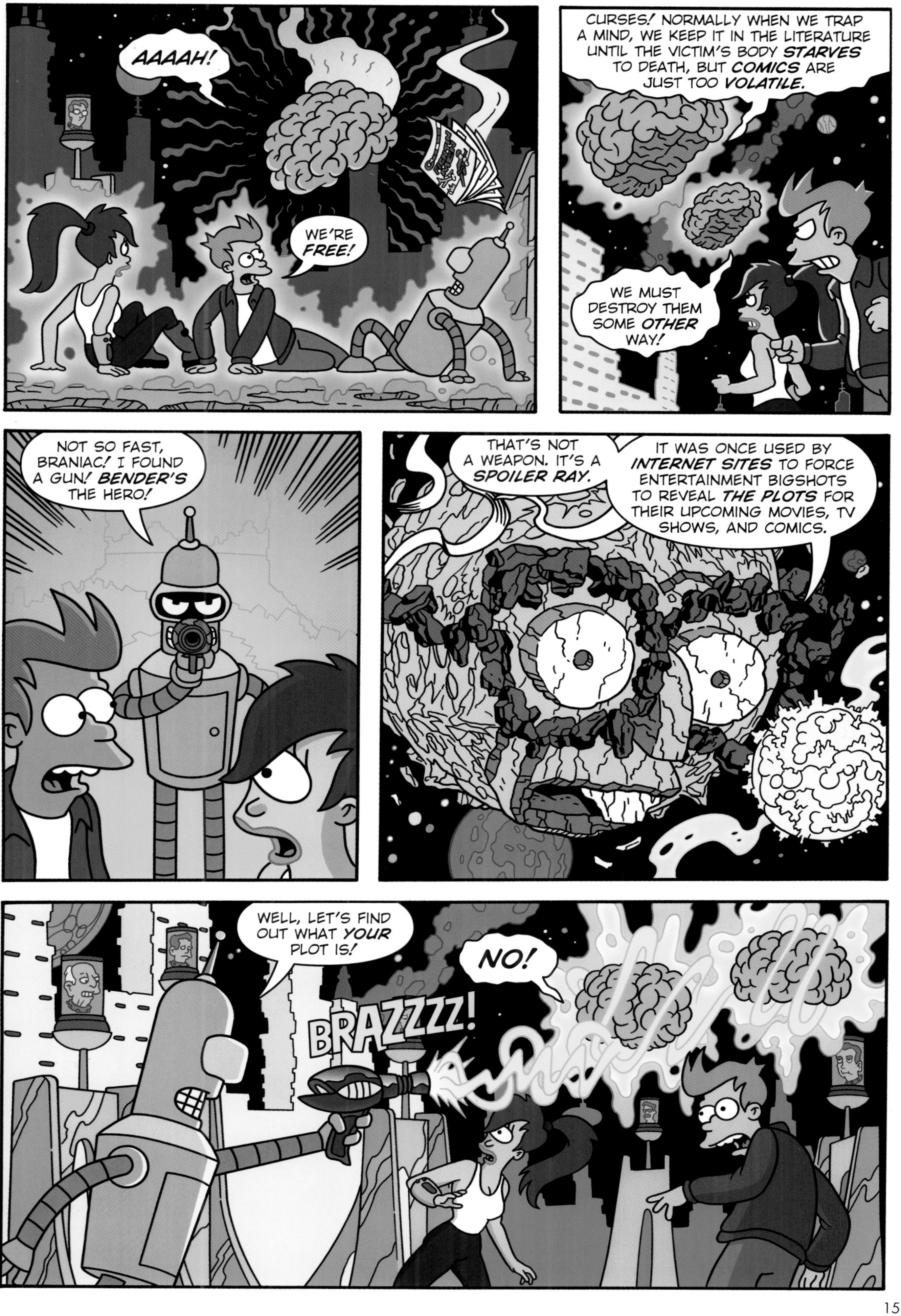
AAAAH!
CURSES! NORMALLY WHEN WE TRAP A MIND, WE KEEP IT IN THE LITERATURE UNTIL THE VICTIM'S BODY STARVES TO DEATH, BUT COMICS ARE JUST TOO VOLATILE.
WE'RE FREE!
WE MUST DESTROY THEM SOME OTHER WAY!
NOT SO FAST, BRANIAC! I FOUND A GUN! BENDER'S THE HERO!
THAT'S NOT A WEAPON. IT'S A SPOILER RAY.
IT WAS ONCE USED BY INTERNET SITES TO FORCE ENTERTAINMENT BIGSHOTS TO REVEAL THE PLOTS FOR THEIR UPCOMING MOVIES, TV SHOWS, AND COMICS.
WELL, LET'S FIND OUT WHAT YOUR PLOT IS!
NO!
BRAZZZZ!

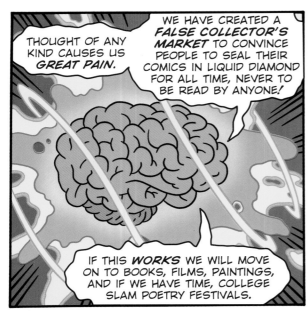

THOUGHT OF ANY KIND CAUSES US *GREAT PAIN.*

WE HAVE CREATED A *FALSE COLLECTOR'S MARKET* TO CONVINCE PEOPLE TO SEAL THEIR COMICS IN LIQUID DIAMOND FOR ALL TIME, NEVER TO BE READ BY ANYONE!

IF THIS *WORKS* WE WILL MOVE ON TO BOOKS, FILMS, PAINTINGS, AND IF WE HAVE TIME, COLLEGE SLAM POETRY FESTIVALS.

WITH *ART* GONE, THE COLLECTIVE I.Q. OF EARTH WILL BE *LOW ENOUGH* FOR US TO INVADE. THEN, WE WILL *CONSUME AND DESTROY YOUR WORLD!*

YOU AND WHAT ARMY?

THIS ONE.

NYAAAAH!

YOU'LL *STILL* NEVER GET AWAY WITH THIS! EVEN IF YOU KILL US, THE STAFF OF *PLANET EXPRESS* WILL AVENGE OUR DEATHS AND *DEFEAT* YOU!

THIS IS A FACTOR WE HAD NOT CONSIDERED...

...UNTIL NOW.

ONE HOUR LATER...

SWEET MANTA RAY OF ST. JAMES BAY BUT YOU'RE AN IDIOT, FRY!

THANKS A LOT, FRY!

HOORAY! A *ROAD TRIP,* AND ZOIDBERG'S *INVITED!*

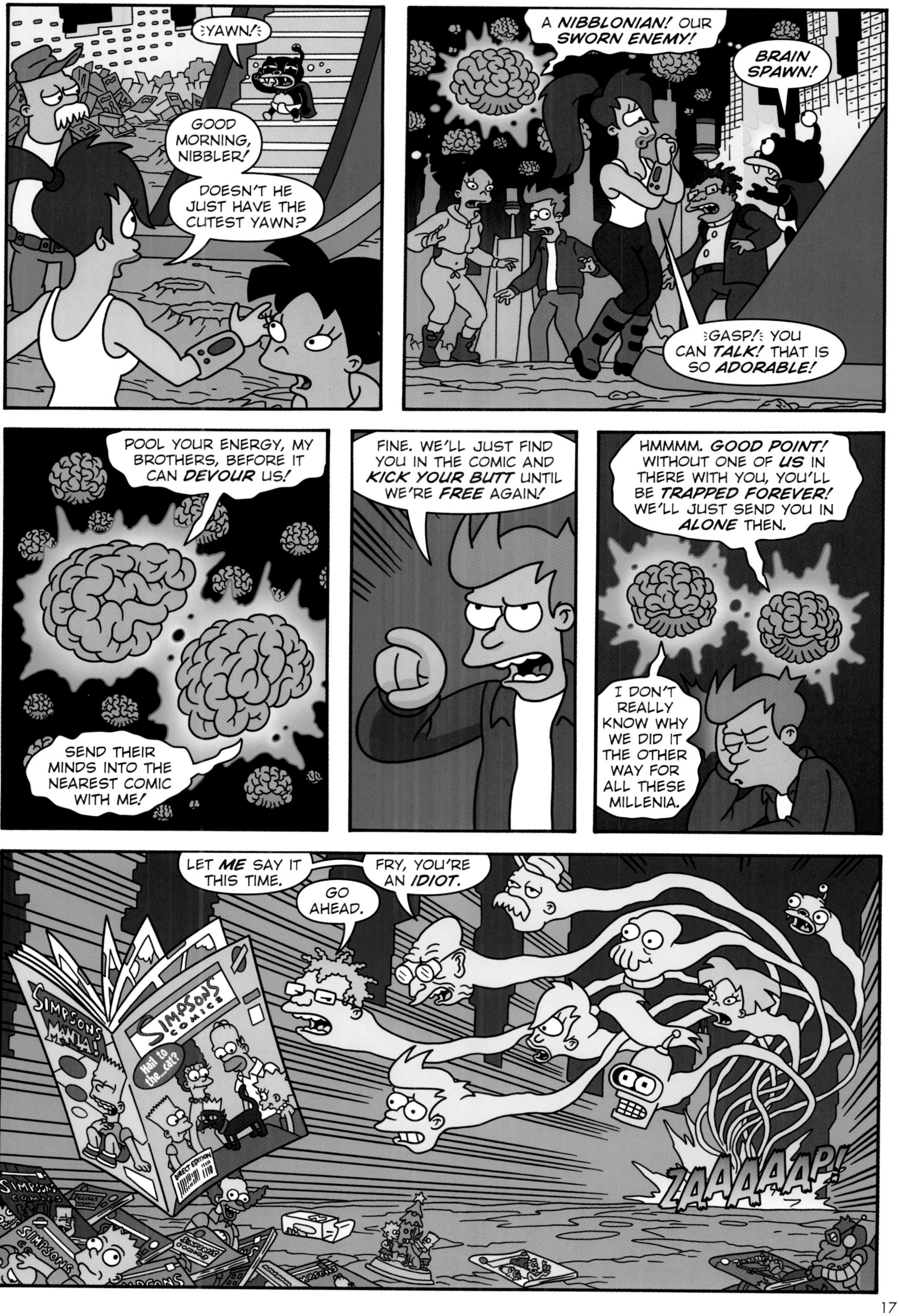
YAWN!
GOOD MORNING, NIBBLER!
DOESN'T HE JUST HAVE THE CUTEST YAWN?
A NIBBLONIAN! OUR SWORN ENEMY!
BRAIN SPAWN!
GASP! YOU CAN TALK! THAT IS SO ADORABLE!
POOL YOUR ENERGY, MY BROTHERS, BEFORE IT CAN DEVOUR US!
SEND THEIR MINDS INTO THE NEAREST COMIC WITH ME!
FINE. WE'LL JUST FIND YOU IN THE COMIC AND KICK YOUR BUTT UNTIL WE'RE FREE AGAIN!
HMMMM. GOOD POINT! WITHOUT ONE OF US IN THERE WITH YOU, YOU'LL BE TRAPPED FOREVER! WE'LL JUST SEND YOU IN ALONE THEN.
I DON'T REALLY KNOW WHY WE DID IT THE OTHER WAY FOR ALL THESE MILLENIA.
LET ME SAY IT THIS TIME.
GO AHEAD.
FRY, YOU'RE AN IDIOT.
SIMPSONS MANIA!
SIMPSONS COMICS
Hail to the...cat?
ZAAAAAP!

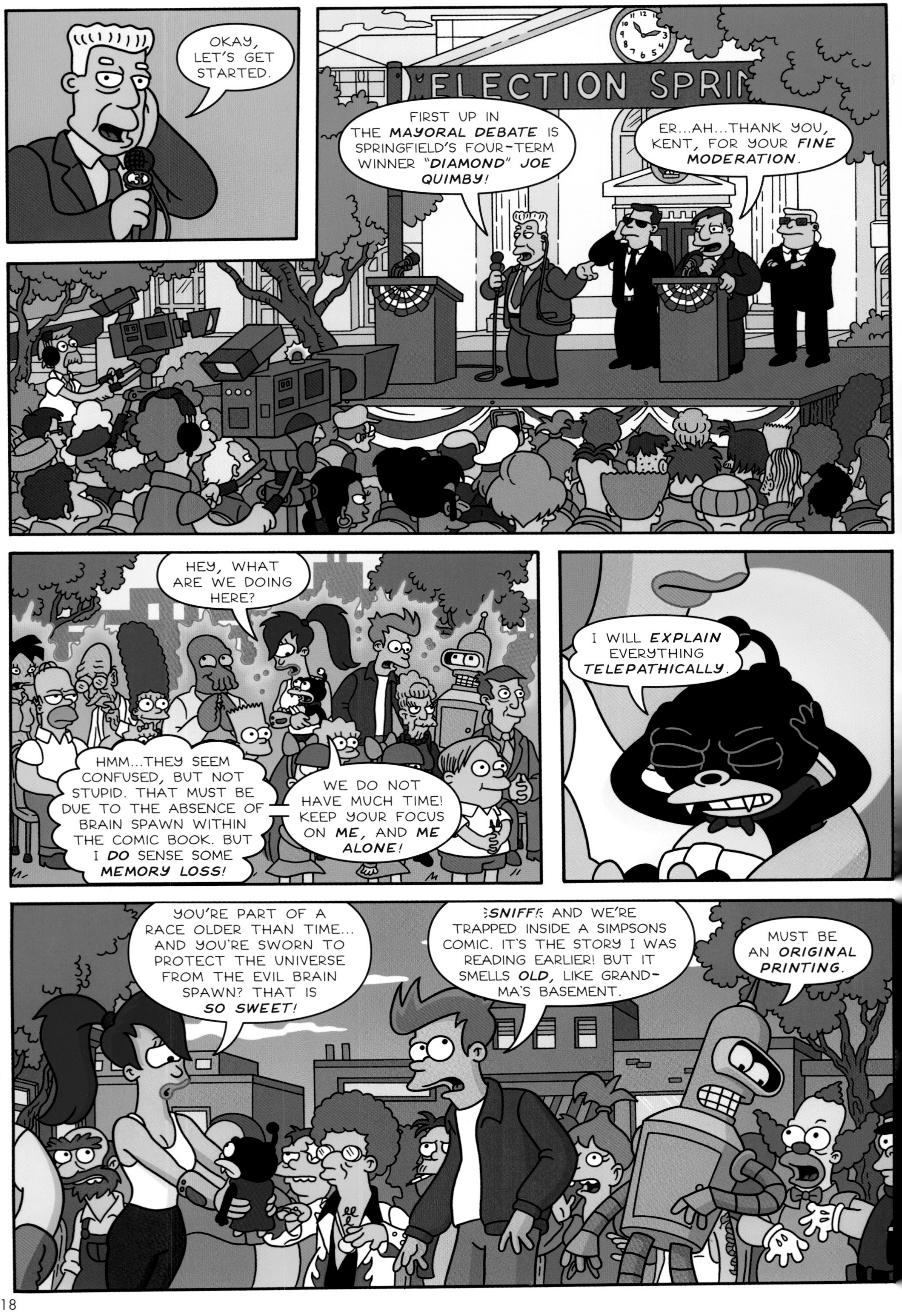
OKAY, LET'S GET STARTED.
ELECTION SPRI
FIRST UP IN THE MAYORAL DEBATE IS SPRINGFIELD'S FOUR-TERM WINNER "DIAMOND" JOE QUIMBY!
ER...AH...THANK YOU, KENT, FOR YOUR FINE MODERATION.
HEY, WHAT ARE WE DOING HERE?
HMM...THEY SEEM CONFUSED, BUT NOT STUPID. THAT MUST BE DUE TO THE ABSENCE OF BRAIN SPAWN WITHIN THE COMIC BOOK. BUT I DO SENSE SOME MEMORY LOSS!
WE DO NOT HAVE MUCH TIME! KEEP YOUR FOCUS ON ME, AND ME ALONE!
I WILL EXPLAIN EVERYTHING TELEPATHICALLY.
YOU'RE PART OF A RACE OLDER THAN TIME... AND YOU'RE SWORN TO PROTECT THE UNIVERSE FROM THE EVIL BRAIN SPAWN? THAT IS SO SWEET!
SNIFF! AND WE'RE TRAPPED INSIDE A SIMPSONS COMIC. IT'S THE STORY I WAS READING EARLIER! BUT IT SMELLS OLD, LIKE GRAND-MA'S BASEMENT.
MUST BE AN ORIGINAL PRINTING.

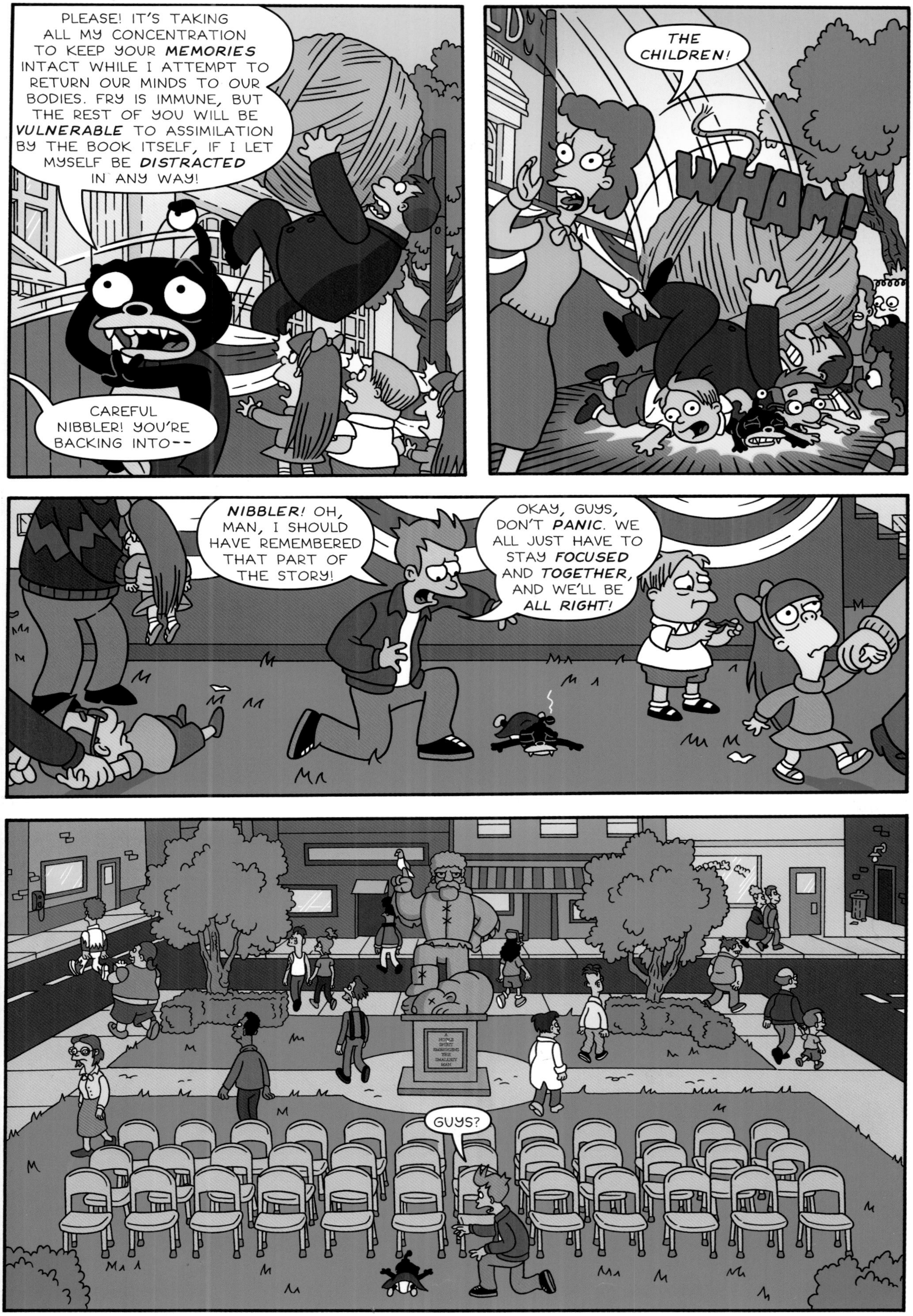
PLEASE! IT'S TAKING ALL MY CONCENTRATION TO KEEP YOUR MEMORIES INTACT WHILE I ATTEMPT TO RETURN OUR MINDS TO OUR BODIES. FRY IS IMMUNE, BUT THE REST OF YOU WILL BE VULNERABLE TO ASSIMILATION BY THE BOOK ITSELF, IF I LET MYSELF BE DISTRACTED IN ANY WAY!
CAREFUL NIBBLER! YOU'RE BACKING INTO--
THE CHILDREN!
WHAM!
NIBBLER! OH, MAN, I SHOULD HAVE REMEMBERED THAT PART OF THE STORY!
OKAY, GUYS, DON'T PANIC. WE ALL JUST HAVE TO STAY FOCUSED AND TOGETHER, AND WE'LL BE ALL RIGHT!
GUYS?

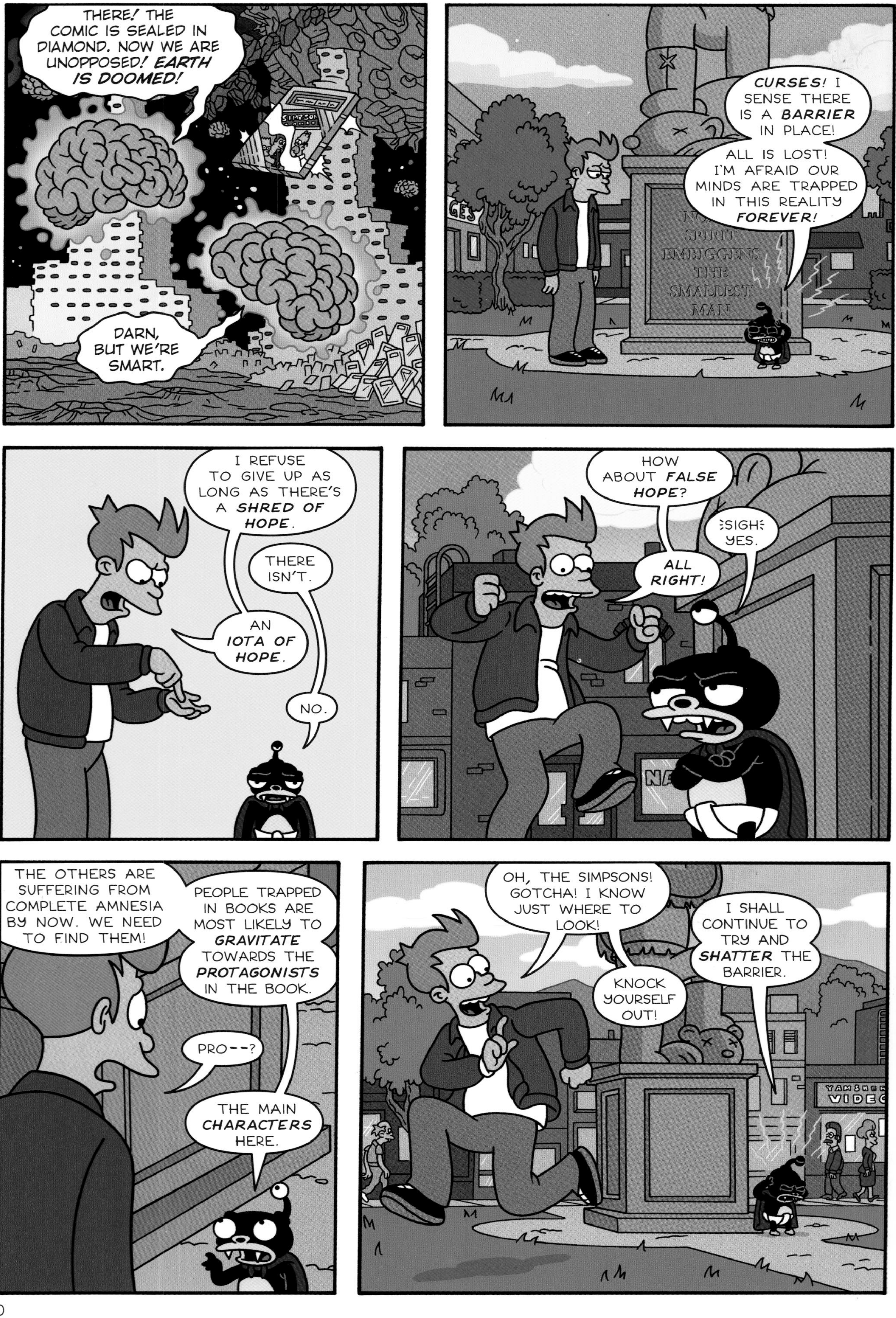
THERE! THE COMIC IS SEALED IN DIAMOND. NOW WE ARE UNOPPOSED! EARTH IS DOOMED!
DARN, BUT WE'RE SMART.
CURSES! I SENSE THERE IS A BARRIER IN PLACE!
ALL IS LOST! I'M AFRAID OUR MINDS ARE TRAPPED IN THIS REALITY FOREVER!
NO SPIRIT EMBIGGENS THE SMALLEST MAN
I REFUSE TO GIVE UP AS LONG AS THERE'S A SHRED OF HOPE.
THERE ISN'T.
AN IOTA OF HOPE.
NO.
HOW ABOUT FALSE HOPE?
:SIGH: YES.
ALL RIGHT!
THE OTHERS ARE SUFFERING FROM COMPLETE AMNESIA BY NOW. WE NEED TO FIND THEM!
PEOPLE TRAPPED IN BOOKS ARE MOST LIKELY TO GRAVITATE TOWARDS THE PROTAGONISTS IN THE BOOK.
PRO--?
THE MAIN CHARACTERS HERE.
OH, THE SIMPSONS! GOTCHA! I KNOW JUST WHERE TO LOOK!
KNOCK YOURSELF OUT!
I SHALL CONTINUE TO TRY AND SHATTER THE BARRIER.

ELSEWHERE...

MAN, I DON'T REMEMBER A THING, AND I REEK OF BOOZE.

SUE'S DINER

WELL, I'VE LEARNED MY LESSON. *I'LL NEVER DRINK AGAIN!*

MOE'S

HEY, A *BAR!*

I THINK I'LL HAVE A FEW BEERS AND CELEBRATE MY *NEW SOBRIETY!*

GIMME A BREW AND KEEP 'EM COMING, MEATBAG!

AW, THAT'S WHAT MY *MA* USED TO CALL ME! THIS ONE'S ON THE HOUSE!

MAN, THAT GUY IN THE *ROBOT SUIT* SURE LIKES HIS DUFF BEER.

MAYBE HE'S THE NEW *DUFF MASCOT!*

WOULD I GET MORE FREE BEER IF I *AM?*

SURE, I'D JUST BILL THE COMPANY.

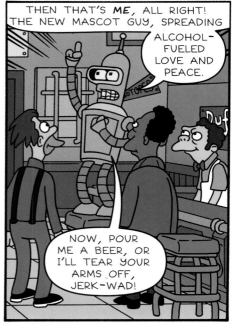

THEN THAT'S *ME,* ALL RIGHT! THE NEW MASCOT GUY, SPREADING ALCOHOL-FUELED LOVE AND PEACE.

NOW, POUR ME A BEER, OR I'LL TEAR YOUR ARMS OFF, JERK-WAD!

21

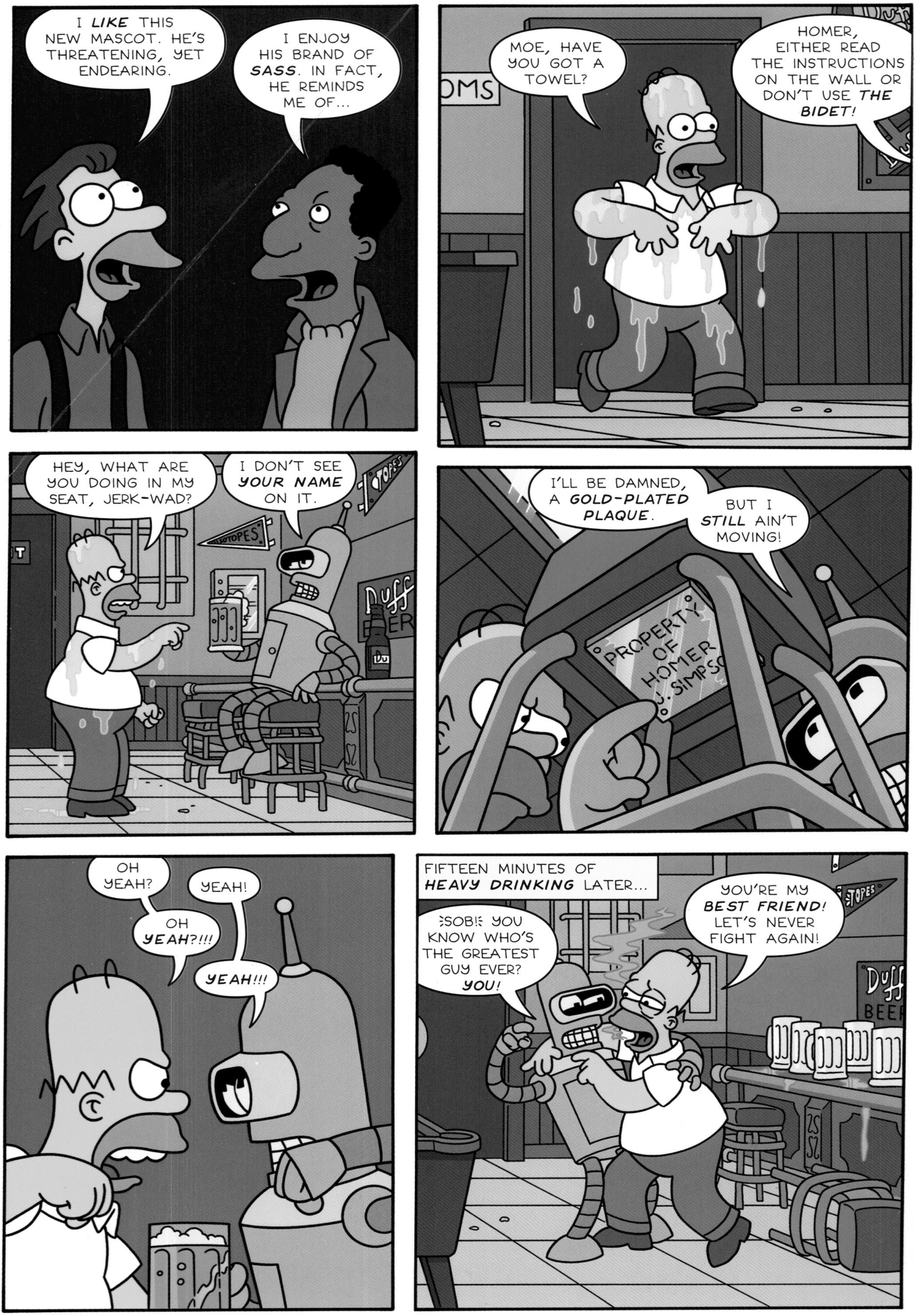

I *LIKE* THIS NEW MASCOT. HE'S THREATENING, YET ENDEARING.
I ENJOY HIS BRAND OF **SASS**. IN FACT, HE REMINDS ME OF...
MOE, HAVE YOU GOT A TOWEL?
HOMER, EITHER READ THE INSTRUCTIONS ON THE WALL OR DON'T USE ***THE BIDET***!
HEY, WHAT ARE YOU DOING IN MY SEAT, JERK-WAD?
I DON'T SEE ***YOUR NAME*** ON IT.
I'LL BE DAMNED, A ***GOLD-PLATED PLAQUE***.
PROPERTY OF HOMER J. SIMPSO
BUT I ***STILL*** AIN'T MOVING!
OH YEAH?
YEAH!
OH ***YEAH***?!!!
YEAH!!!
FIFTEEN MINUTES OF ***HEAVY DRINKING*** LATER...
SOB! YOU KNOW WHO'S THE GREATEST GUY EVER? ***YOU***!
YOU'RE MY ***BEST FRIEND***! LET'S NEVER FIGHT AGAIN!

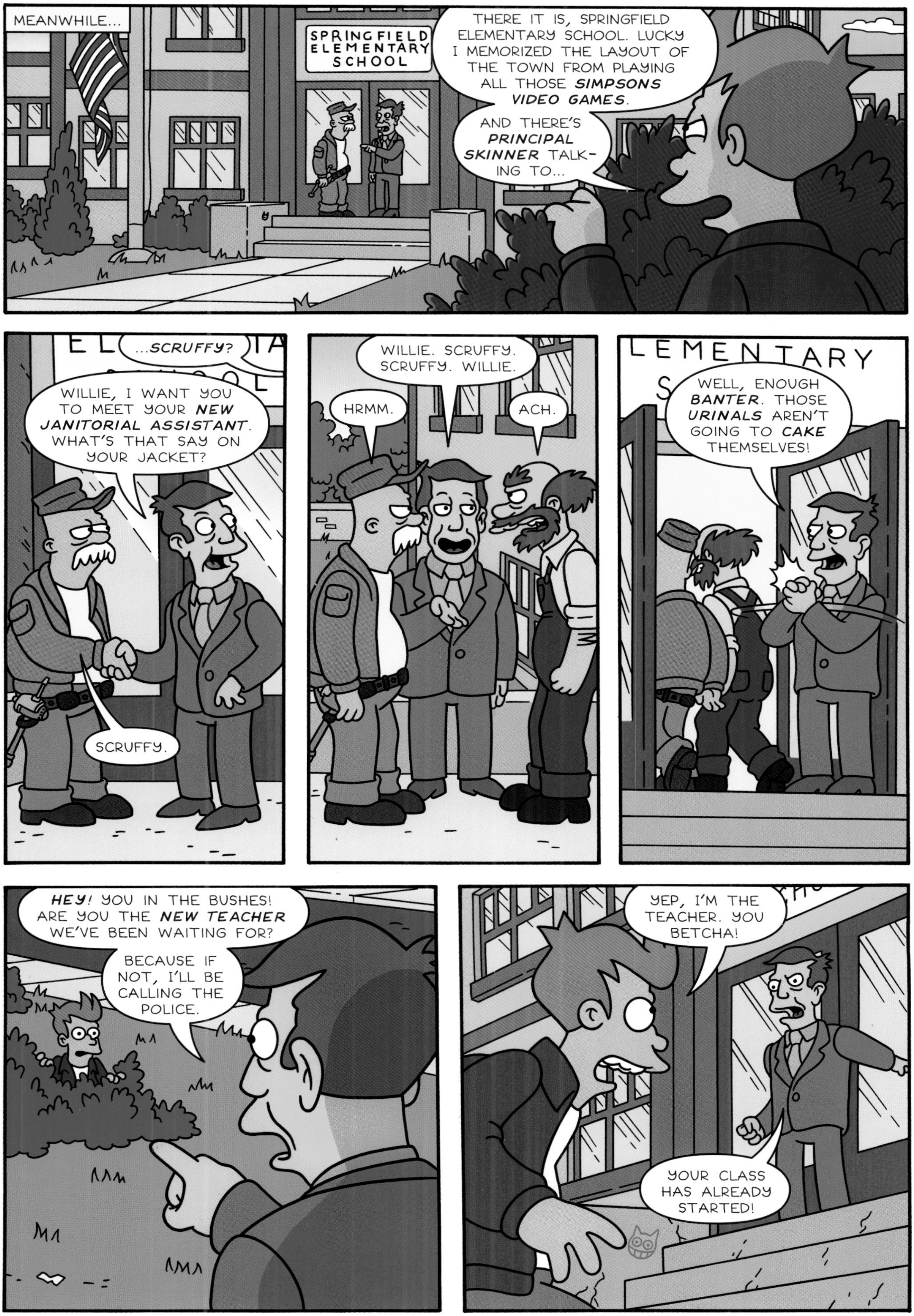
MEANWHILE...
SPRINGFIELD ELEMENTARY SCHOOL
THERE IT IS, SPRINGFIELD ELEMENTARY SCHOOL. LUCKY I MEMORIZED THE LAYOUT OF THE TOWN FROM PLAYING ALL THOSE SIMPSONS VIDEO GAMES.
AND THERE'S PRINCIPAL SKINNER TALKING TO...
...SCRUFFY?
WILLIE, I WANT YOU TO MEET YOUR NEW JANITORIAL ASSISTANT. WHAT'S THAT SAY ON YOUR JACKET?
SCRUFFY.
WILLIE. SCRUFFY. SCRUFFY. WILLIE.
HRMM.
ACH.
LEMENTARY
WELL, ENOUGH BANTER. THOSE URINALS AREN'T GOING TO CAKE THEMSELVES!
HEY! YOU IN THE BUSHES! ARE YOU THE NEW TEACHER WE'VE BEEN WAITING FOR?
BECAUSE IF NOT, I'LL BE CALLING THE POLICE.
YEP, I'M THE TEACHER. YOU BETCHA!
YOUR CLASS HAS ALREADY STARTED!

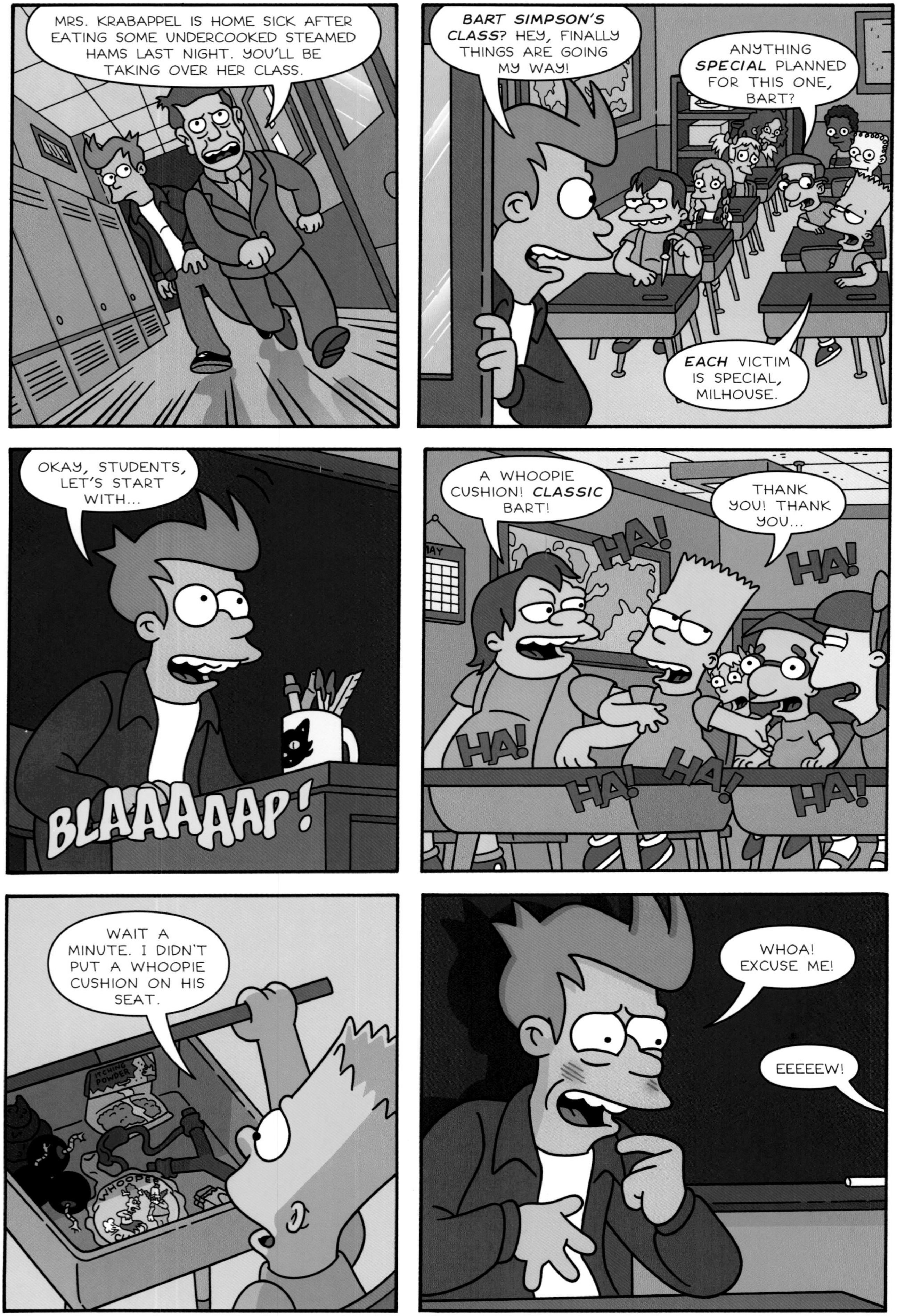
MRS. KRABAPPEL IS HOME SICK AFTER EATING SOME UNDERCOOKED STEAMED HAMS LAST NIGHT. YOU'LL BE TAKING OVER HER CLASS.
BART SIMPSON'S CLASS? HEY, FINALLY THINGS ARE GOING MY WAY!
ANYTHING SPECIAL PLANNED FOR THIS ONE, BART?
EACH VICTIM IS SPECIAL, MILHOUSE.
OKAY, STUDENTS, LET'S START WITH...
BLAAAAAP!
A WHOOPIE CUSHION! CLASSIC BART!
THANK YOU! THANK YOU...
HA!
HA!
HA!
HA!
HA!
HA!
WAIT A MINUTE. I DIDN'T PUT A WHOOPIE CUSHION ON HIS SEAT.
ITCHING POWDER
WHOA! EXCUSE ME!
EEEEEW!

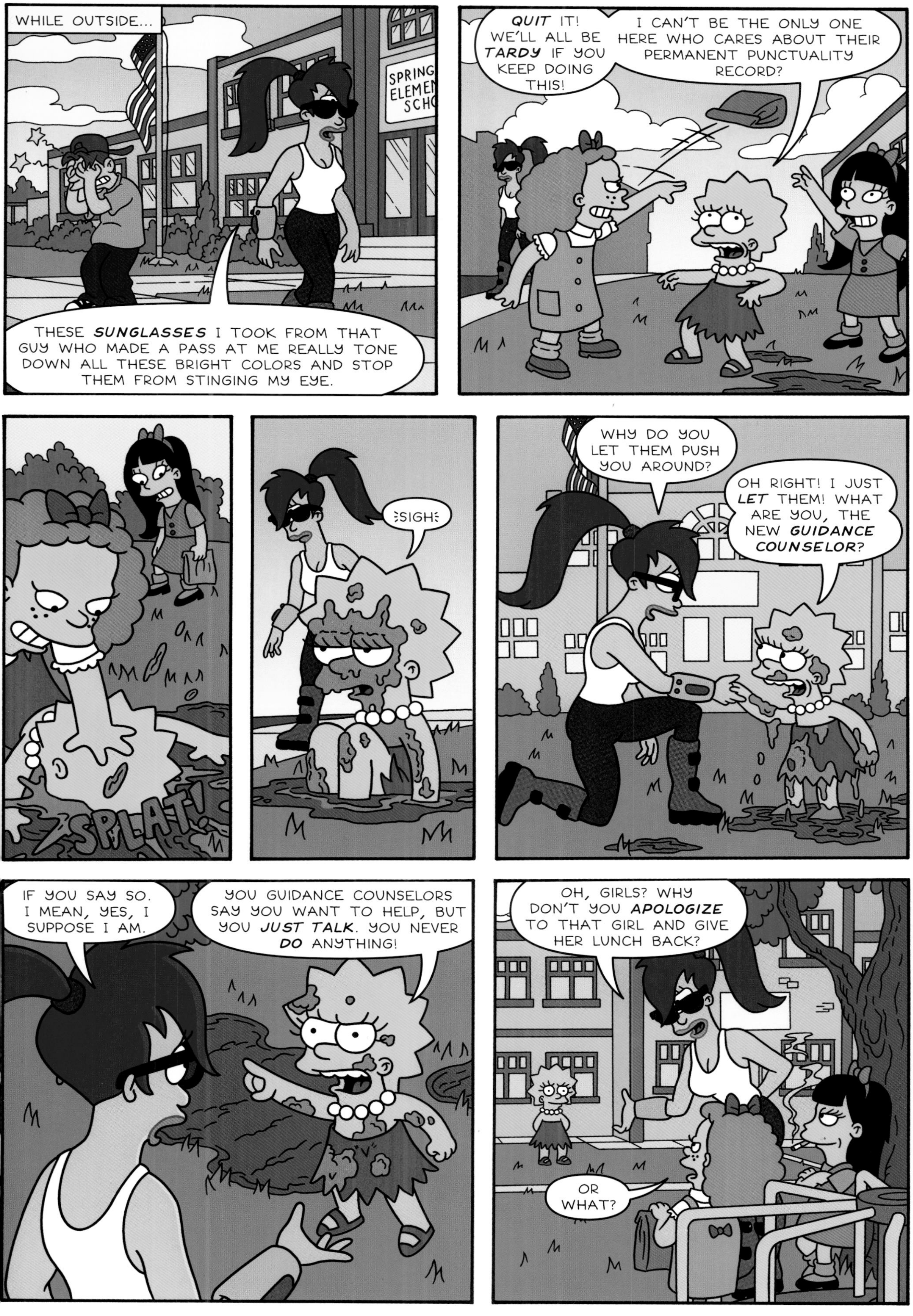
WHILE OUTSIDE...
SPRING ELEMEN SCHO
THESE SUNGLASSES I TOOK FROM THAT GUY WHO MADE A PASS AT ME REALLY TONE DOWN ALL THESE BRIGHT COLORS AND STOP THEM FROM STINGING MY EYE.
QUIT IT! WE'LL ALL BE TARDY IF YOU KEEP DOING THIS!
I CAN'T BE THE ONLY ONE HERE WHO CARES ABOUT THEIR PERMANENT PUNCTUALITY RECORD?
SPLAT!
SIGH
WHY DO YOU LET THEM PUSH YOU AROUND?
OH RIGHT! I JUST LET THEM! WHAT ARE YOU, THE NEW GUIDANCE COUNSELOR?
IF YOU SAY SO. I MEAN, YES, I SUPPOSE I AM.
YOU GUIDANCE COUNSELORS SAY YOU WANT TO HELP, BUT YOU JUST TALK. YOU NEVER DO ANYTHING!
OH, GIRLS? WHY DON'T YOU APOLOGIZE TO THAT GIRL AND GIVE HER LUNCH BACK?
OR WHAT?

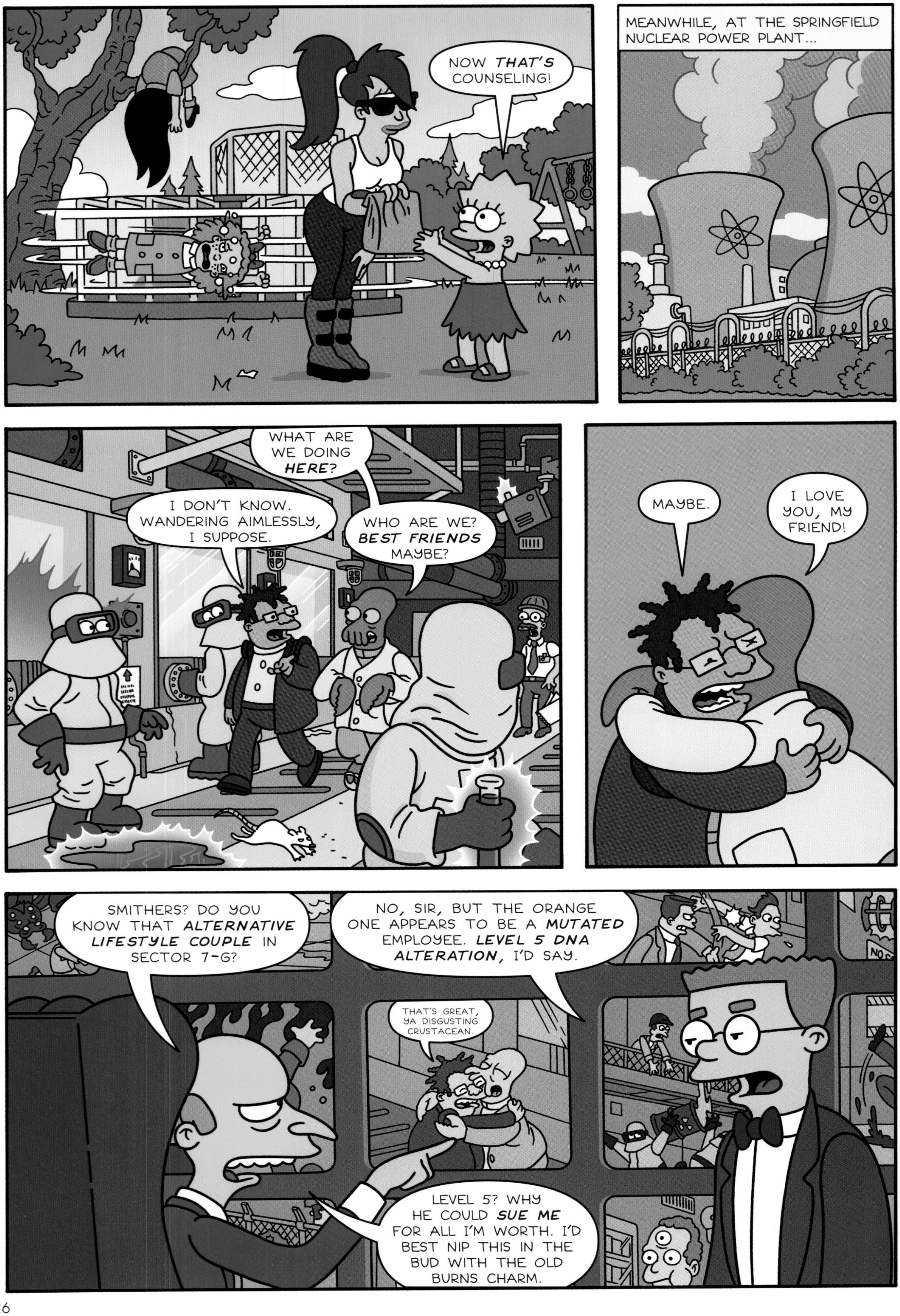
NOW THAT'S COUNSELING!
MEANWHILE, AT THE SPRINGFIELD NUCLEAR POWER PLANT...
WHAT ARE WE DOING HERE?
I DON'T KNOW. WANDERING AIMLESSLY, I SUPPOSE.
WHO ARE WE? BEST FRIENDS MAYBE?
MAYBE.
I LOVE YOU, MY FRIEND!
SMITHERS? DO YOU KNOW THAT ALTERNATIVE LIFESTYLE COUPLE IN SECTOR 7-G?
NO, SIR, BUT THE ORANGE ONE APPEARS TO BE A MUTATED EMPLOYEE. LEVEL 5 DNA ALTERATION, I'D SAY.
THAT'S GREAT, YA DISGUSTING CRUSTACEAN.
LEVEL 5? WHY HE COULD SUE ME FOR ALL I'M WORTH. I'D BEST NIP THIS IN THE BUD WITH THE OLD BURNS CHARM.

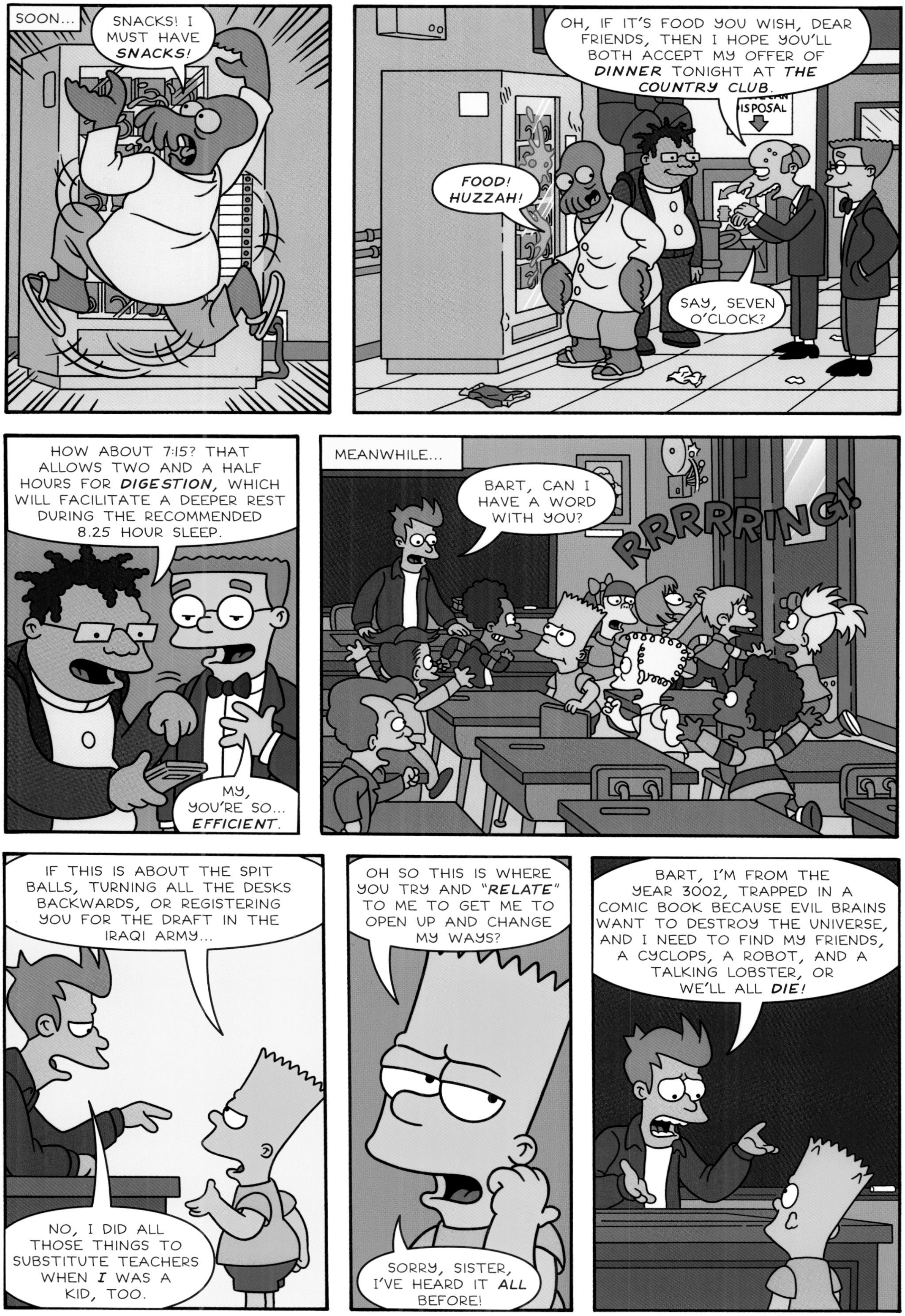
SOON...
SNACKS! I MUST HAVE SNACKS!
OH, IF IT'S FOOD YOU WISH, DEAR FRIENDS, THEN I HOPE YOU'LL BOTH ACCEPT MY OFFER OF DINNER TONIGHT AT THE COUNTRY CLUB.
FOOD! HUZZAH!
SAY, SEVEN O'CLOCK?
HOW ABOUT 7:15? THAT ALLOWS TWO AND A HALF HOURS FOR DIGESTION, WHICH WILL FACILITATE A DEEPER REST DURING THE RECOMMENDED 8.25 HOUR SLEEP.
MY, YOU'RE SO... EFFICIENT.
MEANWHILE...
BART, CAN I HAVE A WORD WITH YOU?
RRRRRING!
IF THIS IS ABOUT THE SPIT BALLS, TURNING ALL THE DESKS BACKWARDS, OR REGISTERING YOU FOR THE DRAFT IN THE IRAQI ARMY...
NO, I DID ALL THOSE THINGS TO SUBSTITUTE TEACHERS WHEN I WAS A KID, TOO.
OH SO THIS IS WHERE YOU TRY AND "RELATE" TO ME TO GET ME TO OPEN UP AND CHANGE MY WAYS?
SORRY, SISTER, I'VE HEARD IT ALL BEFORE!
BART, I'M FROM THE YEAR 3002, TRAPPED IN A COMIC BOOK BECAUSE EVIL BRAINS WANT TO DESTROY THE UNIVERSE, AND I NEED TO FIND MY FRIENDS, A CYCLOPS, A ROBOT, AND A TALKING LOBSTER, OR WE'LL ALL DIE!

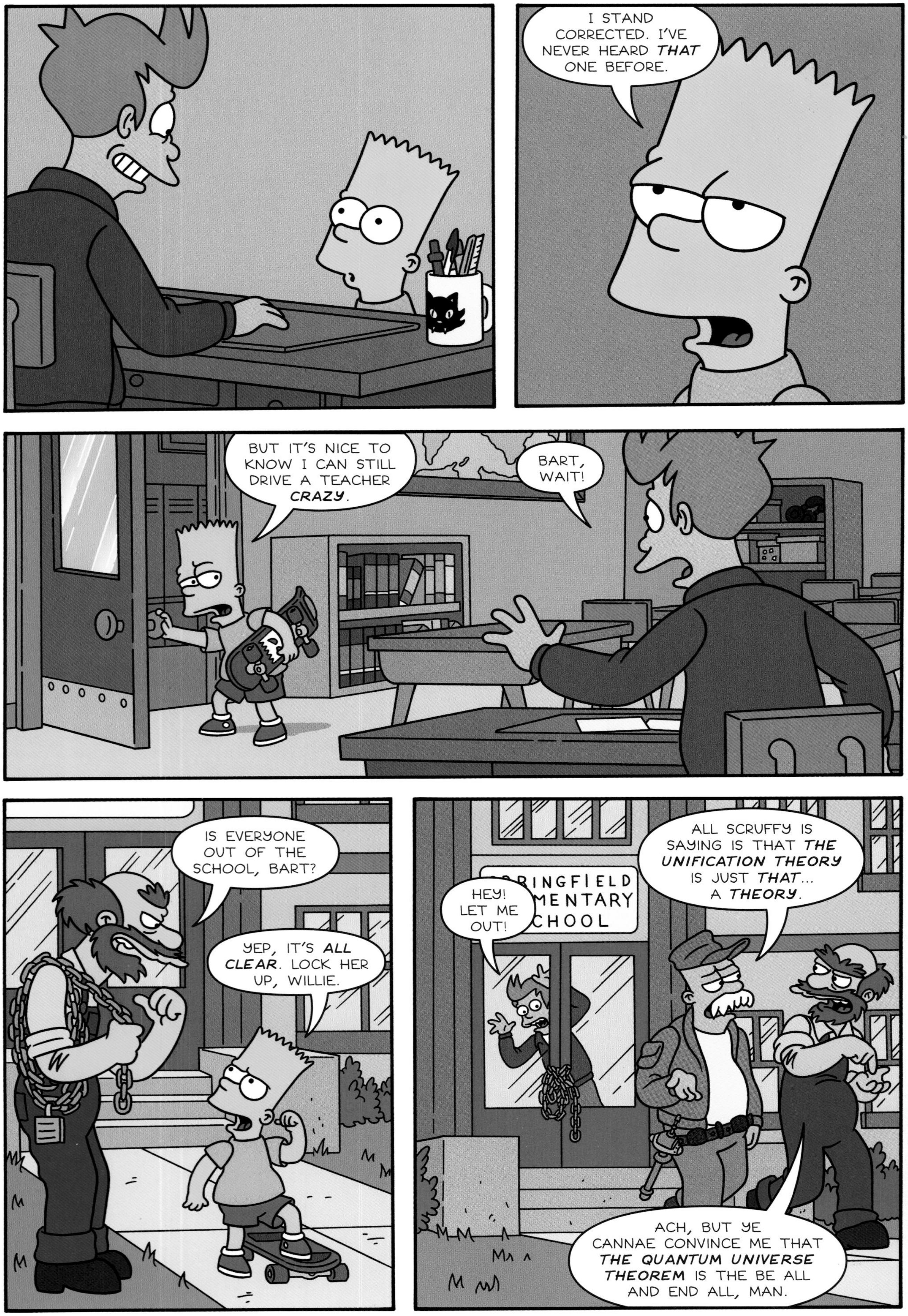

I STAND CORRECTED. I'VE NEVER HEARD **THAT** ONE BEFORE.
BUT IT'S NICE TO KNOW I CAN STILL DRIVE A TEACHER **CRAZY**.
BART, WAIT!
IS EVERYONE OUT OF THE SCHOOL, BART?
YEP, IT'S **ALL CLEAR**. LOCK HER UP, WILLIE.
HEY! LET ME OUT!
ALL SCRUFFY IS SAYING IS THAT **THE UNIFICATION THEORY** IS JUST **THAT**... A **THEORY**.
ACH, BUT YE CANNAE CONVINCE ME THAT **THE QUANTUM UNIVERSE THEOREM** IS THE BE ALL AND END ALL, MAN.

MEANWHILE...

DON'T WALK

NT

MARKET

WHOA! WATCH IT, OLD DUDE!

SCREEEEE!

SPRINGFIELD

BUS

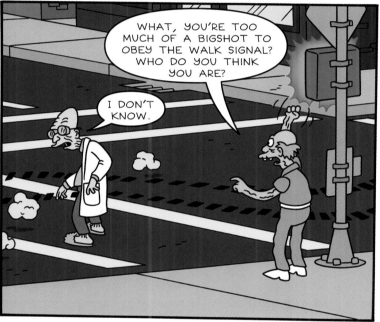

WHAT, YOU'RE TOO MUCH OF A BIGSHOT TO OBEY THE WALK SIGNAL? WHO DO YOU THINK YOU ARE?

I DON'T KNOW.

BUT I *DO* KNOW HOW TO MAKE THAT SIGNAL MORE *EFFICIENT,* USING THIS GUM, COAT HANGER, BROKEN WATCH, AND TIN FOIL.

AW, GIL WAS GONNA RUMMAGE THROUGH THAT CAN!

¡BUENO!

HOLY...!

WOW!

MUCH BETTER!

I'LL SAY! HUBBA, *HUBBA! 23 SKIDOO!*

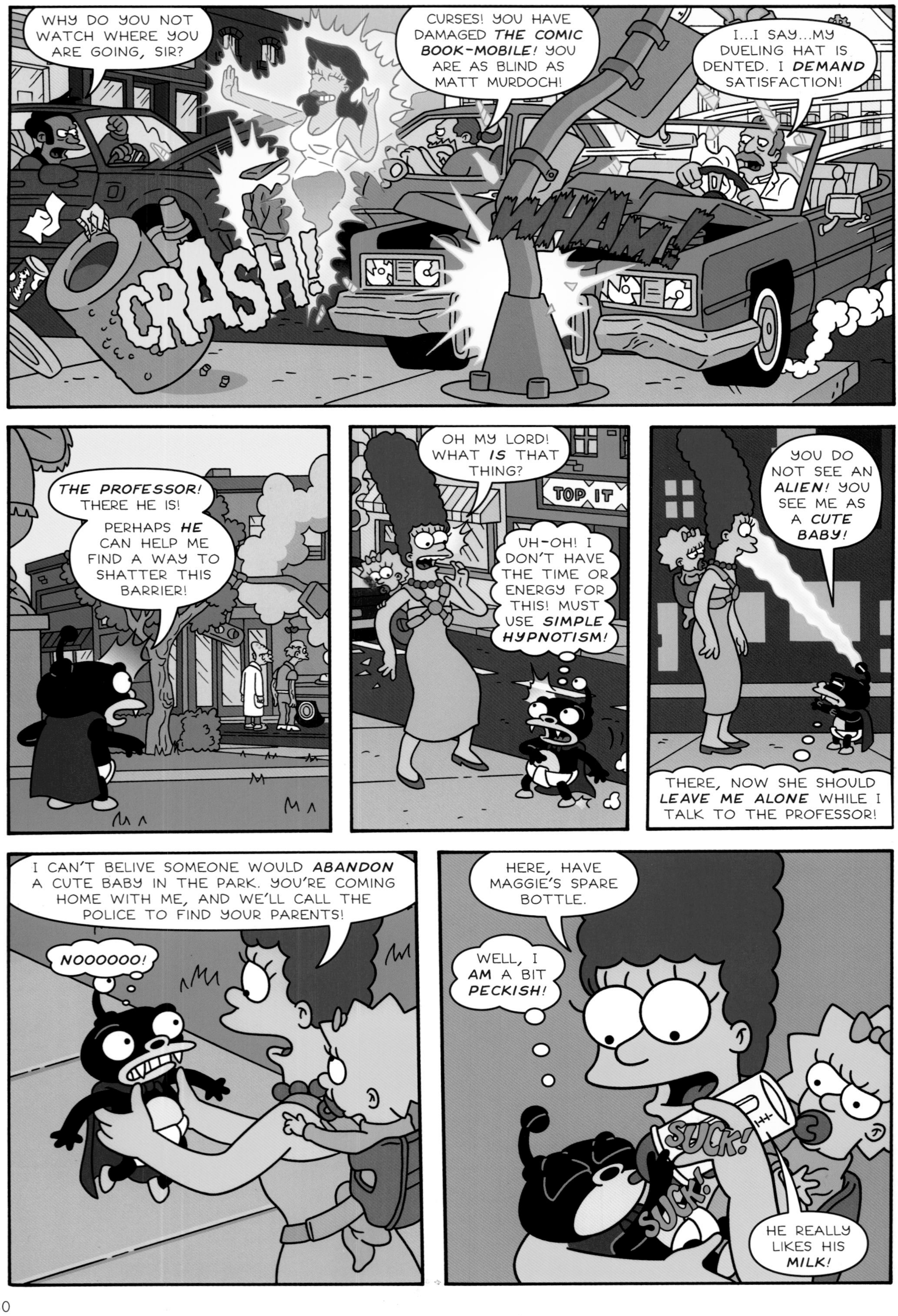
WHY DO YOU NOT WATCH WHERE YOU ARE GOING, SIR?
CURSES! YOU HAVE DAMAGED THE COMIC BOOK-MOBILE! YOU ARE AS BLIND AS MATT MURDOCH!
I...I SAY...MY DUELING HAT IS DENTED. I DEMAND SATISFACTION!
CRASH!
WHAM!
THE PROFESSOR! THERE HE IS!
PERHAPS HE CAN HELP ME FIND A WAY TO SHATTER THIS BARRIER!
OH MY LORD! WHAT IS THAT THING?
TOP IT
UH-OH! I DON'T HAVE THE TIME OR ENERGY FOR THIS! MUST USE SIMPLE HYPNOTISM!
YOU DO NOT SEE AN ALIEN! YOU SEE ME AS A CUTE BABY!
THERE, NOW SHE SHOULD LEAVE ME ALONE WHILE I TALK TO THE PROFESSOR!
I CAN'T BELIVE SOMEONE WOULD ABANDON A CUTE BABY IN THE PARK. YOU'RE COMING HOME WITH ME, AND WE'LL CALL THE POLICE TO FIND YOUR PARENTS!
NOOOOOO!
HERE, HAVE MAGGIE'S SPARE BOTTLE.
WELL, I AM A BIT PECKISH!
SUCK!
SUCK!
HE REALLY LIKES HIS MILK!

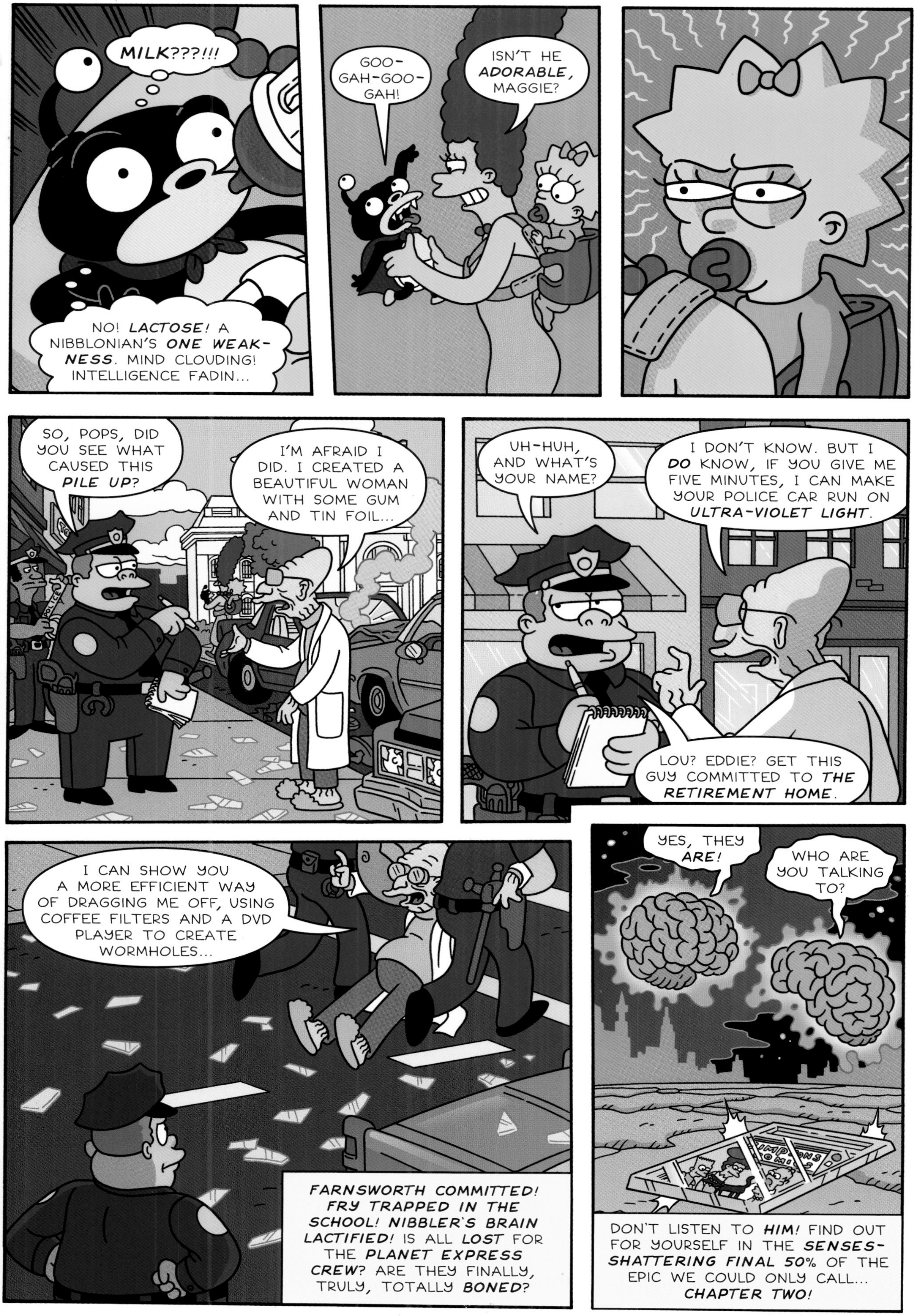
MILK???!!!
NO! LACTOSE! A NIBBLONIAN'S ONE WEAKNESS. MIND CLOUDING! INTELLIGENCE FADIN...
GOO-GAH-GOO-GAH!
ISN'T HE ADORABLE, MAGGIE?
SO, POPS, DID YOU SEE WHAT CAUSED THIS PILE UP?
I'M AFRAID I DID. I CREATED A BEAUTIFUL WOMAN WITH SOME GUM AND TIN FOIL...
UH-HUH, AND WHAT'S YOUR NAME?
I DON'T KNOW. BUT I DO KNOW, IF YOU GIVE ME FIVE MINUTES, I CAN MAKE YOUR POLICE CAR RUN ON ULTRA-VIOLET LIGHT.
LOU? EDDIE? GET THIS GUY COMMITTED TO THE RETIREMENT HOME.
I CAN SHOW YOU A MORE EFFICIENT WAY OF DRAGGING ME OFF, USING COFFEE FILTERS AND A DVD PLAYER TO CREATE WORMHOLES...
FARNSWORTH COMMITTED! FRY TRAPPED IN THE SCHOOL! NIBBLER'S BRAIN LACTIFIED! IS ALL LOST FOR THE PLANET EXPRESS CREW? ARE THEY FINALLY, TRULY, TOTALLY BONED?
YES, THEY ARE!
WHO ARE YOU TALKING TO?
DON'T LISTEN TO HIM! FIND OUT FOR YOURSELF IN THE SENSES-SHATTERING FINAL 50% OF THE EPIC WE COULD ONLY CALL... CHAPTER TWO!

CHAPTER 2: LIQUID DIAMOND IS FOREVER!

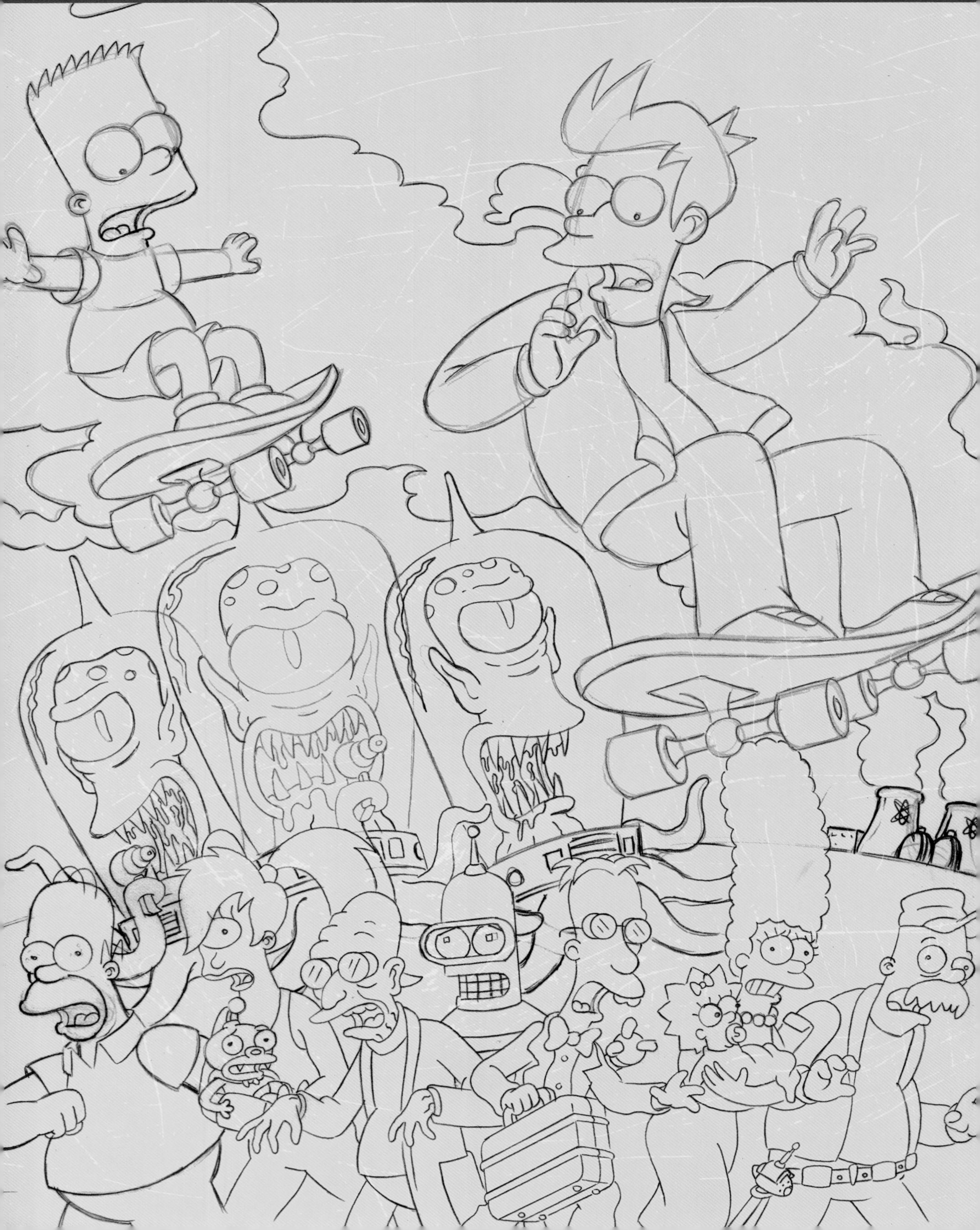

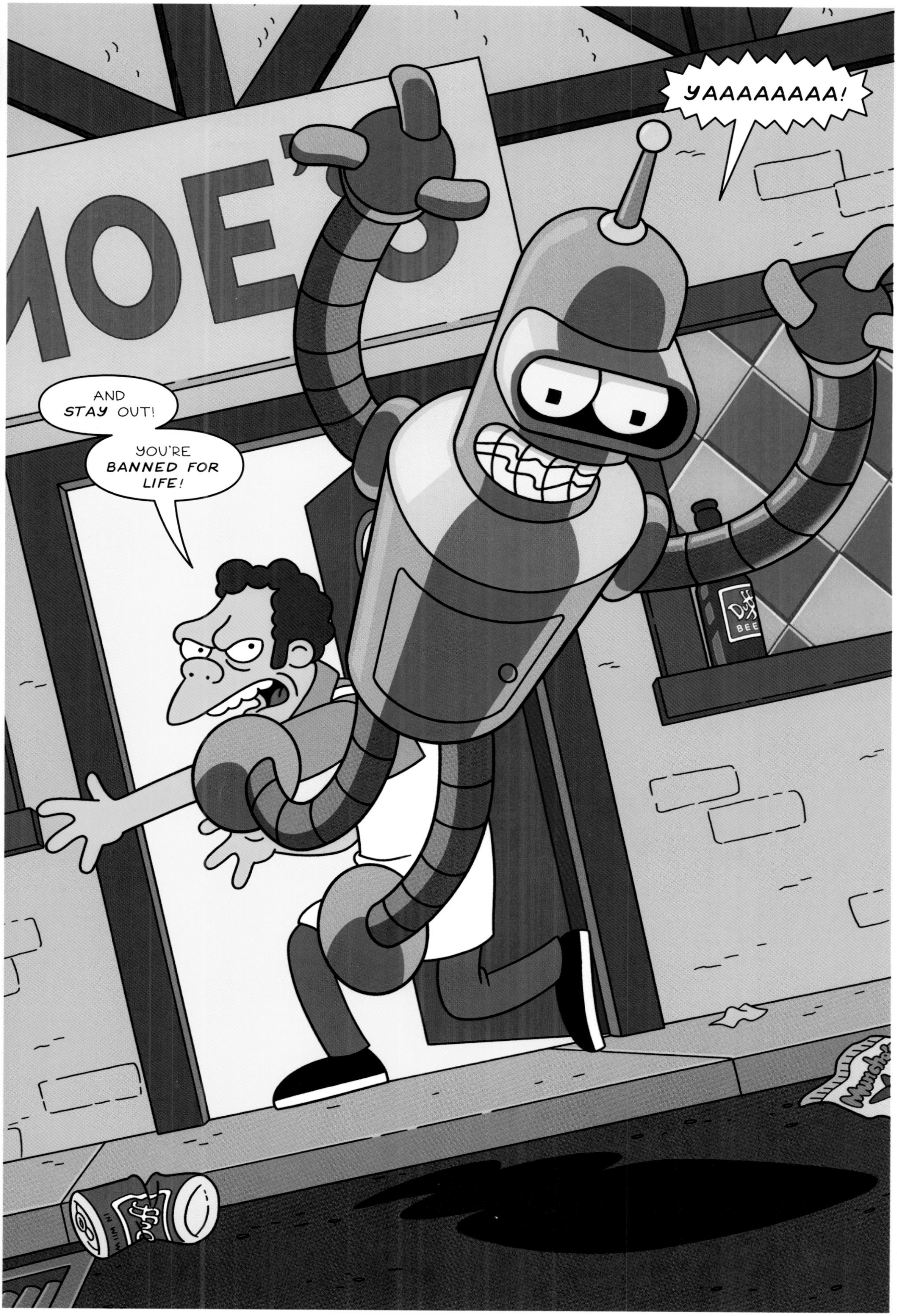
MOE'S
YAAAAAAAAA!
AND STAY OUT!
YOU'RE BANNED FOR LIFE!

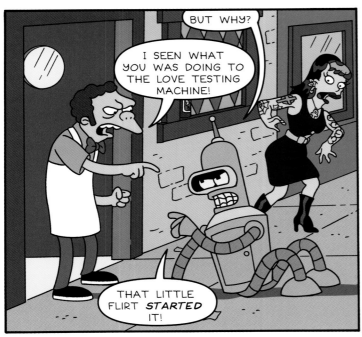

BUT WHY?

I SEEN WHAT YOU WAS DOING TO THE LOVE TESTING MACHINE!

THAT LITTLE FLIRT *STARTED* IT!

WELL, I SHOULD BE GETTING HOME.

I'D GO HOME, TOO...

...IF I *HAD* ONE.

HAND OVER YOUR WALLETS. THIS IS LIKE, *TOTALLY*, A MUGGING.

LATER...

SO YOU *REALLY* DON'T HAVE A PLACE TO STAY TONIGHT?

MAN, IT TOOK A LONG TIME TO GET THIS *TATTOO* OFF HIM, BUT IT WAS WORTH IT. MAN, I LOOK *COOL!*

SADLY, YES. ≡SIGH≡

WELL, DON'T YOU WORRY! ANY *BEST FRIEND* OF MINE WILL ALWAYS HAVE A BED AND SOMETHING TO EAT!

HEY, *FLANDERS!* GIVE MY BEST FRIEND A BED AND SOME-THING TO EAT!

OKILLY-DOKILLY-DO!

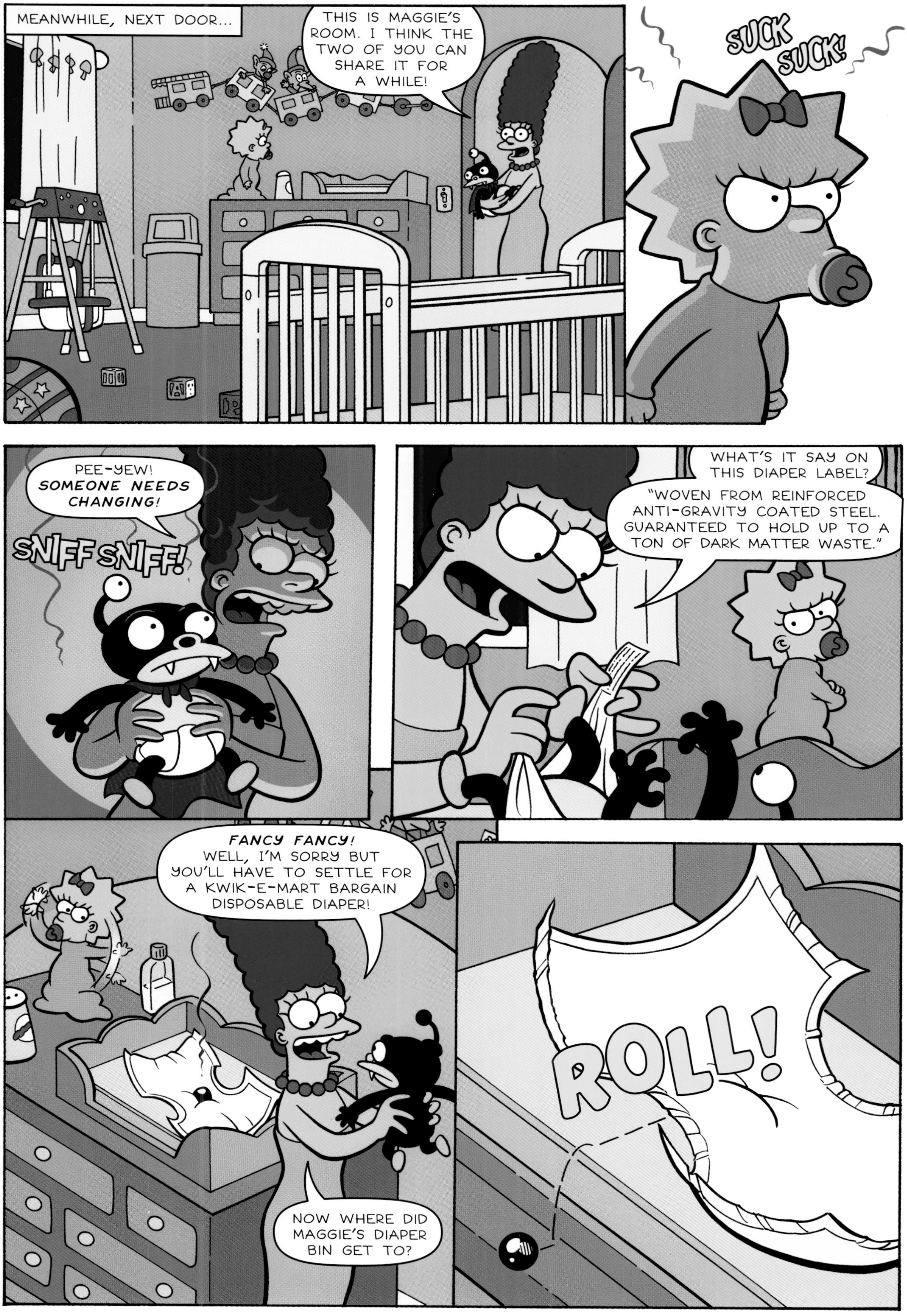
MEANWHILE, NEXT DOOR...
THIS IS MAGGIE'S ROOM. I THINK THE TWO OF YOU CAN SHARE IT FOR A WHILE!
SUCK SUCK!
PEE-YEW! SOMEONE NEEDS CHANGING!
SNIFF SNIFF!
WHAT'S IT SAY ON THIS DIAPER LABEL?
"WOVEN FROM REINFORCED ANTI-GRAVITY COATED STEEL. GUARANTEED TO HOLD UP TO A TON OF DARK MATTER WASTE."
FANCY FANCY! WELL, I'M SORRY BUT YOU'LL HAVE TO SETTLE FOR A KWIK-E-MART BARGAIN DISPOSABLE DIAPER!
NOW WHERE DID MAGGIE'S DIAPER BIN GET TO?
ROLL!

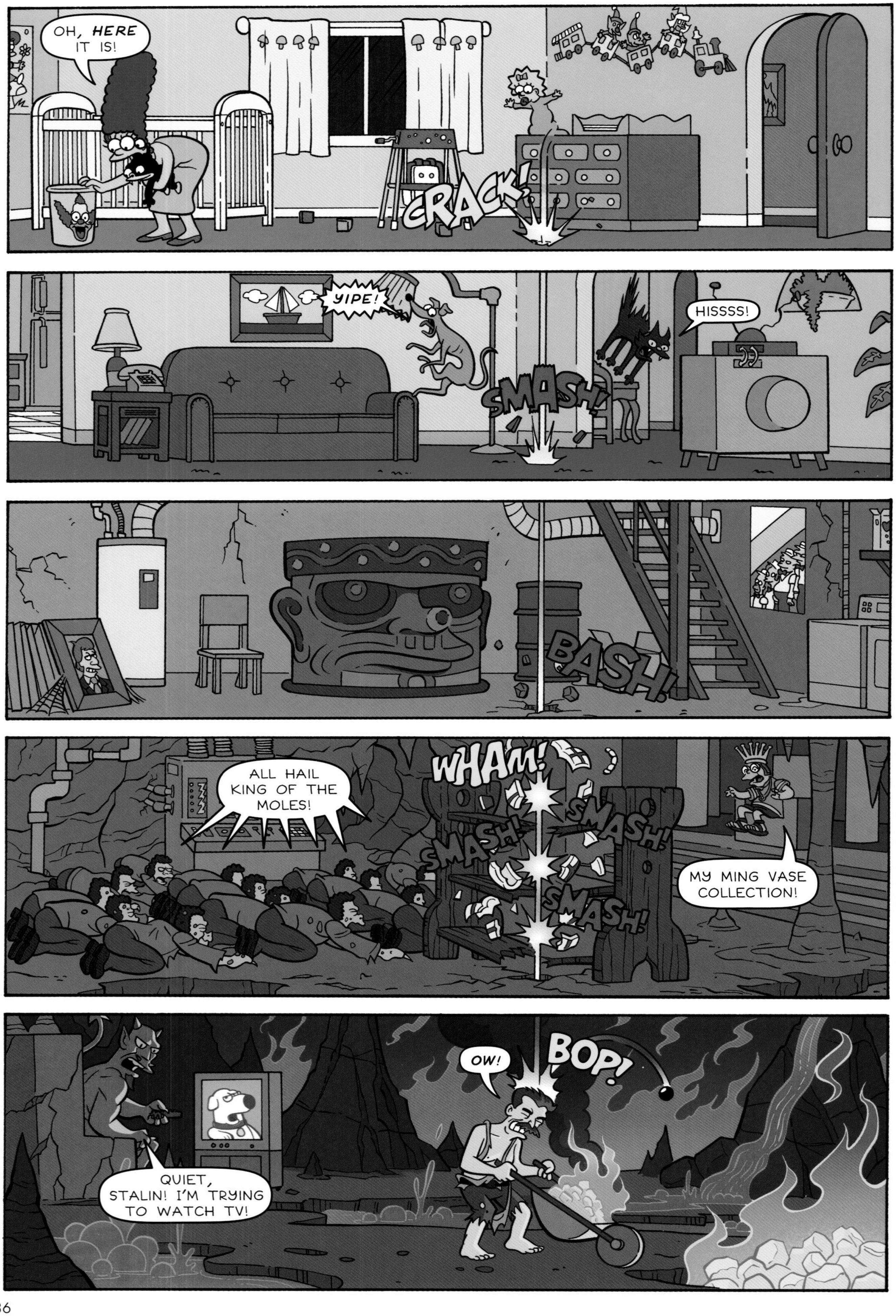
OH, HERE IT IS!
CRACK!
YIPE!
SMASH!
HISSSS!
BASH!
ALL HAIL KING OF THE MOLES!
WHAM!
SMASH!
SMASH!
SMASH!
MY MING VASE COLLECTION!
QUIET, STALIN! I'M TRYING TO WATCH TV!
OW!
BOP!

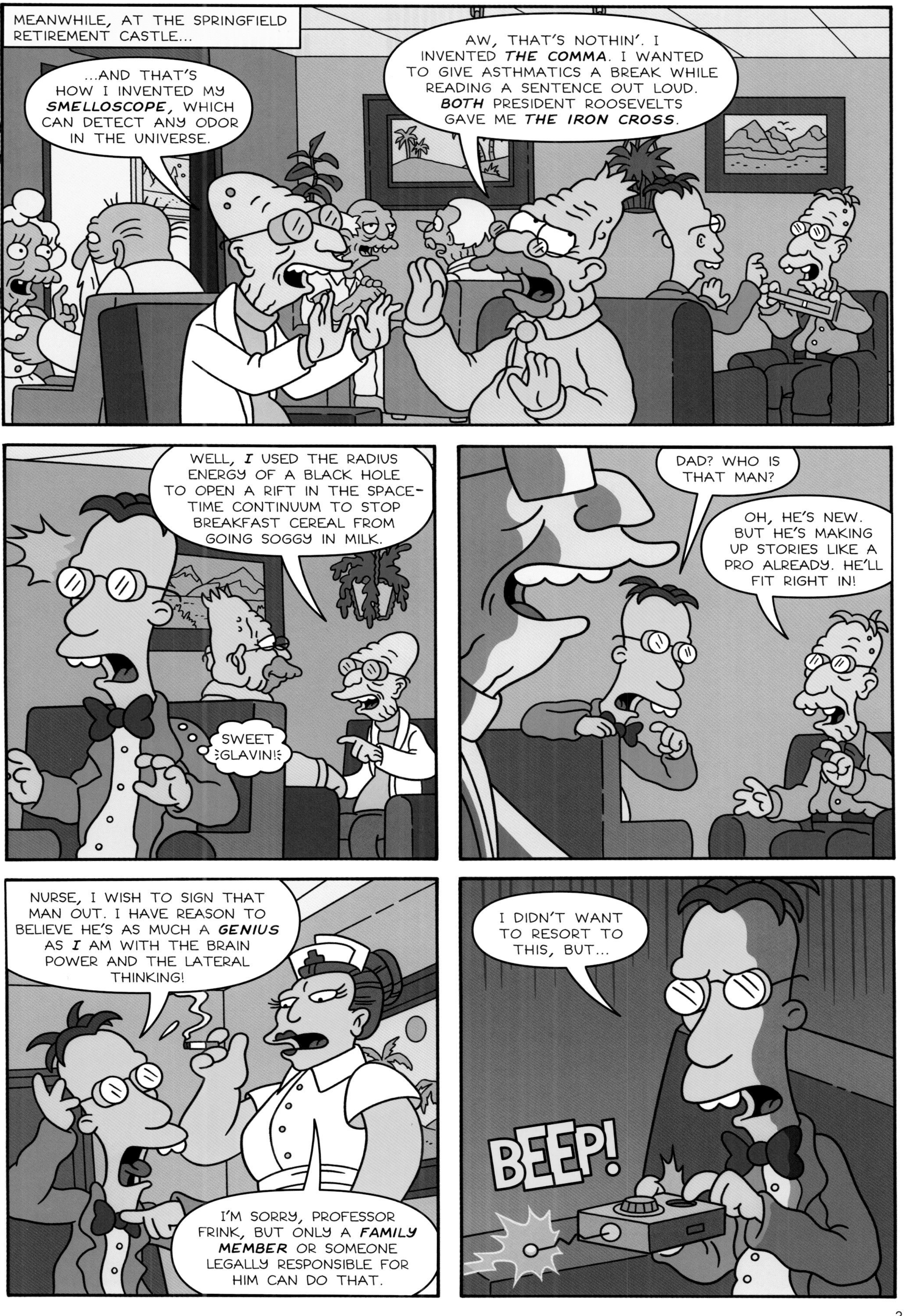
MEANWHILE, AT THE SPRINGFIELD RETIREMENT CASTLE...
...AND THAT'S HOW I INVENTED MY **SMELLOSCOPE,** WHICH CAN DETECT ANY ODOR IN THE UNIVERSE.
AW, THAT'S NOTHIN'. I INVENTED **THE COMMA**. I WANTED TO GIVE ASTHMATICS A BREAK WHILE READING A SENTENCE OUT LOUD. **BOTH** PRESIDENT ROOSEVELTS GAVE ME **THE IRON CROSS**.
WELL, **I** USED THE RADIUS ENERGY OF A BLACK HOLE TO OPEN A RIFT IN THE SPACE-TIME CONTINUUM TO STOP BREAKFAST CEREAL FROM GOING SOGGY IN MILK.
SWEET GLAVIN!
DAD? WHO IS THAT MAN?
OH, HE'S NEW. BUT HE'S MAKING UP STORIES LIKE A PRO ALREADY. HE'LL FIT RIGHT IN!
NURSE, I WISH TO SIGN THAT MAN OUT. I HAVE REASON TO BELIEVE HE'S AS MUCH A **GENIUS** AS **I** AM WITH THE BRAIN POWER AND THE LATERAL THINKING!
I'M SORRY, PROFESSOR FRINK, BUT ONLY A **FAMILY MEMBER** OR SOMEONE LEGALLY RESPONSIBLE FOR HIM CAN DO THAT.
I DIDN'T WANT TO RESORT TO THIS, BUT...
BEEP!

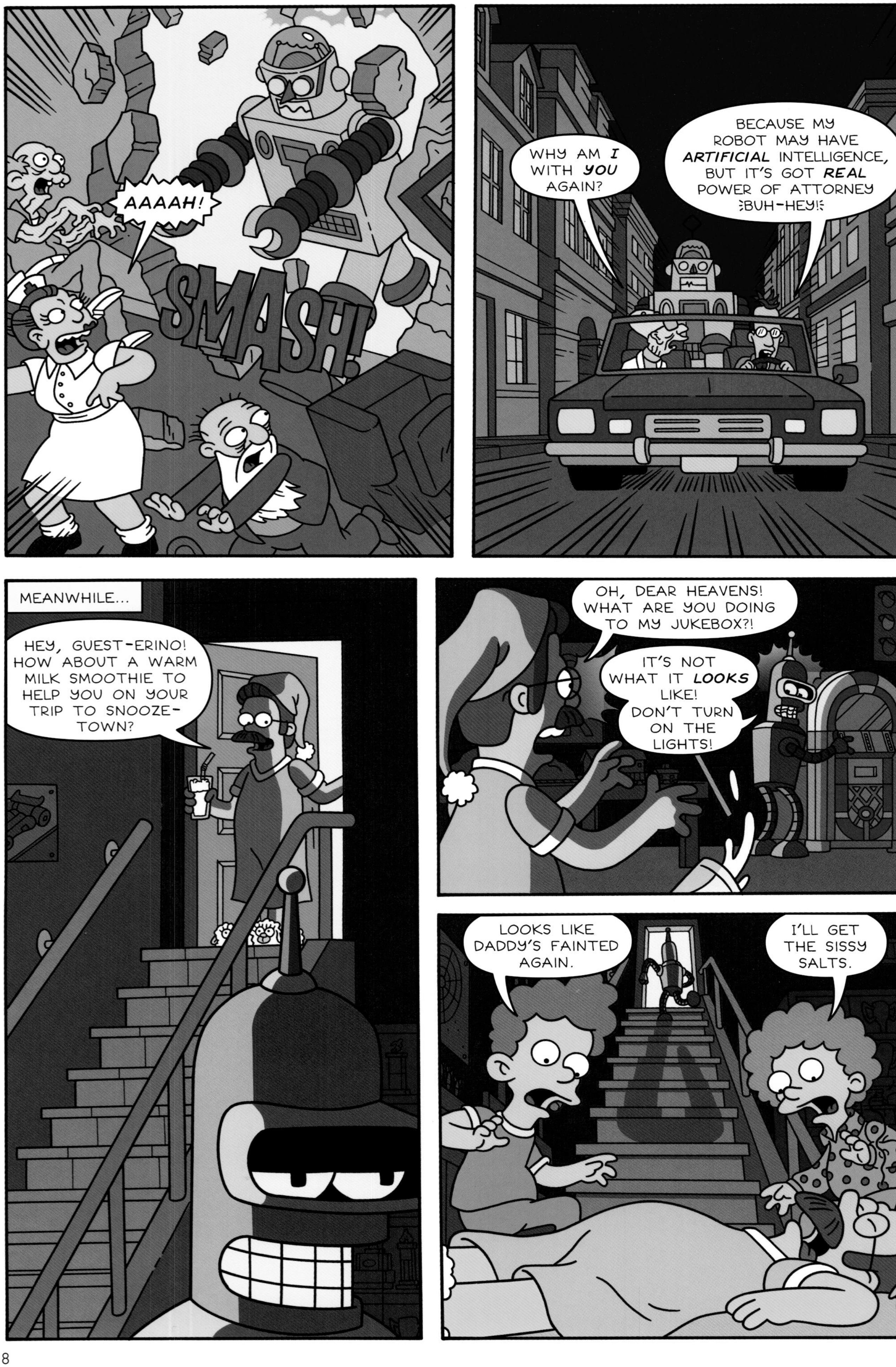
AAAAH!
SMASH!
WHY AM I WITH YOU AGAIN?
BECAUSE MY ROBOT MAY HAVE ARTIFICIAL INTELLIGENCE, BUT IT'S GOT REAL POWER OF ATTORNEY
BUH-HEY!
MEANWHILE...
HEY, GUEST-ERINO! HOW ABOUT A WARM MILK SMOOTHIE TO HELP YOU ON YOUR TRIP TO SNOOZE-TOWN?
OH, DEAR HEAVENS! WHAT ARE YOU DOING TO MY JUKEBOX?!
IT'S NOT WHAT IT LOOKS LIKE! DON'T TURN ON THE LIGHTS!
LOOKS LIKE DADDY'S FAINTED AGAIN.
I'LL GET THE SISSY SALTS.

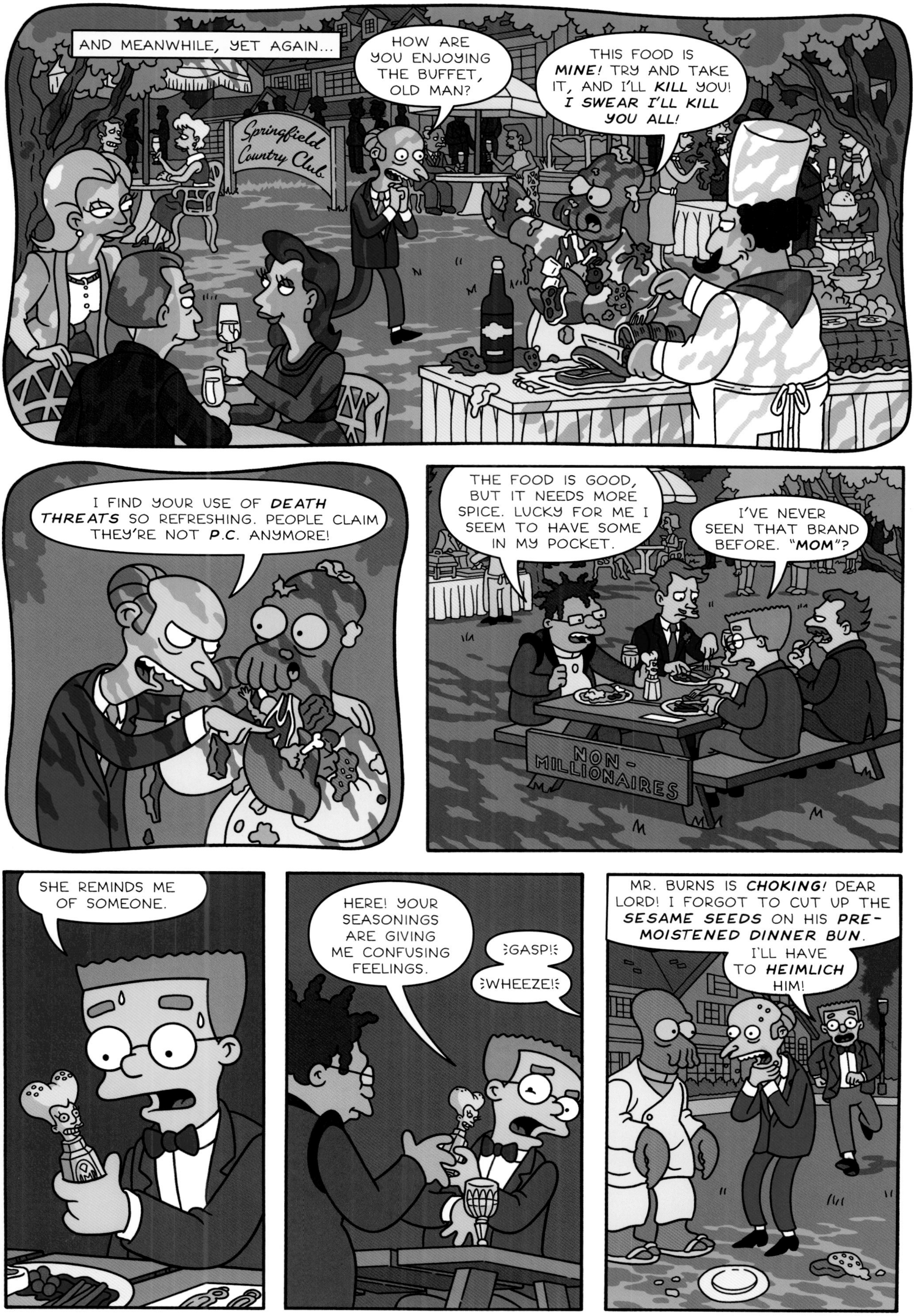

AND MEANWHILE, YET AGAIN...
HOW ARE YOU ENJOYING THE BUFFET, OLD MAN?
THIS FOOD IS MINE! TRY AND TAKE IT, AND I'LL KILL YOU! I SWEAR I'LL KILL YOU ALL!
Springfield Country Club
I FIND YOUR USE OF DEATH THREATS SO REFRESHING. PEOPLE CLAIM THEY'RE NOT P.C. ANYMORE!
THE FOOD IS GOOD, BUT IT NEEDS MORE SPICE. LUCKY FOR ME I SEEM TO HAVE SOME IN MY POCKET.
I'VE NEVER SEEN THAT BRAND BEFORE. "MOM"?
NON-MILLIONAIRES
SHE REMINDS ME OF SOMEONE.
HERE! YOUR SEASONINGS ARE GIVING ME CONFUSING FEELINGS.
GASP!
WHEEZE!
MR. BURNS IS CHOKING! DEAR LORD! I FORGOT TO CUT UP THE SESAME SEEDS ON HIS PRE-MOISTENED DINNER BUN.
I'LL HAVE TO HEIMLICH HIM!

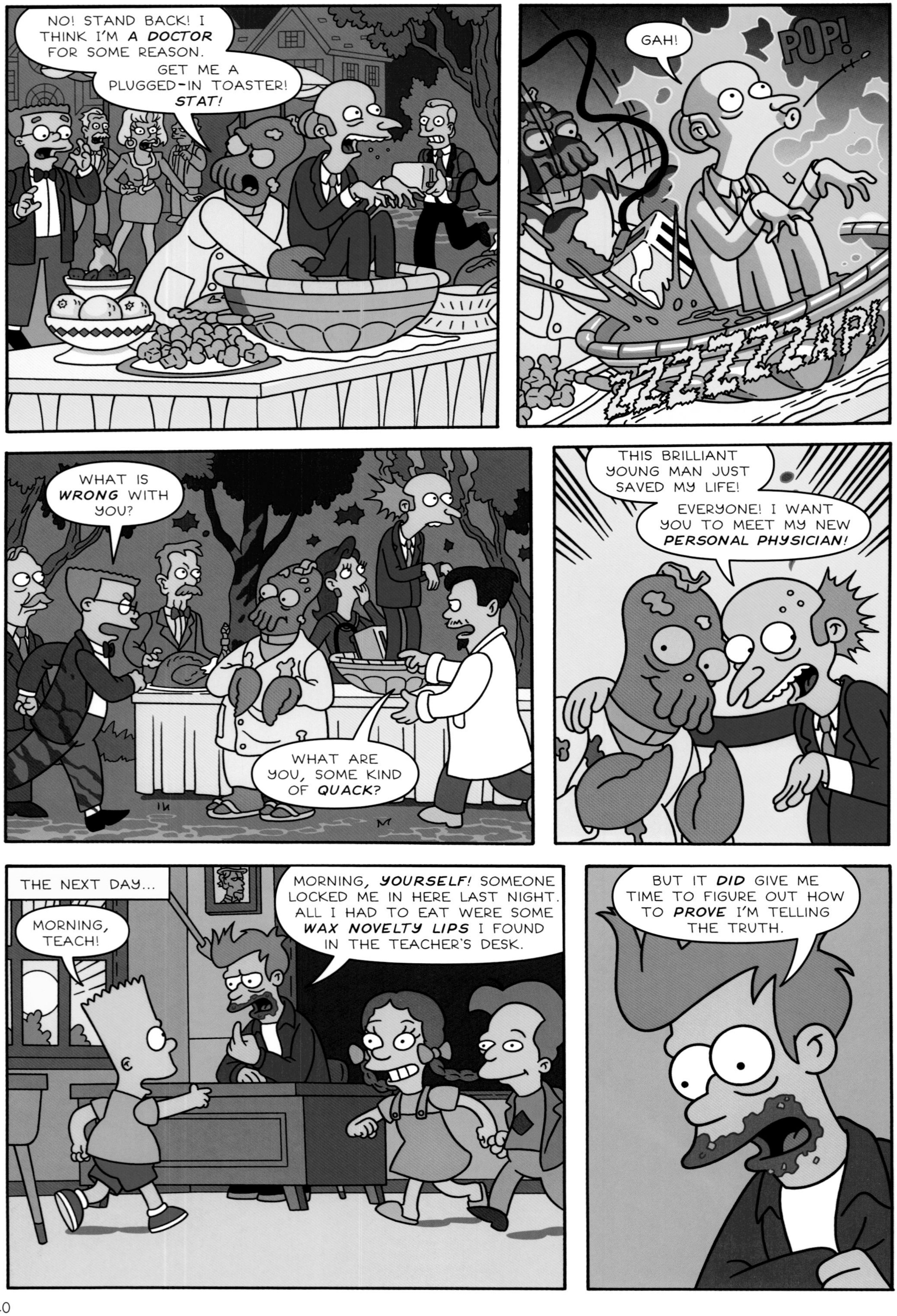
NO! STAND BACK! I THINK I'M **A DOCTOR** FOR SOME REASON.
GET ME A PLUGGED-IN TOASTER! ***STAT!***
GAH!
POP!
ZZZZZAP!
WHAT IS ***WRONG*** WITH YOU?
WHAT ARE YOU, SOME KIND OF ***QUACK?***
THIS BRILLIANT YOUNG MAN JUST SAVED MY LIFE!
EVERYONE! I WANT YOU TO MEET MY NEW ***PERSONAL PHYSICIAN!***
THE NEXT DAY...
MORNING, TEACH!
MORNING, ***YOURSELF!*** SOMEONE LOCKED ME IN HERE LAST NIGHT. ALL I HAD TO EAT WERE SOME ***WAX NOVELTY LIPS*** I FOUND IN THE TEACHER'S DESK.
BUT IT ***DID*** GIVE ME TIME TO FIGURE OUT HOW TO ***PROVE*** I'M TELLING THE TRUTH.

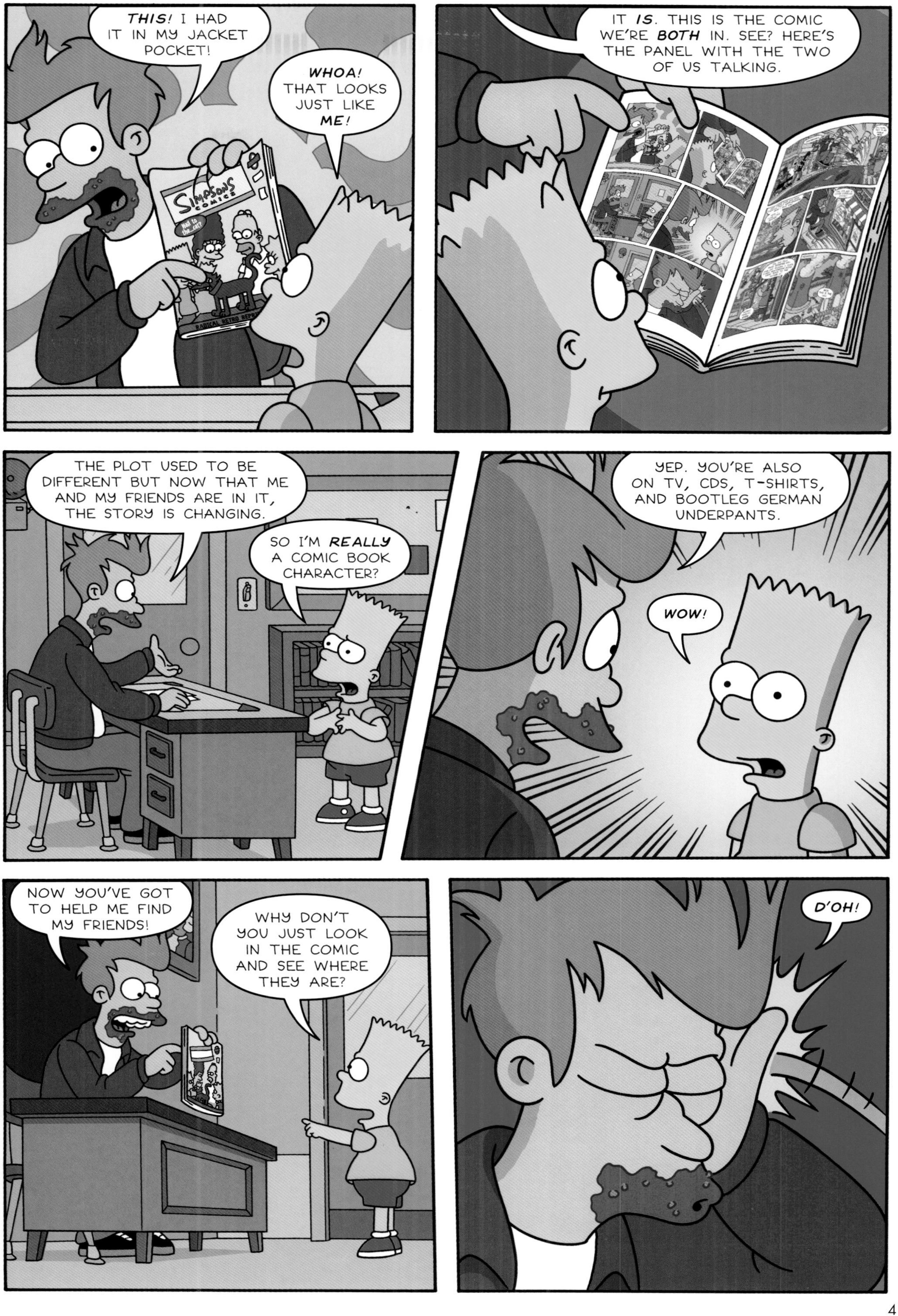
THIS! I HAD IT IN MY JACKET POCKET!
WHOA! THAT LOOKS JUST LIKE ME!
SIMPSONS COMICS
RADICAL RETRO REPR
IT IS. THIS IS THE COMIC WE'RE BOTH IN. SEE? HERE'S THE PANEL WITH THE TWO OF US TALKING.
THE PLOT USED TO BE DIFFERENT BUT NOW THAT ME AND MY FRIENDS ARE IN IT, THE STORY IS CHANGING.
SO I'M REALLY A COMIC BOOK CHARACTER?
YEP. YOU'RE ALSO ON TV, CDS, T-SHIRTS, AND BOOTLEG GERMAN UNDERPANTS.
WOW!
NOW YOU'VE GOT TO HELP ME FIND MY FRIENDS!
WHY DON'T YOU JUST LOOK IN THE COMIC AND SEE WHERE THEY ARE?
D'OH!

COWABUNGA!

OH, PLEASE, THAT IS *SO* EARLY '90's!

JUST MAKE SURE YOU KEEP CHEWING THAT *ANTI-GRAVITY GUM* I GAVE YOU!

HEY, I THINK I SEE BENDER!

AW, IT'S JUST A LOUSY CARDBOARD CUTOUT!

"TAKE ME TO YOUR COMIC BOOKS & BASEBALL CARDS"

YES, WE'RE *OPEN*

OH, BIG TALK FROM SOMEONE RIPPING OFF MICHAEL J. FOX'S FLYING SKATEBOARD SCENE FROM "BACK TO THE FUTURE II"!

WORST TRIBUTE, *EVER!*

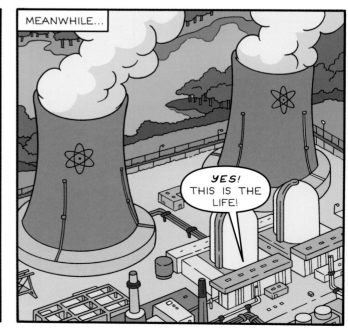

MEANWHILE...

YES! THIS IS THE LIFE!

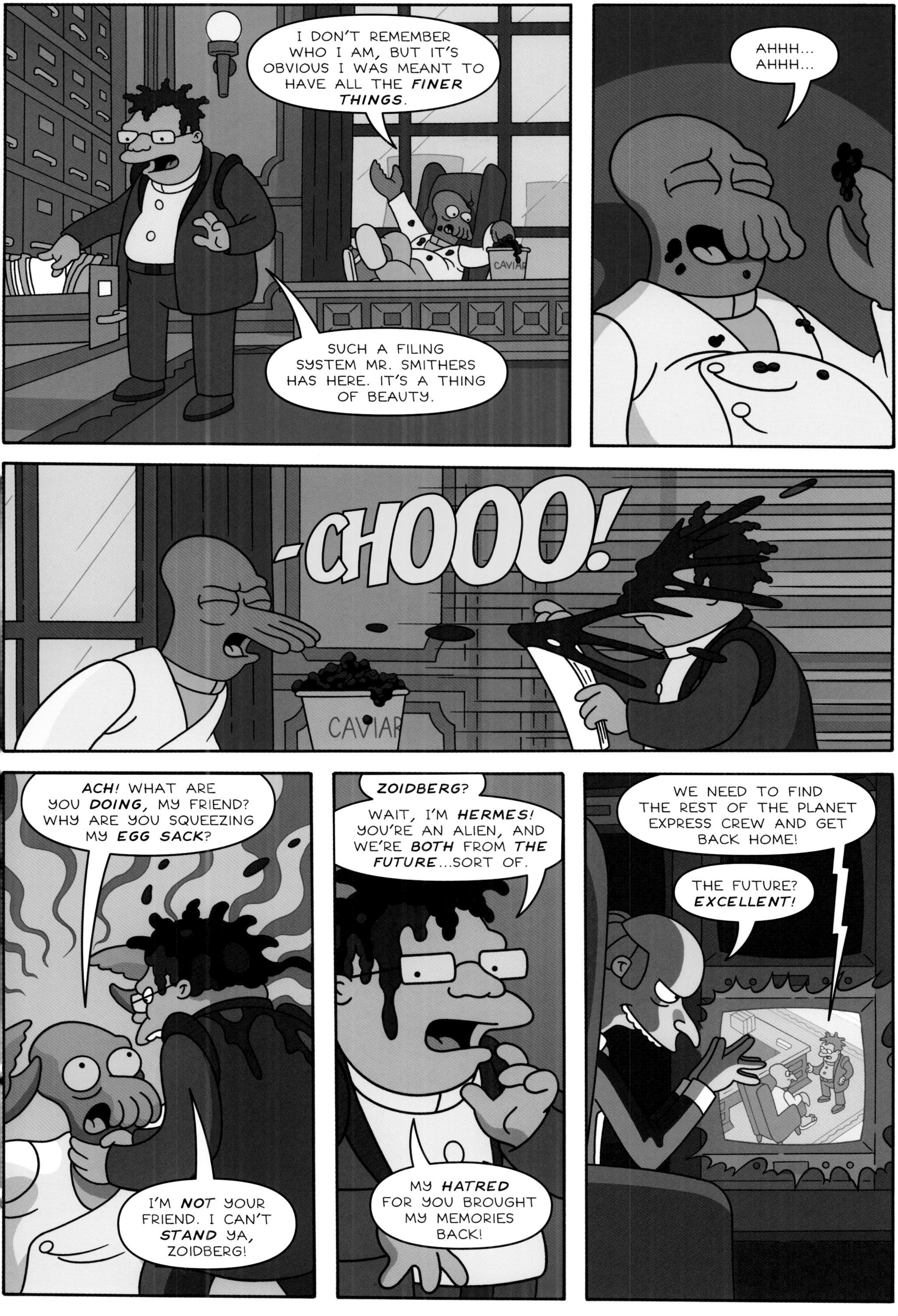
I DON'T REMEMBER WHO I AM, BUT IT'S OBVIOUS I WAS MEANT TO HAVE ALL THE *FINER THINGS*.
SUCH A FILING SYSTEM MR. SMITHERS HAS HERE. IT'S A THING OF BEAUTY.
CAVIAR
AHHH... AHHH...
-CHOOO!
CAVIAR
ACH! WHAT ARE YOU *DOING,* MY FRIEND? WHY ARE YOU SQUEEZING MY *EGG SACK*?
I'M *NOT* YOUR FRIEND. I CAN'T *STAND* YA, ZOIDBERG!
ZOIDBERG?
WAIT, I'M *HERMES*! YOU'RE AN ALIEN, AND WE'RE *BOTH* FROM *THE FUTURE*...SORT OF.
MY *HATRED* FOR YOU BROUGHT MY MEMORIES BACK!
WE NEED TO FIND THE REST OF THE PLANET EXPRESS CREW AND GET BACK HOME!
THE FUTURE? *EXCELLENT*!

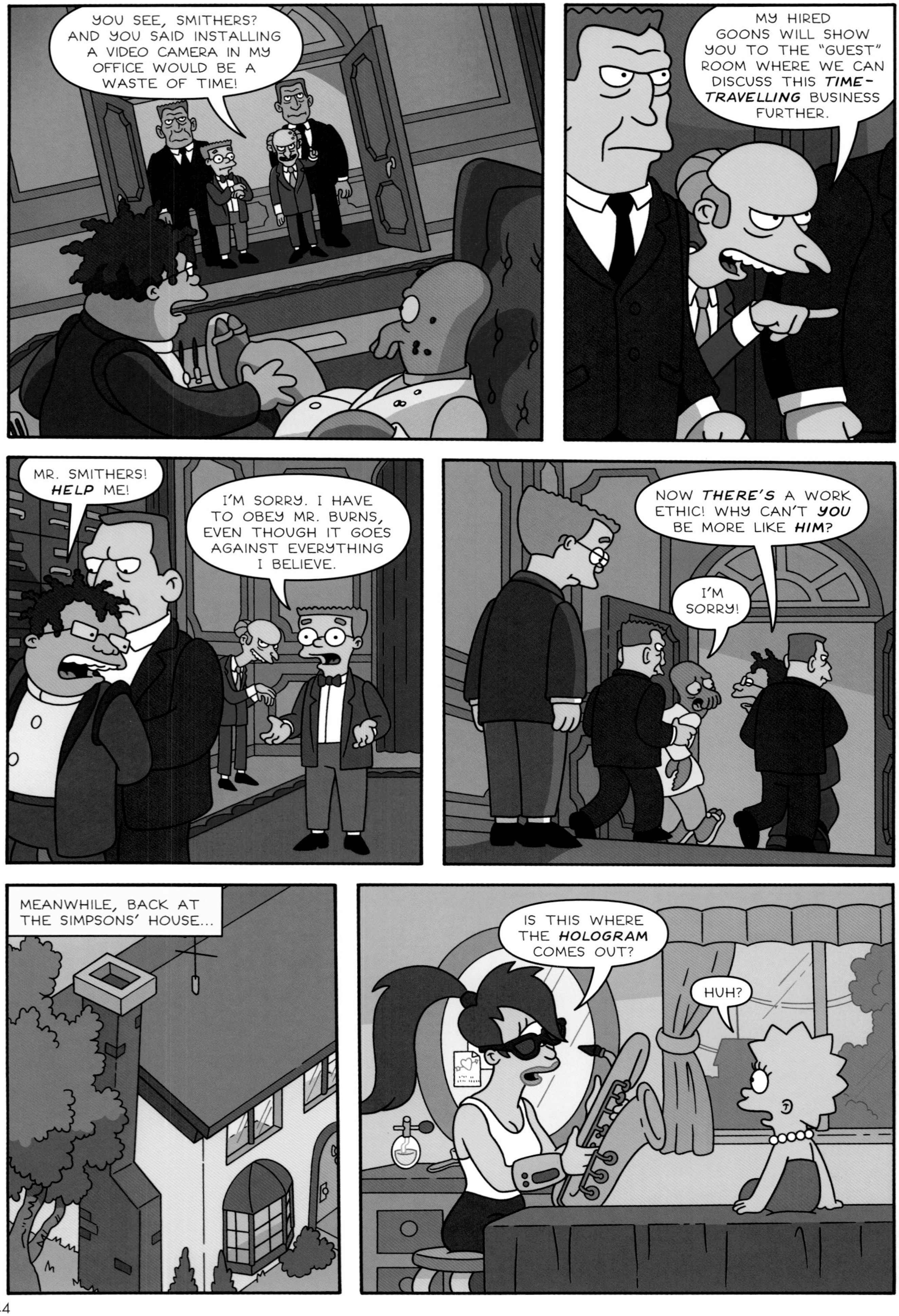
YOU SEE, SMITHERS? AND YOU SAID INSTALLING A VIDEO CAMERA IN MY OFFICE WOULD BE A WASTE OF TIME!
MY HIRED GOONS WILL SHOW YOU TO THE "GUEST" ROOM WHERE WE CAN DISCUSS THIS **TIME-TRAVELLING** BUSINESS FURTHER.
MR. SMITHERS! **HELP** ME!
I'M SORRY. I HAVE TO OBEY MR. BURNS, EVEN THOUGH IT GOES AGAINST EVERYTHING I BELIEVE.
NOW **THERE'S** A WORK ETHIC! WHY CAN'T **YOU** BE MORE LIKE **HIM**?
I'M SORRY!
MEANWHILE, BACK AT THE SIMPSONS' HOUSE...
IS THIS WHERE THE **HOLOGRAM** COMES OUT?
HUH?

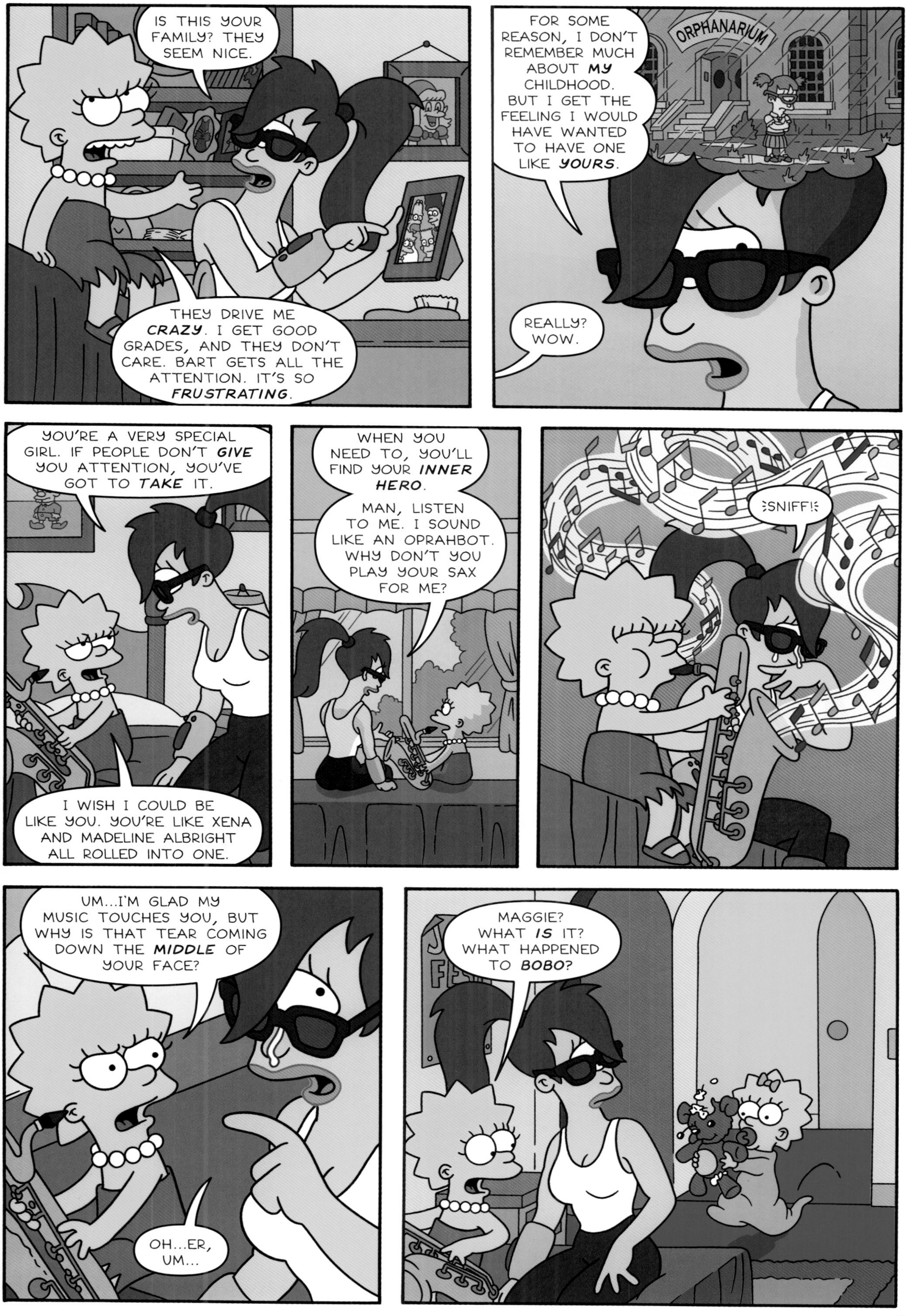
IS THIS YOUR FAMILY? THEY SEEM NICE.
THEY DRIVE ME CRAZY. I GET GOOD GRADES, AND THEY DON'T CARE. BART GETS ALL THE ATTENTION. IT'S SO FRUSTRATING.
ORPHANARIUM
FOR SOME REASON, I DON'T REMEMBER MUCH ABOUT MY CHILDHOOD. BUT I GET THE FEELING I WOULD HAVE WANTED TO HAVE ONE LIKE YOURS.
REALLY? WOW.
YOU'RE A VERY SPECIAL GIRL. IF PEOPLE DON'T GIVE YOU ATTENTION, YOU'VE GOT TO TAKE IT.
I WISH I COULD BE LIKE YOU. YOU'RE LIKE XENA AND MADELINE ALBRIGHT ALL ROLLED INTO ONE.
WHEN YOU NEED TO, YOU'LL FIND YOUR INNER HERO.
MAN, LISTEN TO ME. I SOUND LIKE AN OPRAHBOT. WHY DON'T YOU PLAY YOUR SAX FOR ME?
SNIFF!
UM...I'M GLAD MY MUSIC TOUCHES YOU, BUT WHY IS THAT TEAR COMING DOWN THE MIDDLE OF YOUR FACE?
OH...ER, UM...
MAGGIE? WHAT IS IT? WHAT HAPPENED TO BOBO?

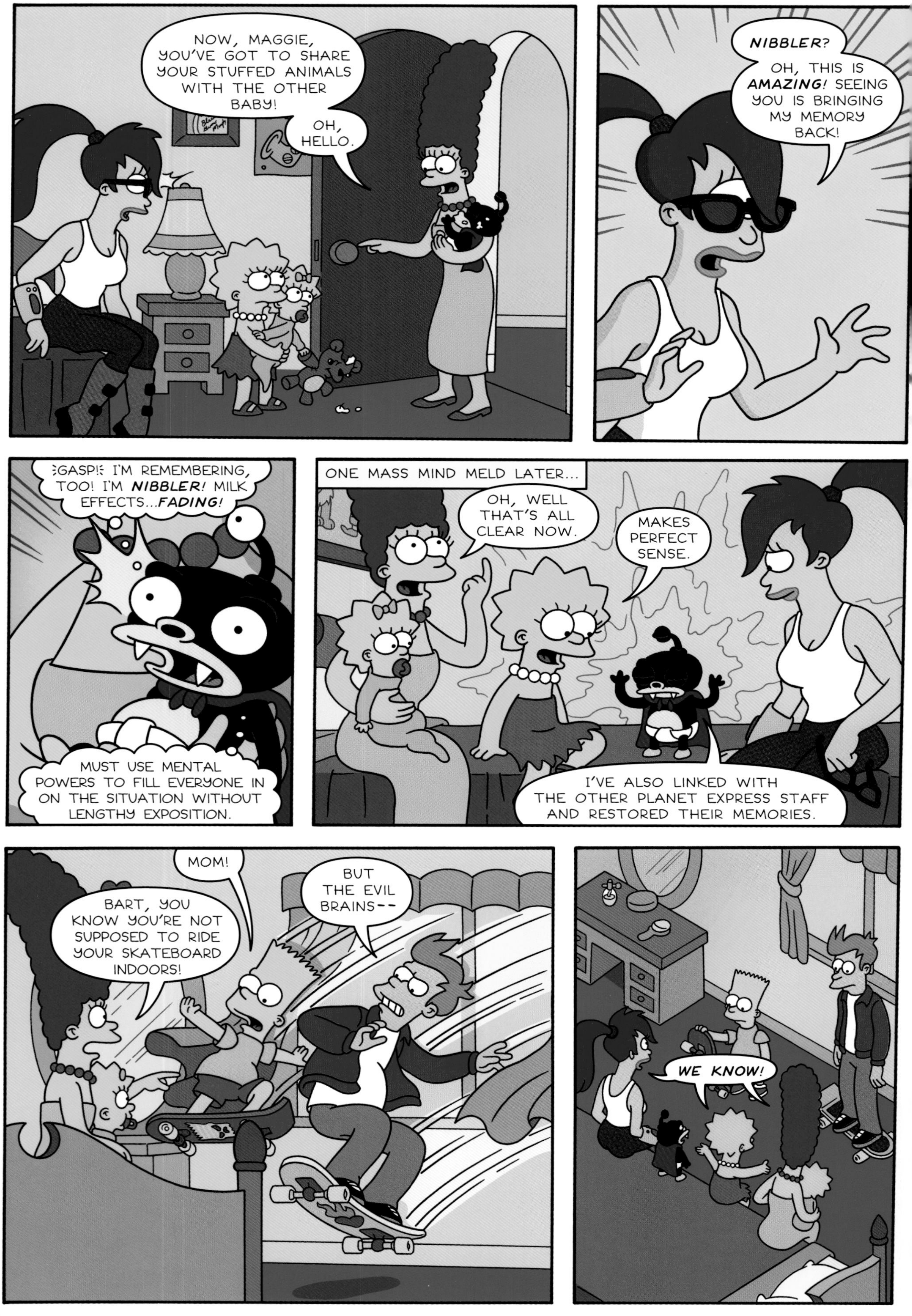
NOW, MAGGIE, YOU'VE GOT TO SHARE YOUR STUFFED ANIMALS WITH THE OTHER BABY!
OH, HELLO.
NIBBLER?
OH, THIS IS AMAZING! SEEING YOU IS BRINGING MY MEMORY BACK!
:GASP!: I'M REMEMBERING, TOO! I'M NIBBLER! MILK EFFECTS...FADING!
MUST USE MENTAL POWERS TO FILL EVERYONE IN ON THE SITUATION WITHOUT LENGTHY EXPOSITION.
ONE MASS MIND MELD LATER...
OH, WELL THAT'S ALL CLEAR NOW.
MAKES PERFECT SENSE.
I'VE ALSO LINKED WITH THE OTHER PLANET EXPRESS STAFF AND RESTORED THEIR MEMORIES.
MOM!
BART, YOU KNOW YOU'RE NOT SUPPOSED TO RIDE YOUR SKATEBOARD INDOORS!
BUT THE EVIL BRAINS--
WE KNOW!

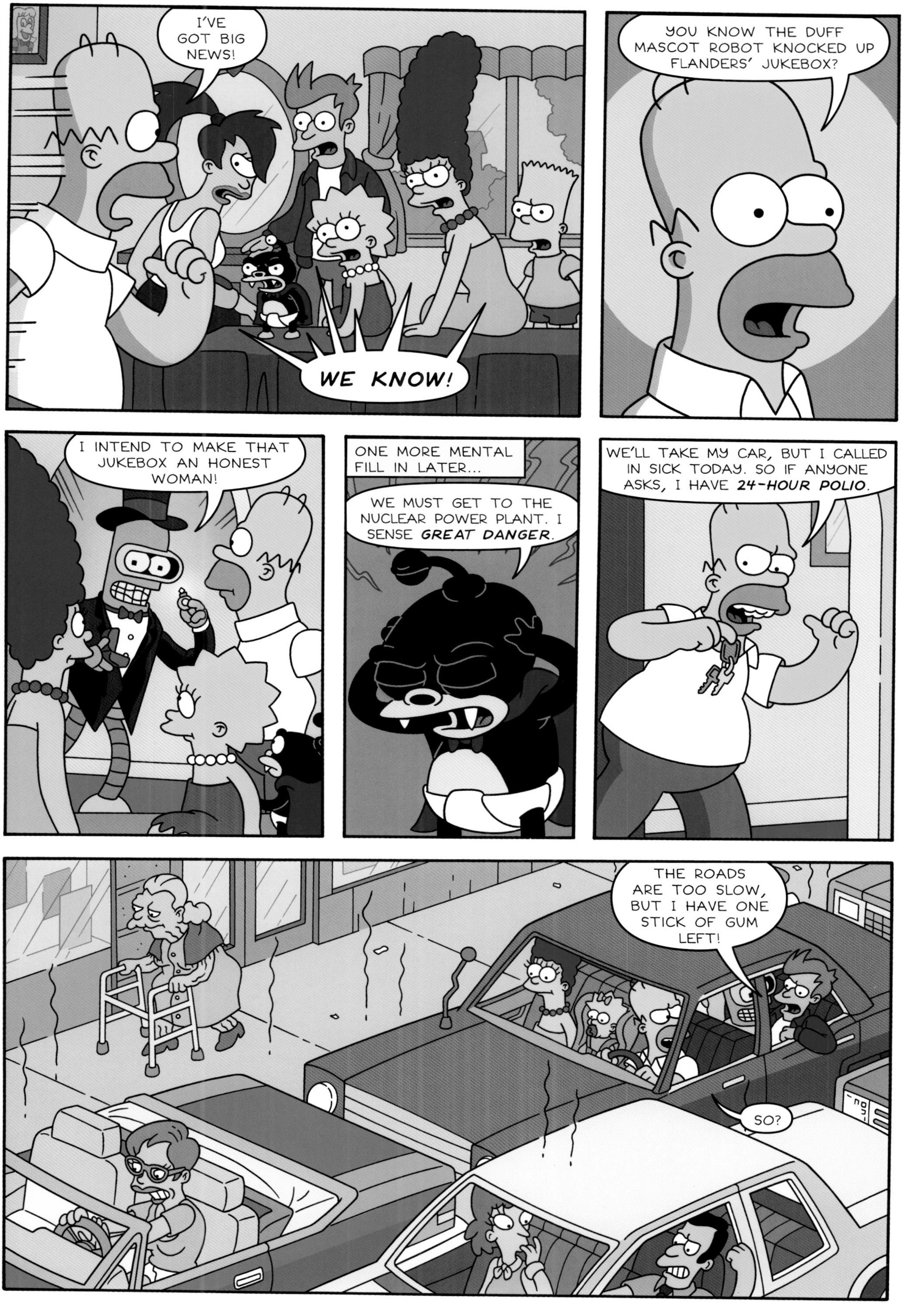
I'VE GOT BIG NEWS!
WE KNOW!
YOU KNOW THE DUFF MASCOT ROBOT KNOCKED UP FLANDERS' JUKEBOX?
I INTEND TO MAKE THAT JUKEBOX AN HONEST WOMAN!
ONE MORE MENTAL FILL IN LATER...
WE MUST GET TO THE NUCLEAR POWER PLANT. I SENSE **GREAT DANGER**.
WE'LL TAKE MY CAR, BUT I CALLED IN SICK TODAY. SO IF ANYONE ASKS, I HAVE **24-HOUR POLIO**.
THE ROADS ARE TOO SLOW, BUT I HAVE ONE STICK OF GUM LEFT!
SO?

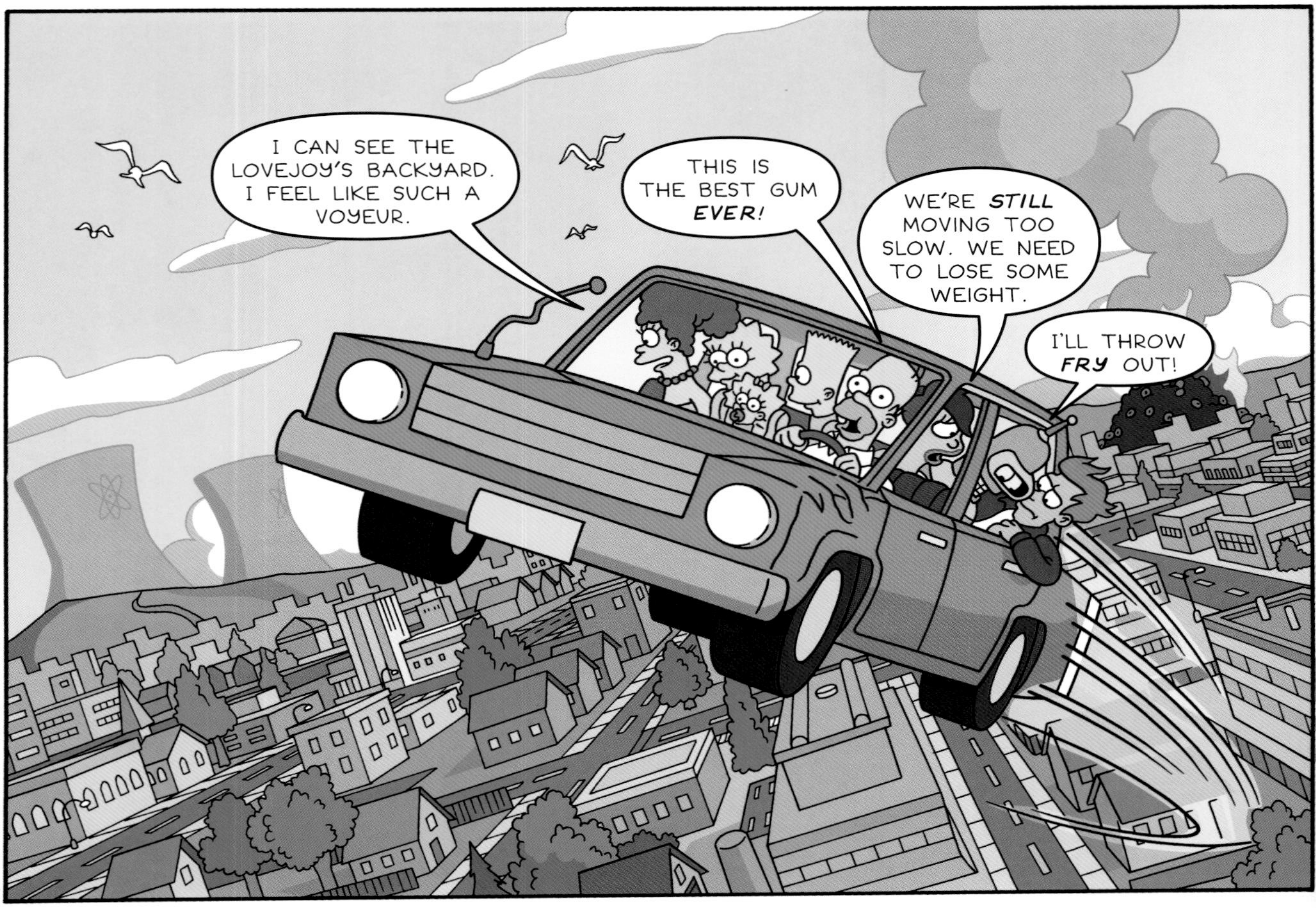
I CAN SEE THE LOVEJOY'S BACKYARD. I FEEL LIKE SUCH A VOYEUR.
THIS IS THE BEST GUM ***EVER!***
WE'RE ***STILL*** MOVING TOO SLOW. WE NEED TO LOSE SOME WEIGHT.
I'LL THROW ***FRY*** OUT!

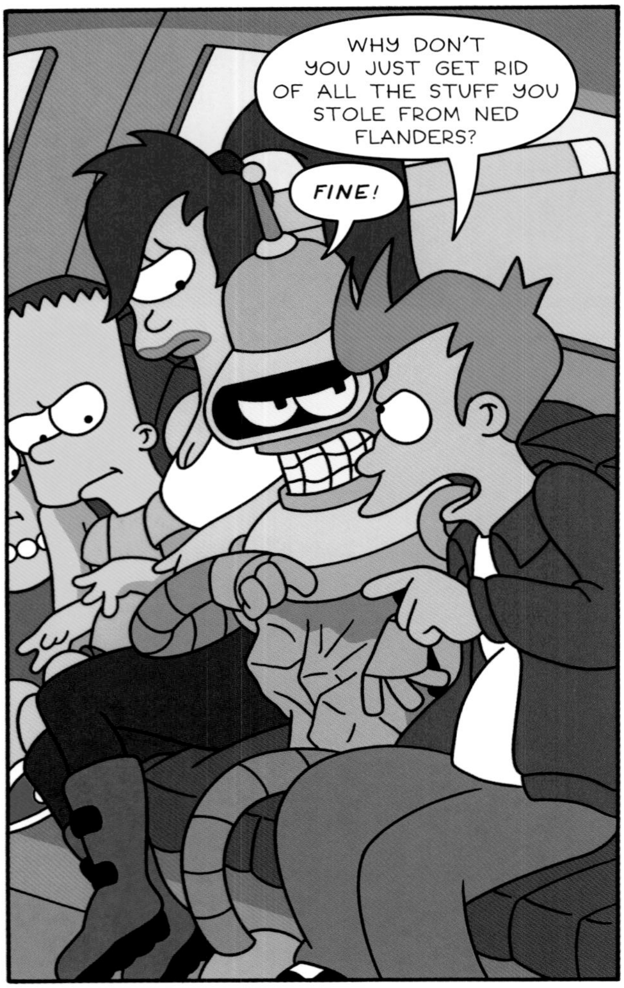
WHY DON'T YOU JUST GET RID OF ALL THE STUFF YOU STOLE FROM NED FLANDERS?
FINE!

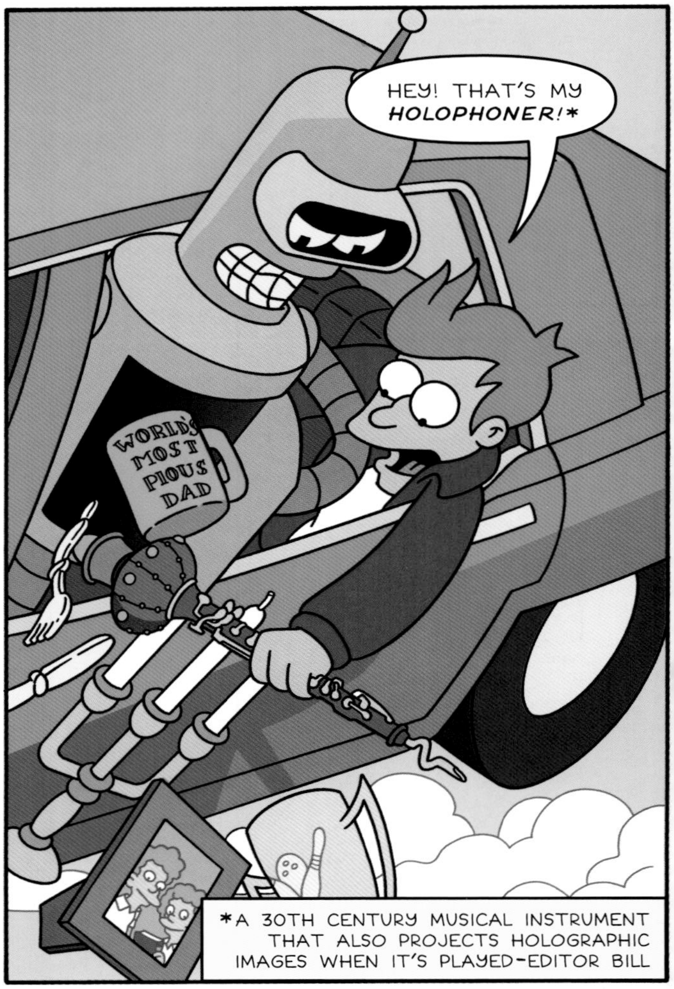
HEY! THAT'S MY ***HOLOPHONER!****
WORLD'S MOST PIOUS DAD

*A 30TH CENTURY MUSICAL INSTRUMENT THAT ALSO PROJECTS HOLOGRAPHIC IMAGES WHEN IT'S PLAYED—EDITOR BILL

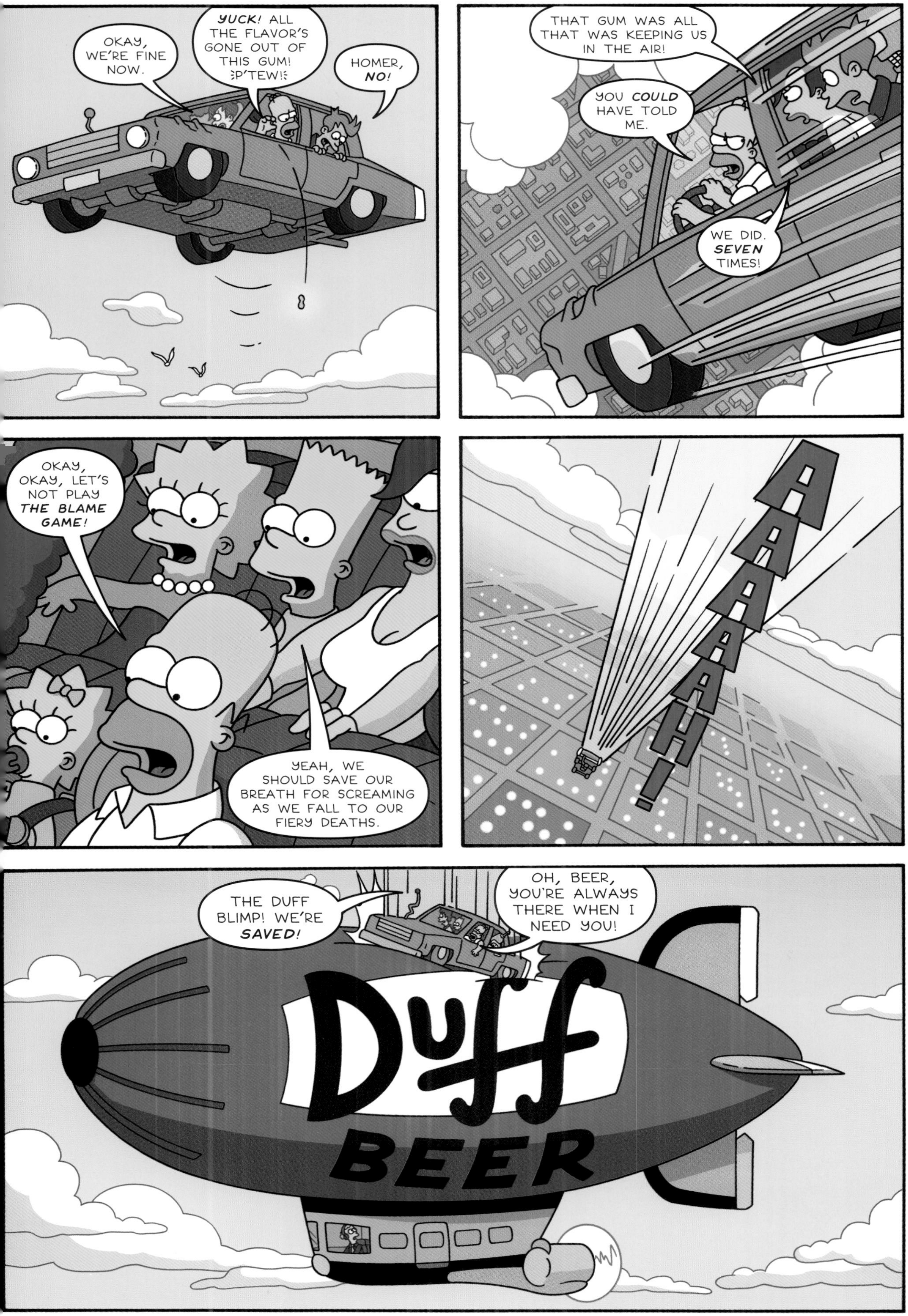

OKAY, WE'RE FINE NOW.
YUCK! ALL THE FLAVOR'S GONE OUT OF THIS GUM! P'TEW!
HOMER, *NO!*
THAT GUM WAS ALL THAT WAS KEEPING US IN THE AIR!
YOU *COULD* HAVE TOLD ME.
WE DID. *SEVEN* TIMES!
OKAY, OKAY, LET'S NOT PLAY *THE BLAME GAME!*
YEAH, WE SHOULD SAVE OUR BREATH FOR SCREAMING AS WE FALL TO OUR FIERY DEATHS.
AAAAAAAH!!
THE DUFF BLIMP! WE'RE *SAVED!*
OH, BEER, YOU'RE ALWAYS THERE WHEN I NEED YOU!
Duff
BEER

AMEN, BROTHER! THIS CALLS FOR A CELEBRATORY SMOKE!
DON'T LIGHT THAT, BENDER!
WHY NOT?
OH.
FWOOOSH!
AAAAAAAH!
CLUNK!
DOES ANYBODY WANT A TOW TO THE POWER PLANT?
PROFESSOR FRINK!
AND PROFESSOR FARNSWORTH!

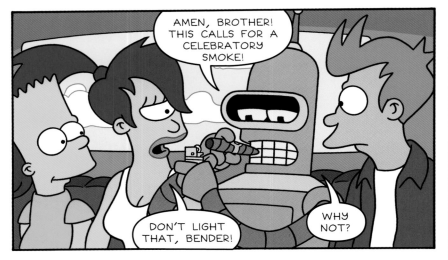

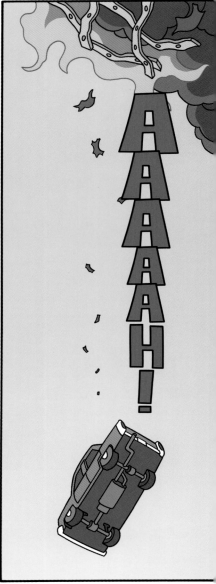

I'M READING AN OVERDRAG RATIO OF TWO.

SOME PERSONS NEED TO LEAVE THE CAR!

WHY IS IT ALWAYS *ME*?

I KNOW WHAT YOU MEAN.

SAY, WHAT KIND OF INSTRUMENT IS THAT?

IT'S A 30TH CENTURY MUSICAL INSTRUMENT THAT ALSO PROJECTS HOLOGRAPHIC IMAGES WHEN-- OH, JUST READ THE THE EDITOR'S NOTE ON PAGE 48! I'M TRYING TO LEARN IT TO IMPRESS LEELA.

WOW!

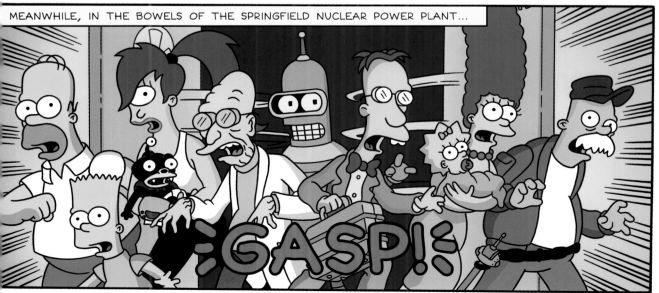

MEANWHILE, IN THE BOWELS OF THE SPRINGFIELD NUCLEAR POWER PLANT...

:·GASP!·:

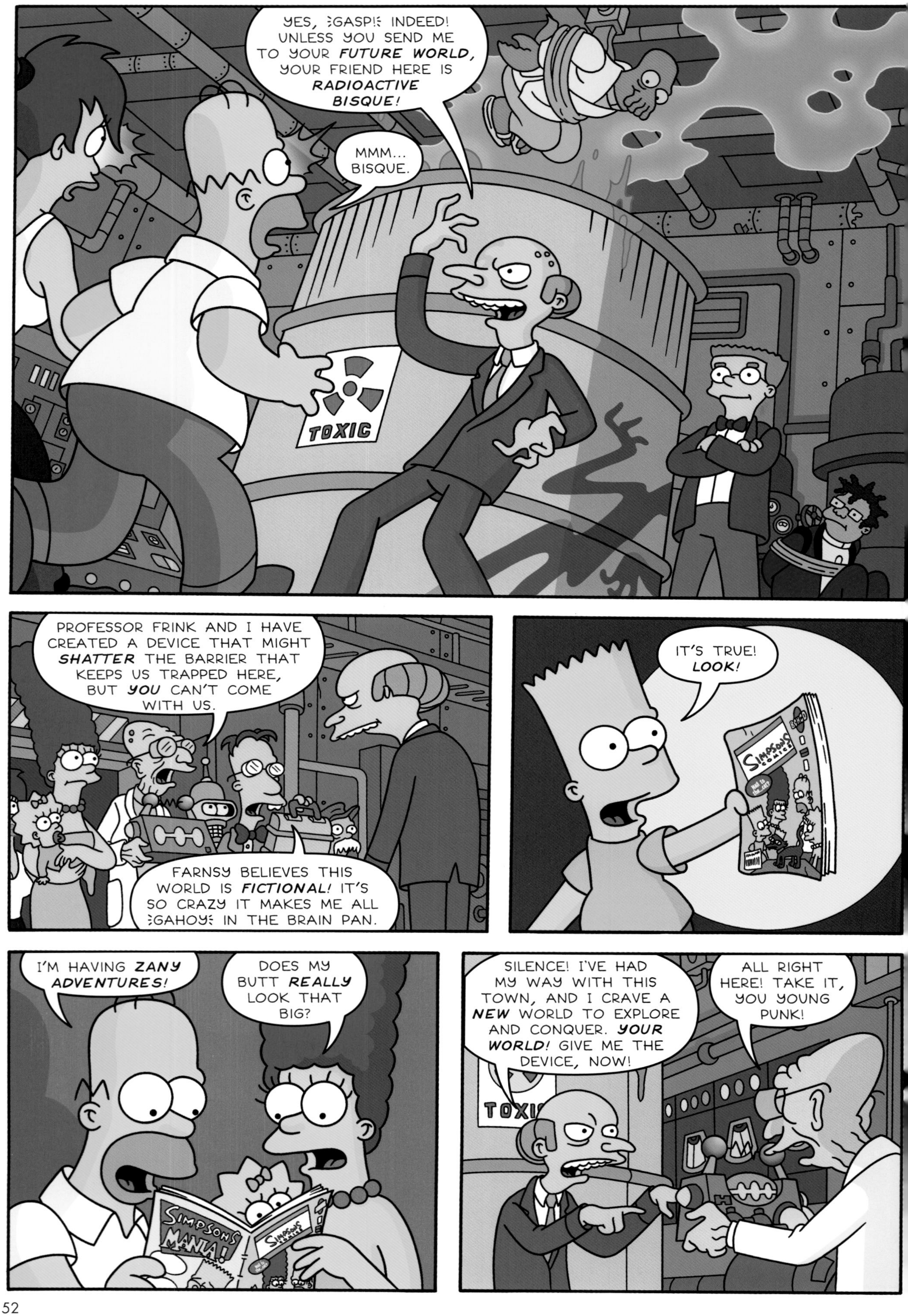
YES, {GASP!} INDEED! UNLESS YOU SEND ME TO YOUR FUTURE WORLD, YOUR FRIEND HERE IS RADIOACTIVE BISQUE!
MMM... BISQUE.
TOXIC
PROFESSOR FRINK AND I HAVE CREATED A DEVICE THAT MIGHT SHATTER THE BARRIER THAT KEEPS US TRAPPED HERE, BUT YOU CAN'T COME WITH US.
FARNSY BELIEVES THIS WORLD IS FICTIONAL! IT'S SO CRAZY IT MAKES ME ALL {GAHOY} IN THE BRAIN PAN.
IT'S TRUE! LOOK!
SIMPSONS COMICS
I'M HAVING ZANY ADVENTURES!
DOES MY BUTT REALLY LOOK THAT BIG?
SIMPSONS MANIA!
SIMPSONS COMICS
SILENCE! I'VE HAD MY WAY WITH THIS TOWN, AND I CRAVE A NEW WORLD TO EXPLORE AND CONQUER. YOUR WORLD! GIVE ME THE DEVICE, NOW!
ALL RIGHT HERE! TAKE IT, YOU YOUNG PUNK!
TOXIC

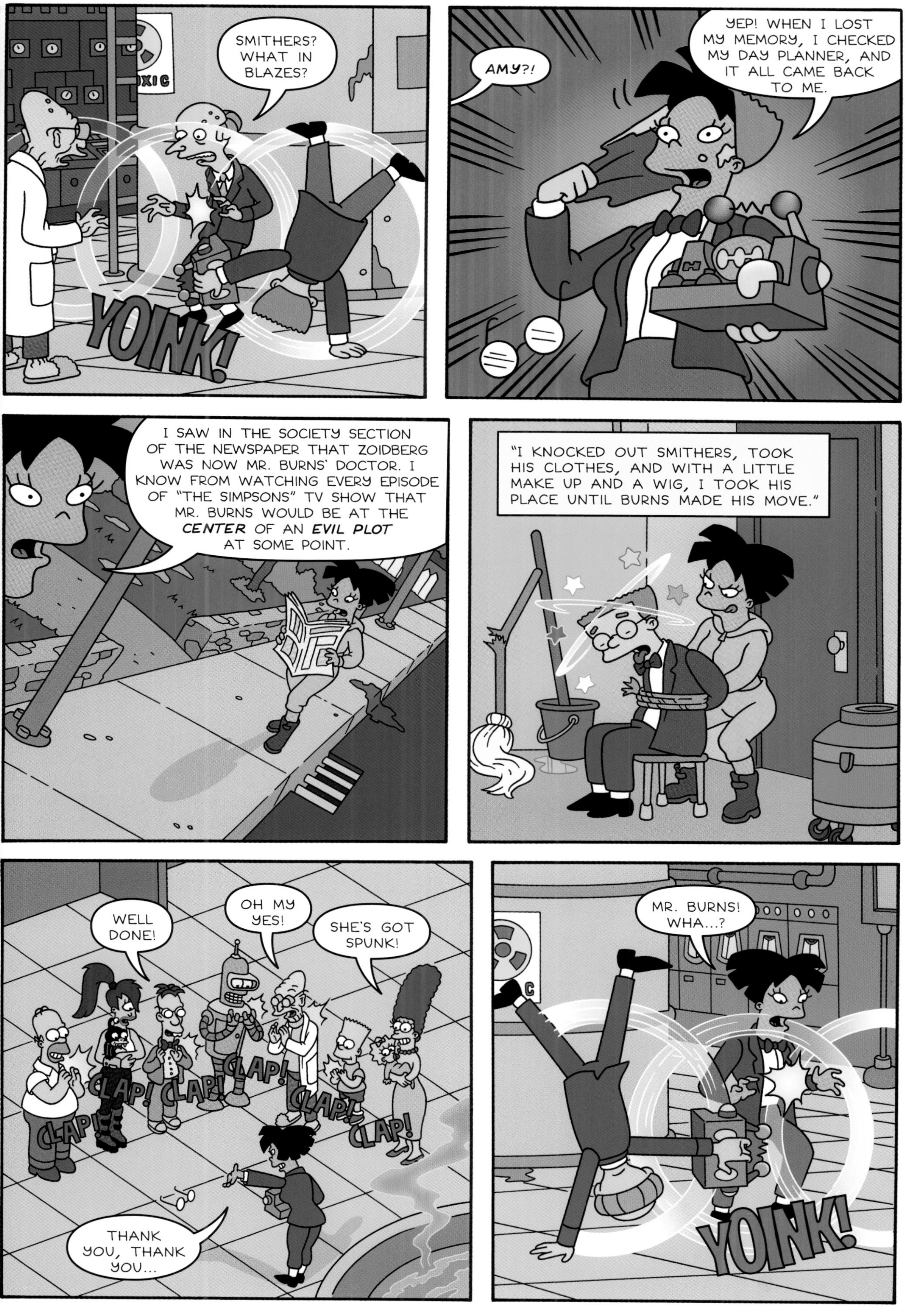
SMITHERS? WHAT IN BLAZES?
YOINK!
AMY?!
YEP! WHEN I LOST MY MEMORY, I CHECKED MY DAY PLANNER, AND IT ALL CAME BACK TO ME.
I SAW IN THE SOCIETY SECTION OF THE NEWSPAPER THAT ZOIDBERG WAS NOW MR. BURNS' DOCTOR. I KNOW FROM WATCHING EVERY EPISODE OF "THE SIMPSONS" TV SHOW THAT MR. BURNS WOULD BE AT THE *CENTER* OF AN *EVIL PLOT* AT SOME POINT.
"I KNOCKED OUT SMITHERS, TOOK HIS CLOTHES, AND WITH A LITTLE MAKE UP AND A WIG, I TOOK HIS PLACE UNTIL BURNS MADE HIS MOVE."
WELL DONE!
OH MY YES!
SHE'S GOT SPUNK!
CLAP! CLAP! CLAP! CLAP! CLAP! CLAP!
THANK YOU, THANK YOU...
MR. BURNS! WHA...?
YOINK!

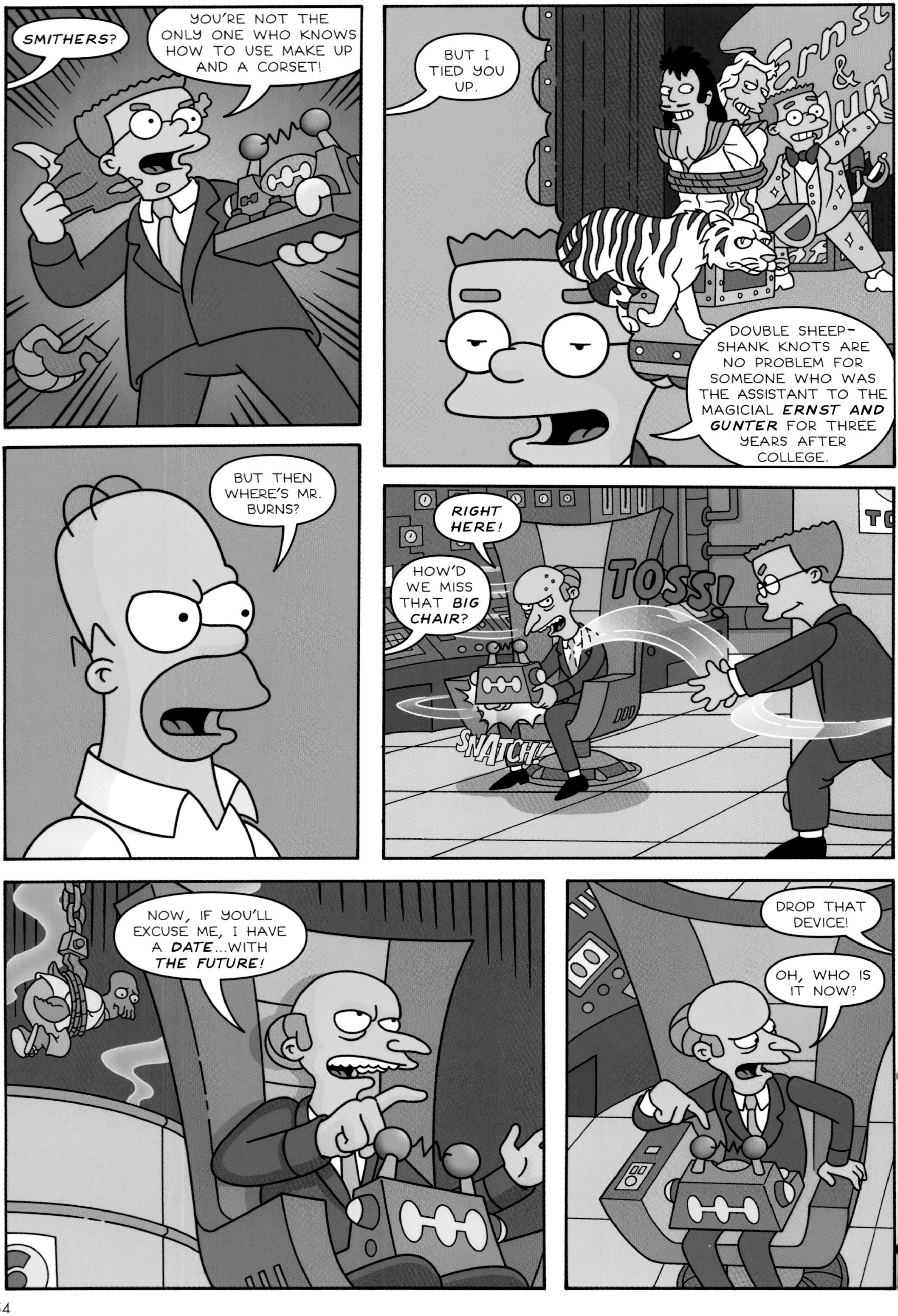
SMITHERS?
YOU'RE NOT THE ONLY ONE WHO KNOWS HOW TO USE MAKE UP AND A CORSET!
BUT I TIED YOU UP.
DOUBLE SHEEP-SHANK KNOTS ARE NO PROBLEM FOR SOMEONE WHO WAS THE ASSISTANT TO THE MAGICIAL **ERNST AND GUNTER** FOR THREE YEARS AFTER COLLEGE.
BUT THEN WHERE'S MR. BURNS?
RIGHT HERE!
HOW'D WE MISS THAT ***BIG CHAIR***?
TOSS!
SNATCH!
NOW, IF YOU'LL EXCUSE ME, I HAVE A ***DATE***...WITH ***THE FUTURE!***
DROP THAT DEVICE!
OH, WHO IS IT NOW?

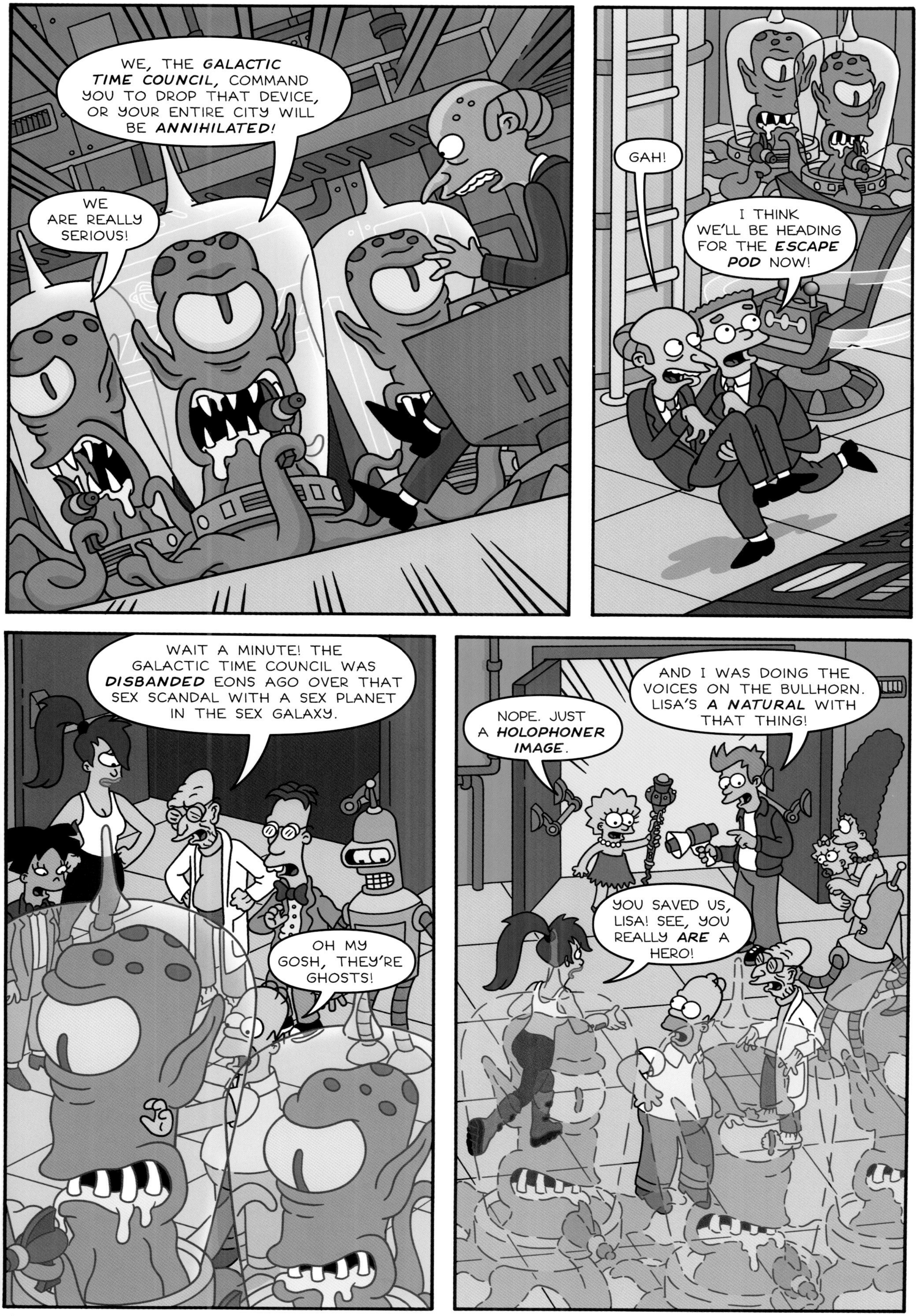
WE, THE **GALACTIC TIME COUNCIL,** COMMAND YOU TO DROP THAT DEVICE, OR YOUR ENTIRE CITY WILL BE **ANNIHILATED!**
WE ARE REALLY SERIOUS!
GAH!
I THINK WE'LL BE HEADING FOR THE **ESCAPE POD** NOW!
WAIT A MINUTE! THE GALACTIC TIME COUNCIL WAS **DISBANDED** EONS AGO OVER THAT SEX SCANDAL WITH A SEX PLANET IN THE SEX GALAXY.
OH MY GOSH, THEY'RE GHOSTS!
NOPE. JUST A **HOLOPHONER IMAGE**.
AND I WAS DOING THE VOICES ON THE BULLHORN. LISA'S **A NATURAL** WITH THAT THING!
YOU SAVED US, LISA! SEE, YOU REALLY **ARE** A HERO!

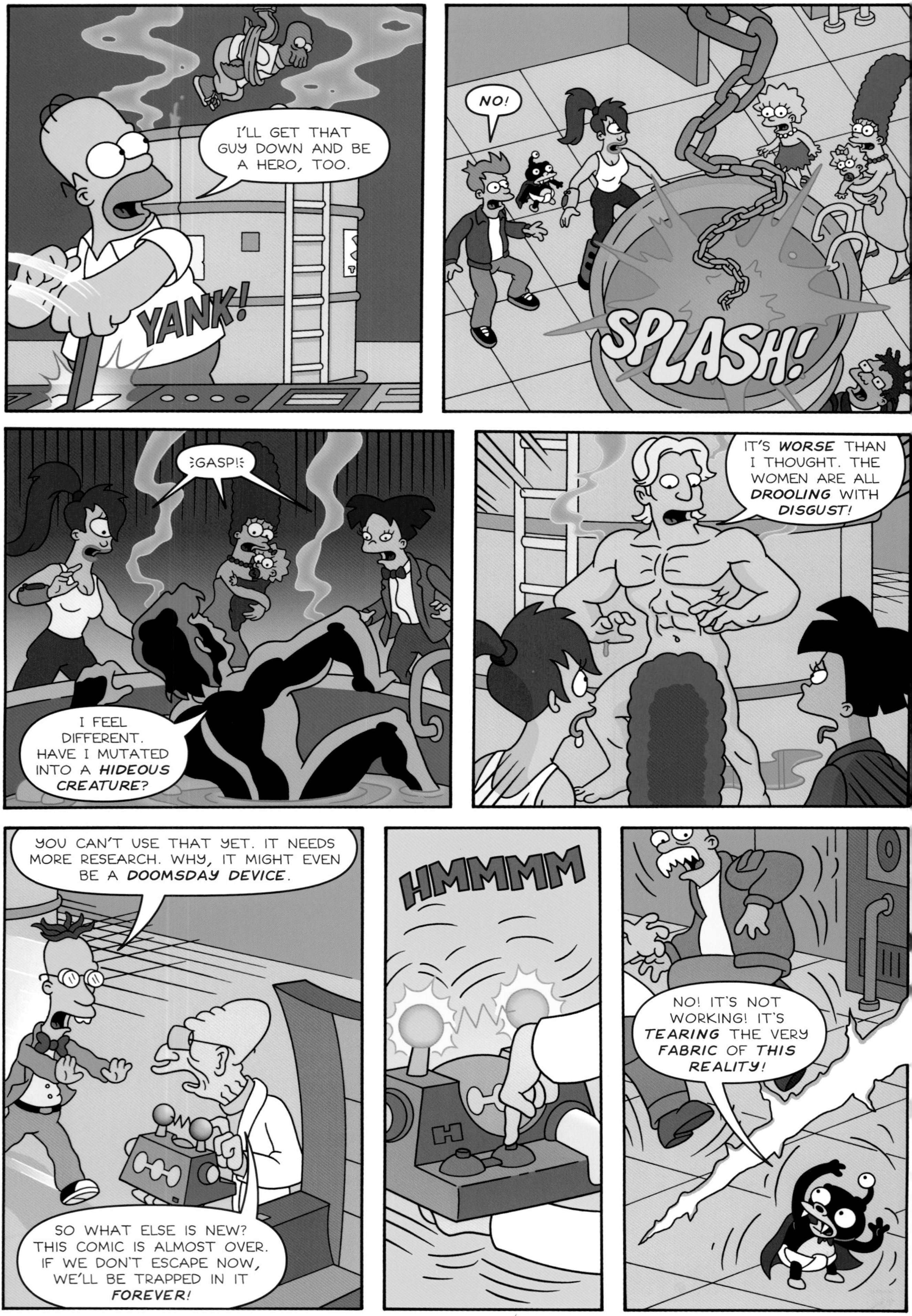
I'LL GET THAT GUY DOWN AND BE A HERO, TOO.
YANK!
NO!
SPLASH!
GASP!
I FEEL DIFFERENT. HAVE I MUTATED INTO A **HIDEOUS CREATURE**?
IT'S **WORSE** THAN I THOUGHT. THE WOMEN ARE ALL **DROOLING** WITH **DISGUST**!
YOU CAN'T USE THAT YET. IT NEEDS MORE RESEARCH. WHY, IT MIGHT EVEN BE A **DOOMSDAY DEVICE**.
SO WHAT ELSE IS NEW? THIS COMIC IS ALMOST OVER. IF WE DON'T ESCAPE NOW, WE'LL BE TRAPPED IN IT **FOREVER**!
HMMMM
NO! IT'S NOT WORKING! IT'S **TEARING** THE VERY **FABRIC** OF **THIS REALITY**!

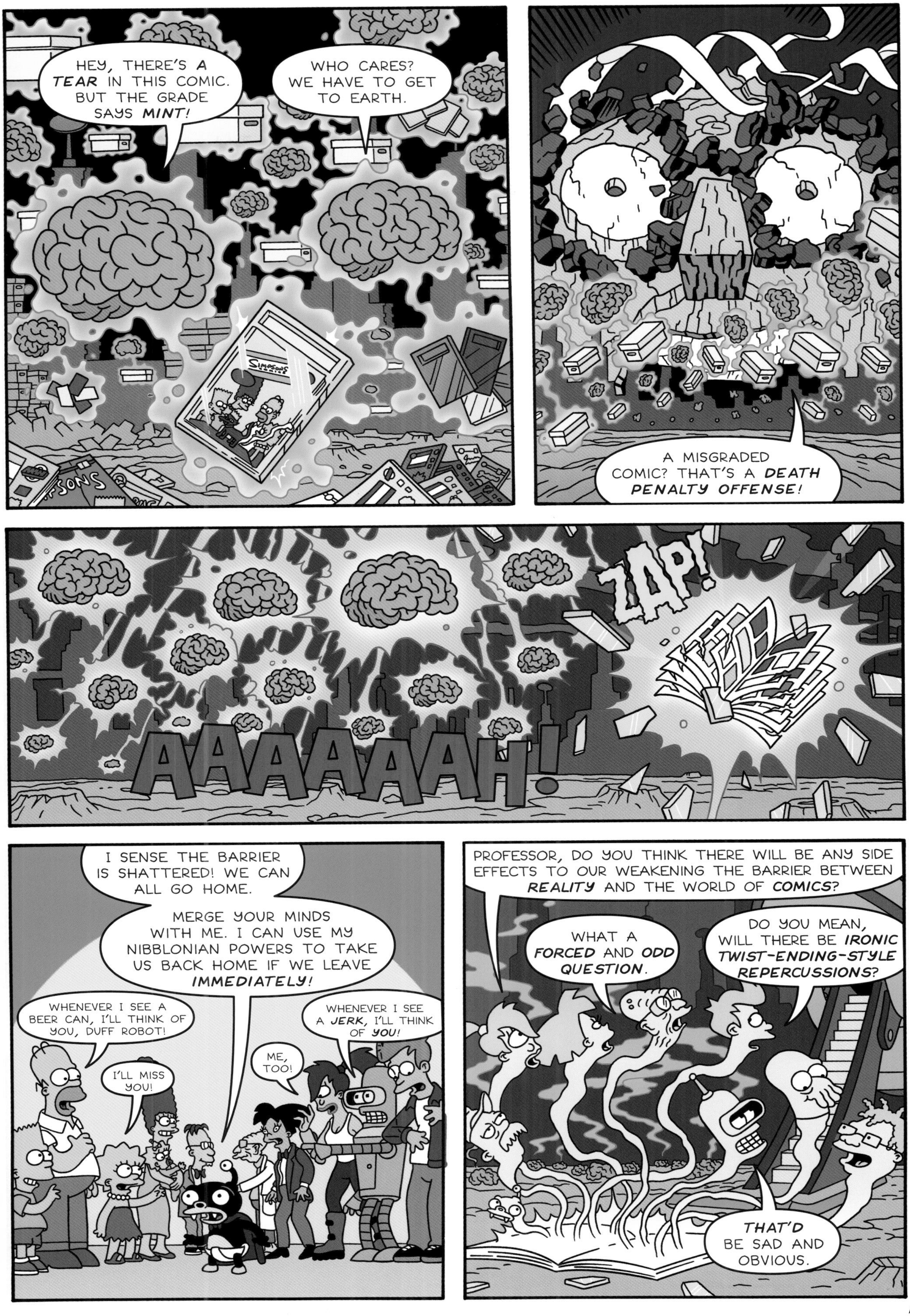
HEY, THERE'S A TEAR IN THIS COMIC. BUT THE GRADE SAYS MINT!
WHO CARES? WE HAVE TO GET TO EARTH.
A MISGRADED COMIC? THAT'S A DEATH PENALTY OFFENSE!
ZAP!
AAAAAAAH!
I SENSE THE BARRIER IS SHATTERED! WE CAN ALL GO HOME.
MERGE YOUR MINDS WITH ME. I CAN USE MY NIBBLONIAN POWERS TO TAKE US BACK HOME IF WE LEAVE IMMEDIATELY!
WHENEVER I SEE A BEER CAN, I'LL THINK OF YOU, DUFF ROBOT!
I'LL MISS YOU!
ME, TOO!
WHENEVER I SEE A JERK, I'LL THINK OF YOU!
PROFESSOR, DO YOU THINK THERE WILL BE ANY SIDE EFFECTS TO OUR WEAKENING THE BARRIER BETWEEN REALITY AND THE WORLD OF COMICS?
WHAT A FORCED AND ODD QUESTION.
DO YOU MEAN, WILL THERE BE IRONIC TWIST-ENDING-STYLE REPERCUSSIONS?
THAT'D BE SAD AND OBVIOUS.

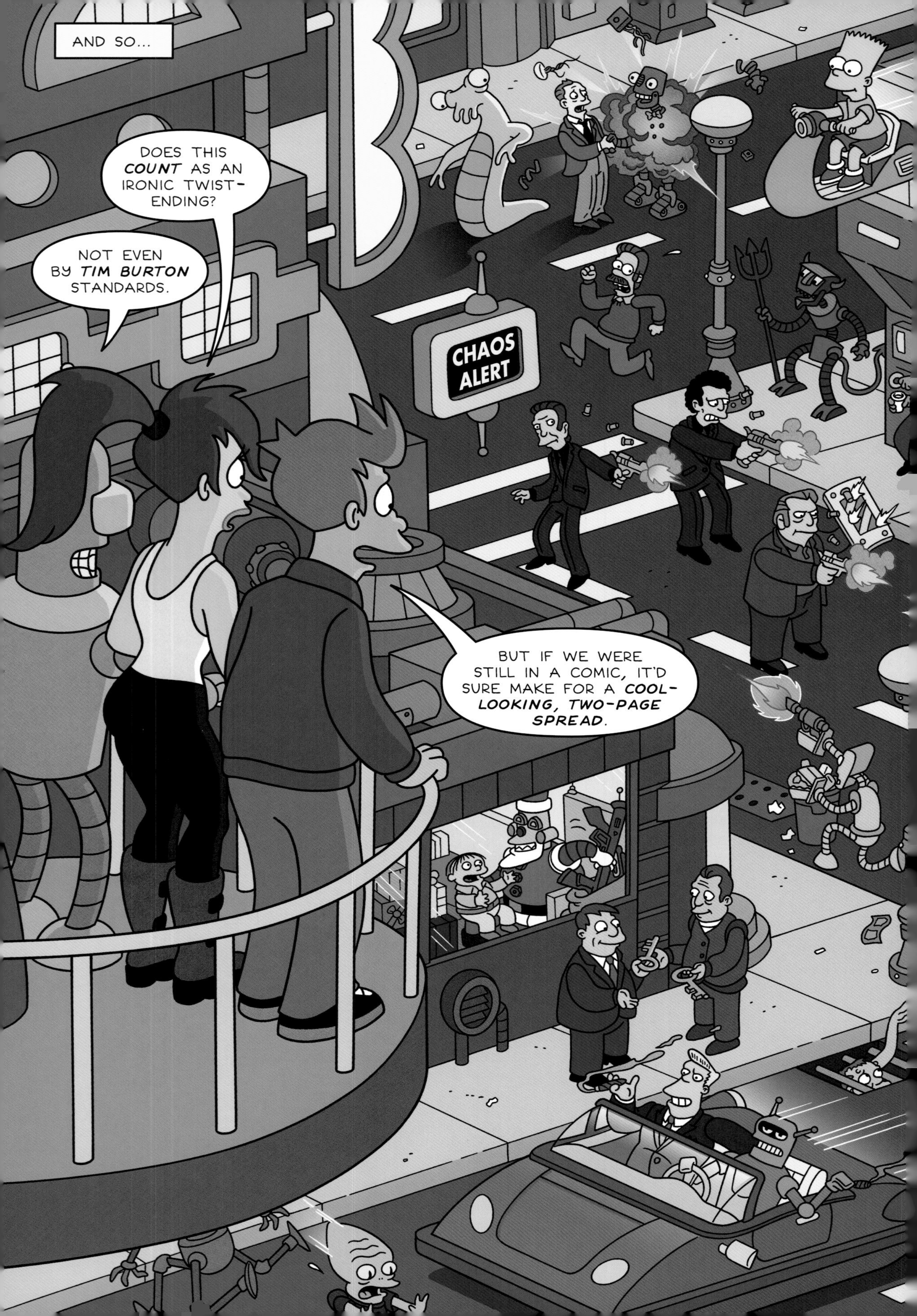
AND SO...
DOES THIS COUNT AS AN IRONIC TWIST-ENDING?
NOT EVEN BY TIM BURTON STANDARDS.
CHAOS ALERT
BUT IF WE WERE STILL IN A COMIC, IT'D SURE MAKE FOR A COOL-LOOKING, TWO-PAGE SPREAD.

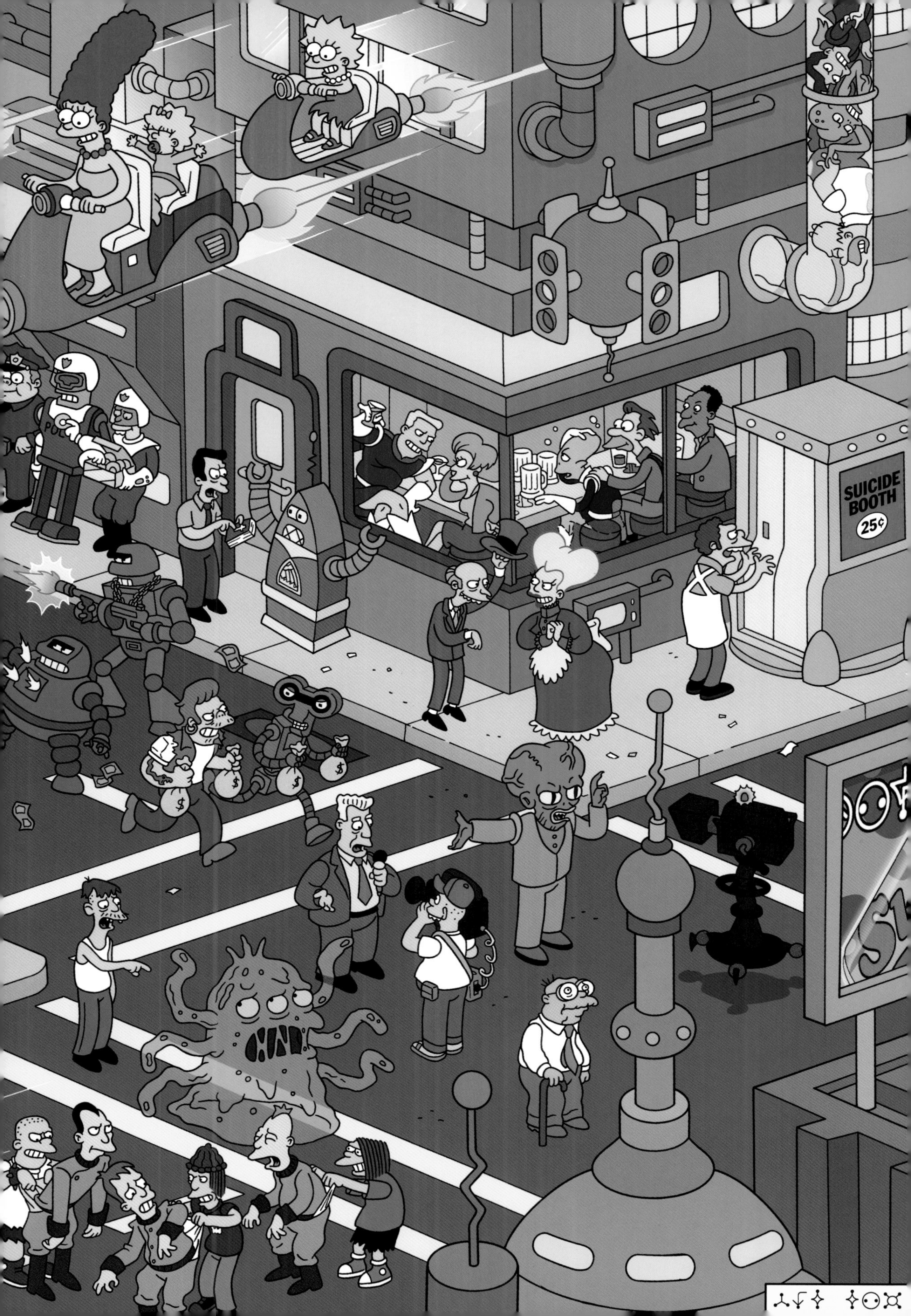
SUICIDE BOOTH
25¢

INTERLUDE: HAIL TO THE CAT

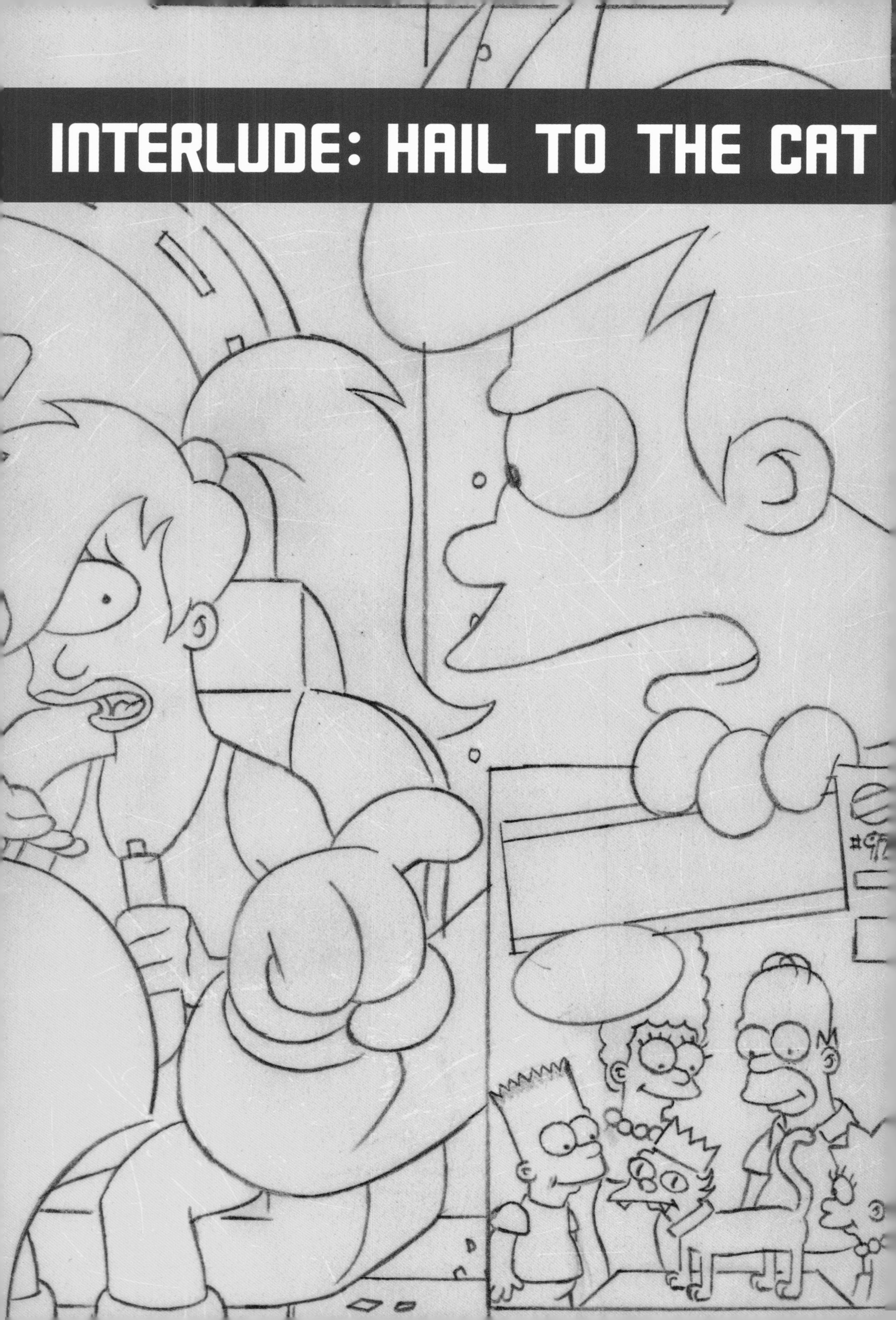

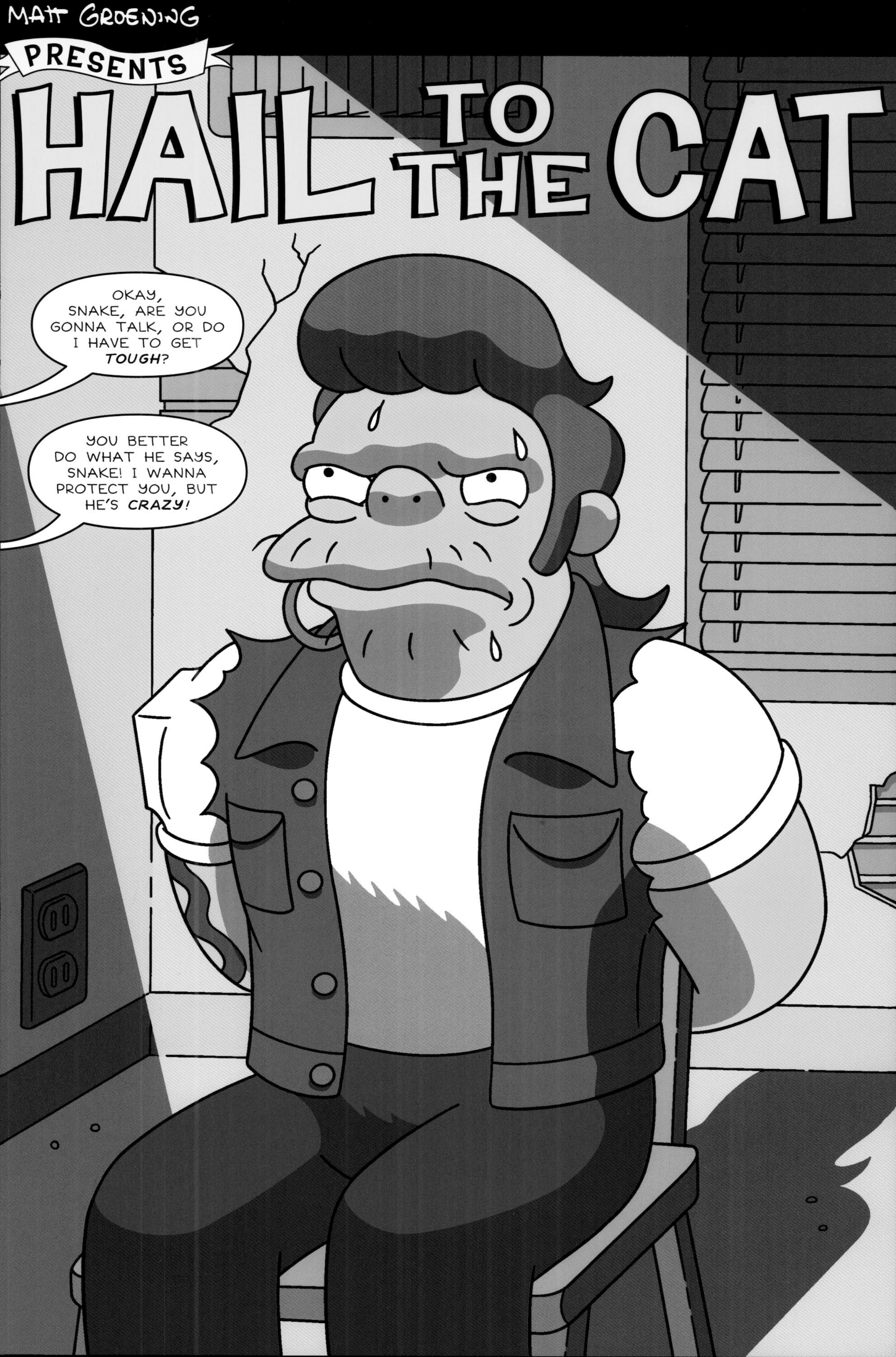
MATT GROENING
PRESENTS
HAIL TO THE CAT
OKAY, SNAKE, ARE YOU GONNA TALK, OR DO I HAVE TO GET *TOUGH*?
YOU BETTER DO WHAT HE SAYS, SNAKE! I WANNA PROTECT YOU, BUT HE'S *CRAZY*!

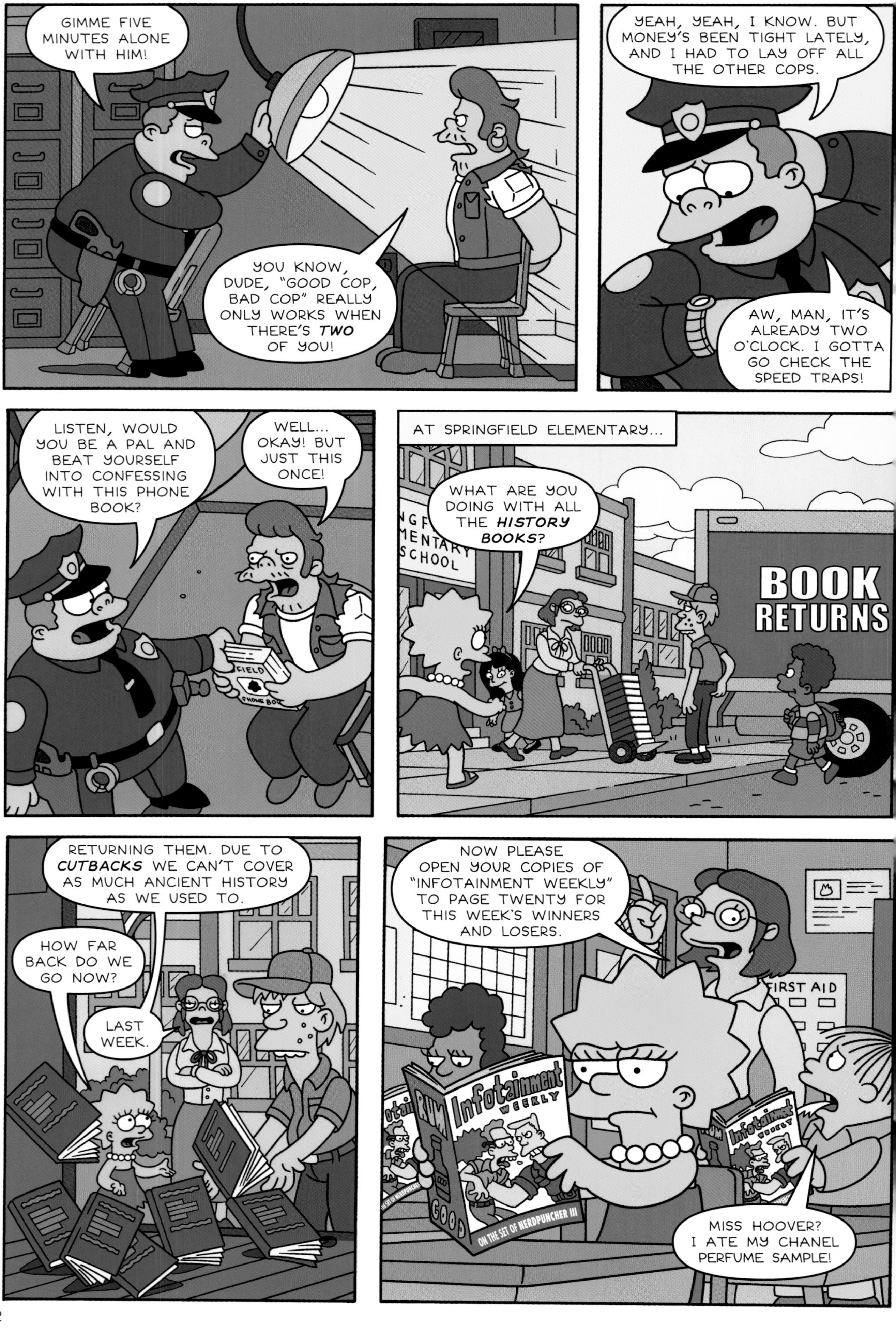
GIMME FIVE MINUTES ALONE WITH HIM!
YOU KNOW, DUDE, "GOOD COP, BAD COP" REALLY ONLY WORKS WHEN THERE'S *TWO* OF YOU!
YEAH, YEAH, I KNOW. BUT MONEY'S BEEN TIGHT LATELY, AND I HAD TO LAY OFF ALL THE OTHER COPS.
AW, MAN, IT'S ALREADY TWO O'CLOCK. I GOTTA GO CHECK THE SPEED TRAPS!
LISTEN, WOULD YOU BE A PAL AND BEAT YOURSELF INTO CONFESSING WITH THIS PHONE BOOK?
WELL... OKAY! BUT JUST THIS ONCE!
FIELD
AT SPRINGFIELD ELEMENTARY...
WHAT ARE YOU DOING WITH ALL THE ***HISTORY BOOKS***?
BOOK RETURNS
RETURNING THEM. DUE TO ***CUTBACKS*** WE CAN'T COVER AS MUCH ANCIENT HISTORY AS WE USED TO.
HOW FAR BACK DO WE GO NOW?
LAST WEEK.
NOW PLEASE OPEN YOUR COPIES OF "INFOTAINMENT WEEKLY" TO PAGE TWENTY FOR THIS WEEK'S WINNERS AND LOSERS.
FIRST AID
Infotainment WEEKLY
ON THE SET OF NERDPUNCHER III
MISS HOOVER? I ATE MY CHANEL PERFUME SAMPLE!

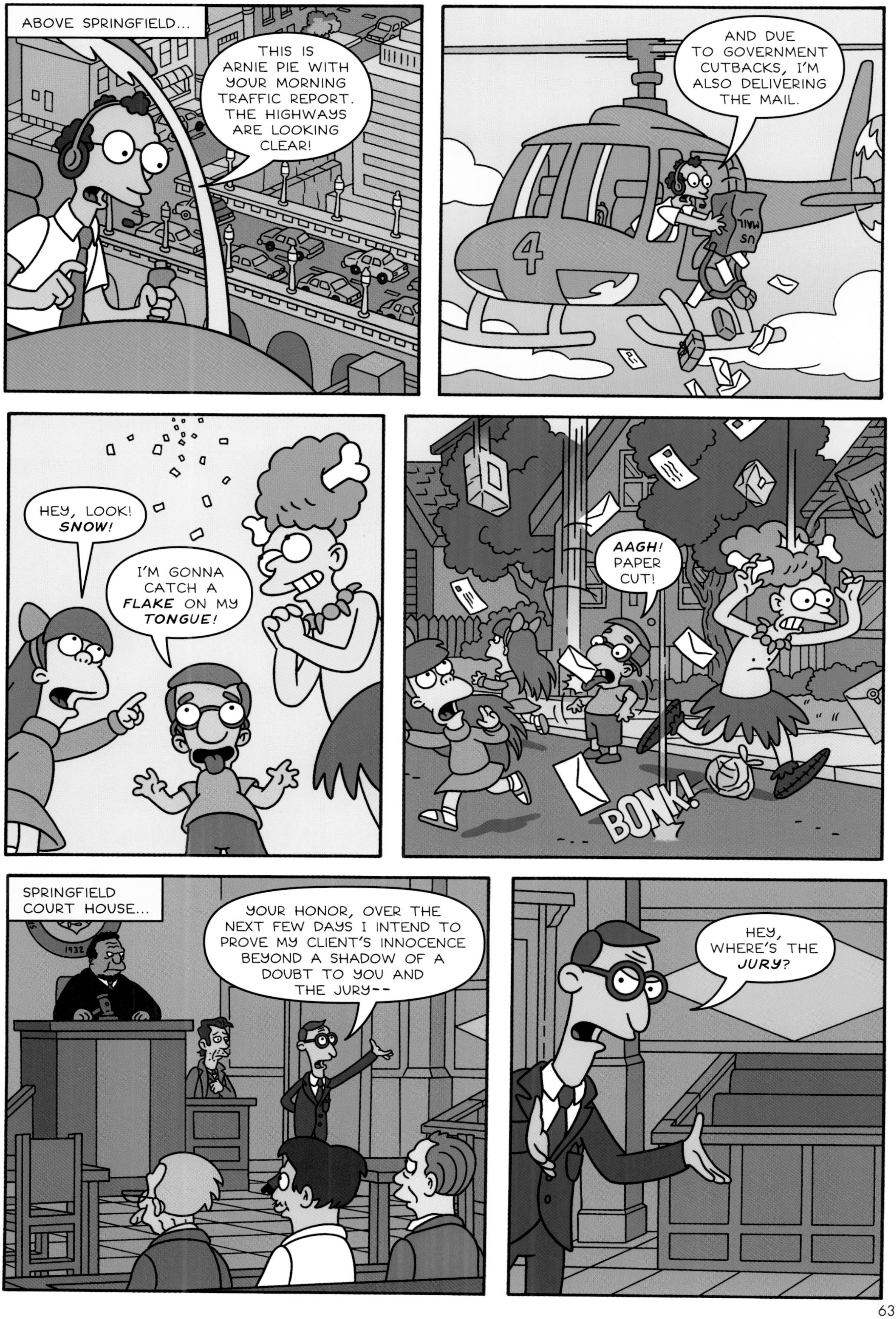
ABOVE SPRINGFIELD...
THIS IS ARNIE PIE WITH YOUR MORNING TRAFFIC REPORT. THE HIGHWAYS ARE LOOKING CLEAR!
AND DUE TO GOVERNMENT CUTBACKS, I'M ALSO DELIVERING THE MAIL.
4
US MAIL
HEY, LOOK! ***SNOW***!
I'M GONNA CATCH A ***FLAKE*** ON MY ***TONGUE***!
AAGH! PAPER CUT!
BONK!
SPRINGFIELD COURT HOUSE...
1932
YOUR HONOR, OVER THE NEXT FEW DAYS I INTEND TO PROVE MY CLIENT'S INNOCENCE BEYOND A SHADOW OF A DOUBT TO YOU AND THE JURY--
HEY, WHERE'S THE ***JURY***?

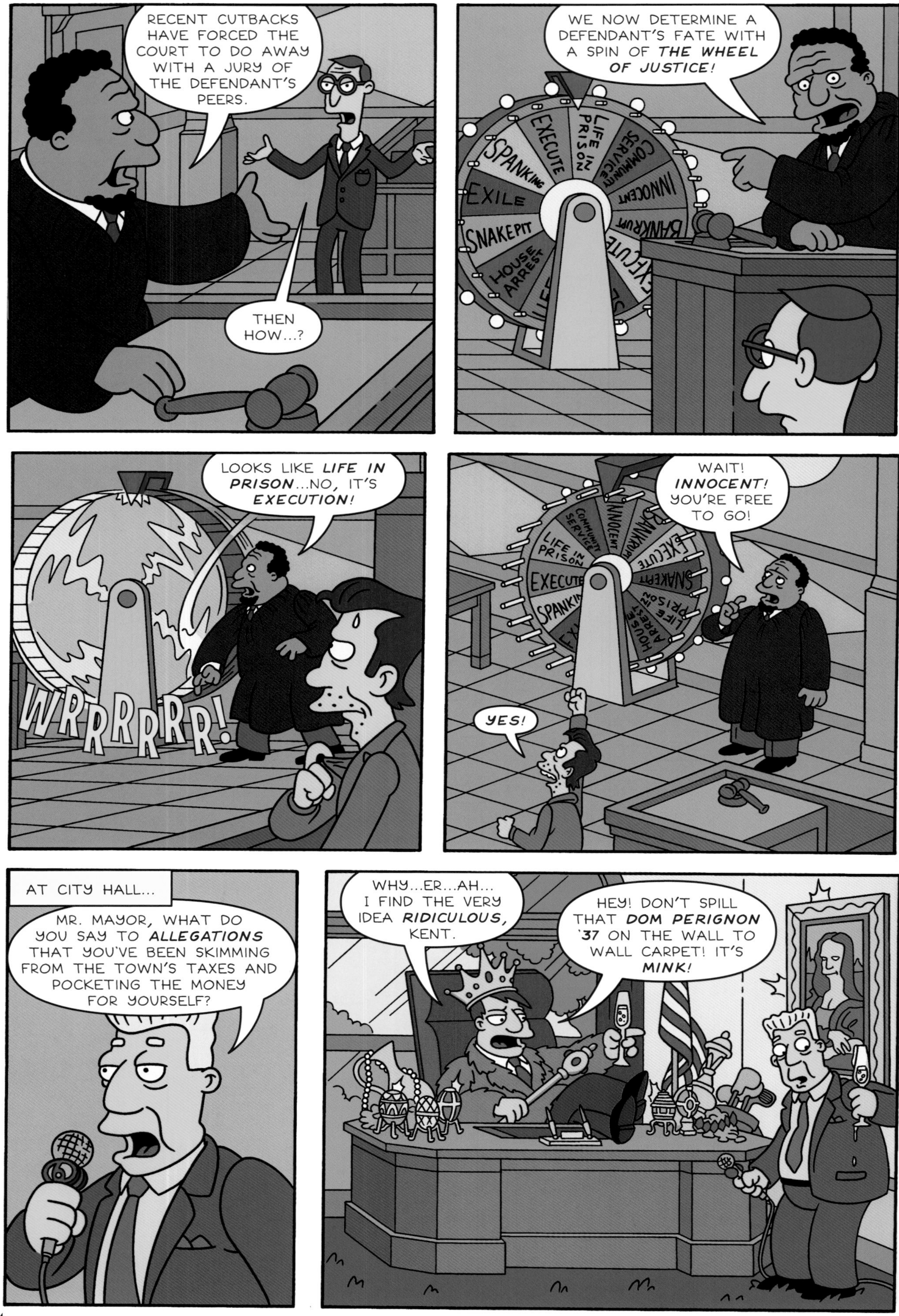
RECENT CUTBACKS HAVE FORCED THE COURT TO DO AWAY WITH A JURY OF THE DEFENDANT'S PEERS.
THEN HOW...?
WE NOW DETERMINE A DEFENDANT'S FATE WITH A SPIN OF THE WHEEL OF JUSTICE!
EXECUTE
LIFE IN PRISON
COMMUNITY SERVICE
INNOCENT
BANKRUPT
SPANKING
EXILE
SNAKEPIT
HOUSE ARREST
LOOKS LIKE LIFE IN PRISON...NO, IT'S EXECUTION!
WRRRRRR!
WAIT! INNOCENT! YOU'RE FREE TO GO!
YES!
AT CITY HALL...
MR. MAYOR, WHAT DO YOU SAY TO ALLEGATIONS THAT YOU'VE BEEN SKIMMING FROM THE TOWN'S TAXES AND POCKETING THE MONEY FOR YOURSELF?
WHY...ER...AH... I FIND THE VERY IDEA RIDICULOUS, KENT.
HEY! DON'T SPILL THAT DOM PERIGNON '37 ON THE WALL TO WALL CARPET! IT'S MINK!

THAT MAYOR QUIMBY! SOMEONE SHOULD REALLY DO SOMETHING ABOUT HIM!

YOU CAN'T FIGHT CITY HALL, MARGE.

MOTHRA DID. HE DESTROYED TOYKO CITY HALL IN THE 1964 FILM "GODZILLA VS. MOTHRA."

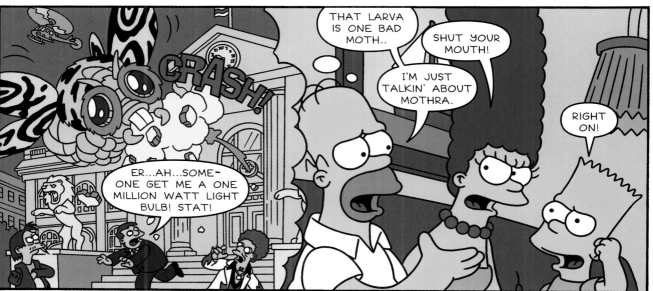

CRASH!

ER...AH...SOME-ONE GET ME A ONE MILLION WATT LIGHT BULB! STAT!

THAT LARVA IS ONE BAD MOTH..

I'M JUST TALKIN' ABOUT MOTHRA.

SHUT YOUR MOUTH!

RIGHT ON!

I'M DOING A CLASS PROJECT ON THE CORRUPTION OF THE CITY ELECTION PROCESS.

DAD! LISA'S BORING ME!

STOP BORING YOUR BROTHER, LISA!

WELL, I WANT TO HEAR ABOUT YOUR PROJECT, HONEY. I'M SURE IT'S NOT BORING AT ALL.

I'M RECREATING AN ELECTION USING SANTA'S LITTLE HELPER AND SNOWBALL II! I'VE CALCULATED THE POLITICAL RATIO OF...

SNOOORE!

SNIZZZ!

SNXXXX!

:SIGH!:

THE NEXT DAY AT SCHOOL...

LISA, YOU CAN BEGIN YOUR PRESENTATION. IF ANY-ONE NEEDS ME, I'LL BE IN THE TEACHER'S LOUNGE TESTING AN EXPERIMENTAL ANTI-DEPRESSION DRUG.

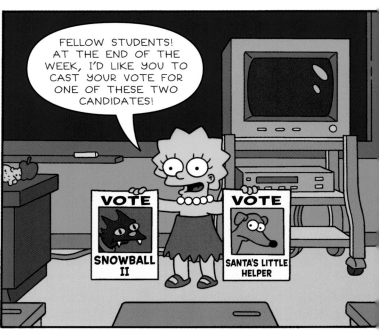

FELLOW STUDENTS! AT THE END OF THE WEEK, I'D LIKE YOU TO CAST YOUR VOTE FOR ONE OF THESE TWO CANDIDATES!

VOTE SNOWBALL II

VOTE SANTA'S LITTLE HELPER

BUT FIRST...A COUPLE OF PAID POLITICAL ANNOUNCEMENTS.

SANTA'S LITTLE HELPER CLAIMS TO BE *MAN'S BEST FRIEND*.

"BUT WHAT'S HE HIDING?"

"HE SAYS HE DOESN'T HAVE FLEAS."

"THEN WHY IS HE BITING HIS BUTT?"

"DON'T BACK A BUTT BITER!"

"VOTE SNOWBALL II!"

IF HE *LIES* ABOUT THE FLEAS, HOW CAN WE TRUST HIM ON THE *TOUGH* ISSUES?

I'M VOTING FOR FROSTY THE SNOWMAN II!

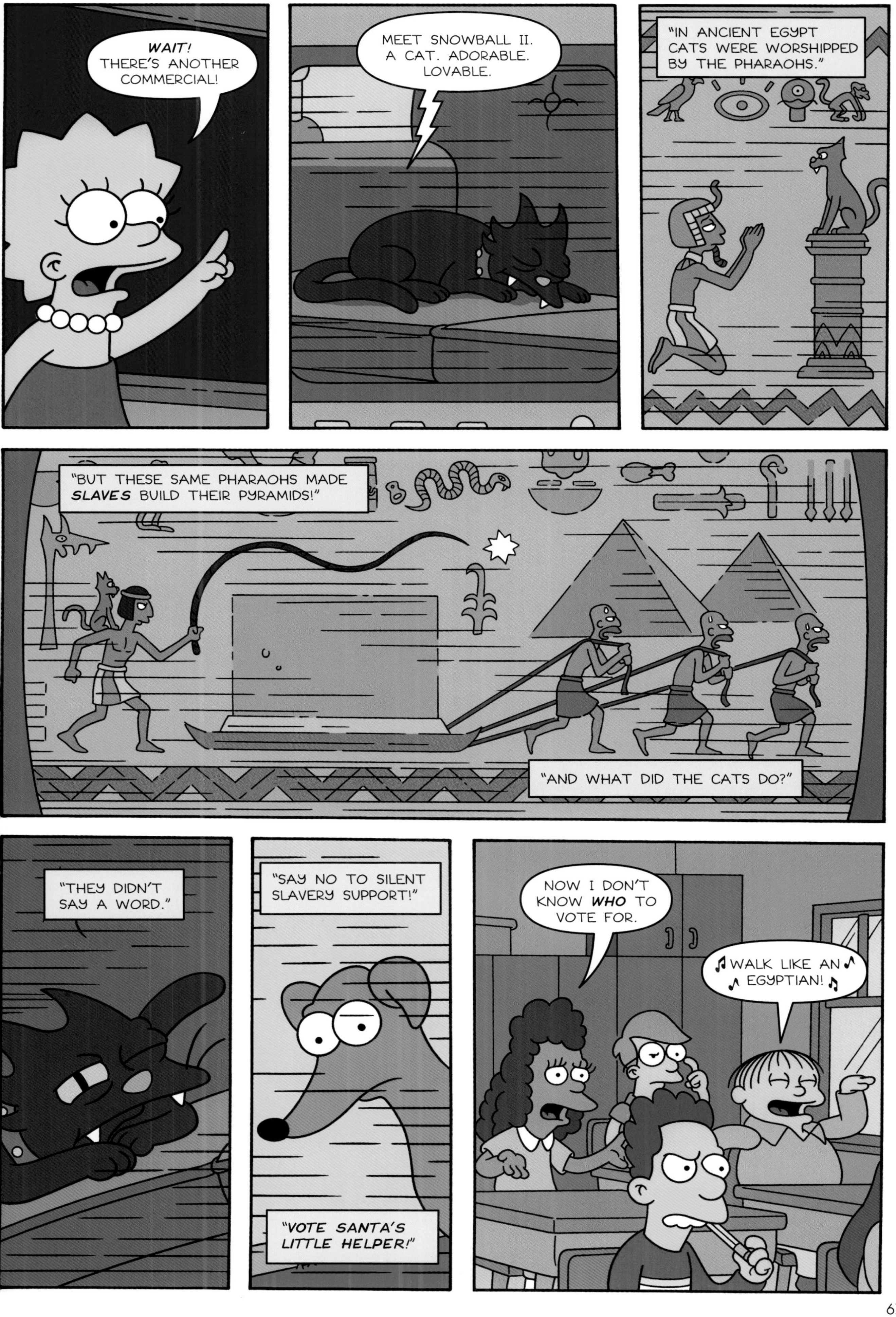

WAIT! THERE'S ANOTHER COMMERCIAL!
MEET SNOWBALL II. A CAT. ADORABLE. LOVABLE.
"IN ANCIENT EGYPT CATS WERE WORSHIPPED BY THE PHARAOHS."
"BUT THESE SAME PHARAOHS MADE *SLAVES* BUILD THEIR PYRAMIDS!"
"AND WHAT DID THE CATS DO?"
"THEY DIDN'T SAY A WORD."
"SAY NO TO SILENT SLAVERY SUPPORT!"
"VOTE SANTA'S LITTLE HELPER!"
NOW I DON'T KNOW *WHO* TO VOTE FOR.
♫ WALK LIKE AN ♪ ♪ EGYPTIAN! ♫

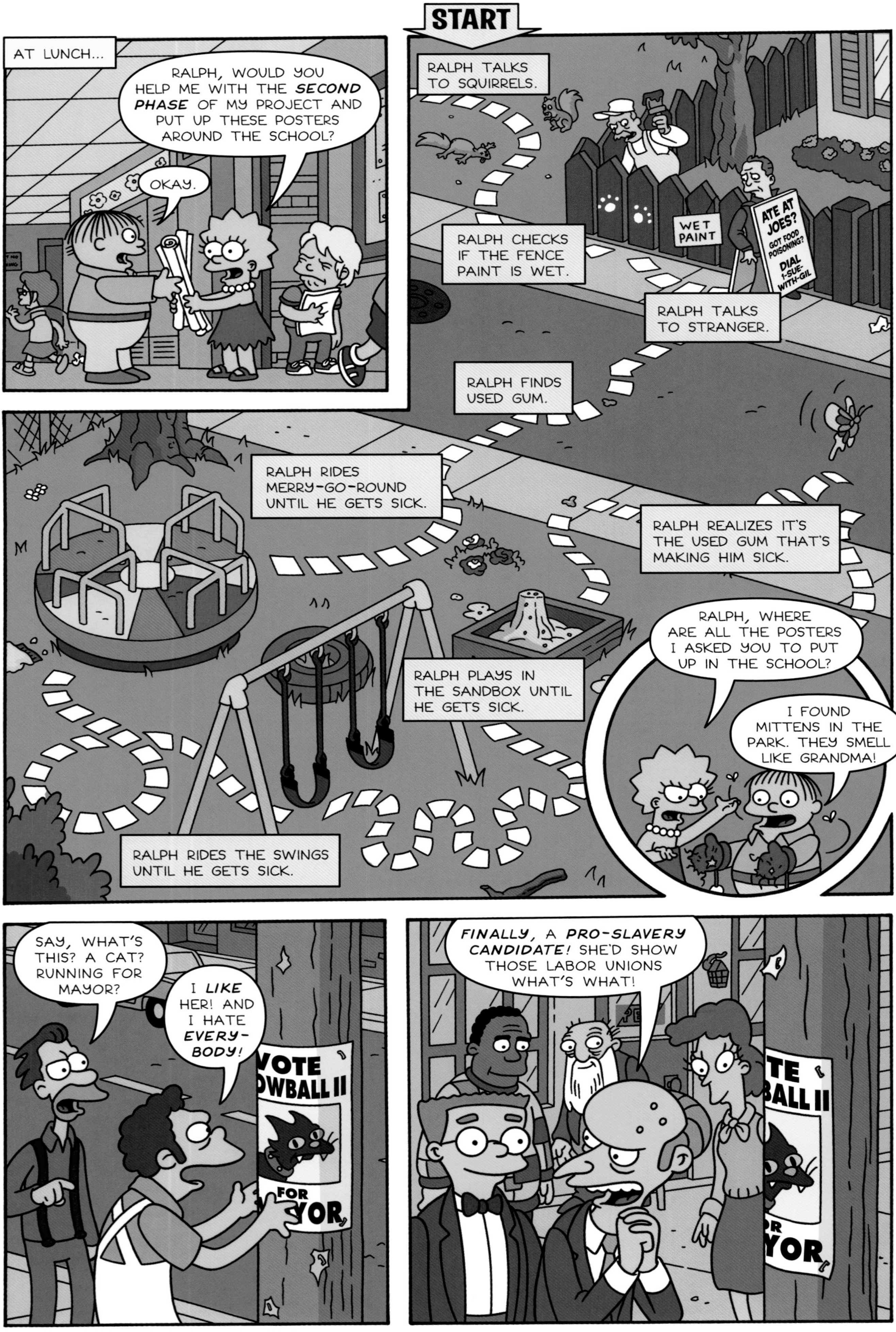
START
AT LUNCH...
RALPH, WOULD YOU HELP ME WITH THE *SECOND PHASE* OF MY PROJECT AND PUT UP THESE POSTERS AROUND THE SCHOOL?
OKAY.
RALPH TALKS TO SQUIRRELS.
RALPH CHECKS IF THE FENCE PAINT IS WET.
WET PAINT
ATE AT JOES? GOT FOOD POISONING? DIAL 1-SUE-WITH-GIL
RALPH TALKS TO STRANGER.
RALPH FINDS USED GUM.
RALPH RIDES MERRY-GO-ROUND UNTIL HE GETS SICK.
RALPH REALIZES IT'S THE USED GUM THAT'S MAKING HIM SICK.
RALPH PLAYS IN THE SANDBOX UNTIL HE GETS SICK.
RALPH RIDES THE SWINGS UNTIL HE GETS SICK.
RALPH, WHERE ARE ALL THE POSTERS I ASKED YOU TO PUT UP IN THE SCHOOL?
I FOUND MITTENS IN THE PARK. THEY SMELL LIKE GRANDMA!
SAY, WHAT'S THIS? A CAT? RUNNING FOR MAYOR?
I *LIKE* HER! AND I HATE *EVERYBODY*!
VOTE
OWBALL II
FOR
YOR
FINALLY, A *PRO-SLAVERY CANDIDATE*! SHE'D SHOW THOSE LABOR UNIONS WHAT'S WHAT!
TE
BALL II
OR
YOR

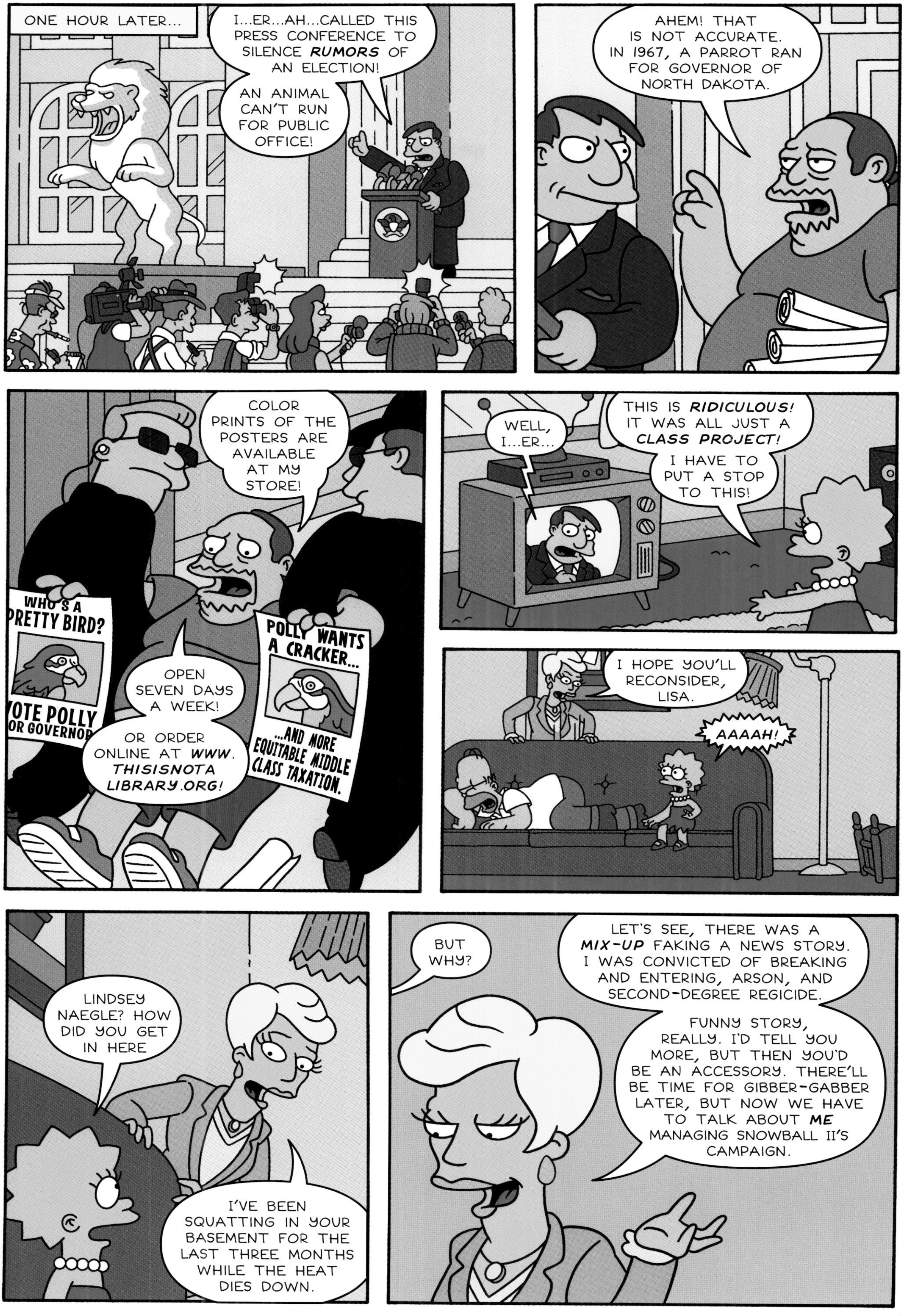
ONE HOUR LATER...
I...ER...AH...CALLED THIS PRESS CONFERENCE TO SILENCE **RUMORS** OF AN ELECTION!
AN ANIMAL CAN'T RUN FOR PUBLIC OFFICE!
AHEM! THAT IS NOT ACCURATE. IN 1967, A PARROT RAN FOR GOVERNOR OF NORTH DAKOTA.
COLOR PRINTS OF THE POSTERS ARE AVAILABLE AT MY STORE!
WHO'S A PRETTY BIRD? VOTE POLLY FOR GOVERNOR
POLLY WANTS A CRACKER... ...AND MORE EQUITABLE MIDDLE CLASS TAXATION.
OPEN SEVEN DAYS A WEEK!
OR ORDER ONLINE AT *WWW.THISISNOTA LIBRARY.ORG!*
WELL, I...ER...
THIS IS ***RIDICULOUS!*** IT WAS ALL JUST A ***CLASS PROJECT!***
I HAVE TO PUT A STOP TO THIS!
I HOPE YOU'LL RECONSIDER, LISA.
AAAAH!
LINDSEY NAEGLE? HOW DID YOU GET IN HERE
I'VE BEEN SQUATTING IN YOUR BASEMENT FOR THE LAST THREE MONTHS WHILE THE HEAT DIES DOWN.
BUT WHY?
LET'S SEE, THERE WAS A ***MIX-UP*** FAKING A NEWS STORY. I WAS CONVICTED OF BREAKING AND ENTERING, ARSON, AND SECOND-DEGREE REGICIDE.
FUNNY STORY, REALLY. I'D TELL YOU MORE, BUT THEN YOU'D BE AN ACCESSORY. THERE'LL BE TIME FOR GIBBER-GABBER LATER, BUT NOW WE HAVE TO TALK ABOUT **ME** MANAGING SNOWBALL II'S CAMPAIGN.

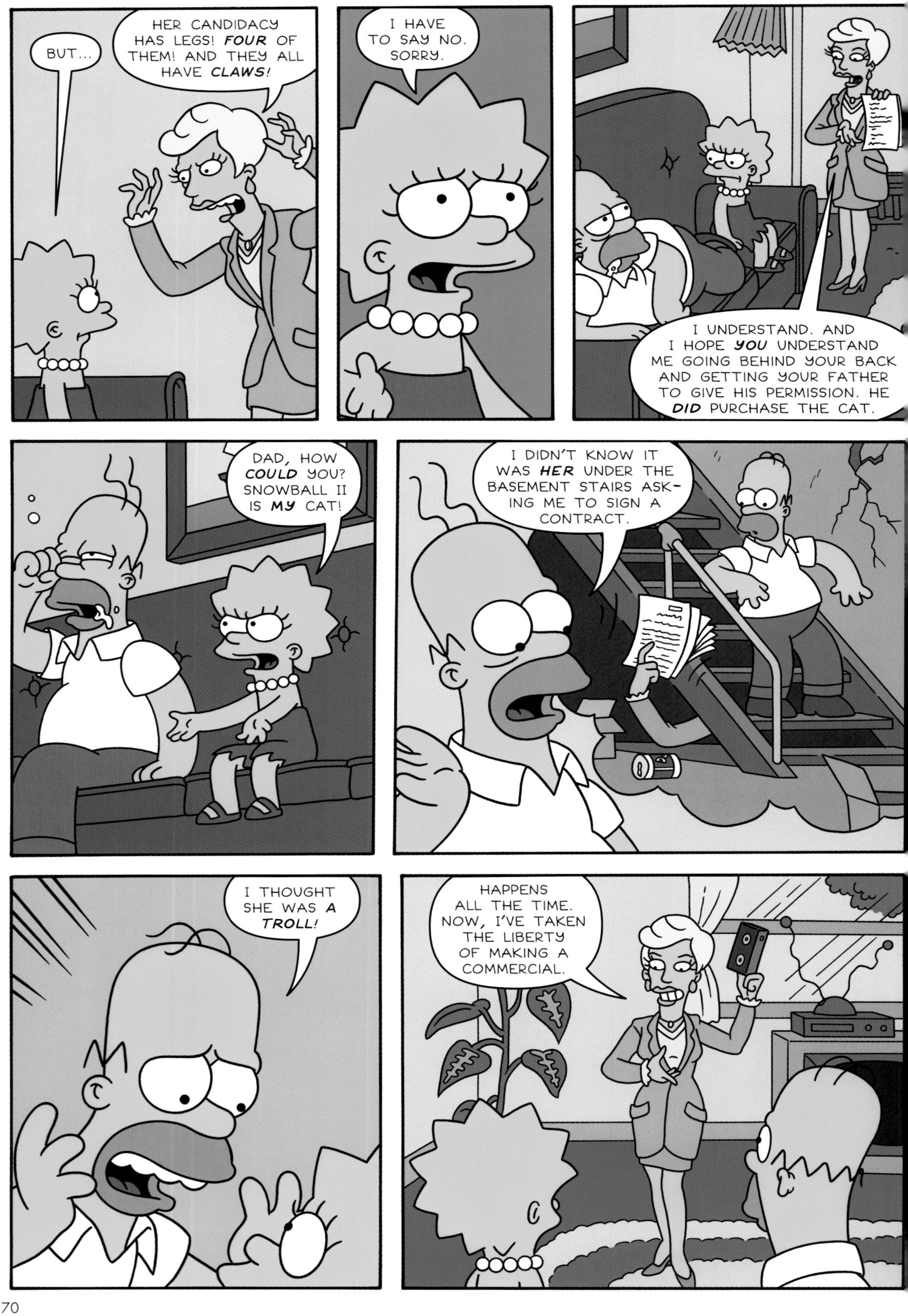
BUT...
HER CANDIDACY HAS LEGS! FOUR OF THEM! AND THEY ALL HAVE CLAWS!
I HAVE TO SAY NO. SORRY.
I UNDERSTAND. AND I HOPE YOU UNDERSTAND ME GOING BEHIND YOUR BACK AND GETTING YOUR FATHER TO GIVE HIS PERMISSION. HE DID PURCHASE THE CAT.
DAD, HOW COULD YOU? SNOWBALL II IS MY CAT!
I DIDN'T KNOW IT WAS HER UNDER THE BASEMENT STAIRS ASKING ME TO SIGN A CONTRACT.
I THOUGHT SHE WAS A TROLL!
HAPPENS ALL THE TIME. NOW, I'VE TAKEN THE LIBERTY OF MAKING A COMMERCIAL.

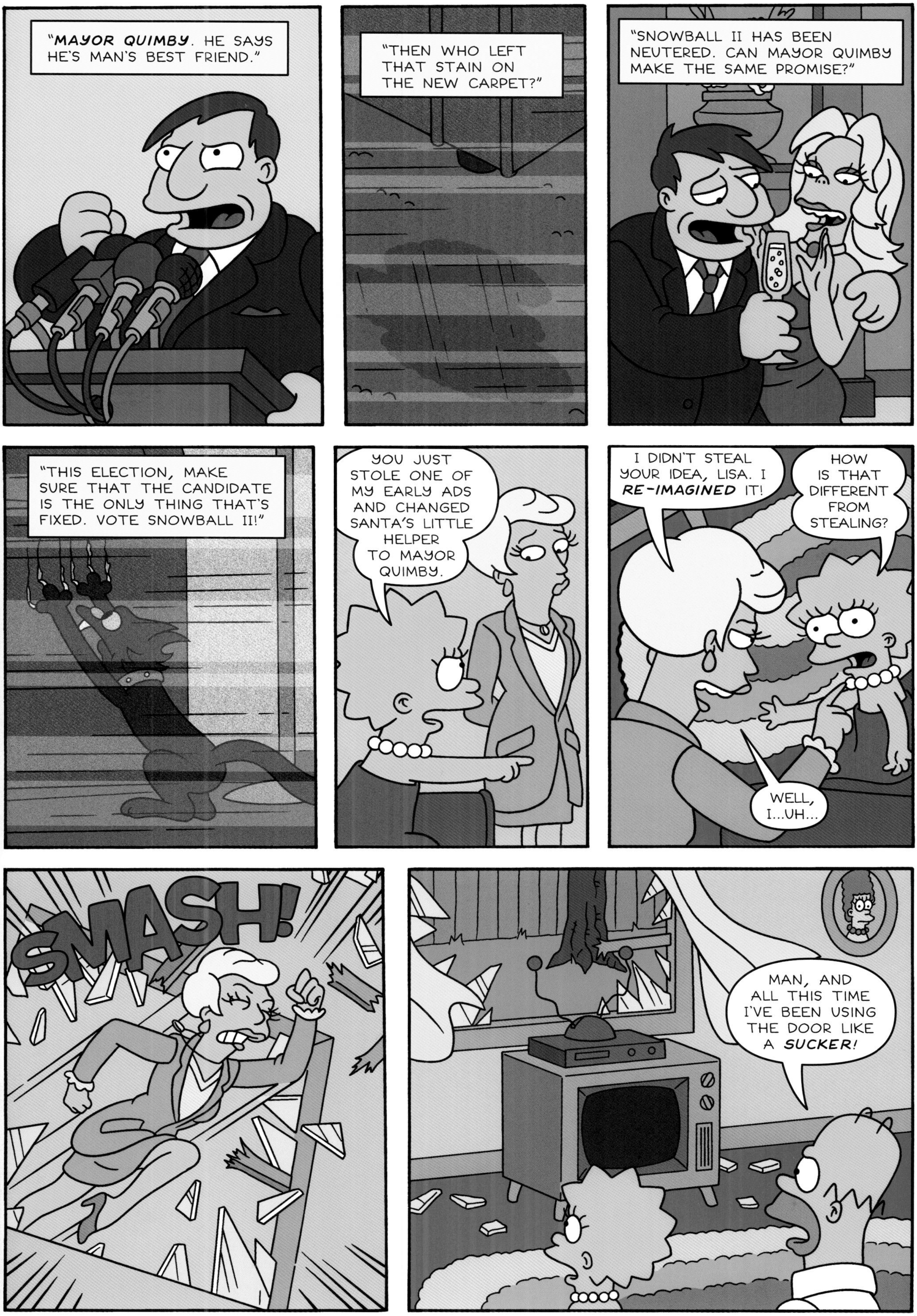
"MAYOR QUIMBY. HE SAYS HE'S MAN'S BEST FRIEND."
"THEN WHO LEFT THAT STAIN ON THE NEW CARPET?"
"SNOWBALL II HAS BEEN NEUTERED. CAN MAYOR QUIMBY MAKE THE SAME PROMISE?"
"THIS ELECTION, MAKE SURE THAT THE CANDIDATE IS THE ONLY THING THAT'S FIXED. VOTE SNOWBALL II!"
YOU JUST STOLE ONE OF MY EARLY ADS AND CHANGED SANTA'S LITTLE HELPER TO MAYOR QUIMBY.
I DIDN'T STEAL YOUR IDEA, LISA. I RE-IMAGINED IT!
HOW IS THAT DIFFERENT FROM STEALING?
WELL, I...UH...
SMASH!
MAN, AND ALL THIS TIME I'VE BEEN USING THE DOOR LIKE A SUCKER!

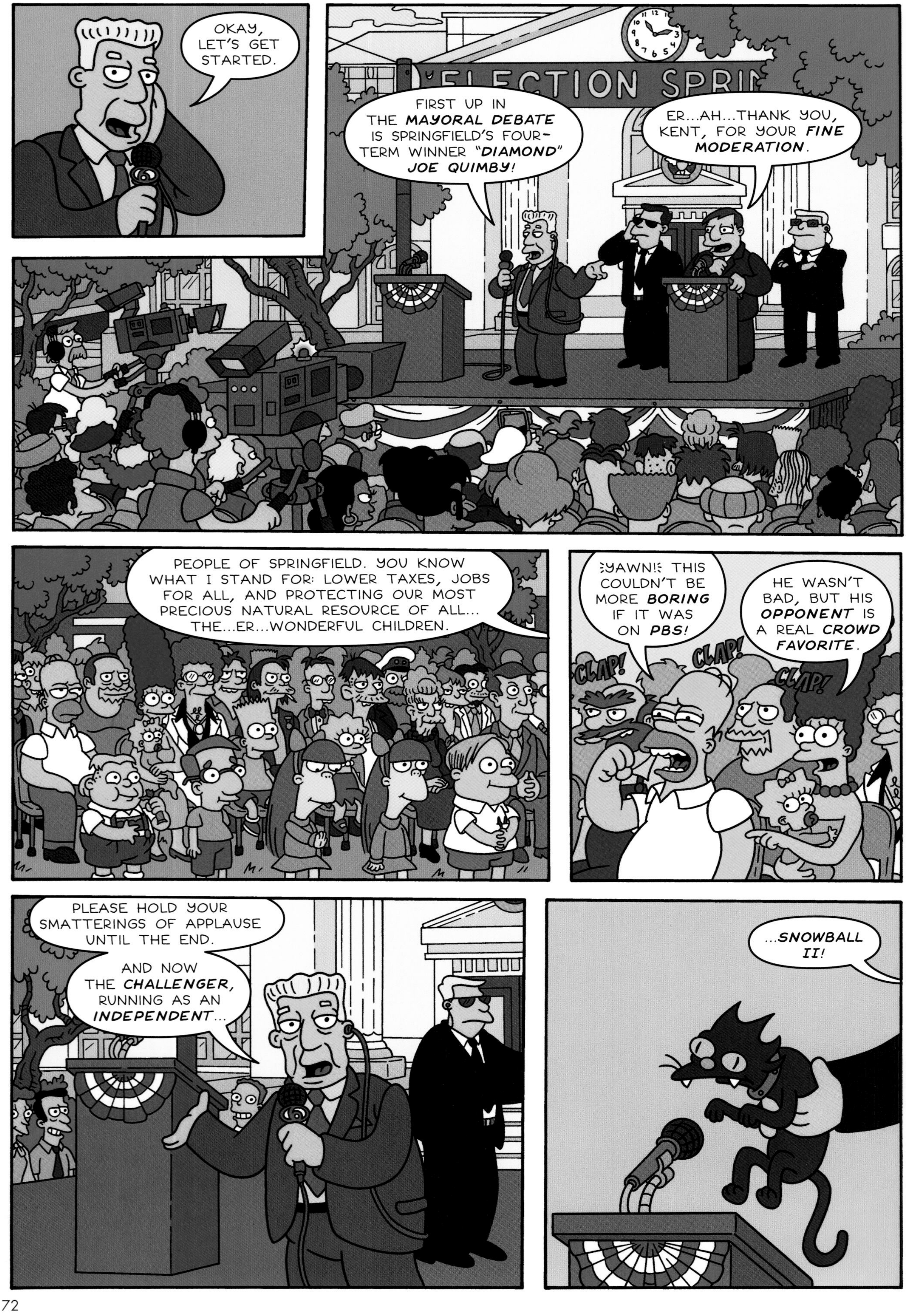
OKAY, LET'S GET STARTED.
ELECTION SPRIN
FIRST UP IN THE MAYORAL DEBATE IS SPRINGFIELD'S FOUR-TERM WINNER "DIAMOND" JOE QUIMBY!
ER...AH...THANK YOU, KENT, FOR YOUR FINE MODERATION.
PEOPLE OF SPRINGFIELD. YOU KNOW WHAT I STAND FOR: LOWER TAXES, JOBS FOR ALL, AND PROTECTING OUR MOST PRECIOUS NATURAL RESOURCE OF ALL... THE...ER...WONDERFUL CHILDREN.
YAWN! THIS COULDN'T BE MORE BORING IF IT WAS ON PBS!
HE WASN'T BAD, BUT HIS OPPONENT IS A REAL CROWD FAVORITE.
CLAP!
CLAP!
CLAP!
PLEASE HOLD YOUR SMATTERINGS OF APPLAUSE UNTIL THE END.
AND NOW THE CHALLENGER, RUNNING AS AN INDEPENDENT...
...SNOWBALL II!

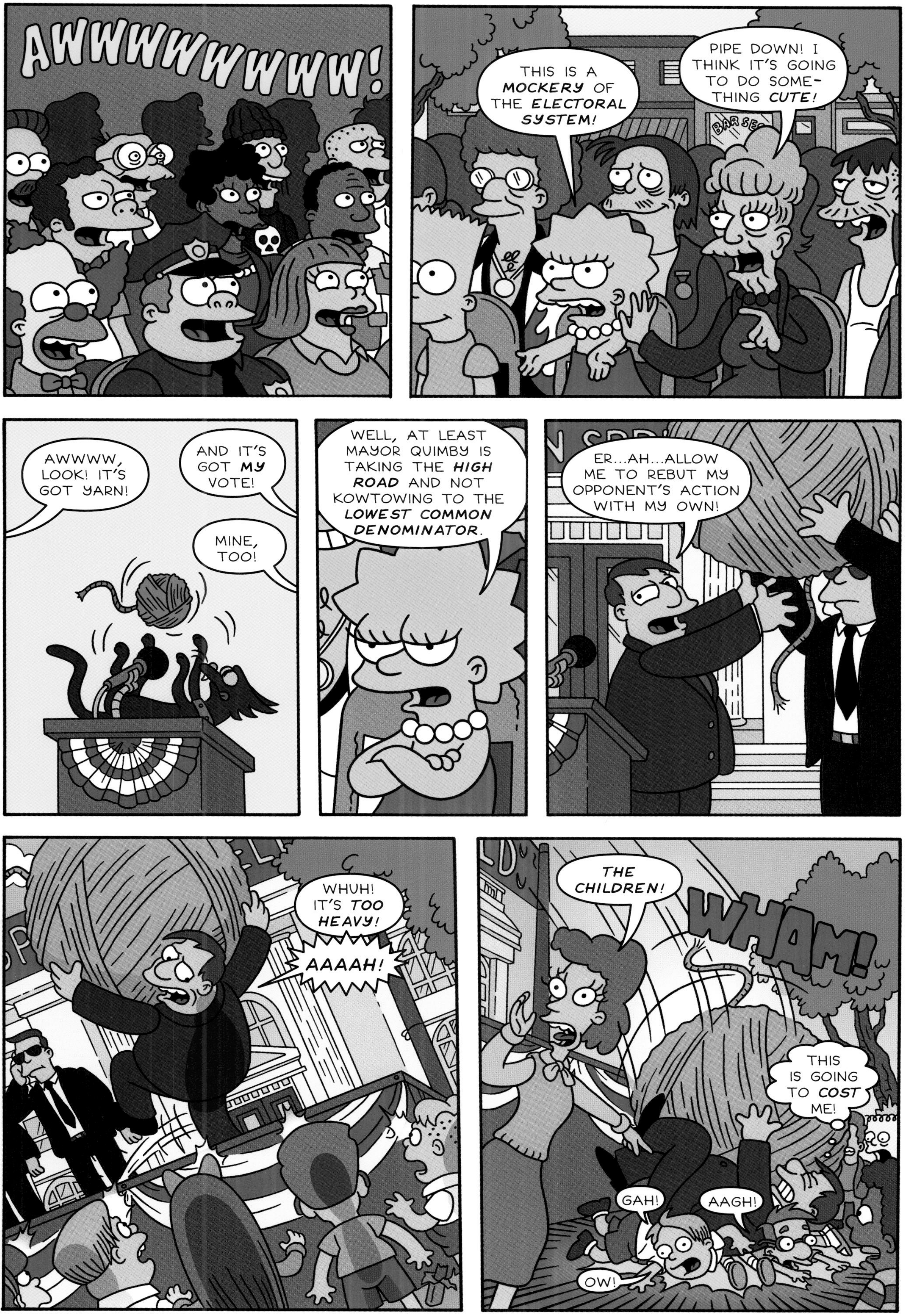
AWWWWWWWWW!
THIS IS A MOCKERY OF THE ELECTORAL SYSTEM!
PIPE DOWN! I THINK IT'S GOING TO DO SOME-THING CUTE!
AWWWW, LOOK! IT'S GOT YARN!
AND IT'S GOT MY VOTE!
MINE, TOO!
WELL, AT LEAST MAYOR QUIMBY IS TAKING THE HIGH ROAD AND NOT KOWTOWING TO THE LOWEST COMMON DENOMINATOR.
ER...AH...ALLOW ME TO REBUT MY OPPONENT'S ACTION WITH MY OWN!
WHUH! IT'S TOO HEAVY!
AAAAH!
THE CHILDREN!
WHAM!
THIS IS GOING TO COST ME!
GAH!
AAGH!
OW!

AND IN A *LAND-SLIDE VICTORY*... *SNOWBALL II* IS THE NEW MAYOR OF SPRINGFIELD!

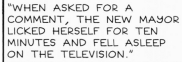

"WHEN ASKED FOR A COMMENT, THE NEW MAYOR LICKED HERSELF FOR TEN MINUTES AND FELL ASLEEP ON THE TELEVISION."

ISN'T THAT *ADORABLE*, HOMER?

HOMER! GET OFF THE TV!

OH, WAY TO HAVE A *DOUBLE STANDARD*, MARGE!

"AND WHAT ABOUT FORMER MAYOR QUIMBY?"

I'M NOT LEAVING!

HE'S GOT A PRETTY GOOD GRIP, CHIEF.

GREASE HIM DOWN, BOYS!

SLIP!

FEATHER PILLOW, HOME DELIVERY SERVICE

WHOOOMP!

HEY! WATCH IT, PALLY!

WELL, AT LEAST I'M LEAVING WITH MY DIGNITY.

HAW, HAW!

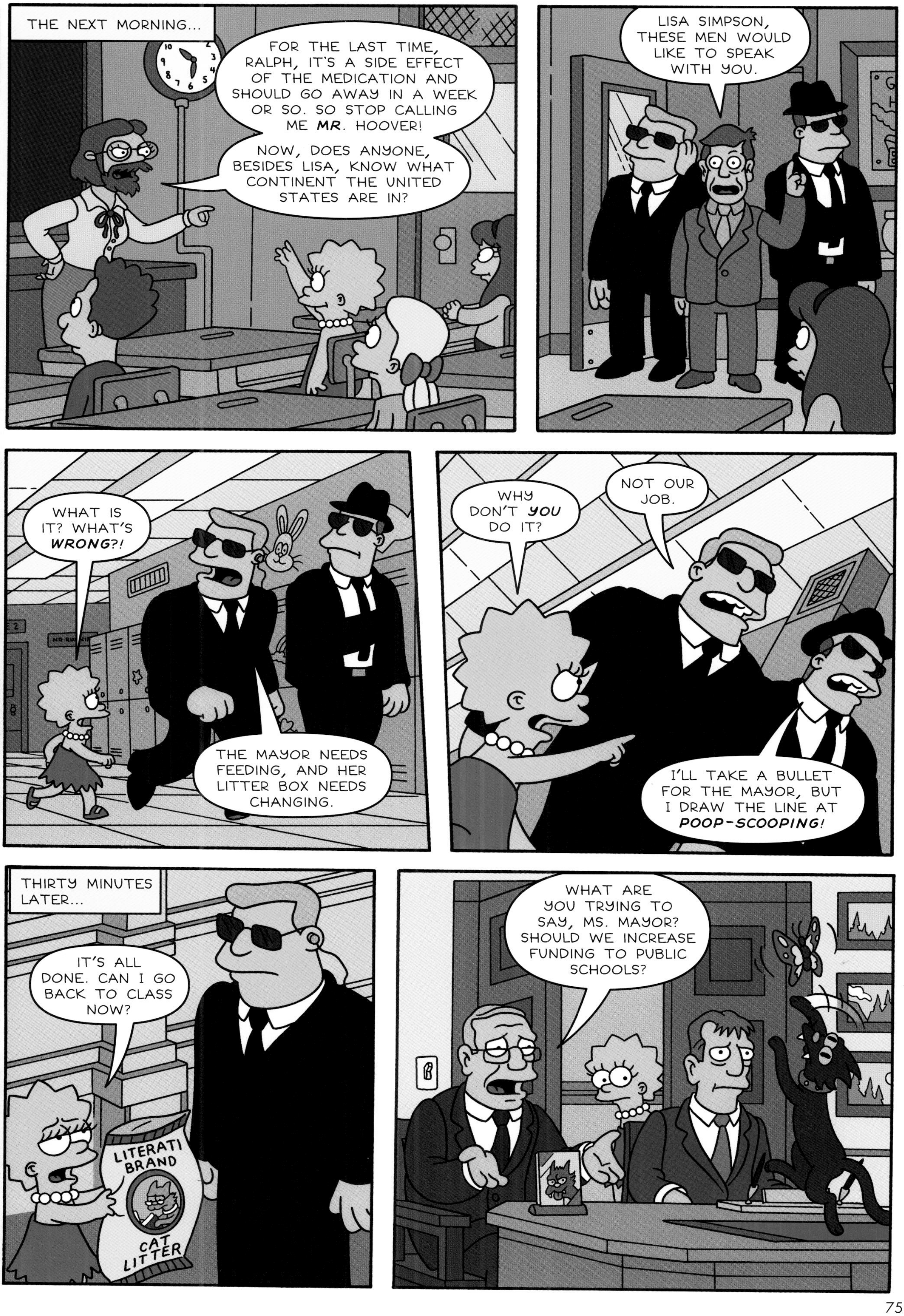
THE NEXT MORNING...
FOR THE LAST TIME, RALPH, IT'S A SIDE EFFECT OF THE MEDICATION AND SHOULD GO AWAY IN A WEEK OR SO. SO STOP CALLING ME *MR*. HOOVER!
NOW, DOES ANYONE, BESIDES LISA, KNOW WHAT CONTINENT THE UNITED STATES ARE IN?
LISA SIMPSON, THESE MEN WOULD LIKE TO SPEAK WITH YOU.
WHAT IS IT? WHAT'S *WRONG*?!
THE MAYOR NEEDS FEEDING, AND HER LITTER BOX NEEDS CHANGING.
WHY DON'T *YOU* DO IT?
NOT OUR JOB.
I'LL TAKE A BULLET FOR THE MAYOR, BUT I DRAW THE LINE AT *POOP-SCOOPING*!
THIRTY MINUTES LATER...
IT'S ALL DONE. CAN I GO BACK TO CLASS NOW?
LITERATI BRAND
CAT LITTER
WHAT ARE YOU TRYING TO SAY, MS. MAYOR? SHOULD WE INCREASE FUNDING TO PUBLIC SCHOOLS?

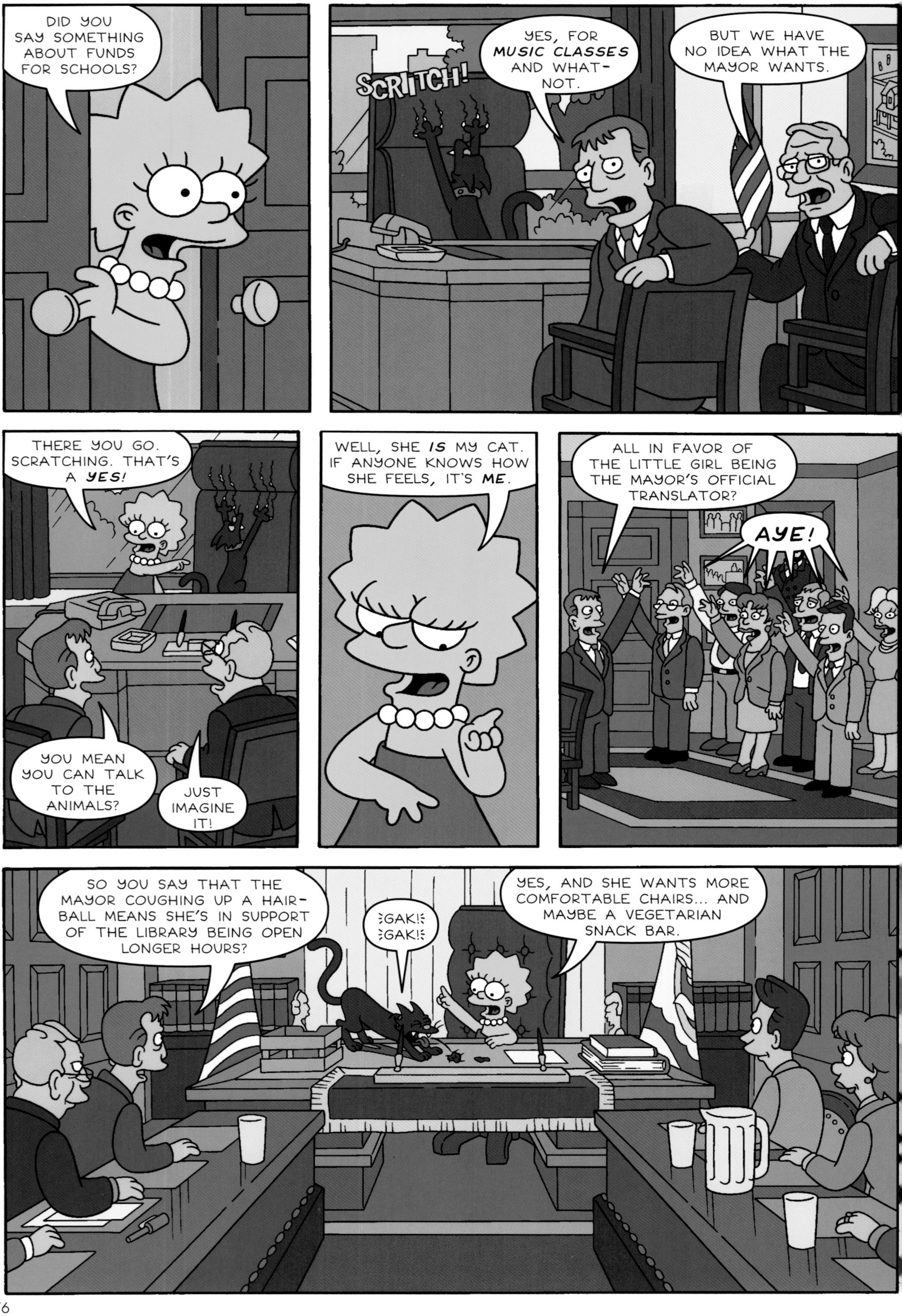
DID YOU SAY SOMETHING ABOUT FUNDS FOR SCHOOLS?
SCRITCH!
YES, FOR *MUSIC CLASSES* AND WHAT-NOT.
BUT WE HAVE NO IDEA WHAT THE MAYOR WANTS.
THERE YOU GO. SCRATCHING. THAT'S A *YES!*
YOU MEAN YOU CAN TALK TO THE ANIMALS?
JUST IMAGINE IT!
WELL, SHE *IS* MY CAT. IF ANYONE KNOWS HOW SHE FEELS, IT'S *ME*.
ALL IN FAVOR OF THE LITTLE GIRL BEING THE MAYOR'S OFFICIAL TRANSLATOR?
AYE!
SO YOU SAY THAT THE MAYOR COUGHING UP A HAIR-BALL MEANS SHE'S IN SUPPORT OF THE LIBRARY BEING OPEN LONGER HOURS?
GAK! GAK!
YES, AND SHE WANTS MORE COMFORTABLE CHAIRS... AND MAYBE A VEGETARIAN SNACK BAR.

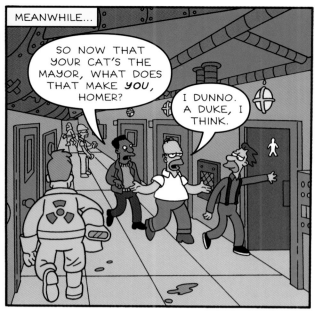

MEANWHILE...

SO NOW THAT YOUR CAT'S THE MAYOR, WHAT DOES THAT MAKE *YOU*, HOMER?

I DUNNO. A DUKE, I THINK.

FRESH URINAL CAKE, SIR?

MAYOR QUIMBY?

BURNS IS A

SORRY, I MEAN *EX*-MAYOR QUIMBY.

JUST CALL ME JOE. THAT'S ALL I AM, A REGULAR, WORTHLESS JOE, LIKE ALL OF YOU.

HEY!!

IS A

WHAT ARE YOU DOING HERE?

WHAT ELSE IS THERE FOR ME? I HAVE NO SKILLS EXCEPT BILKING AND...ER...PHILANDERING!

BURNS

HEY, HOMER'S EVEN LESS SKILLED THAN YOU, AND HE'S THE PLANT SAFETY INSPECTOR.

I WONDER WHAT WOULD HAPPEN IF I AIM THESE HAND DRYERS AT EACH OTHER.

BILL 3:16

SOAP-O-DISPENSE

Jenn

MAYBE YOU'RE RIGHT. MAYBE THERE *IS* HOPE.

FWOOOSH!!

YOU WASH YOUR HANDS?

NATHAN LOVES ALL THE GIRLS

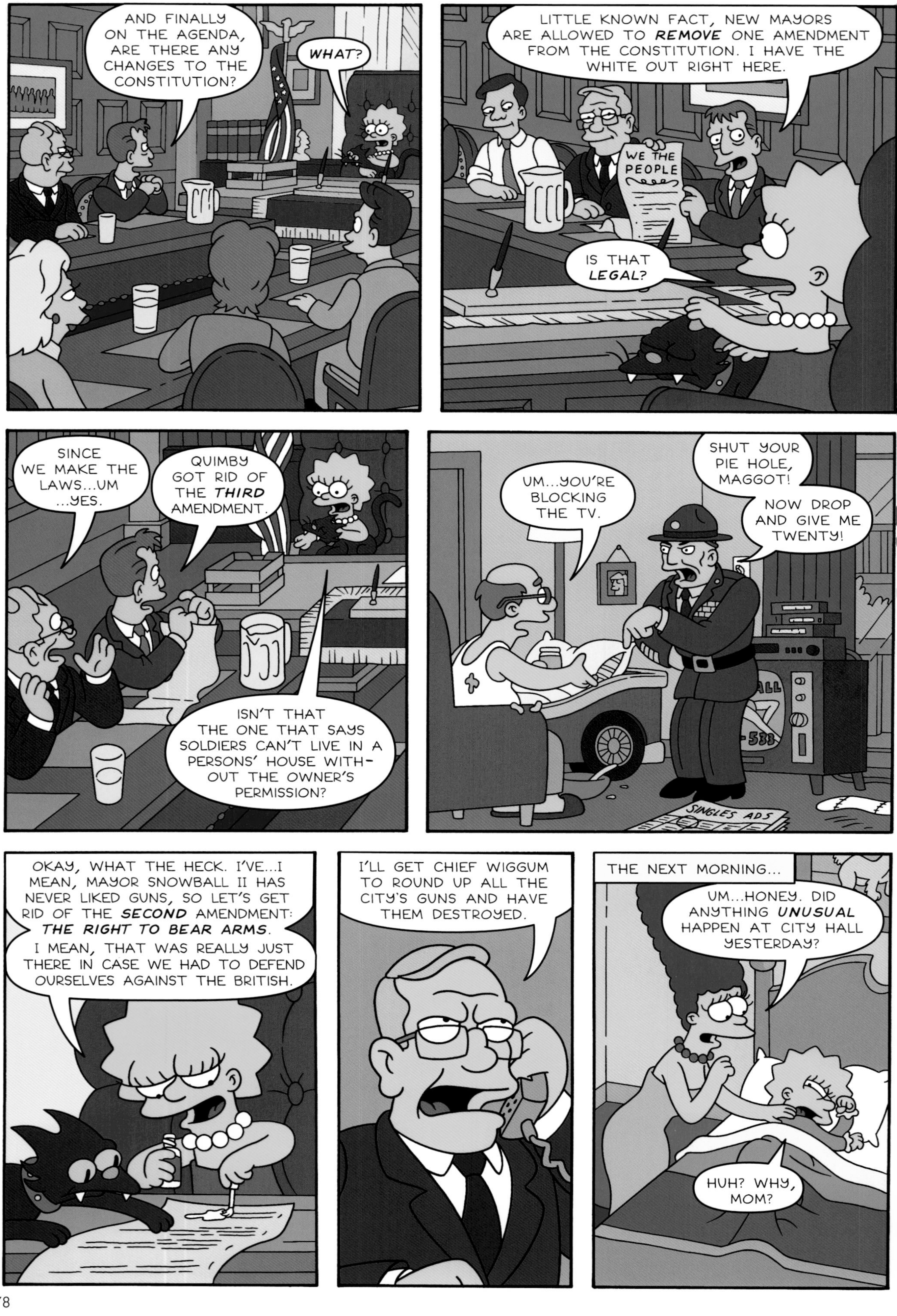
AND FINALLY ON THE AGENDA, ARE THERE ANY CHANGES TO THE CONSTITUTION?
WHAT?
LITTLE KNOWN FACT, NEW MAYORS ARE ALLOWED TO REMOVE ONE AMENDMENT FROM THE CONSTITUTION. I HAVE THE WHITE OUT RIGHT HERE.
WE THE PEOPLE
IS THAT LEGAL?
SINCE WE MAKE THE LAWS...UM ...YES.
QUIMBY GOT RID OF THE THIRD AMENDMENT.
ISN'T THAT THE ONE THAT SAYS SOLDIERS CAN'T LIVE IN A PERSONS' HOUSE WITH-OUT THE OWNER'S PERMISSION?
UM...YOU'RE BLOCKING THE TV.
SHUT YOUR PIE HOLE, MAGGOT!
NOW DROP AND GIVE ME TWENTY!
SINGLES ADS
OKAY, WHAT THE HECK. I'VE...I MEAN, MAYOR SNOWBALL II HAS NEVER LIKED GUNS, SO LET'S GET RID OF THE SECOND AMENDMENT: THE RIGHT TO BEAR ARMS.
I MEAN, THAT WAS REALLY JUST THERE IN CASE WE HAD TO DEFEND OURSELVES AGAINST THE BRITISH.
I'LL GET CHIEF WIGGUM TO ROUND UP ALL THE CITY'S GUNS AND HAVE THEM DESTROYED.
THE NEXT MORNING...
UM...HONEY. DID ANYTHING UNUSUAL HAPPEN AT CITY HALL YESTERDAY?
HUH? WHY, MOM?

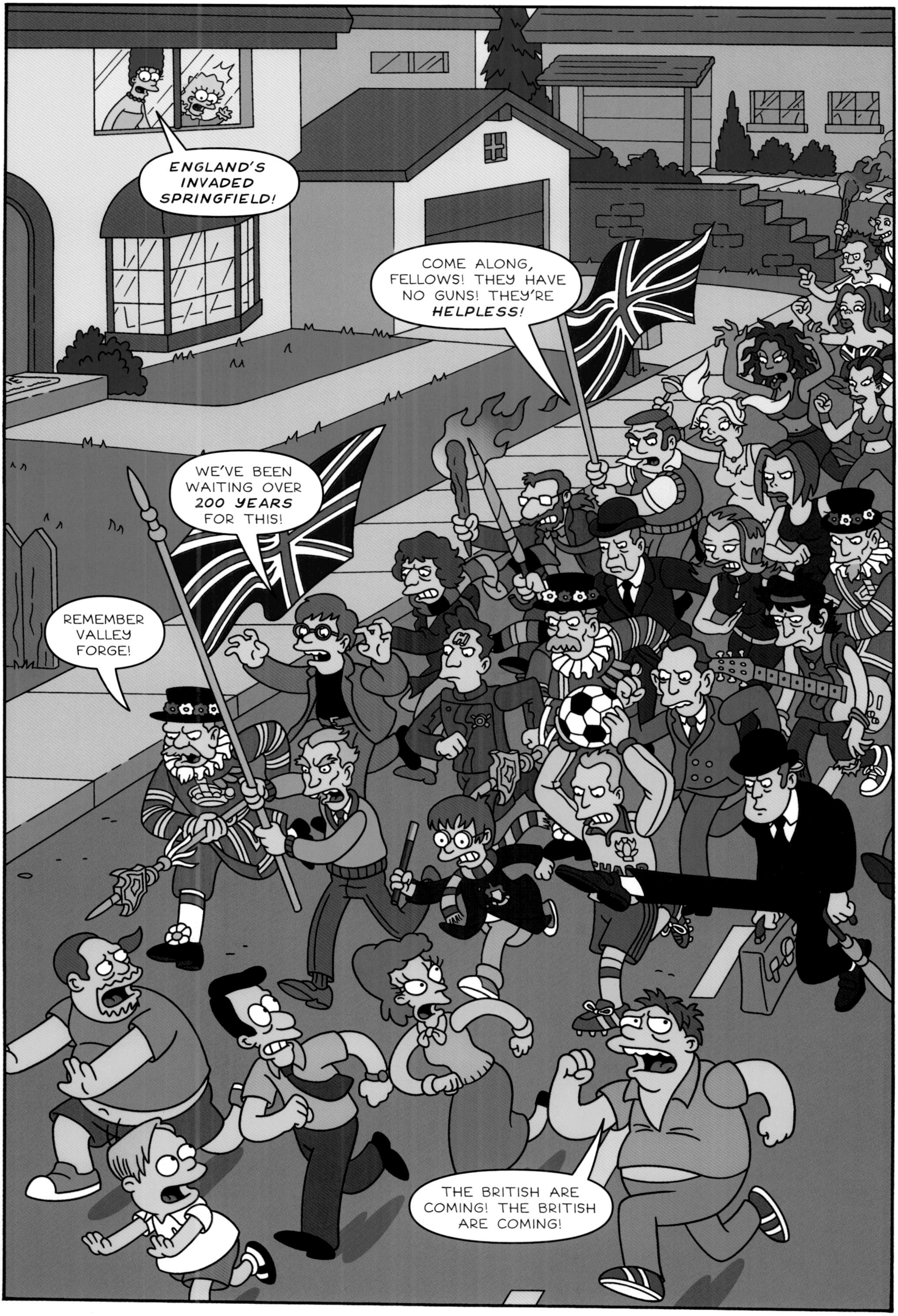
ENGLAND'S INVADED SPRINGFIELD!
COME ALONG, FELLOWS! THEY HAVE NO GUNS! THEY'RE HELPLESS!
WE'VE BEEN WAITING OVER 200 YEARS FOR THIS!
REMEMBER VALLEY FORGE!
THE BRITISH ARE COMING! THE BRITISH ARE COMING!

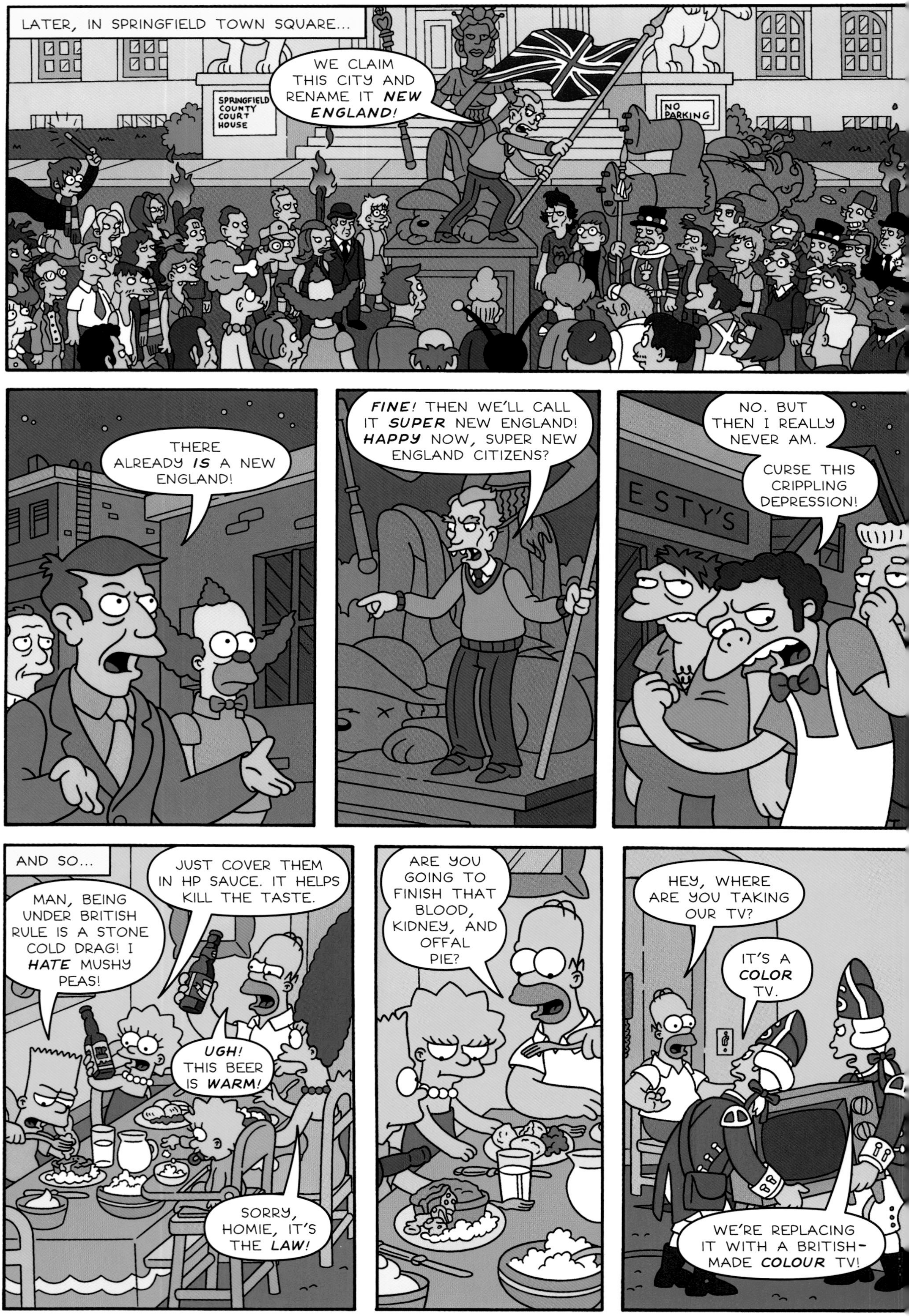

LATER, IN SPRINGFIELD TOWN SQUARE...
SPRINGFIELD COUNTY COURT HOUSE
NO PARKING
WE CLAIM THIS CITY AND RENAME IT **NEW ENGLAND!**
THERE ALREADY **IS** A NEW ENGLAND!
FINE! THEN WE'LL CALL IT **SUPER** NEW ENGLAND! **HAPPY** NOW, SUPER NEW ENGLAND CITIZENS?
ESTY'S
NO. BUT THEN I REALLY NEVER AM.
CURSE THIS CRIPPLING DEPRESSION!
AND SO...
MAN, BEING UNDER BRITISH RULE IS A STONE COLD DRAG! I **HATE** MUSHY PEAS!
JUST COVER THEM IN HP SAUCE. IT HELPS KILL THE TASTE.
UGH! THIS BEER IS **WARM!**
SORRY, HOMIE, IT'S THE **LAW!**
ARE YOU GOING TO FINISH THAT BLOOD, KIDNEY, AND OFFAL PIE?
HEY, WHERE ARE YOU TAKING OUR TV?
IT'S A **COLOR** TV.
WE'RE REPLACING IT WITH A BRITISH-MADE **COLOUR** TV!

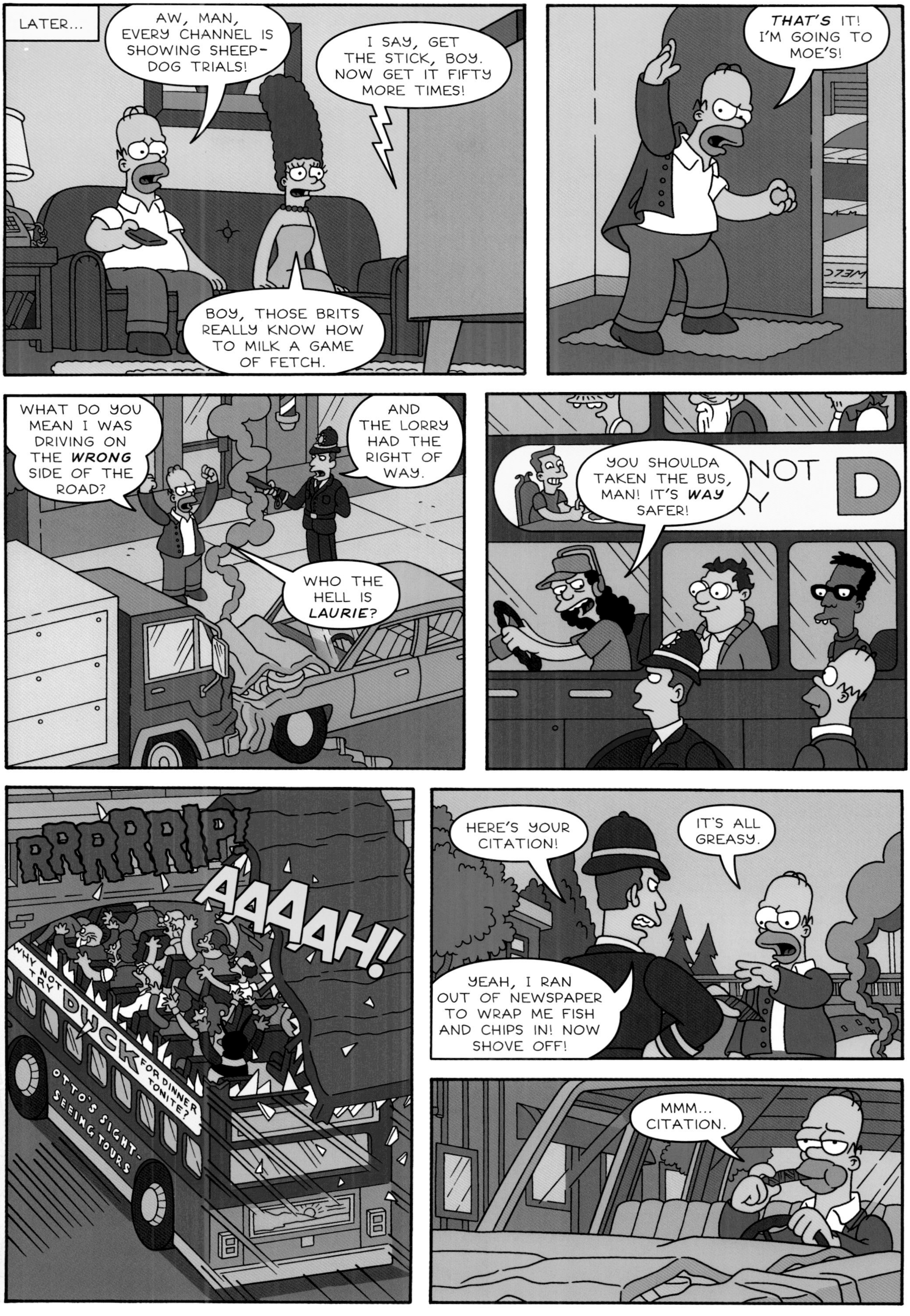

LATER...
AW, MAN, EVERY CHANNEL IS SHOWING SHEEP-DOG TRIALS!
I SAY, GET THE STICK, BOY. NOW GET IT FIFTY MORE TIMES!
BOY, THOSE BRITS REALLY KNOW HOW TO MILK A GAME OF FETCH.
THAT'S IT! I'M GOING TO MOE'S!
WHAT DO YOU MEAN I WAS DRIVING ON THE WRONG SIDE OF THE ROAD?
AND THE LORRY HAD THE RIGHT OF WAY.
WHO THE HELL IS LAURIE?
YOU SHOULDA TAKEN THE BUS, MAN! IT'S WAY SAFER!
RRRRRIP!
AAAAH!
WHY NOT TRY DUCK FOR DINNER TONITE?
OTTO'S SIGHT-SEEING TOURS
HERE'S YOUR CITATION!
IT'S ALL GREASY.
YEAH, I RAN OUT OF NEWSPAPER TO WRAP ME FISH AND CHIPS IN! NOW SHOVE OFF!
MMM... CITATION.

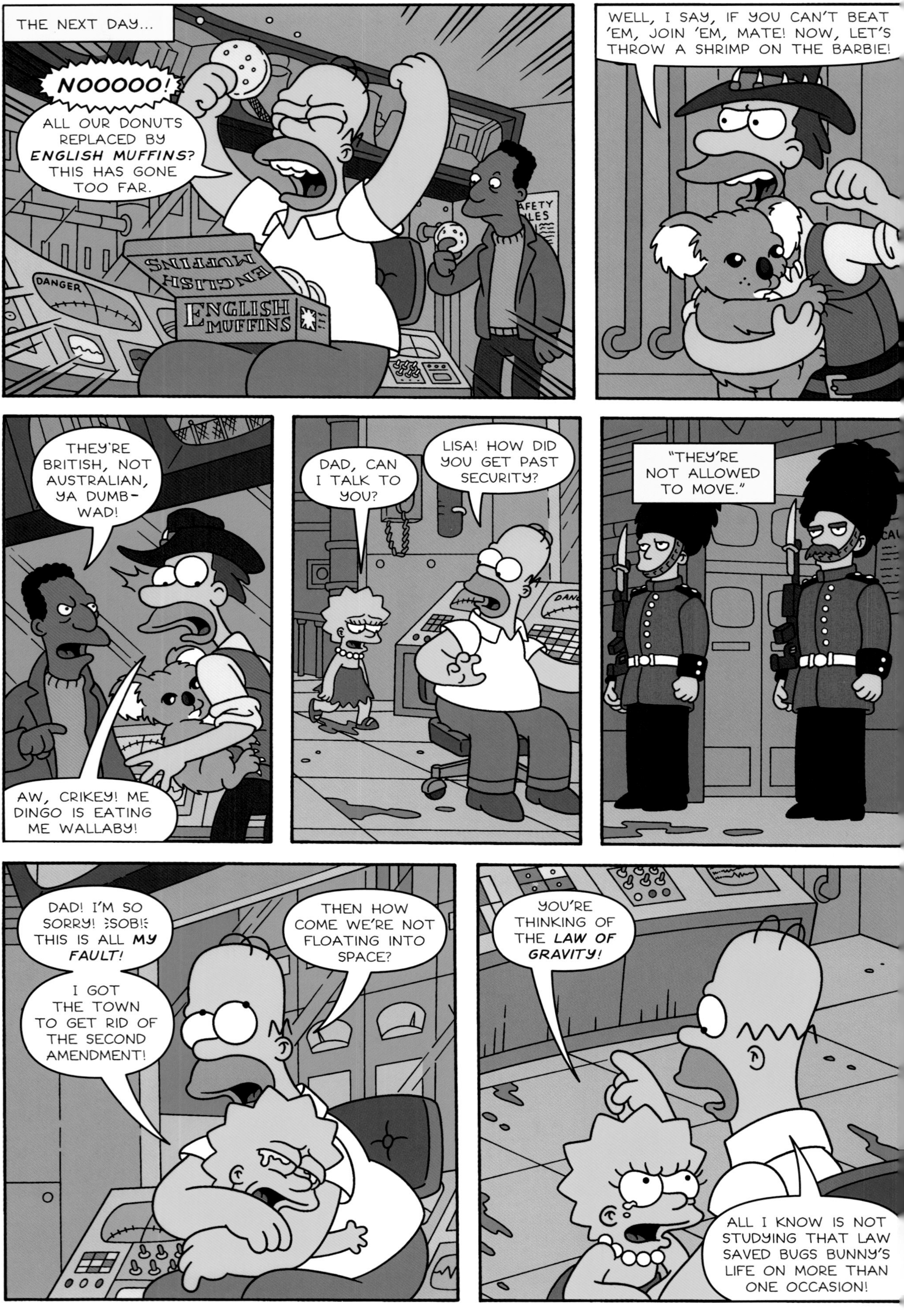
THE NEXT DAY...
NOOOOO!
ALL OUR DONUTS REPLACED BY ***ENGLISH MUFFINS***? THIS HAS GONE TOO FAR.
ENGLISH MUFFINS
DANGER
WELL, I SAY, IF YOU CAN'T BEAT 'EM, JOIN 'EM, MATE! NOW, LET'S THROW A SHRIMP ON THE BARBIE!
THEY'RE BRITISH, NOT AUSTRALIAN, YA DUMB-WAD!
AW, CRIKEY! ME DINGO IS EATING ME WALLABY!
DAD, CAN I TALK TO YOU?
LISA! HOW DID YOU GET PAST SECURITY?
"THEY'RE NOT ALLOWED TO MOVE."
DAD! I'M SO SORRY! SOB! THIS IS ALL ***MY FAULT!***
I GOT THE TOWN TO GET RID OF THE SECOND AMENDMENT!
THEN HOW COME WE'RE NOT FLOATING INTO SPACE?
YOU'RE THINKING OF THE ***LAW OF GRAVITY!***
ALL I KNOW IS NOT STUDYING THAT LAW SAVED BUGS BUNNY'S LIFE ON MORE THAN ONE OCCASION!

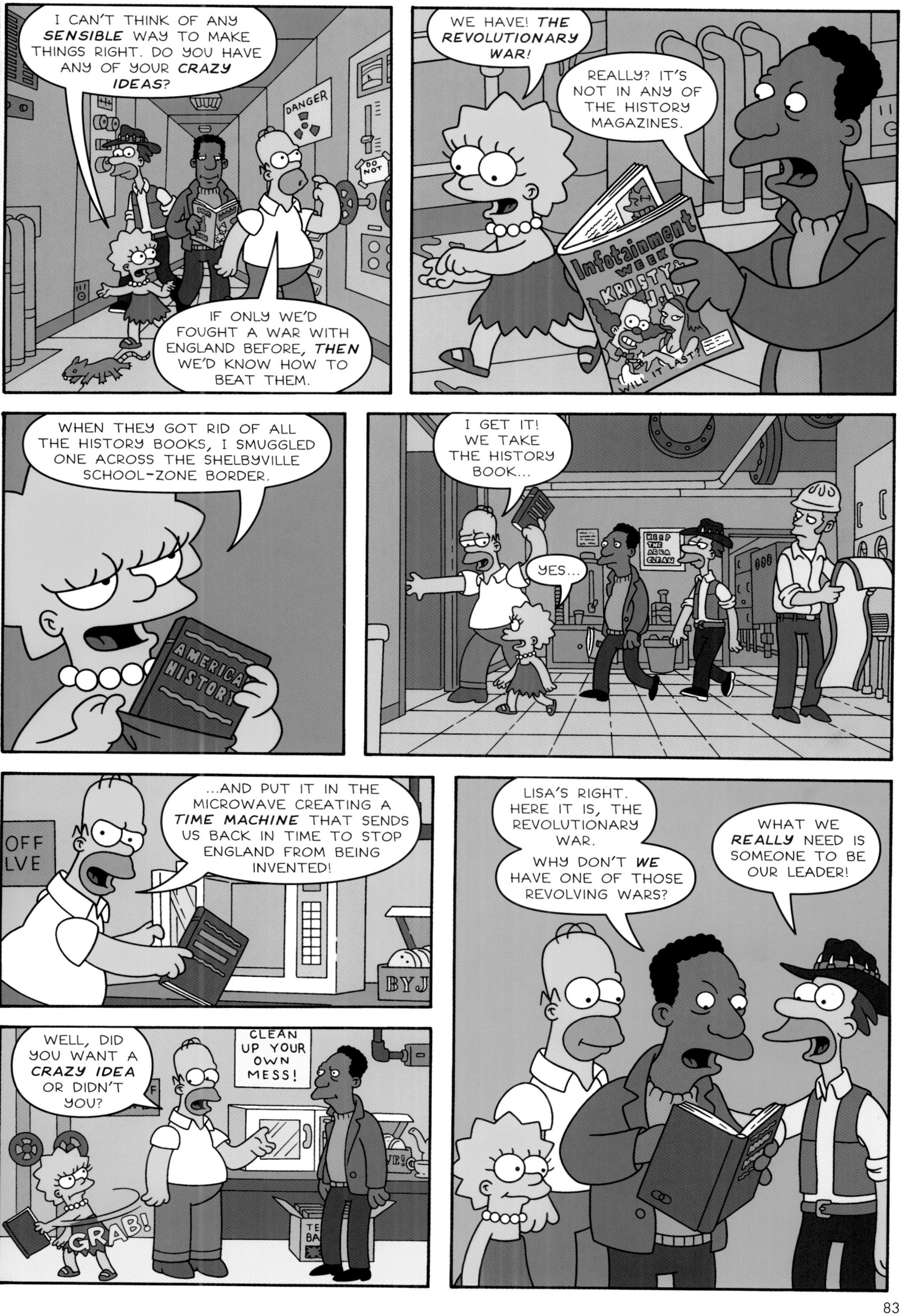
I CAN'T THINK OF ANY **SENSIBLE** WAY TO MAKE THINGS RIGHT. DO YOU HAVE ANY OF YOUR **CRAZY IDEAS**?
DANGER
DO NOT
IF ONLY WE'D FOUGHT A WAR WITH ENGLAND BEFORE, **THEN** WE'D KNOW HOW TO BEAT THEM.
WE HAVE! ***THE REVOLUTIONARY WAR!***
REALLY? IT'S NOT IN ANY OF THE HISTORY MAGAZINES.
Infotainment
WILL IT LAST?
WHEN THEY GOT RID OF ALL THE HISTORY BOOKS, I SMUGGLED ONE ACROSS THE SHELBYVILLE SCHOOL-ZONE BORDER.
I GET IT! WE TAKE THE HISTORY BOOK...
YES...
KEEP THE AREA CLEAN
...AND PUT IT IN THE MICROWAVE CREATING A ***TIME MACHINE*** THAT SENDS US BACK IN TIME TO STOP ENGLAND FROM BEING INVENTED!
WELL, DID YOU WANT A ***CRAZY IDEA*** OR DIDN'T YOU?
CLEAN UP YOUR OWN MESS!
GRAB!
LISA'S RIGHT. HERE IT IS, THE REVOLUTIONARY WAR.
WHY DON'T **WE** HAVE ONE OF THOSE REVOLVING WARS?
WHAT WE ***REALLY*** NEED IS SOMEONE TO BE OUR LEADER!

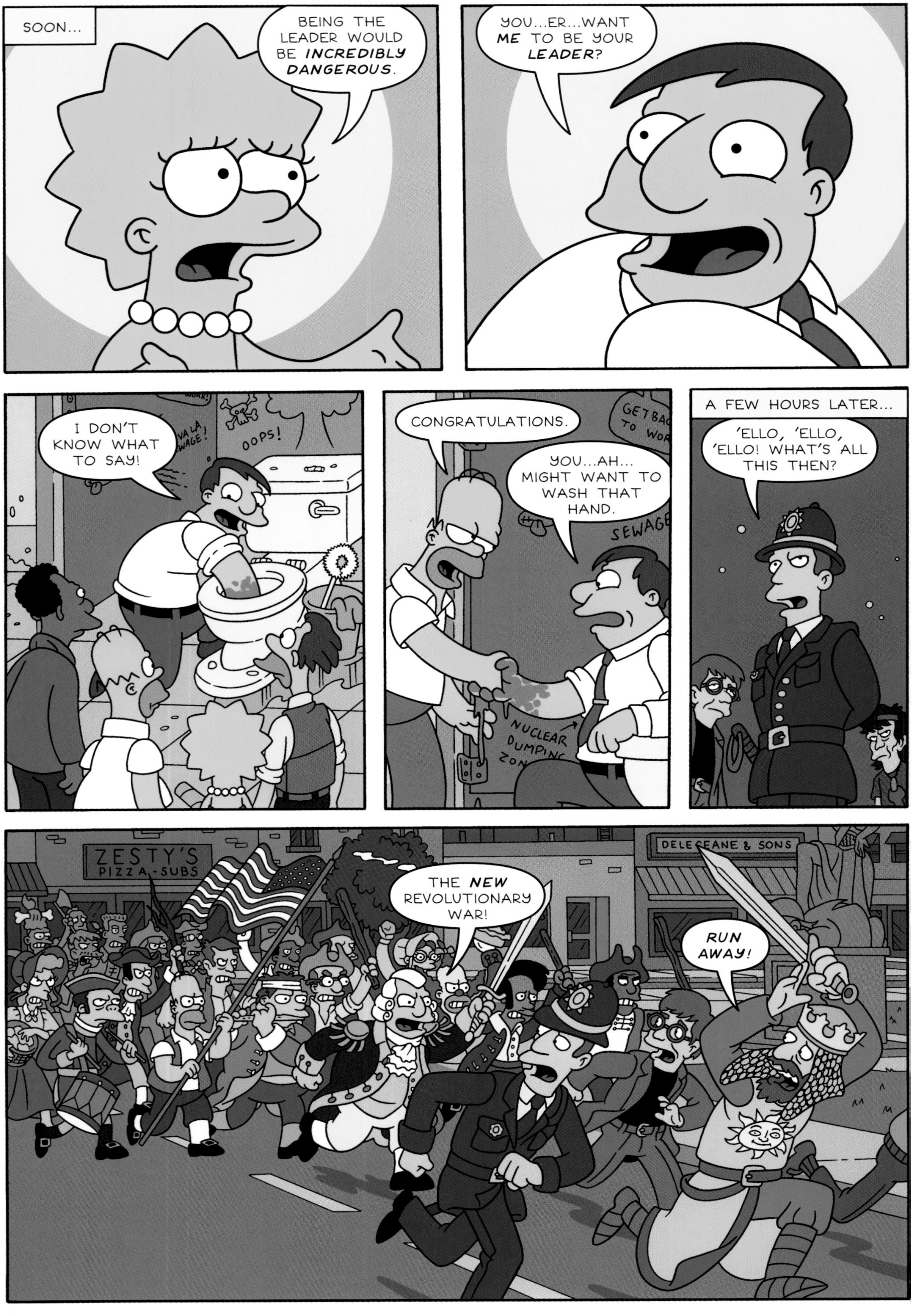
SOON...
BEING THE LEADER WOULD BE INCREDIBLY DANGEROUS.
YOU...ER...WANT ME TO BE YOUR LEADER?
I DON'T KNOW WHAT TO SAY!
OOPS!
CONGRATULATIONS.
YOU...AH... MIGHT WANT TO WASH THAT HAND.
SEWAGE
NUCLEAR DUMPING
A FEW HOURS LATER...
'ELLO, 'ELLO, 'ELLO! WHAT'S ALL THIS THEN?
ZESTY'S PIZZA-SUBS
THE NEW REVOLUTIONARY WAR!
RUN AWAY!

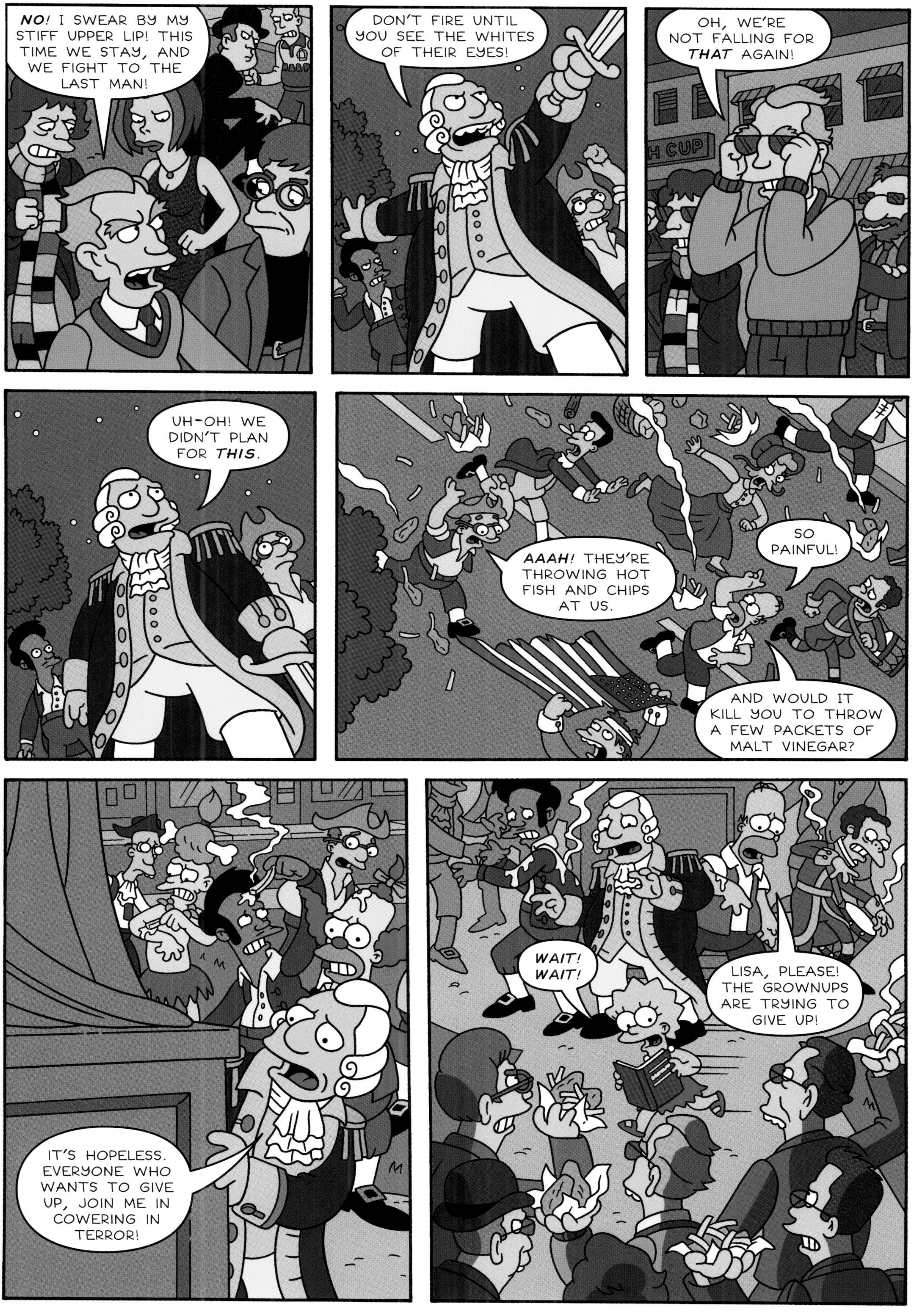
NO! I SWEAR BY MY STIFF UPPER LIP! THIS TIME WE STAY, AND WE FIGHT TO THE LAST MAN!
DON'T FIRE UNTIL YOU SEE THE WHITES OF THEIR EYES!
OH, WE'RE NOT FALLING FOR THAT AGAIN!
UH-OH! WE DIDN'T PLAN FOR THIS.
AAAH! THEY'RE THROWING HOT FISH AND CHIPS AT US.
SO PAINFUL!
AND WOULD IT KILL YOU TO THROW A FEW PACKETS OF MALT VINEGAR?
IT'S HOPELESS. EVERYONE WHO WANTS TO GIVE UP, JOIN ME IN COWERING IN TERROR!
WAIT! WAIT!
LISA, PLEASE! THE GROWNUPS ARE TRYING TO GIVE UP!

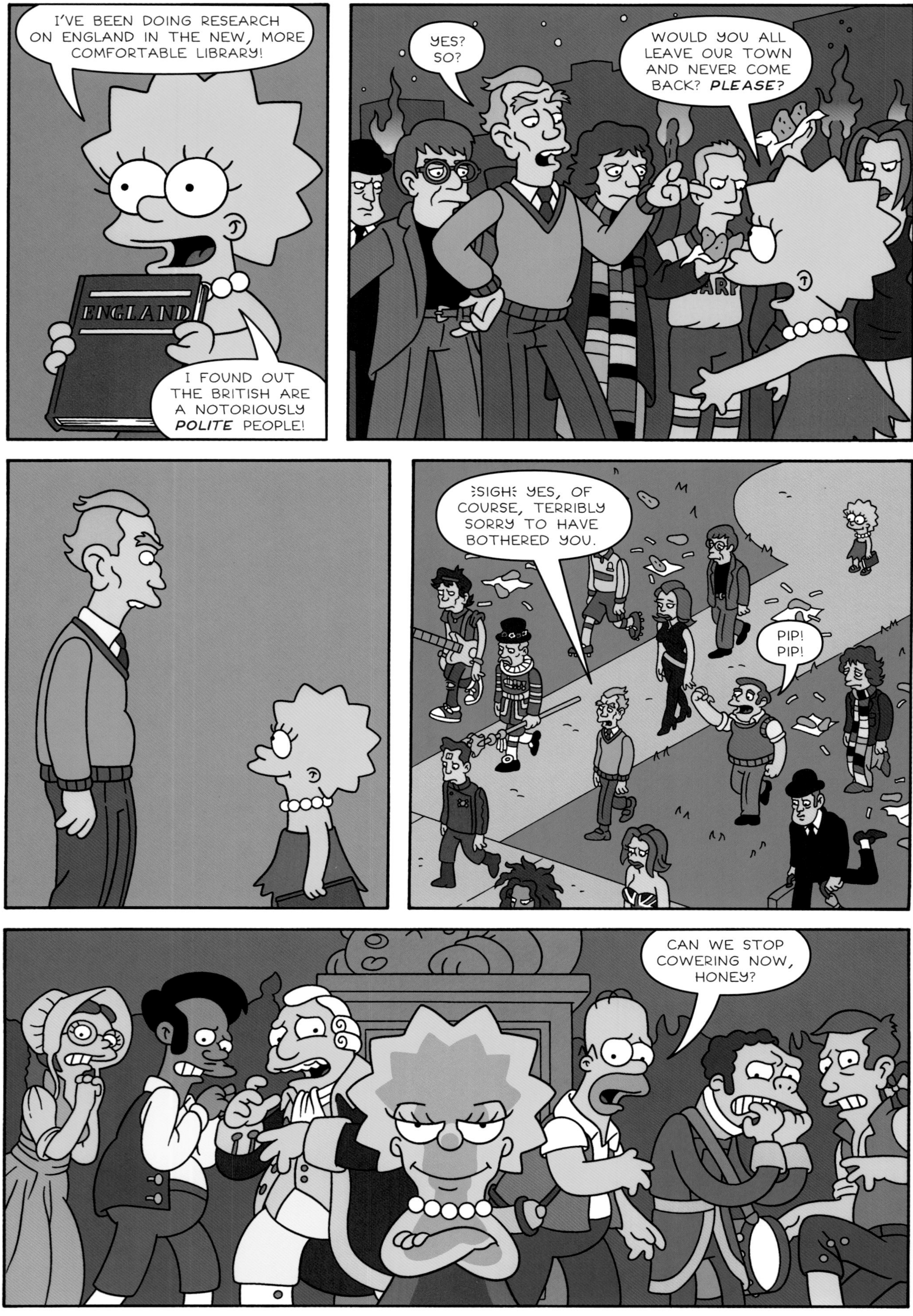
I'VE BEEN DOING RESEARCH ON ENGLAND IN THE NEW, MORE COMFORTABLE LIBRARY!
ENGLAND
I FOUND OUT THE BRITISH ARE A NOTORIOUSLY *POLITE* PEOPLE!
YES? SO?
WOULD YOU ALL LEAVE OUR TOWN AND NEVER COME BACK? *PLEASE*?
:SIGH: YES, OF COURSE, TERRIBLY SORRY TO HAVE BOTHERED YOU.
PIP! PIP!
CAN WE STOP COWERING NOW, HONEY?

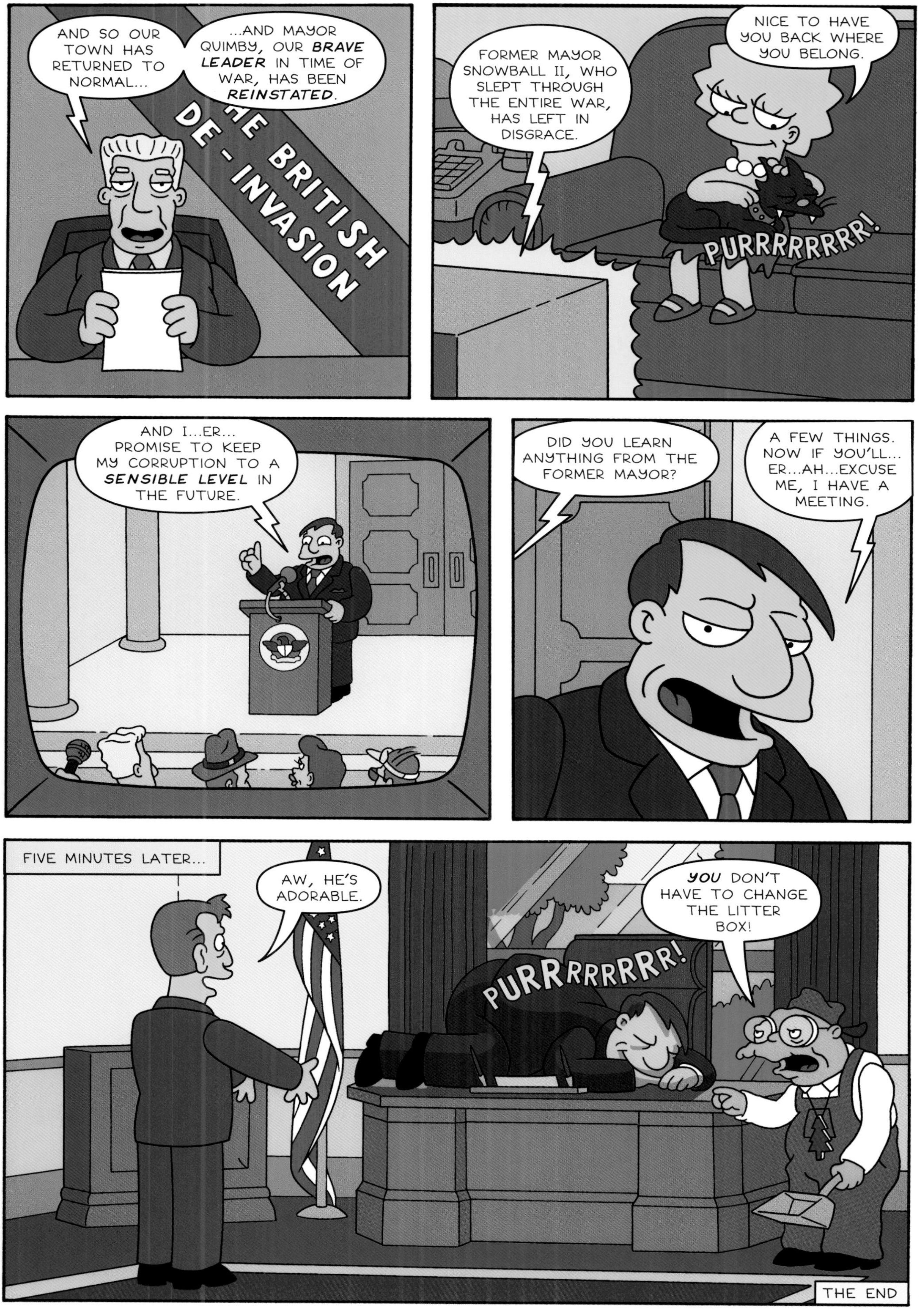
AND SO OUR TOWN HAS RETURNED TO NORMAL...
...AND MAYOR QUIMBY, OUR BRAVE LEADER IN TIME OF WAR, HAS BEEN REINSTATED.
DE-INVASION
FORMER MAYOR SNOWBALL II, WHO SLEPT THROUGH THE ENTIRE WAR, HAS LEFT IN DISGRACE.
NICE TO HAVE YOU BACK WHERE YOU BELONG.
PURRRRRRRR!
AND I...ER... PROMISE TO KEEP MY CORRUPTION TO A SENSIBLE LEVEL IN THE FUTURE.
DID YOU LEARN ANYTHING FROM THE FORMER MAYOR?
A FEW THINGS. NOW IF YOU'LL... ER...AH...EXCUSE ME, I HAVE A MEETING.
FIVE MINUTES LATER...
AW, HE'S ADORABLE.
YOU DON'T HAVE TO CHANGE THE LITTER BOX!
PURRRRRRRR!
THE END

WHO'S WHO IN THE NEW REVOLUTIONARY WAR?

How many of you realized that England has been camped at our borders for 234 years, just waiting for a chance to take back what was once part of the British Empire? And how many of you were able to identify all the British celebs, lords, ladies, dukes, duchesses, knights and knightresses that Simpsons Comics writer Ian Boothby and artist James Lloyd crammed into the Springfield town square on page 79 of this here comic book?* If you can't name them all, we've mapped out a handy dandy key to all the British radicals, rebels, and revolutionaries who have taken Springfield by storm!

* You must realize that as Canadian citizens, Ian and James are subjects of the British government and have risked all to bring you the comedy you have come to expect. All letters of personal thanks should be sent directly to them c/o The Tower of London.

1. **Harry Potter**
2. **David Beckham**
3. **Minister of Silly Walks (John Cleese)**
4. **Elton John**
5. **Arnold Rimmer from *Red Dwarf* (Chris Barrie)**
6. **Prince Charles**
7. **Dr. Who (Tom Baker)**
8. **Ringo Starr**
9. **Mr. John Steed (Patrick Macnee)**
10. **Mrs. Emma Peel (Diana Rigg)**
11. **Keith Richards**
12. **Posh Spice**
13. **Baby Spice**
14. **Scary Spice**
15. **Sporty Spice**
16. **Ginger Spice**
17. **Johnny Rotten**
18. **Tommy Cooper**

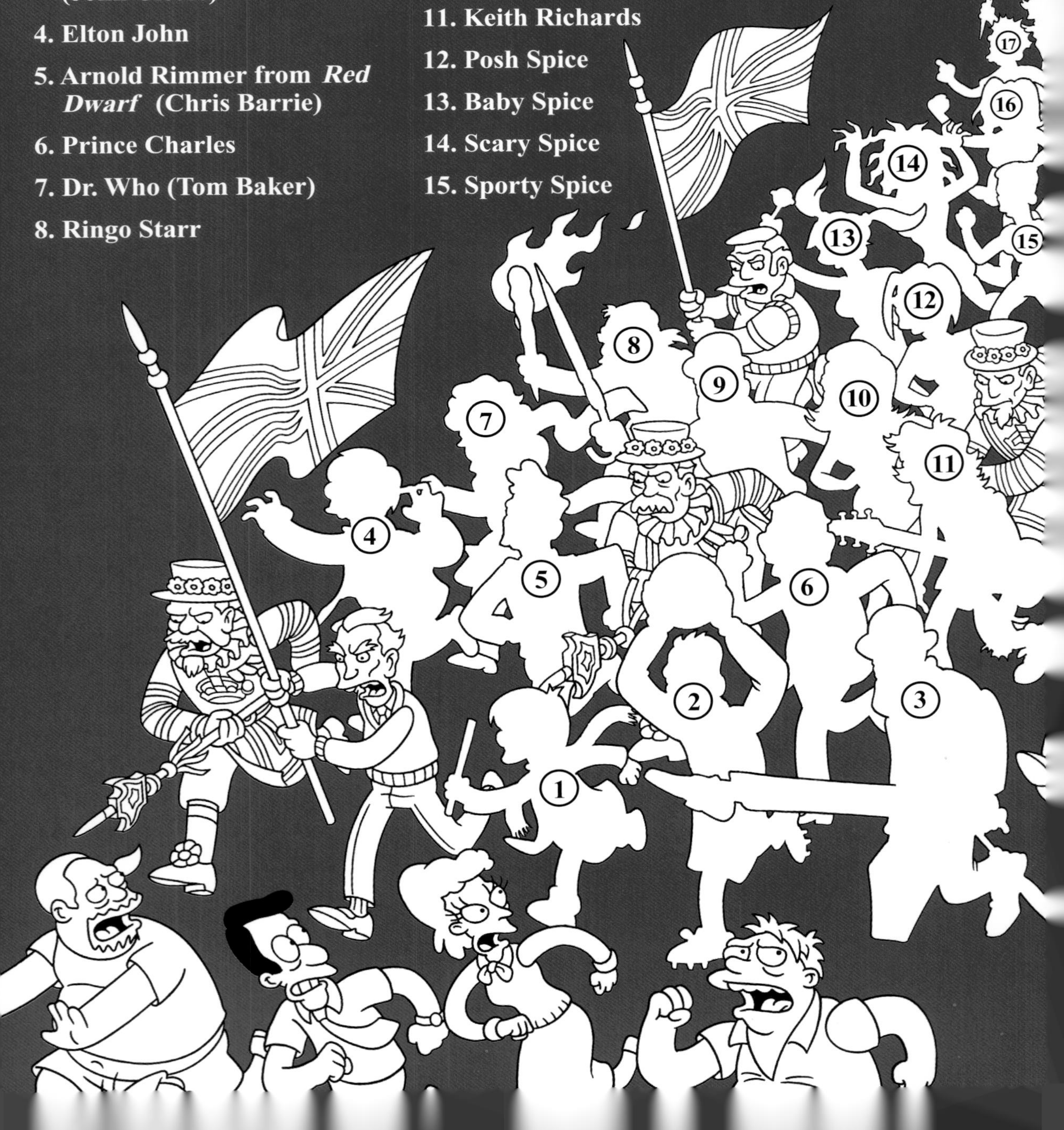
18
17
16
14
13
15
12
8
9
10
7
11
4
5
6
2
3
1

CHAPTER 3: SLAVES OF NEW NEW YORK!

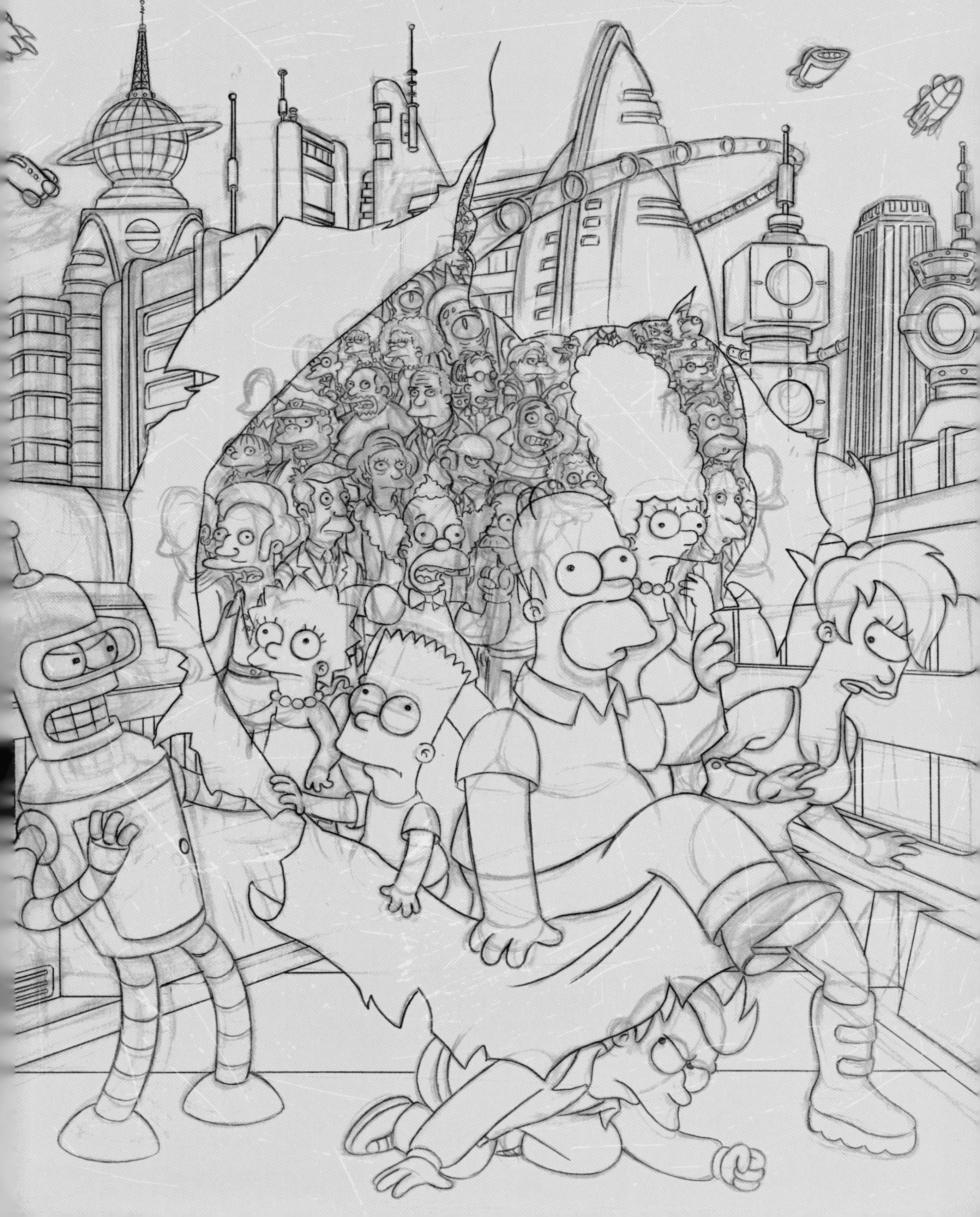

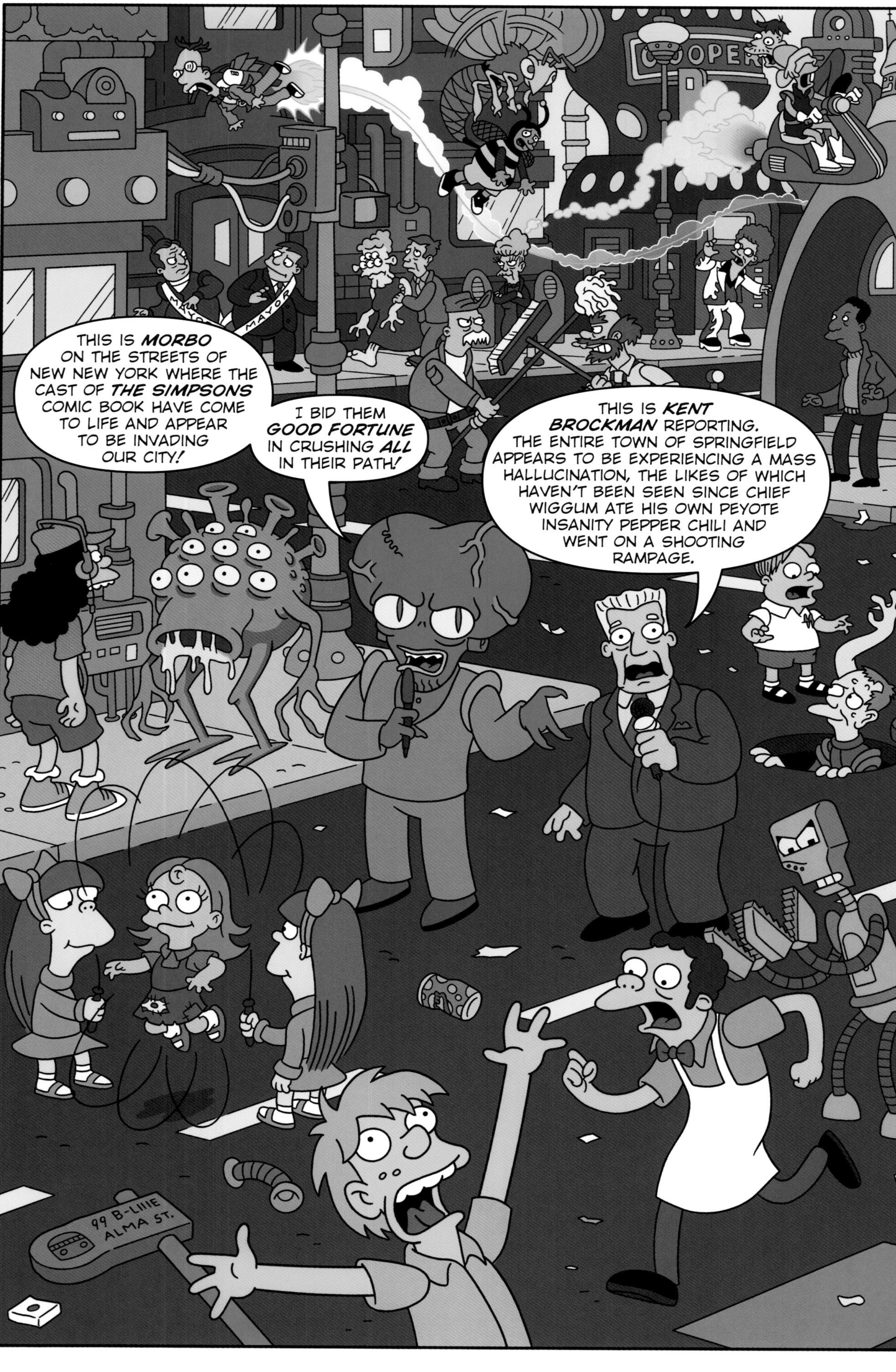
THIS IS MORBO ON THE STREETS OF NEW NEW YORK WHERE THE CAST OF THE SIMPSONS COMIC BOOK HAVE COME TO LIFE AND APPEAR TO BE INVADING OUR CITY!
I BID THEM GOOD FORTUNE IN CRUSHING ALL IN THEIR PATH!
THIS IS KENT BROCKMAN REPORTING. THE ENTIRE TOWN OF SPRINGFIELD APPEARS TO BE EXPERIENCING A MASS HALLUCINATION, THE LIKES OF WHICH HAVEN'T BEEN SEEN SINCE CHIEF WIGGUM ATE HIS OWN PEYOTE INSANITY PEPPER CHILI AND WENT ON A SHOOTING RAMPAGE.
MAYOR
MAYOR
99 B-LIIIE ALMA ST.

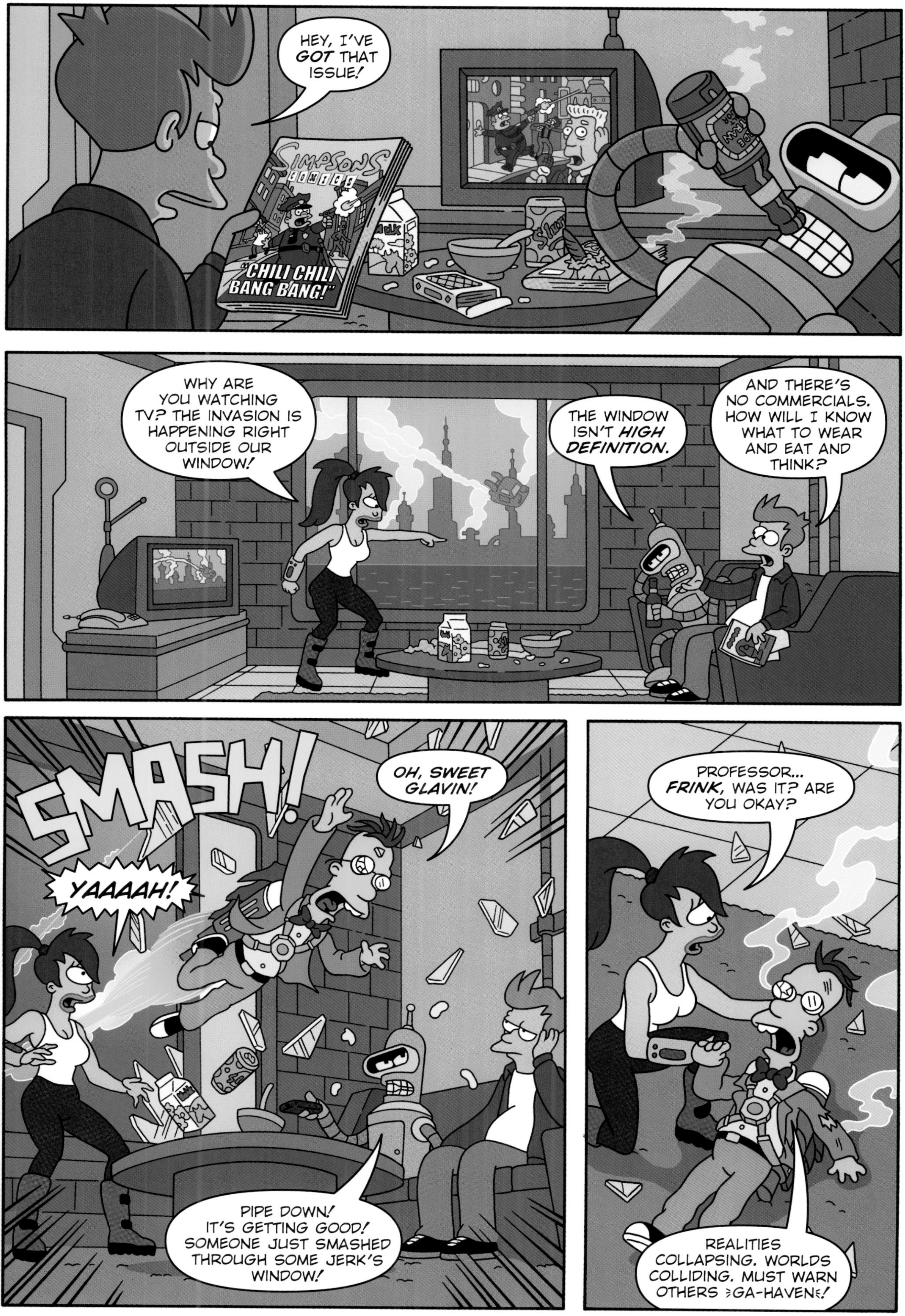
HEY, I'VE **GOT** THAT ISSUE!
SIMPSONS COMICS
"CHILI CHILI BANG BANG!"
WHY ARE YOU WATCHING TV? THE INVASION IS HAPPENING RIGHT OUTSIDE OUR WINDOW!
THE WINDOW ISN'T ***HIGH DEFINITION.***
AND THERE'S NO COMMERCIALS. HOW WILL I KNOW WHAT TO WEAR AND EAT AND THINK?
SMASH!
YAAAAH!
OH, SWEET GLAVIN!
PIPE DOWN! IT'S GETTING GOOD! SOMEONE JUST SMASHED THROUGH SOME JERK'S WINDOW!
PROFESSOR... ***FRINK***, WAS IT? ARE YOU OKAY?
REALITIES COLLAPSING. WORLDS COLLIDING. MUST WARN OTHERS ≥GA-HAVEN≤!

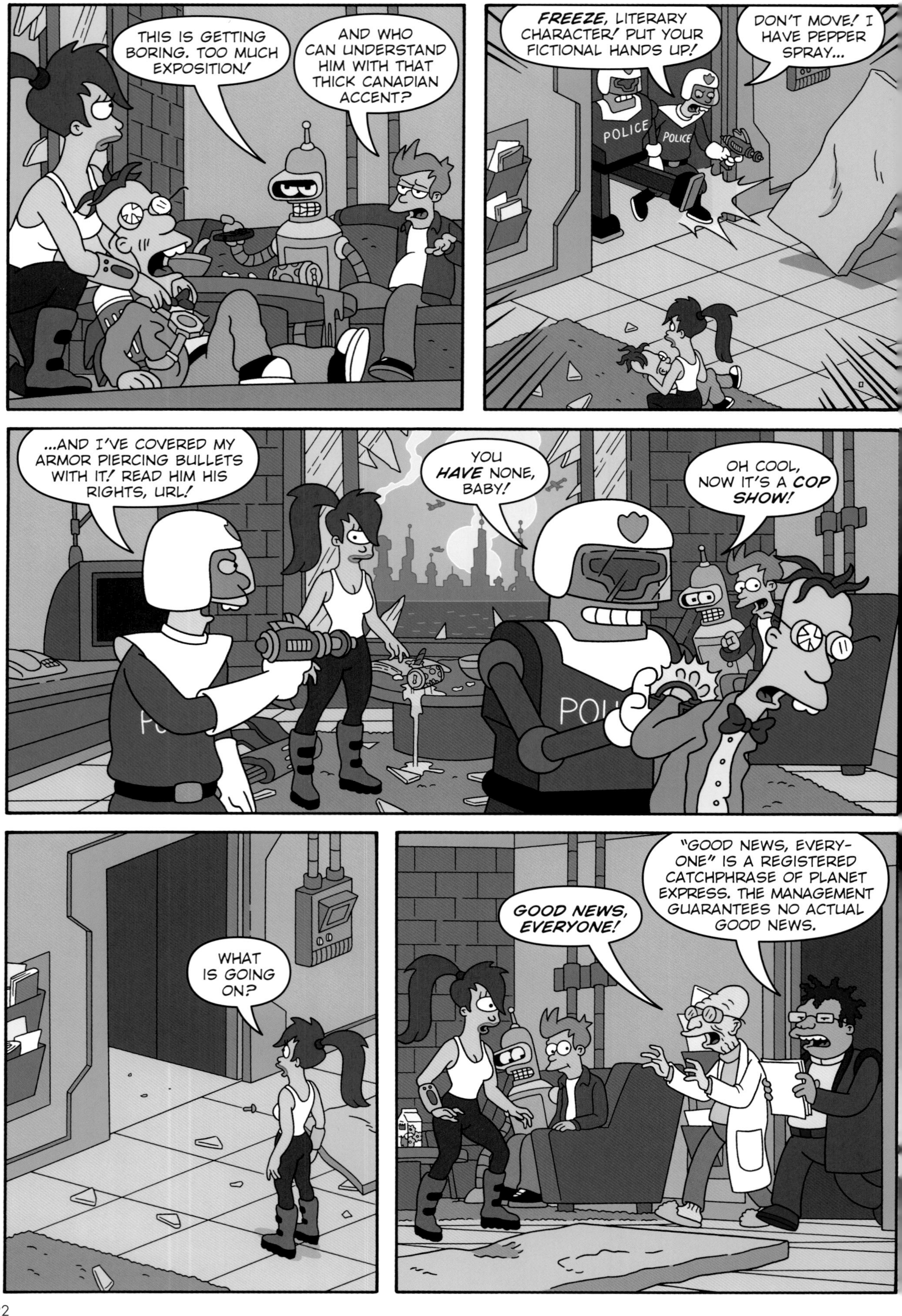
THIS IS GETTING BORING. TOO MUCH EXPOSITION!
AND WHO CAN UNDERSTAND HIM WITH THAT THICK CANADIAN ACCENT?
FREEZE, LITERARY CHARACTER! PUT YOUR FICTIONAL HANDS UP!
DON'T MOVE! I HAVE PEPPER SPRAY...
POLICE
POLICE
...AND I'VE COVERED MY ARMOR PIERCING BULLETS WITH IT! READ HIM HIS RIGHTS, URL!
YOU HAVE NONE, BABY!
OH COOL, NOW IT'S A COP SHOW!
WHAT IS GOING ON?
GOOD NEWS, EVERYONE!
"GOOD NEWS, EVERY-ONE" IS A REGISTERED CATCHPHRASE OF PLANET EXPRESS. THE MANAGEMENT GUARANTEES NO ACTUAL GOOD NEWS.

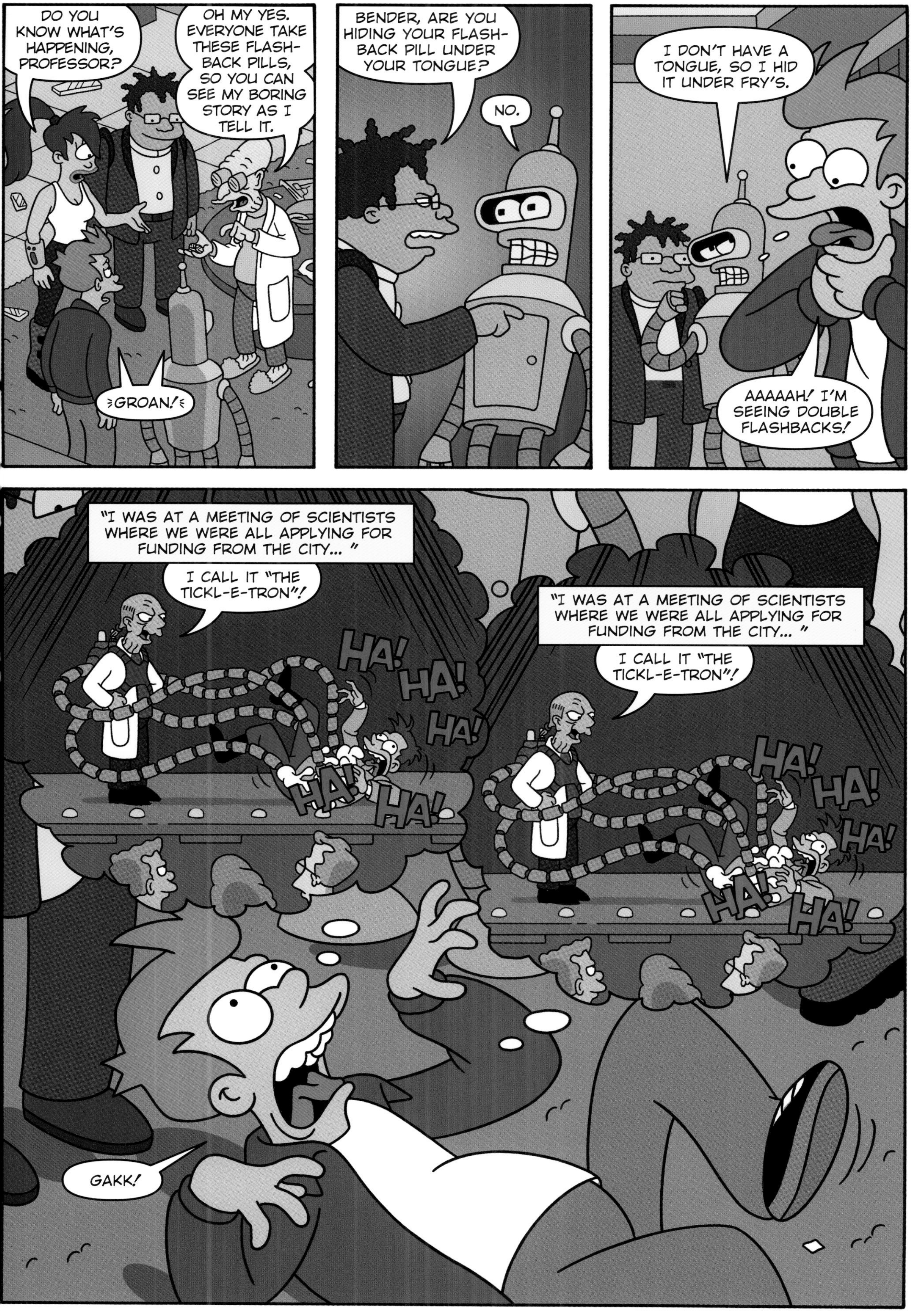
DO YOU KNOW WHAT'S HAPPENING, PROFESSOR?
OH MY YES. EVERYONE TAKE THESE FLASH-BACK PILLS, SO YOU CAN SEE MY BORING STORY AS I TELL IT.
GROAN!
BENDER, ARE YOU HIDING YOUR FLASH-BACK PILL UNDER YOUR TONGUE?
NO.
I DON'T HAVE A TONGUE, SO I HID IT UNDER FRY'S.
AAAAAH! I'M SEEING DOUBLE FLASHBACKS!
"I WAS AT A MEETING OF SCIENTISTS WHERE WE WERE ALL APPLYING FOR FUNDING FROM THE CITY... "
I CALL IT "THE TICKL-E-TRON"!
HA! HA! HA! HA! HA!
"I WAS AT A MEETING OF SCIENTISTS WHERE WE WERE ALL APPLYING FOR FUNDING FROM THE CITY... "
I CALL IT "THE TICKL-E-TRON"!
HA! HA! HA! HA! HA!
GAKK!

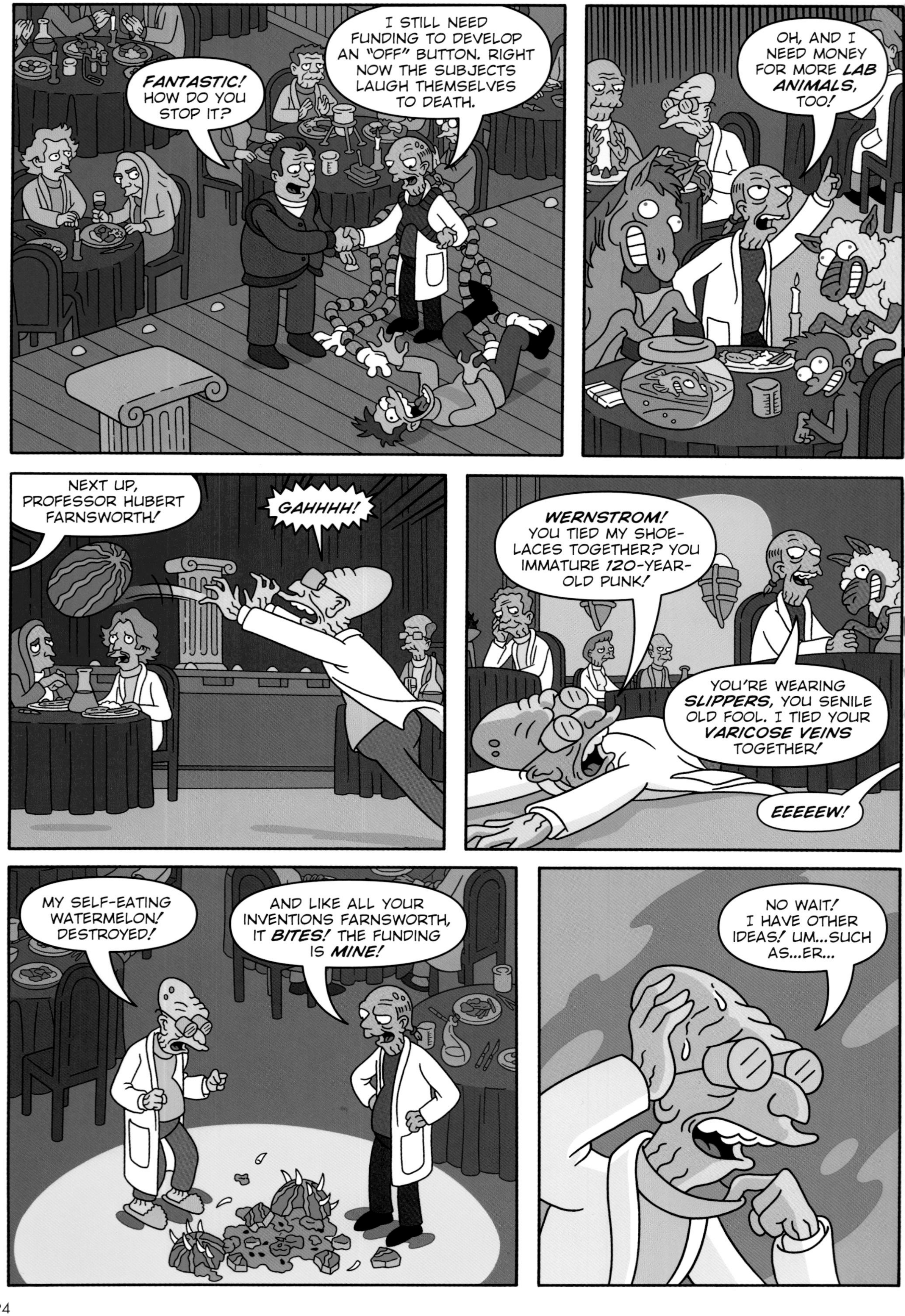

FANTASTIC! HOW DO YOU STOP IT?
I STILL NEED FUNDING TO DEVELOP AN "OFF" BUTTON. RIGHT NOW THE SUBJECTS LAUGH THEMSELVES TO DEATH.
OH, AND I NEED MONEY FOR MORE LAB ANIMALS, TOO!
NEXT UP, PROFESSOR HUBERT FARNSWORTH!
GAHHHH!
WERNSTROM! YOU TIED MY SHOE-LACES TOGETHER? YOU IMMATURE 120-YEAR-OLD PUNK!
YOU'RE WEARING SLIPPERS, YOU SENILE OLD FOOL. I TIED YOUR VARICOSE VEINS TOGETHER!
EEEEEW!
MY SELF-EATING WATERMELON! DESTROYED!
AND LIKE ALL YOUR INVENTIONS FARNSWORTH, IT BITES! THE FUNDING IS MINE!
NO WAIT! I HAVE OTHER IDEAS! UM...SUCH AS...ER...

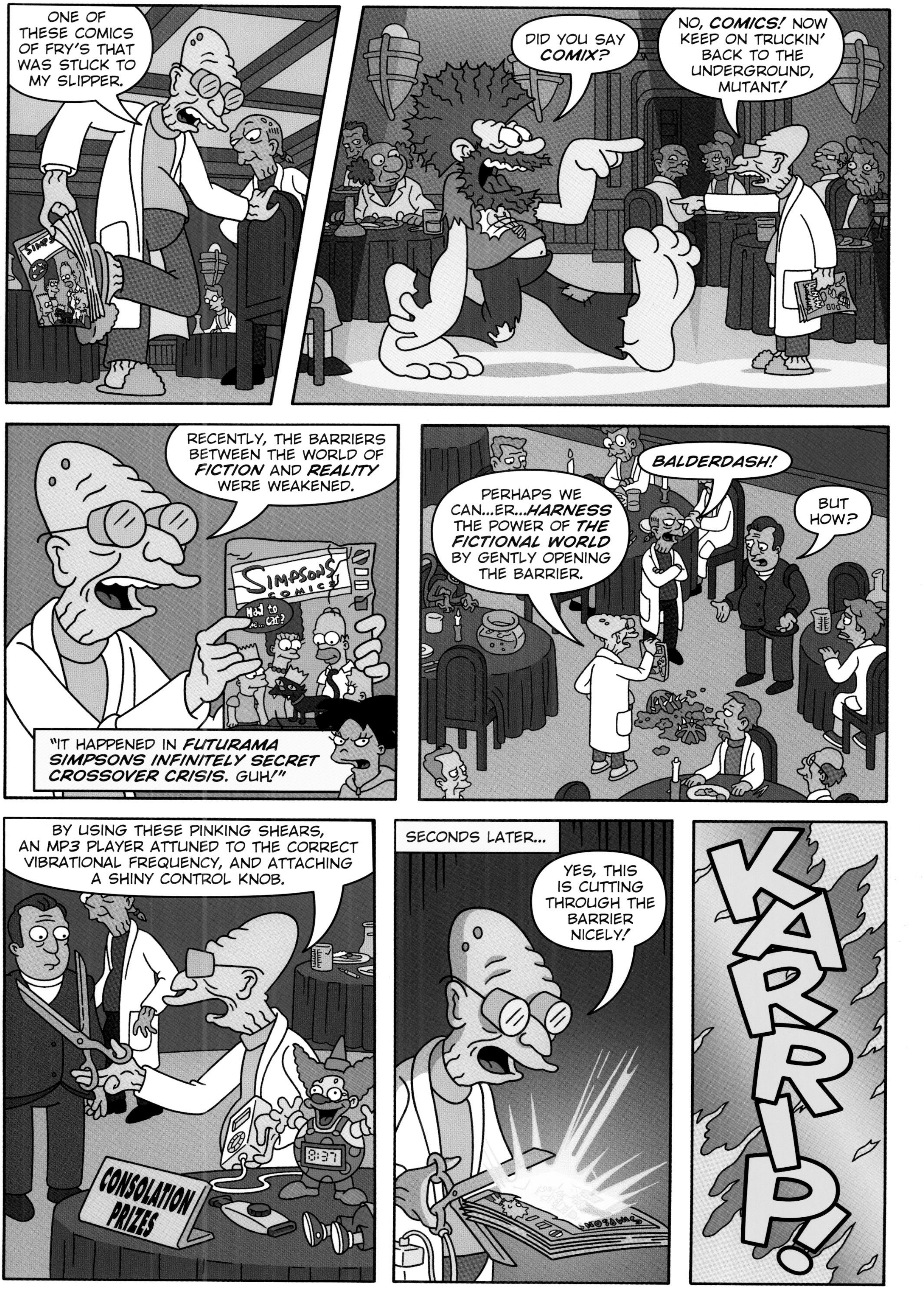
ONE OF THESE COMICS OF FRY'S THAT WAS STUCK TO MY SLIPPER.
DID YOU SAY COMIX?
NO, COMICS! NOW KEEP ON TRUCKIN' BACK TO THE UNDERGROUND, MUTANT!
RECENTLY, THE BARRIERS BETWEEN THE WORLD OF FICTION AND REALITY WERE WEAKENED.
SIMPSONS COMICS
"IT HAPPENED IN FUTURAMA SIMPSONS INFINITELY SECRET CROSSOVER CRISIS. GUH!"
PERHAPS WE CAN...ER...HARNESS THE POWER OF THE FICTIONAL WORLD BY GENTLY OPENING THE BARRIER.
BALDERDASH!
BUT HOW?
BY USING THESE PINKING SHEARS, AN MP3 PLAYER ATTUNED TO THE CORRECT VIBRATIONAL FREQUENCY, AND ATTACHING A SHINY CONTROL KNOB.
CONSOLATION PRIZES
8:37
SECONDS LATER...
YES, THIS IS CUTTING THROUGH THE BARRIER NICELY!
KARRIP!

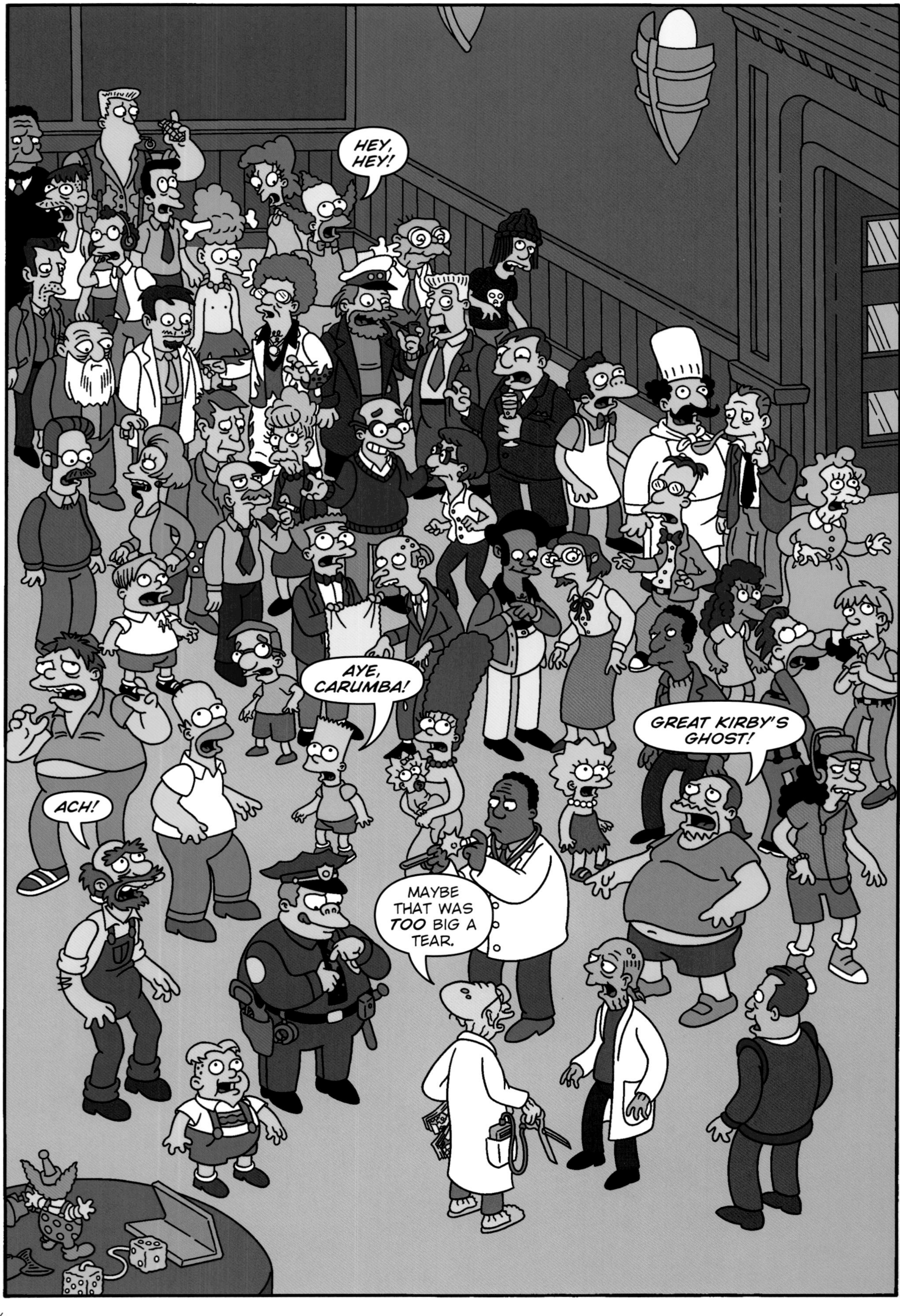
HEY, HEY!
AYE, CARUMBA!
GREAT KIRBY'S GHOST!
ACH!
MAYBE THAT WAS *TOO* BIG A TEAR.

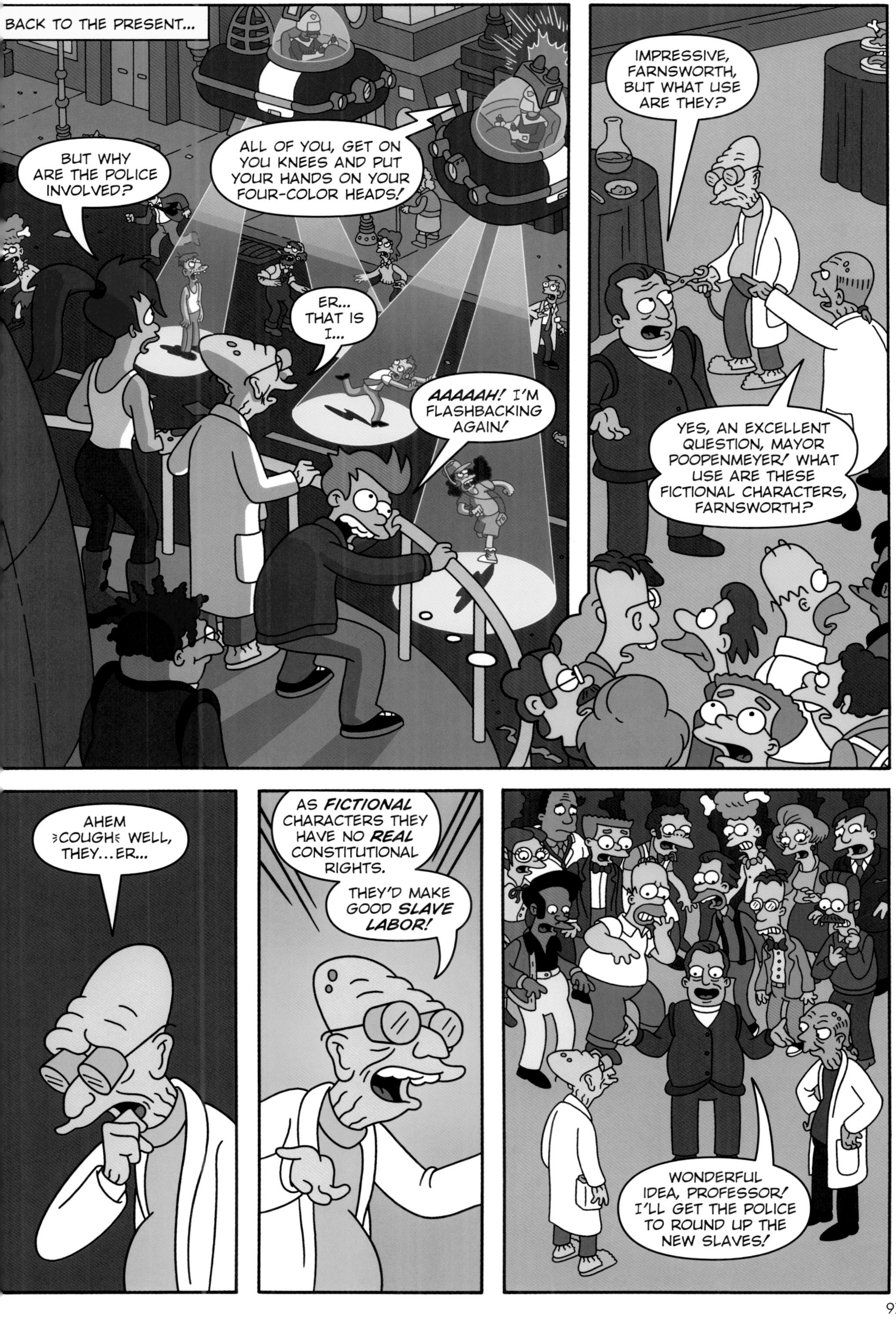
BACK TO THE PRESENT...
BUT WHY ARE THE POLICE INVOLVED?
ALL OF YOU, GET ON YOU KNEES AND PUT YOUR HANDS ON YOUR FOUR-COLOR HEADS!
ER... THAT IS I...
AAAAAH! I'M FLASHBACKING AGAIN!
IMPRESSIVE, FARNSWORTH, BUT WHAT USE ARE THEY?
YES, AN EXCELLENT QUESTION, MAYOR POOPENMEYER! WHAT USE ARE THESE FICTIONAL CHARACTERS, FARNSWORTH?
AHEM *COUGH* WELL, THEY...ER...
AS FICTIONAL CHARACTERS THEY HAVE NO REAL CONSTITUTIONAL RIGHTS.
THEY'D MAKE GOOD SLAVE LABOR!
WONDERFUL IDEA, PROFESSOR! I'LL GET THE POLICE TO ROUND UP THE NEW SLAVES!

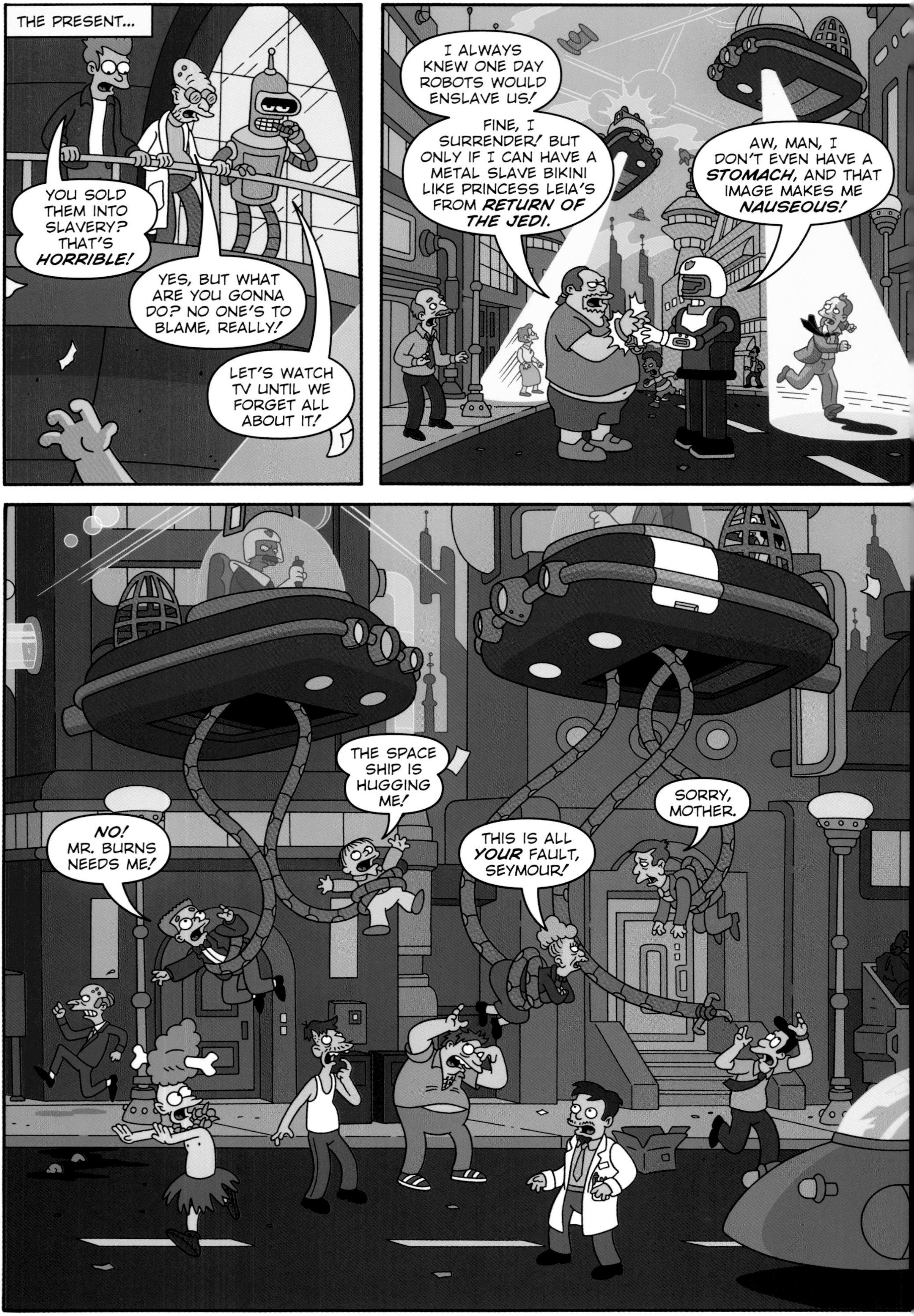
THE PRESENT...
YOU SOLD THEM INTO SLAVERY? THAT'S HORRIBLE!
YES, BUT WHAT ARE YOU GONNA DO? NO ONE'S TO BLAME, REALLY!
LET'S WATCH TV UNTIL WE FORGET ALL ABOUT IT!
I ALWAYS KNEW ONE DAY ROBOTS WOULD ENSLAVE US!
FINE, I SURRENDER! BUT ONLY IF I CAN HAVE A METAL SLAVE BIKINI LIKE PRINCESS LEIA'S FROM RETURN OF THE JEDI.
AW, MAN, I DON'T EVEN HAVE A STOMACH, AND THAT IMAGE MAKES ME NAUSEOUS!
NO! MR. BURNS NEEDS ME!
THE SPACE SHIP IS HUGGING ME!
THIS IS ALL YOUR FAULT, SEYMOUR!
SORRY, MOTHER.

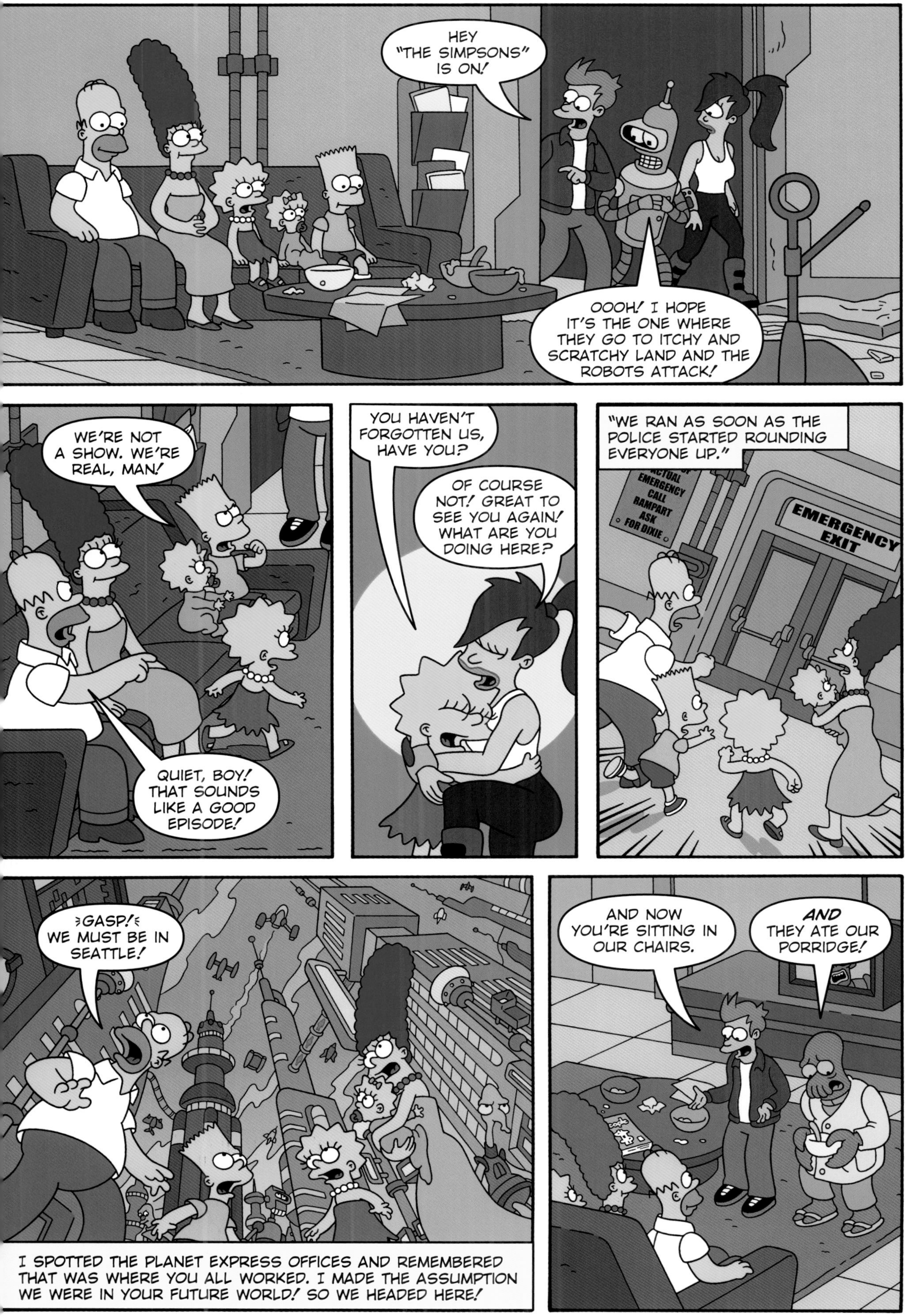
HEY "THE SIMPSONS" IS ON!
OOOH! I HOPE IT'S THE ONE WHERE THEY GO TO ITCHY AND SCRATCHY LAND AND THE ROBOTS ATTACK!
WE'RE NOT A SHOW. WE'RE REAL, MAN!
QUIET, BOY! THAT SOUNDS LIKE A GOOD EPISODE!
YOU HAVEN'T FORGOTTEN US, HAVE YOU?
OF COURSE NOT! GREAT TO SEE YOU AGAIN! WHAT ARE YOU DOING HERE?
"WE RAN AS SOON AS THE POLICE STARTED ROUNDING EVERYONE UP."
EMERGENCY CALL RAMPART ASK FOR DIXIE
EMERGENCY EXIT
GASP! WE MUST BE IN SEATTLE!
I SPOTTED THE PLANET EXPRESS OFFICES AND REMEMBERED THAT WAS WHERE YOU ALL WORKED. I MADE THE ASSUMPTION WE WERE IN YOUR FUTURE WORLD! SO WE HEADED HERE!
AND NOW YOU'RE SITTING IN OUR CHAIRS.
AND THEY ATE OUR PORRIDGE!

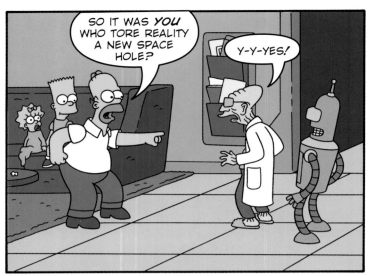

SO IT WAS *YOU* WHO TORE REALITY A NEW SPACE HOLE?

Y-Y-YES!

WHEW! I THOUGHT IT WAS *ME!* FINALLY *SOMETHING* THAT'S NOT MY FAULT!

THE POLICE! THEY'RE BACK!

YOU'VE GOT TO HIDE US!

I CAN'T THINK OF A PLACE WITH YOU SHAKING MY BRAIN!

HELLO AGAIN, WE SPOTTED SOME OTHER FICTIONAL PEOPLE OR "FICS" IN THE NEIGHBORHOOD. YOU SEEN THEM?

IS THERE A REWARD?

BENDER!

SMITTY, OVER HERE!

WHAT? THESE ARE MY LIFE-SIZED SIMPSONS ACTION FIGURES. I GOT THEM ON EBUY!

ARE THOSE THE *ARTICULATED* OR THE *BENDY* KIND?

BENDY.

CRACK!

MMMF!

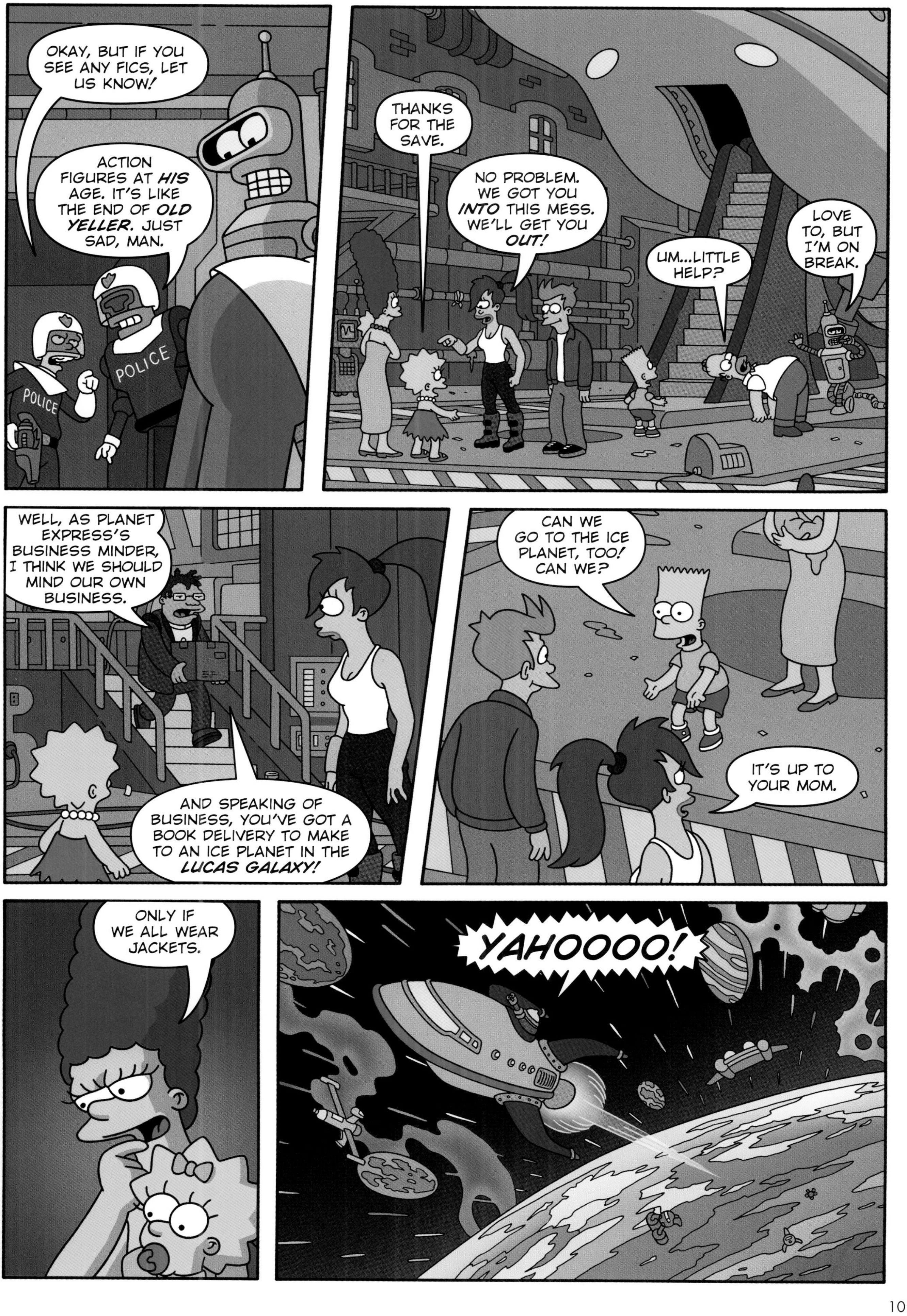
OKAY, BUT IF YOU SEE ANY FICS, LET US KNOW!
ACTION FIGURES AT *HIS* AGE. IT'S LIKE THE END OF ***OLD YELLER***. JUST SAD, MAN.
POLICE
POLICE
THANKS FOR THE SAVE.
NO PROBLEM. WE GOT YOU ***INTO*** THIS MESS. WE'LL GET YOU ***OUT!***
UM...LITTLE HELP?
LOVE TO, BUT I'M ON BREAK.
WELL, AS PLANET EXPRESS'S BUSINESS MINDER, I THINK WE SHOULD MIND OUR OWN BUSINESS.
AND SPEAKING OF BUSINESS, YOU'VE GOT A BOOK DELIVERY TO MAKE TO AN ICE PLANET IN THE ***LUCAS GALAXY!***
CAN WE GO TO THE ICE PLANET, TOO! CAN WE?
IT'S UP TO YOUR MOM.
ONLY IF WE ALL WEAR JACKETS.
YAHOOOO!

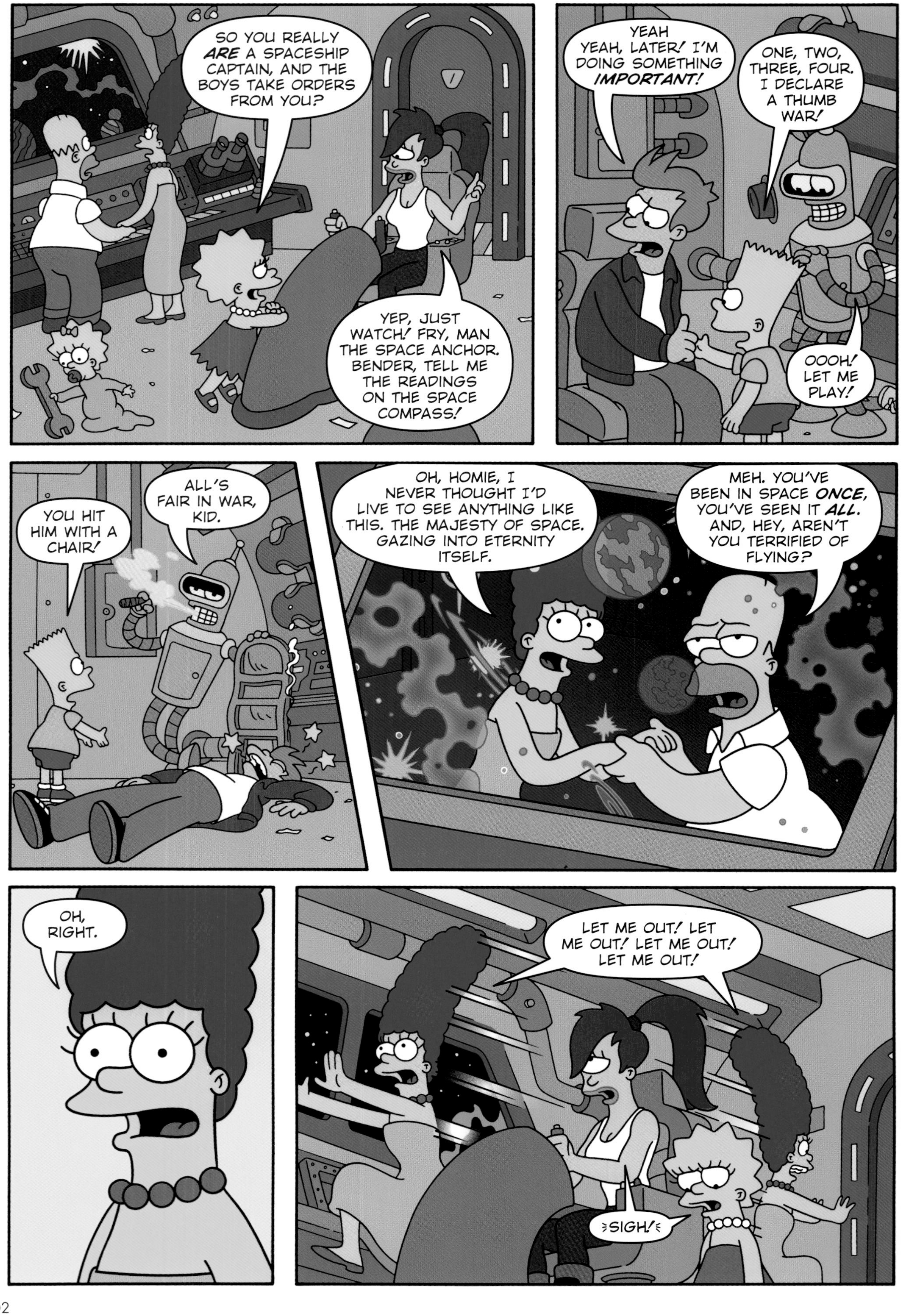
SO YOU REALLY ARE A SPACESHIP CAPTAIN, AND THE BOYS TAKE ORDERS FROM YOU?
YEP, JUST WATCH! FRY, MAN THE SPACE ANCHOR. BENDER, TELL ME THE READINGS ON THE SPACE COMPASS!
YEAH YEAH, LATER! I'M DOING SOMETHING IMPORTANT!
ONE, TWO, THREE, FOUR. I DECLARE A THUMB WAR!
OOOH! LET ME PLAY!
YOU HIT HIM WITH A CHAIR!
ALL'S FAIR IN WAR, KID.
OH, HOMIE, I NEVER THOUGHT I'D LIVE TO SEE ANYTHING LIKE THIS. THE MAJESTY OF SPACE. GAZING INTO ETERNITY ITSELF.
MEH. YOU'VE BEEN IN SPACE ONCE, YOU'VE SEEN IT ALL. AND, HEY, AREN'T YOU TERRIFIED OF FLYING?
OH, RIGHT.
LET ME OUT! LET ME OUT! LET ME OUT! LET ME OUT!
SIGH!

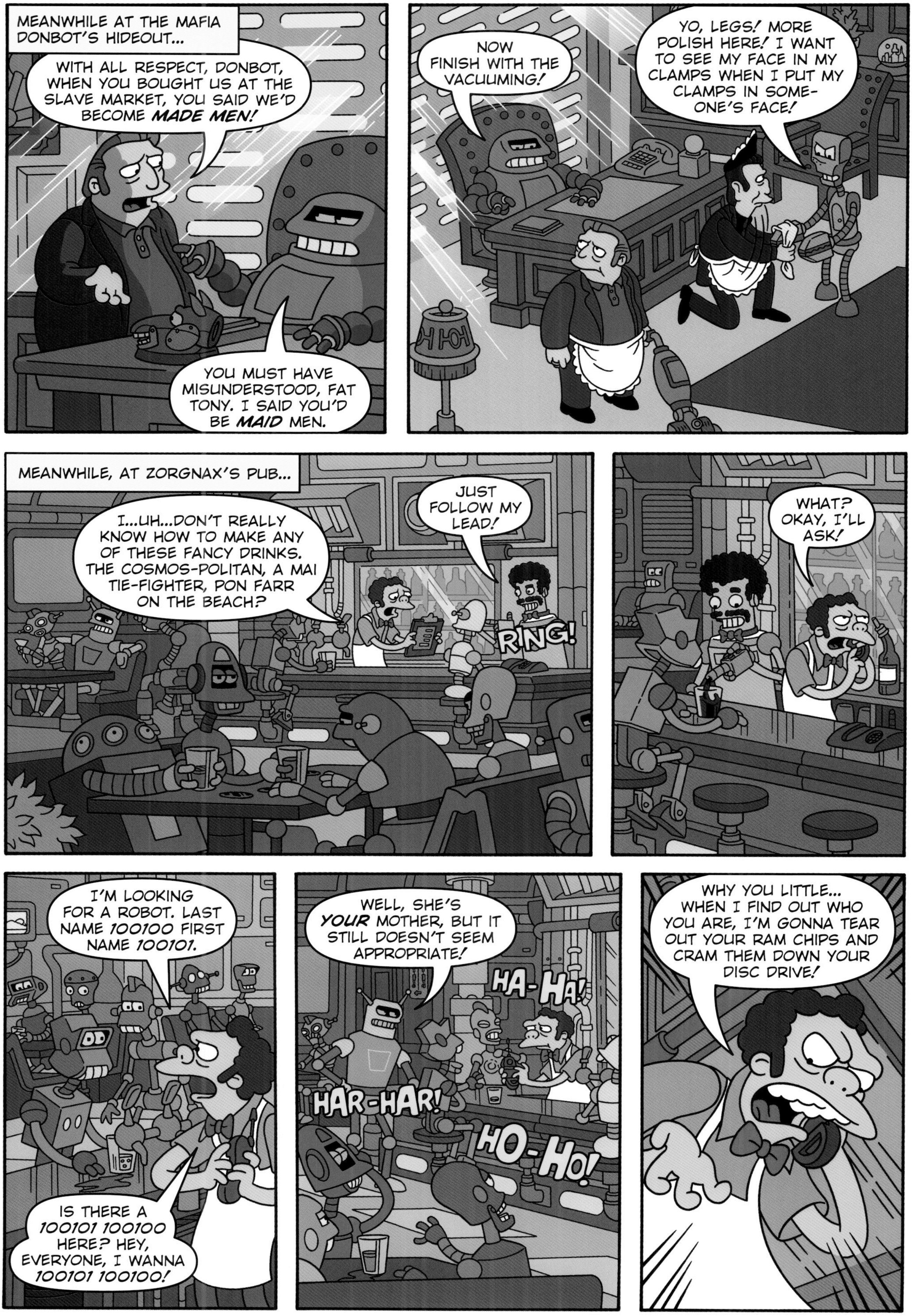

MEANWHILE AT THE MAFIA DONBOT'S HIDEOUT...
WITH ALL RESPECT, DONBOT, WHEN YOU BOUGHT US AT THE SLAVE MARKET, YOU SAID WE'D BECOME MADE MEN!
YOU MUST HAVE MISUNDERSTOOD, FAT TONY. I SAID YOU'D BE MAID MEN.
NOW FINISH WITH THE VACUUMING!
YO, LEGS! MORE POLISH HERE! I WANT TO SEE MY FACE IN MY CLAMPS WHEN I PUT MY CLAMPS IN SOME-ONE'S FACE!
MEANWHILE, AT ZORGNAX'S PUB...
I...UH...DON'T REALLY KNOW HOW TO MAKE ANY OF THESE FANCY DRINKS. THE COSMOS-POLITAN, A MAI TIE-FIGHTER, PON FARR ON THE BEACH?
JUST FOLLOW MY LEAD!
RING!
WHAT? OKAY, I'LL ASK!
I'M LOOKING FOR A ROBOT. LAST NAME 100100 FIRST NAME 100101.
IS THERE A 100101 100100 HERE? HEY, EVERYONE, I WANNA 100101 100100!
WELL, SHE'S YOUR MOTHER, BUT IT STILL DOESN'T SEEM APPROPRIATE!
HA-HA!
HAR-HAR!
HO-HO!
WHY YOU LITTLE... WHEN I FIND OUT WHO YOU ARE, I'M GONNA TEAR OUT YOUR RAM CHIPS AND CRAM THEM DOWN YOUR DISC DRIVE!

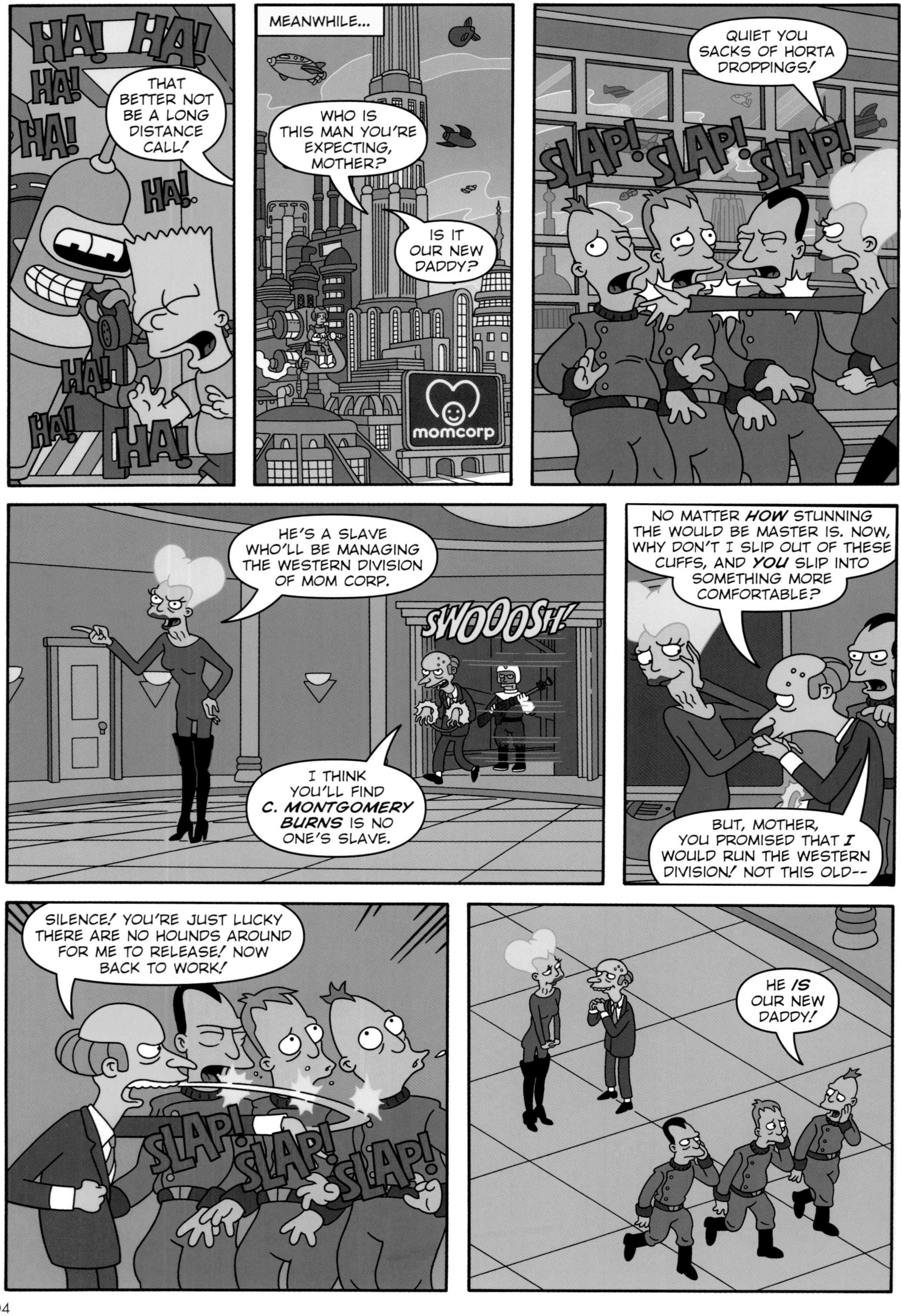
HA! HA! HA! HA!
THAT BETTER NOT BE A LONG DISTANCE CALL!
HA!
HA! HA! HA!
MEANWHILE...
WHO IS THIS MAN YOU'RE EXPECTING, MOTHER?
IS IT OUR NEW DADDY?
momcorp
QUIET YOU SACKS OF HORTA DROPPINGS!
SLAP! SLAP! SLAP!
HE'S A SLAVE WHO'LL BE MANAGING THE WESTERN DIVISION OF MOM CORP.
SWOOOSH!
I THINK YOU'LL FIND ***C. MONTGOMERY BURNS*** IS NO ONE'S SLAVE.
NO MATTER ***HOW*** STUNNING THE WOULD BE MASTER IS. NOW, WHY DON'T I SLIP OUT OF THESE CUFFS, AND ***YOU*** SLIP INTO SOMETHING MORE COMFORTABLE?
BUT, MOTHER, YOU PROMISED THAT ***I*** WOULD RUN THE WESTERN DIVISION! NOT THIS OLD--
SILENCE! YOU'RE JUST LUCKY THERE ARE NO HOUNDS AROUND FOR ME TO RELEASE! NOW BACK TO WORK!
SLAP! SLAP! SLAP!
HE ***IS*** OUR NEW DADDY!

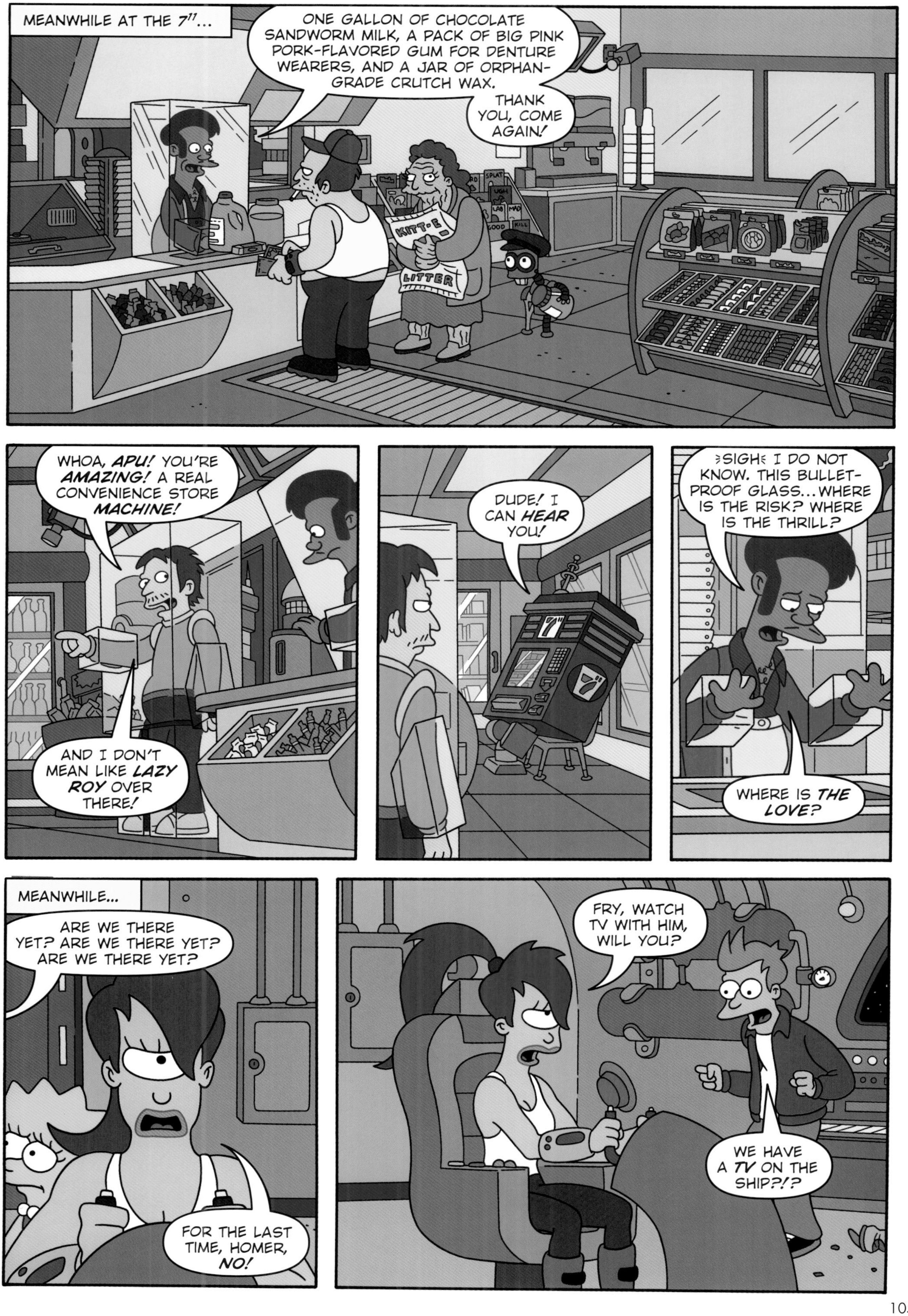
MEANWHILE AT THE 7″...
ONE GALLON OF CHOCOLATE SANDWORM MILK, A PACK OF BIG PINK PORK-FLAVORED GUM FOR DENTURE WEARERS, AND A JAR OF ORPHAN-GRADE CRUTCH WAX.
THANK YOU, COME AGAIN!
KITT-E
LITTER
WHOA, ***APU!*** YOU'RE ***AMAZING!*** A REAL CONVENIENCE STORE ***MACHINE!***
AND I DON'T MEAN LIKE ***LAZY ROY*** OVER THERE!
DUDE! I CAN ***HEAR*** YOU!
SIGH I DO NOT KNOW. THIS BULLET-PROOF GLASS...WHERE IS THE RISK? WHERE IS THE THRILL?
WHERE IS ***THE LOVE?***
MEANWHILE...
ARE WE THERE YET? ARE WE THERE YET? ARE WE THERE YET?
FOR THE LAST TIME, HOMER, ***NO!***
FRY, WATCH TV WITH HIM, WILL YOU?
WE HAVE A ***TV*** ON THE SHIP?!?

HI THERE! I'M *MALFUNCTIONING EDDIE*, AND DO *I* HAVE DEAL FOR *YOU!*

TELL 'EM, GIL!

WELL, JUST LOOK AT WHAT WE GOT HERE! A REAL BEAUTY, BARELY DRIVEN BY A SPROCKET FACTORY EMPLOYEE...

...BEFORE HE WAS KILLED IN A TREADMILL ACCIDENT WHILE WALKING HIS DOG.

AND THIS DREAM HERE... COMPACT OUTSIDE, ROOMY INSIDE!

OL' GIL HIMSELF HAS BEEN DRIVING THIS BABY HERE ALL WEEK LONG!

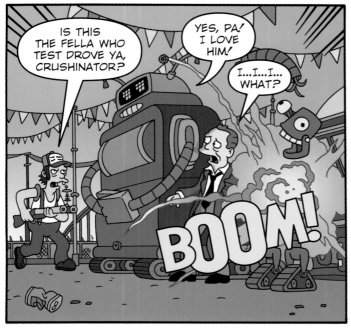

IS THIS THE FELLA WHO TEST DROVE YA, CRUSHINATOR?

YES, PA! I LOVE HIM!

I...I...I... WHAT?

BOOM!

SO COME ON DOWN TO *MALFUNCTIONING EDDIE'S*, WHERE YOU'LL LOVE OUR CARS ALMOST AS MUCH AS *WE* DO!

I NOW PRONOUNCE YOU MAN AND VEHICLE!

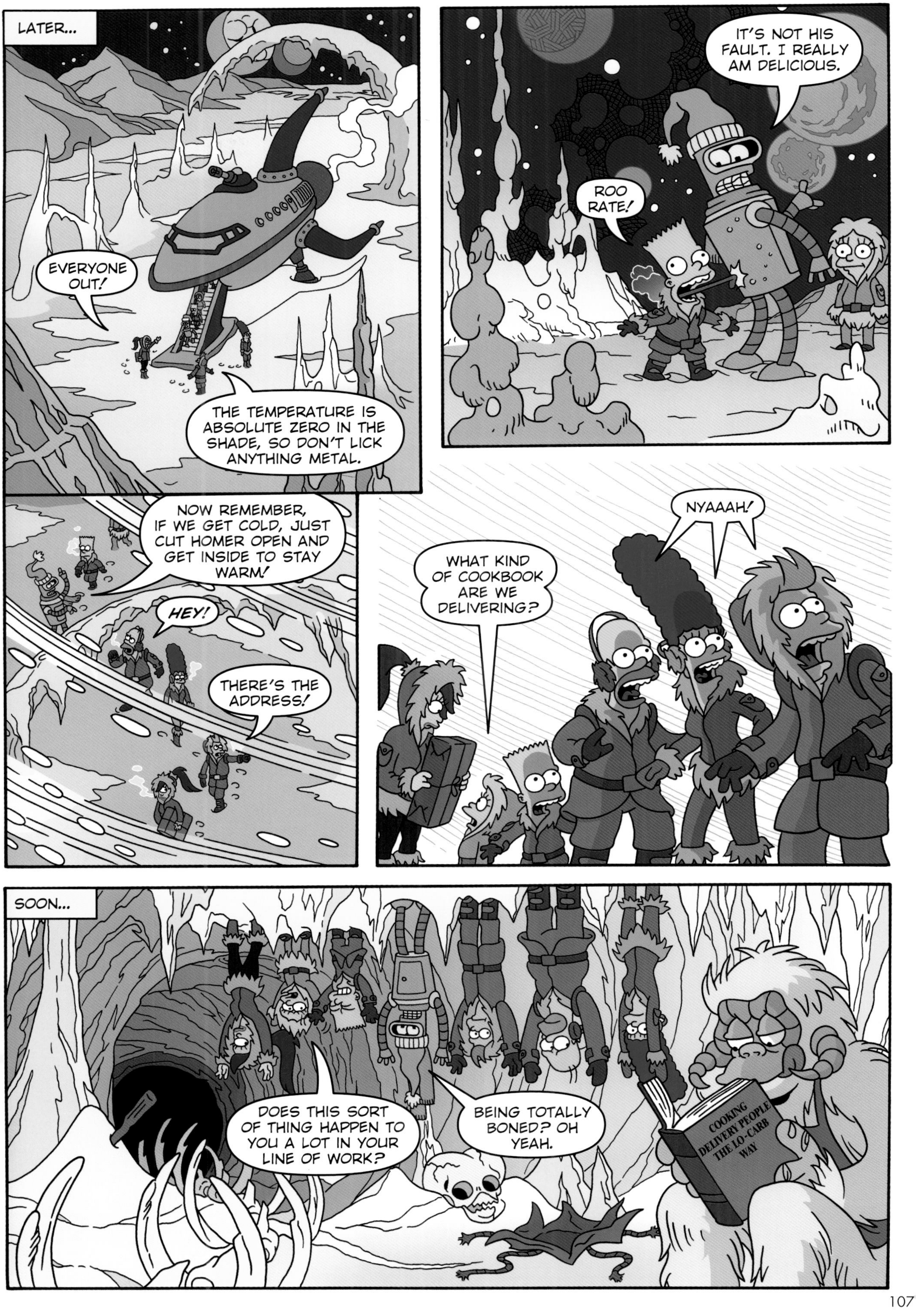
LATER...
EVERYONE OUT!
THE TEMPERATURE IS ABSOLUTE ZERO IN THE SHADE, SO DON'T LICK ANYTHING METAL.
IT'S NOT HIS FAULT. I REALLY AM DELICIOUS.
ROO RATE!
NOW REMEMBER, IF WE GET COLD, JUST CUT HOMER OPEN AND GET INSIDE TO STAY WARM!
HEY!
THERE'S THE ADDRESS!
WHAT KIND OF COOKBOOK ARE WE DELIVERING?
NYAAAH!
SOON...
DOES THIS SORT OF THING HAPPEN TO YOU A LOT IN YOUR LINE OF WORK?
BEING TOTALLY BONED? OH YEAH.
COOKING DELIVERY PEOPLE THE LO-CARB WAY

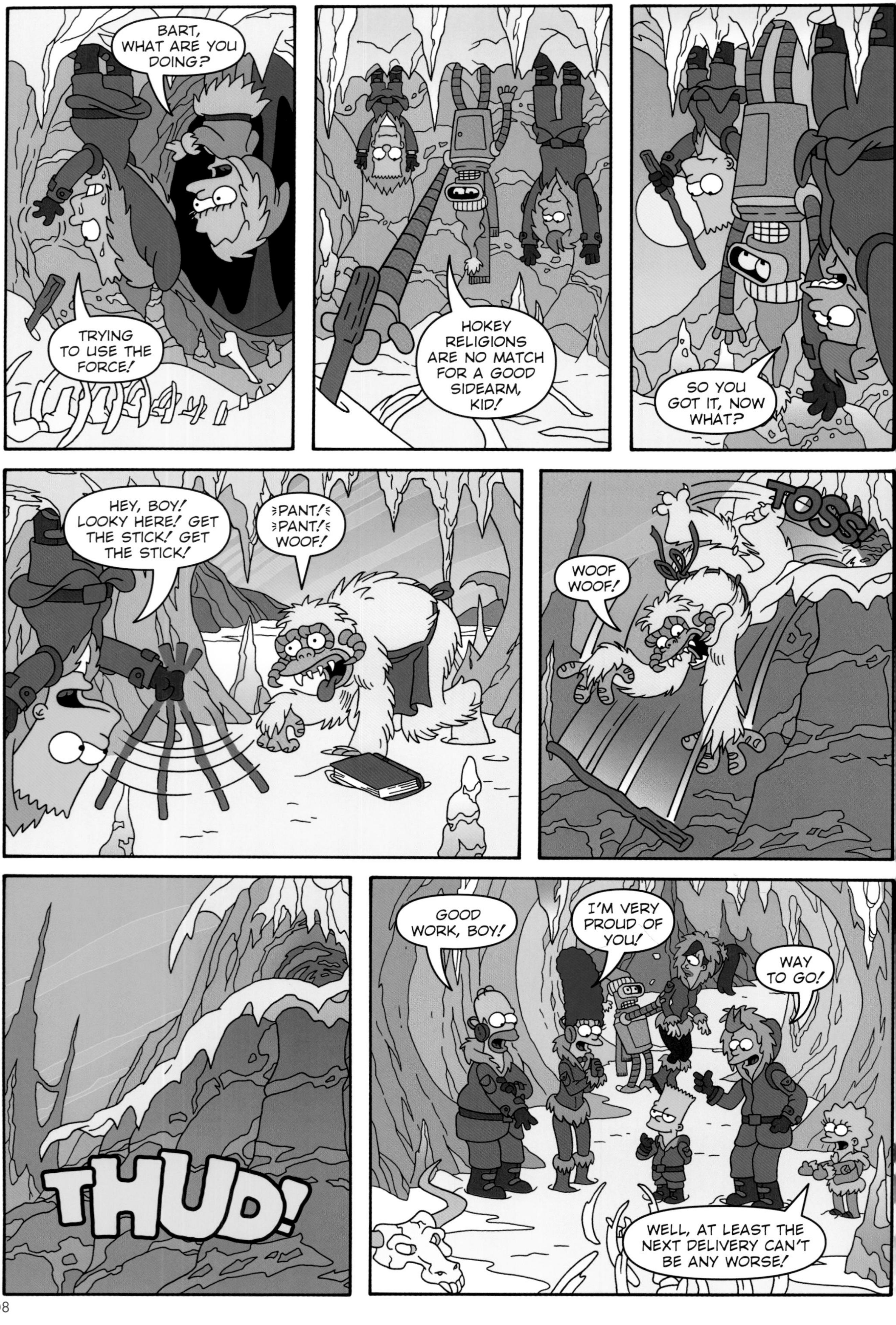
BART, WHAT ARE YOU DOING?
TRYING TO USE THE FORCE!
HOKEY RELIGIONS ARE NO MATCH FOR A GOOD SIDEARM, KID!
SO YOU GOT IT, NOW WHAT?
HEY, BOY! LOOKY HERE! GET THE STICK! GET THE STICK!
PANT! PANT! WOOF!
WOOF WOOF!
TOSS!
THUD!
GOOD WORK, BOY!
I'M VERY PROUD OF YOU!
WAY TO GO!
WELL, AT LEAST THE NEXT DELIVERY CAN'T BE ANY WORSE!

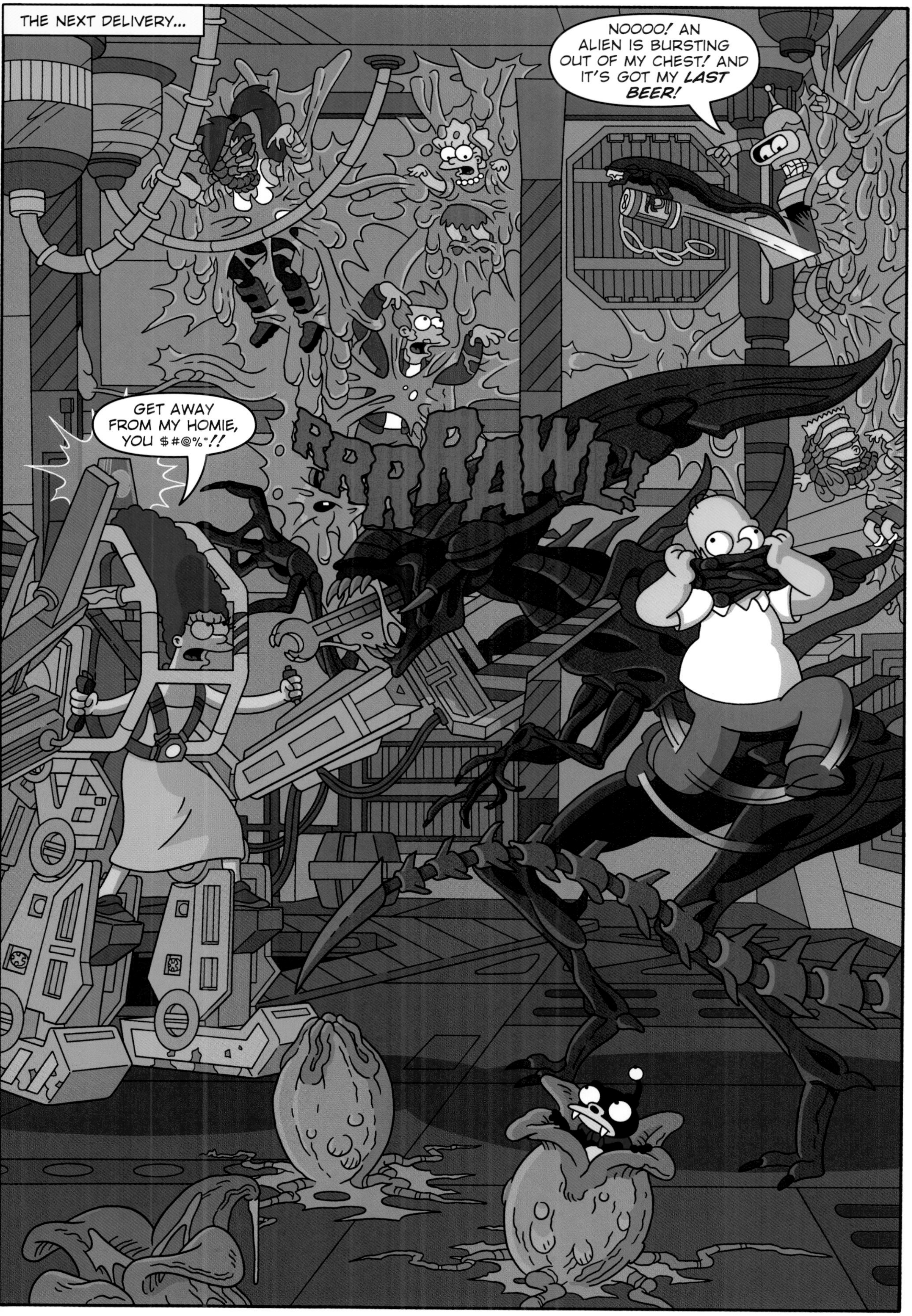
THE NEXT DELIVERY...
NOOOO! AN ALIEN IS BURSTING OUT OF MY CHEST! AND IT'S GOT MY LAST BEER!
GET AWAY FROM MY HOMIE, YOU $#@%*!!
RRRRAWL!

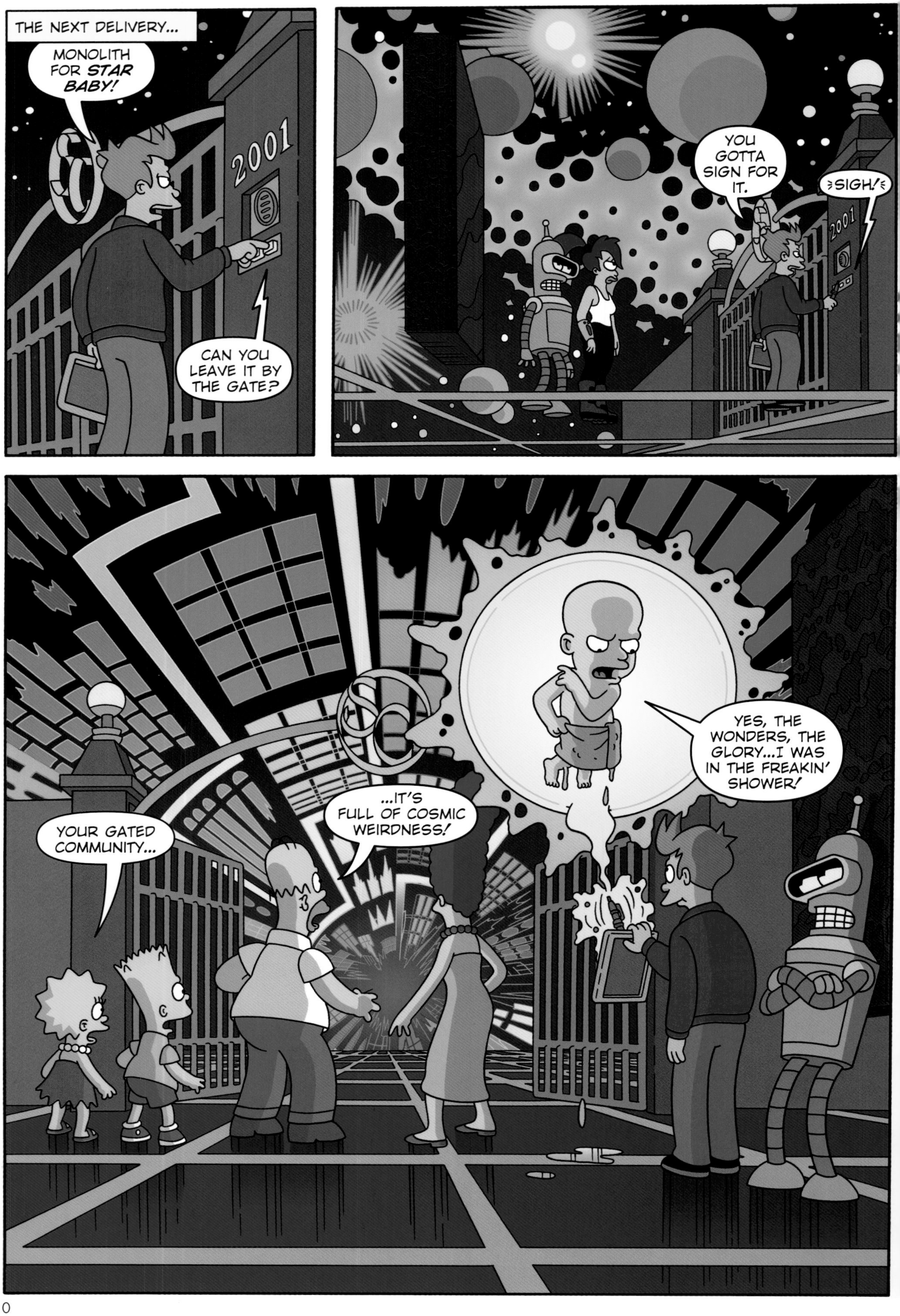
THE NEXT DELIVERY...
MONOLITH FOR **STAR BABY!**
2001
CAN YOU LEAVE IT BY THE GATE?
YOU GOTTA SIGN FOR IT.
SIGH!
2001
YOUR GATED COMMUNITY...
...IT'S FULL OF COSMIC WEIRDNESS!
YES, THE WONDERS, THE GLORY...I WAS IN THE FREAKIN' SHOWER!

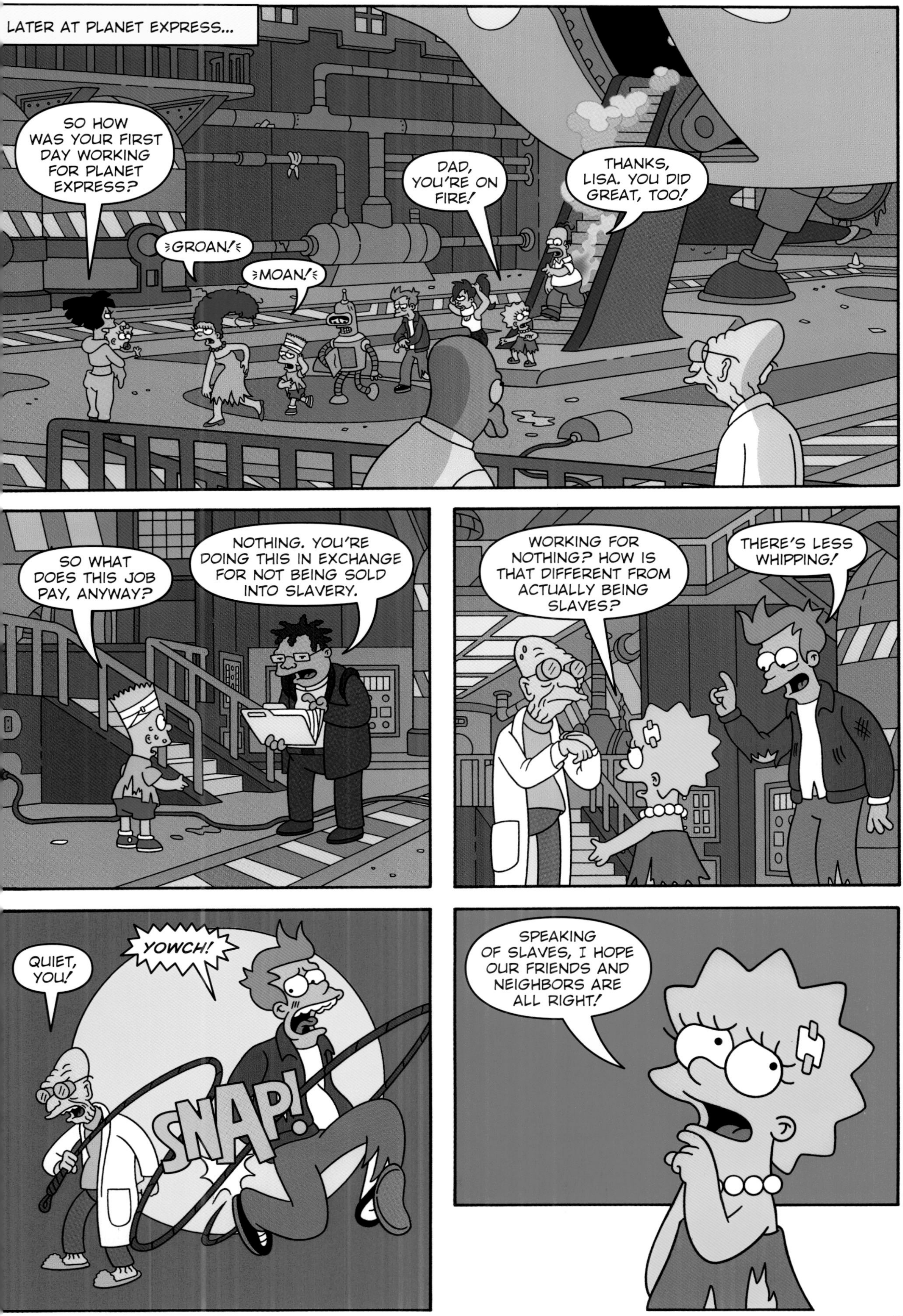

LATER AT PLANET EXPRESS...
SO HOW WAS YOUR FIRST DAY WORKING FOR PLANET EXPRESS?
GROAN!
MOAN!
DAD, YOU'RE ON FIRE!
THANKS, LISA. YOU DID GREAT, TOO!
SO WHAT DOES THIS JOB PAY, ANYWAY?
NOTHING. YOU'RE DOING THIS IN EXCHANGE FOR NOT BEING SOLD INTO SLAVERY.
WORKING FOR NOTHING? HOW IS THAT DIFFERENT FROM ACTUALLY BEING SLAVES?
THERE'S LESS WHIPPING!
QUIET, YOU!
YOWCH!
SNAP!
SPEAKING OF SLAVES, I HOPE OUR FRIENDS AND NEIGHBORS ARE ALL RIGHT!

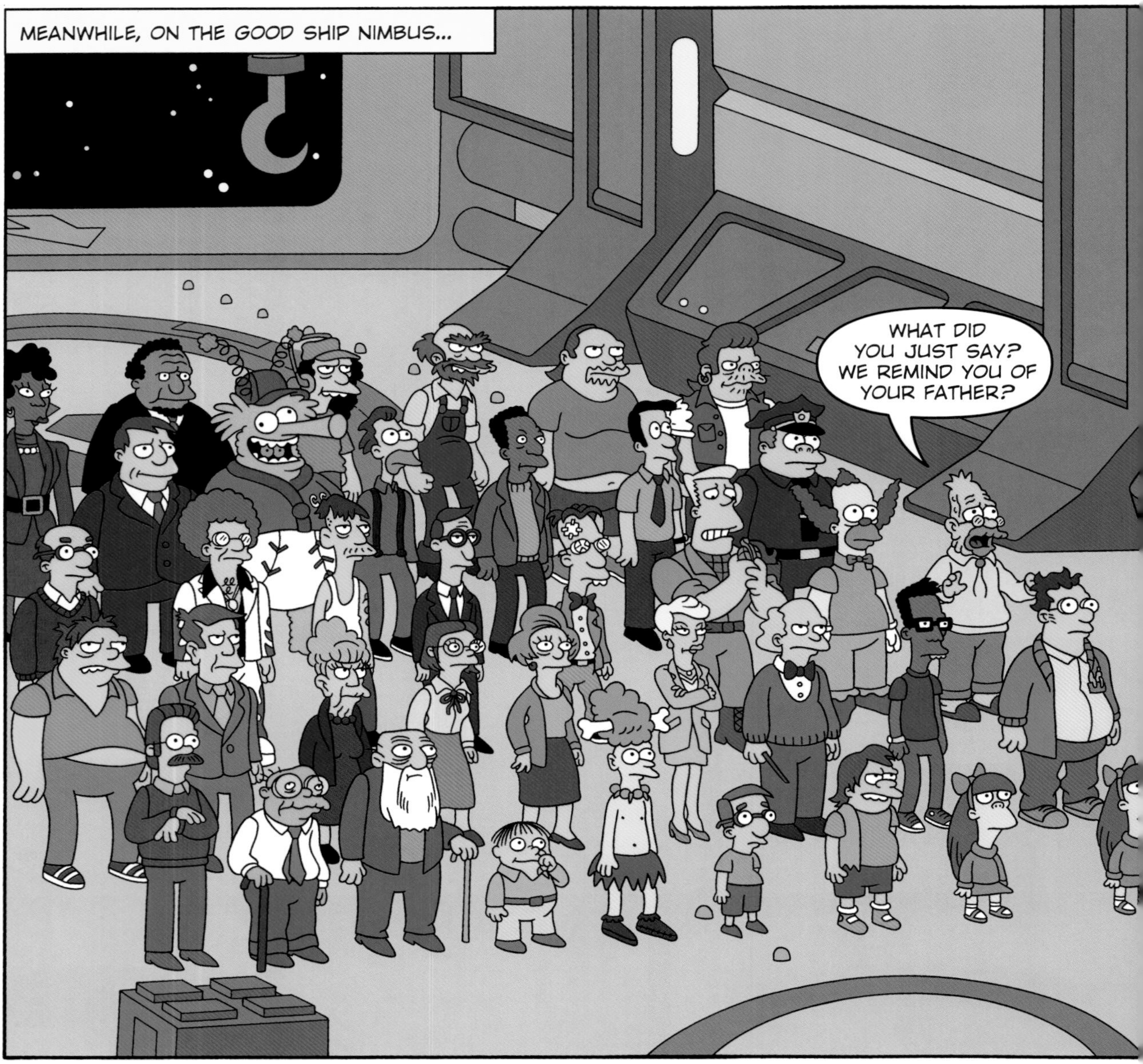
MEANWHILE, ON THE GOOD SHIP NIMBUS...
WHAT DID YOU JUST SAY? WE REMIND YOU OF YOUR FATHER?

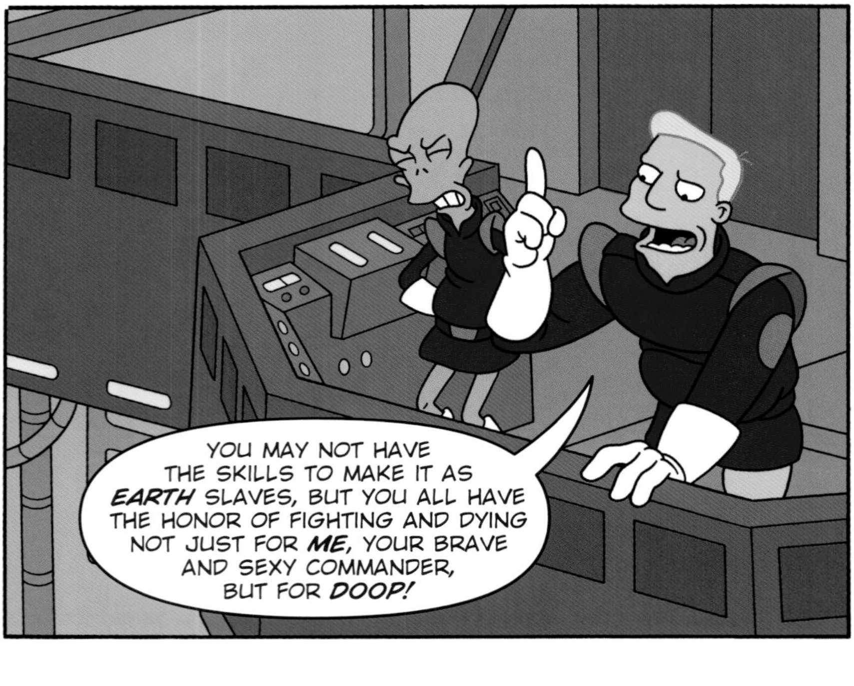
YOU MAY NOT HAVE THE SKILLS TO MAKE IT AS *EARTH* SLAVES, BUT YOU ALL HAVE THE HONOR OF FIGHTING AND DYING NOT JUST FOR *ME*, YOUR BRAVE AND SEXY COMMANDER, BUT FOR *DOOP!*

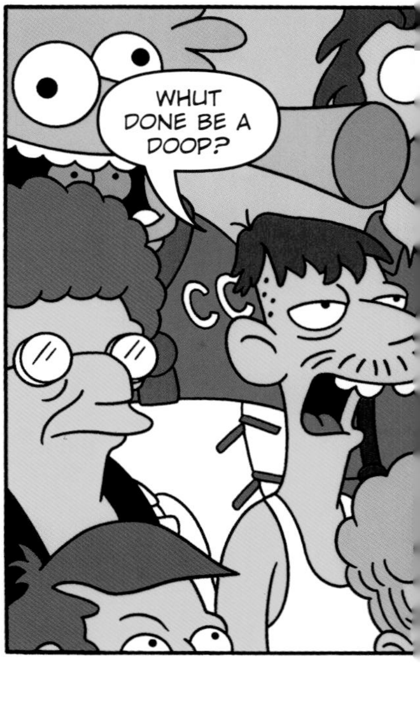
WHUT DONE BE A DOOP?

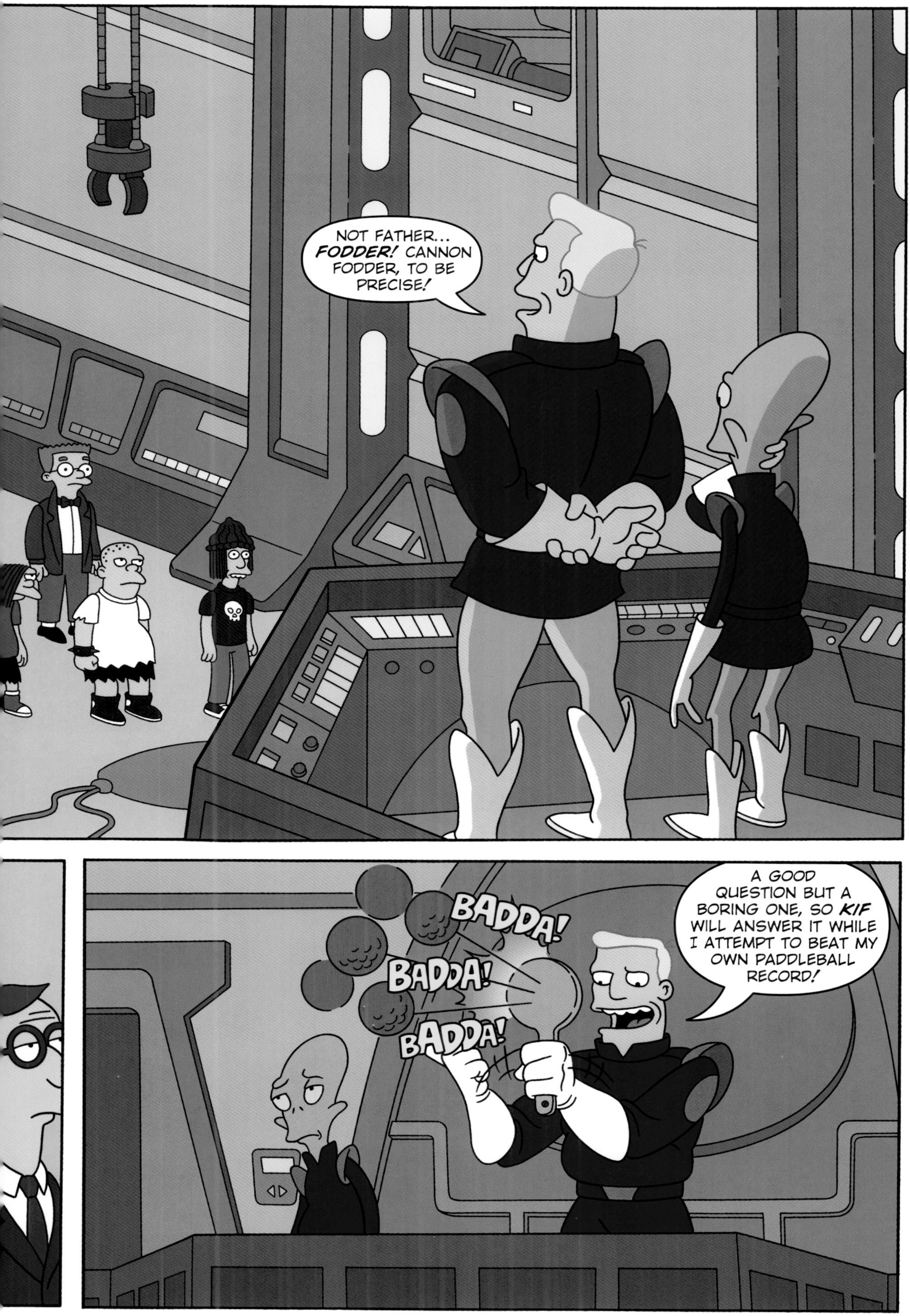
NOT FATHER... **FODDER!** CANNON FODDER, TO BE PRECISE!
BADDA!
BADDA!
BADDA!
A GOOD QUESTION BUT A BORING ONE, SO **KIF** WILL ANSWER IT WHILE I ATTEMPT TO BEAT MY OWN PADDLEBALL RECORD!

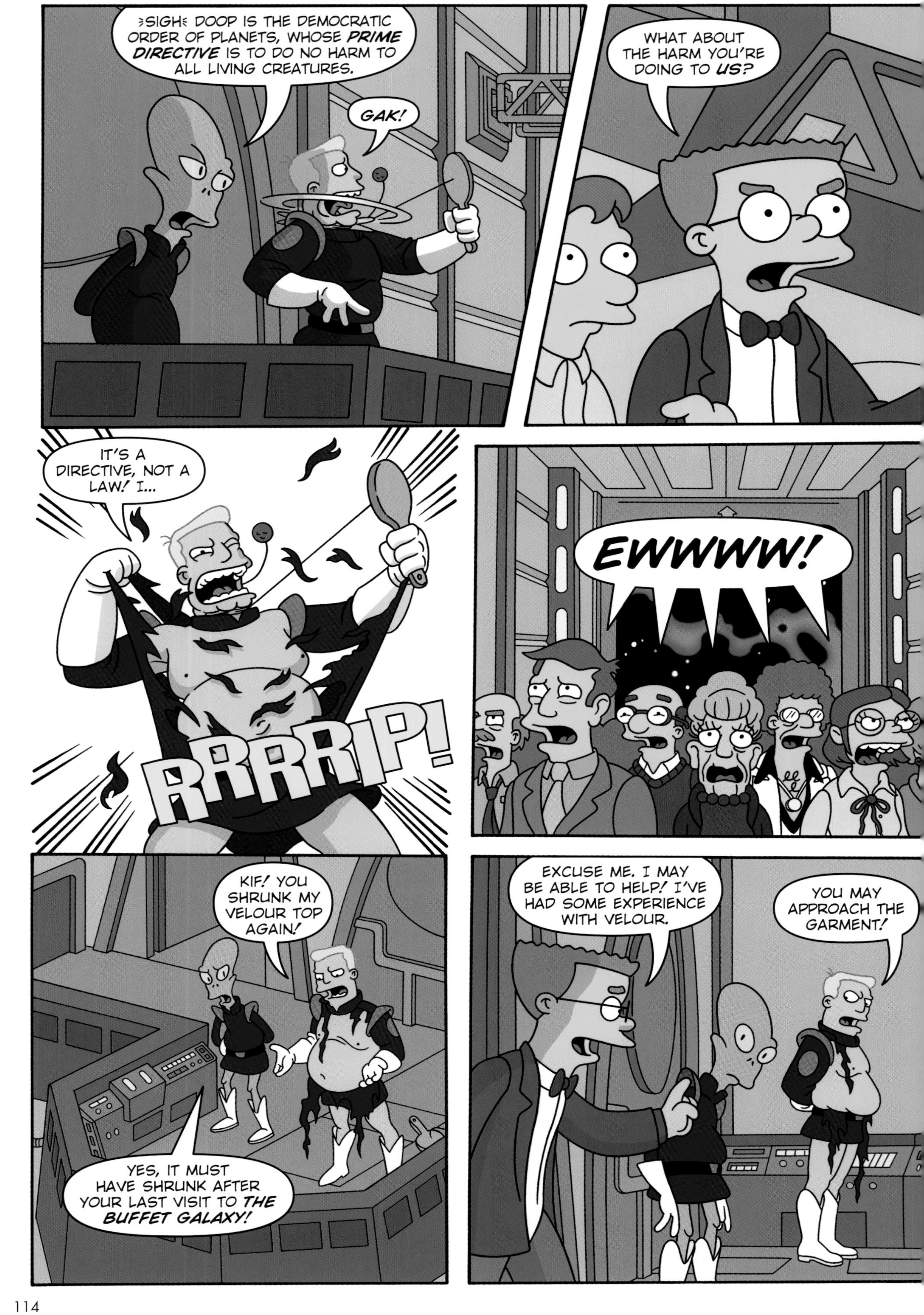

≥SIGH≤ DOOP IS THE DEMOCRATIC ORDER OF PLANETS, WHOSE *PRIME DIRECTIVE* IS TO DO NO HARM TO ALL LIVING CREATURES.
GAK!
WHAT ABOUT THE HARM YOU'RE DOING TO *US*?
IT'S A DIRECTIVE, NOT A LAW! I...
RRRRIP!
EWWWW!
KIF! YOU SHRUNK MY VELOUR TOP AGAIN!
YES, IT MUST HAVE SHRUNK AFTER YOUR LAST VISIT TO *THE BUFFET GALAXY!*
EXCUSE ME. I MAY BE ABLE TO HELP! I'VE HAD SOME EXPERIENCE WITH VELOUR.
YOU MAY APPROACH THE GARMENT!

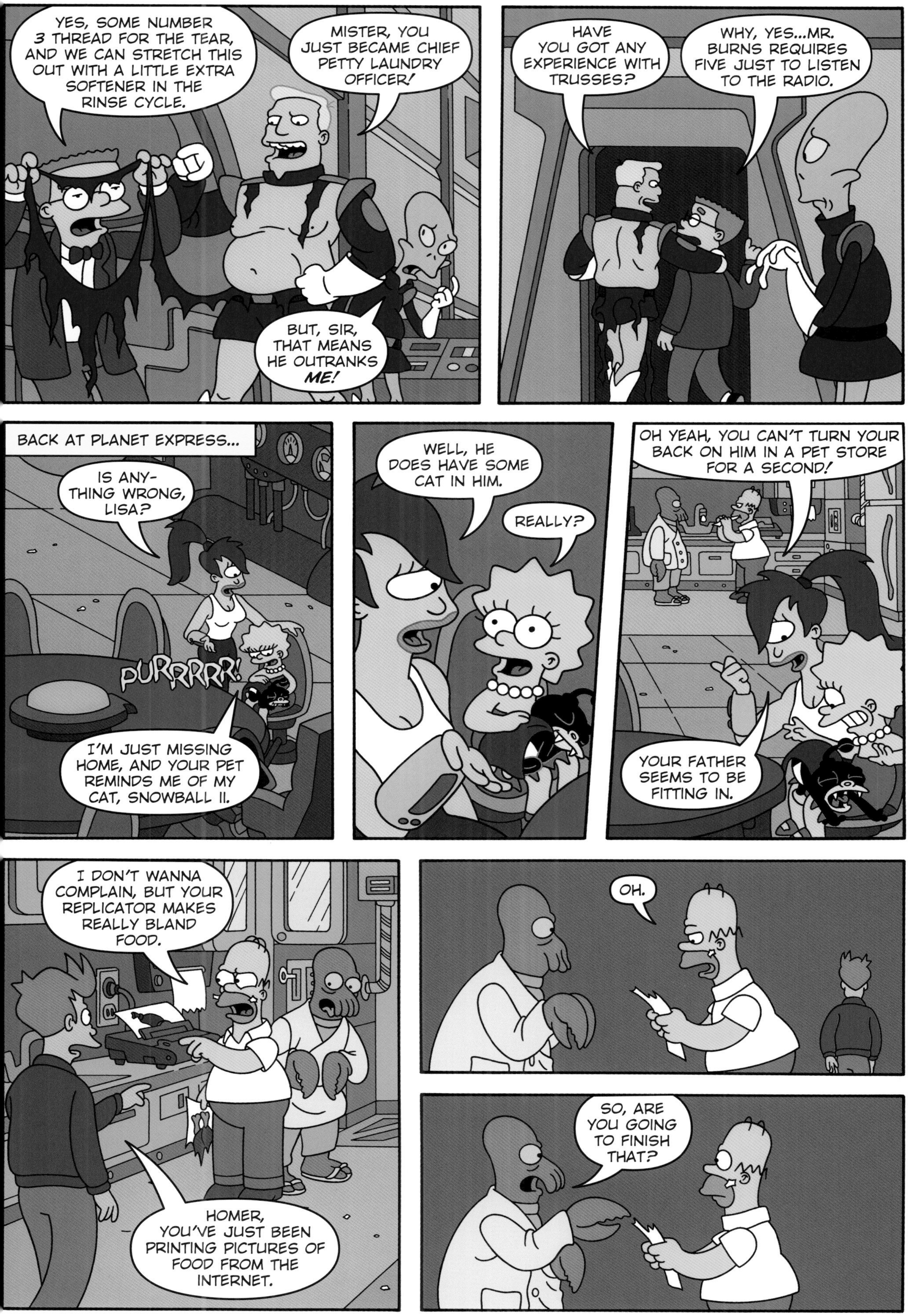

YES, SOME NUMBER 3 THREAD FOR THE TEAR, AND WE CAN STRETCH THIS OUT WITH A LITTLE EXTRA SOFTENER IN THE RINSE CYCLE.
MISTER, YOU JUST BECAME CHIEF PETTY LAUNDRY OFFICER!
BUT, SIR, THAT MEANS HE OUTRANKS *ME!*
HAVE YOU GOT ANY EXPERIENCE WITH TRUSSES?
WHY, YES...MR. BURNS REQUIRES FIVE JUST TO LISTEN TO THE RADIO.
BACK AT PLANET EXPRESS...
IS ANY-THING WRONG, LISA?
PURRRRR!
I'M JUST MISSING HOME, AND YOUR PET REMINDS ME OF MY CAT, SNOWBALL II.
WELL, HE DOES HAVE SOME CAT IN HIM.
REALLY?
OH YEAH, YOU CAN'T TURN YOUR BACK ON HIM IN A PET STORE FOR A SECOND!
YOUR FATHER SEEMS TO BE FITTING IN.
I DON'T WANNA COMPLAIN, BUT YOUR REPLICATOR MAKES REALLY BLAND FOOD.
HOMER, YOU'VE JUST BEEN PRINTING PICTURES OF FOOD FROM THE INTERNET.
OH.
SO, ARE YOU GOING TO FINISH THAT?

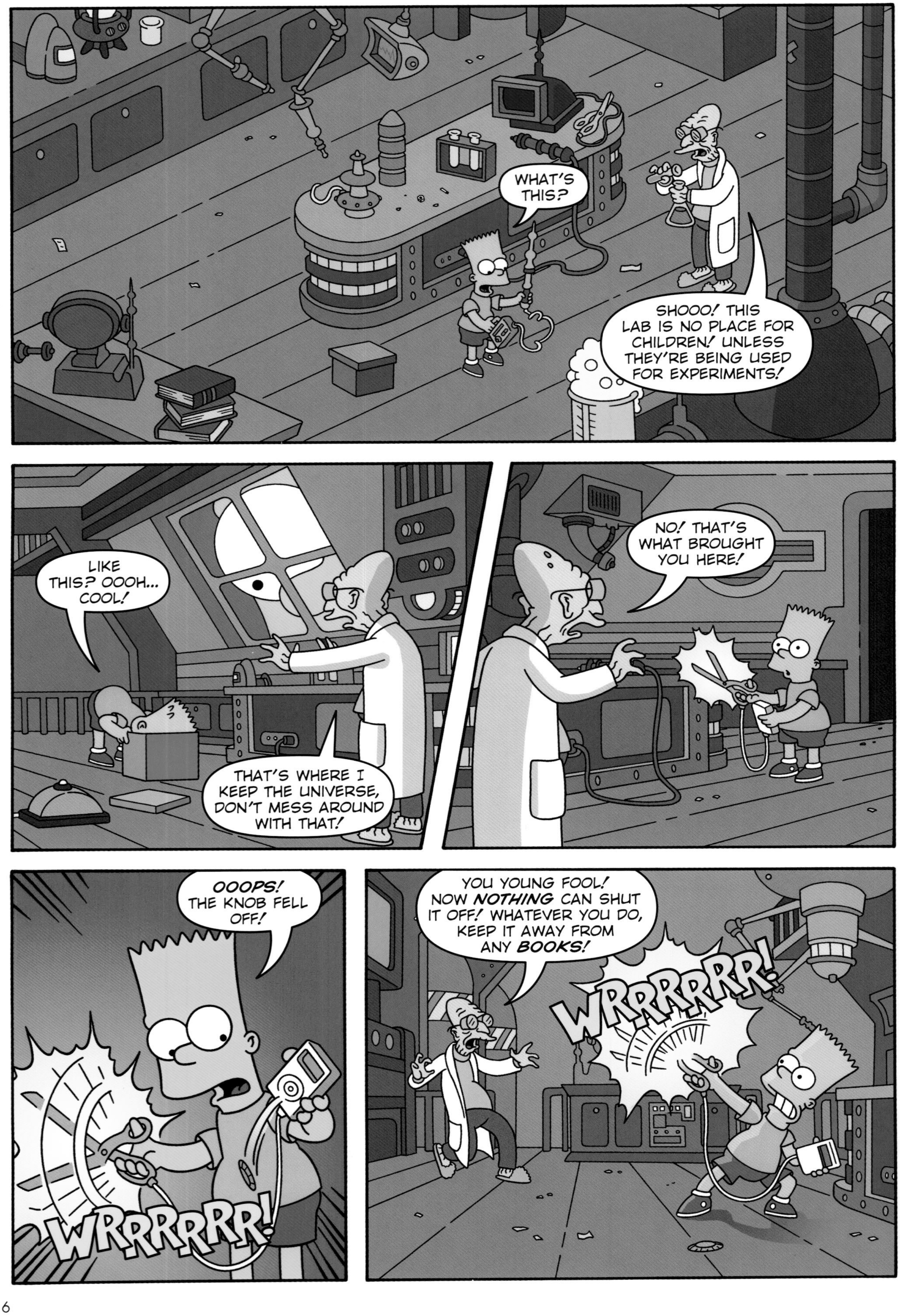
WHAT'S THIS?
SHOOO! THIS LAB IS NO PLACE FOR CHILDREN! UNLESS THEY'RE BEING USED FOR EXPERIMENTS!
LIKE THIS? OOOH... COOL!
THAT'S WHERE I KEEP THE UNIVERSE, DON'T MESS AROUND WITH THAT!
NO! THAT'S WHAT BROUGHT YOU HERE!
OOOPS! THE KNOB FELL OFF!
WRRRRRR!
YOU YOUNG FOOL! NOW NOTHING CAN SHUT IT OFF! WHATEVER YOU DO, KEEP IT AWAY FROM ANY BOOKS!
WRRRRRR!

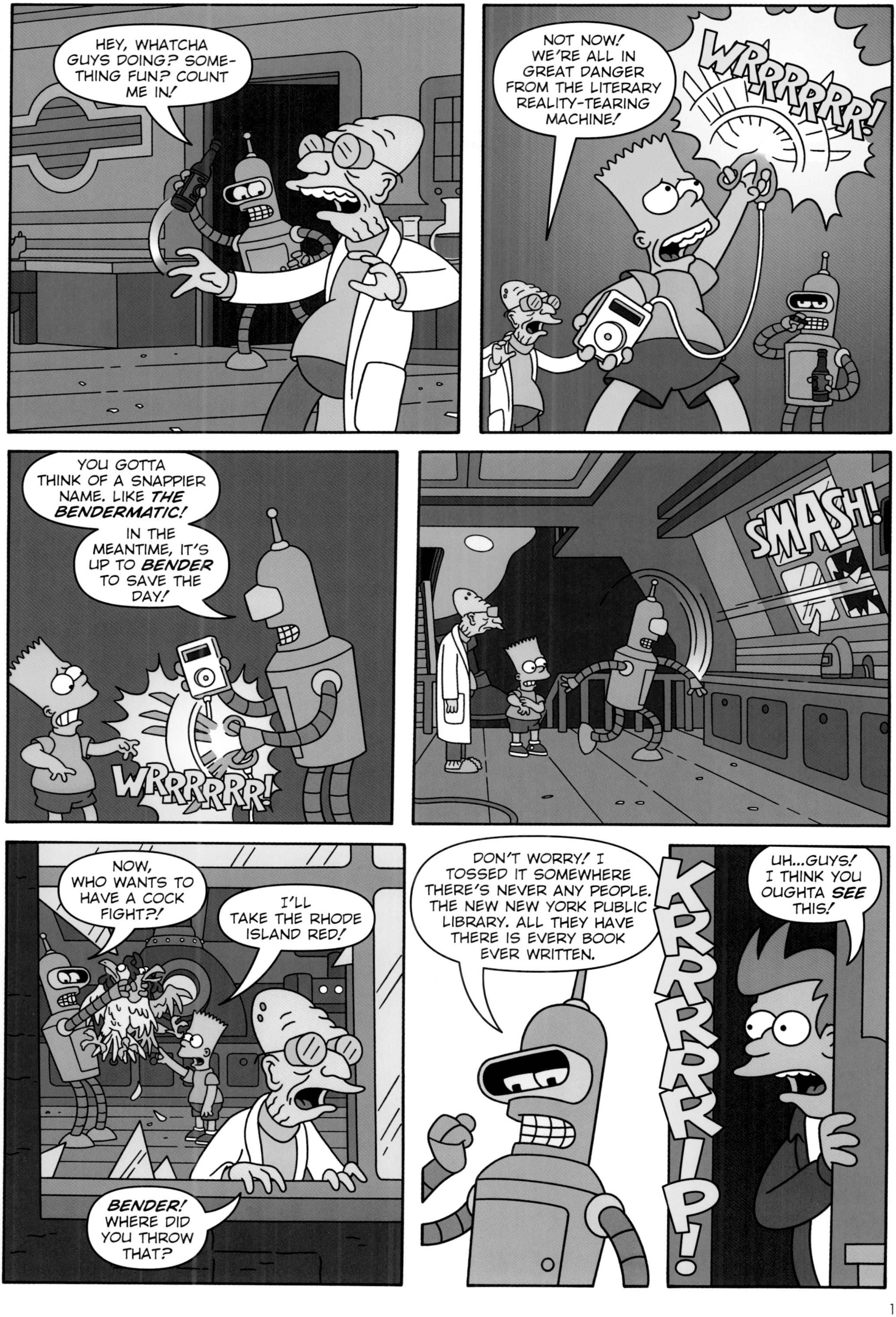
HEY, WHATCHA GUYS DOING? SOME-THING FUN? COUNT ME IN!
NOT NOW! WE'RE ALL IN GREAT DANGER FROM THE LITERARY REALITY-TEARING MACHINE!
WRRRRRRR!
YOU GOTTA THINK OF A SNAPPIER NAME. LIKE THE BENDERMATIC!
IN THE MEANTIME, IT'S UP TO BENDER TO SAVE THE DAY!
WRRRRRRR!
SMASH!
NOW, WHO WANTS TO HAVE A COCK FIGHT?!
I'LL TAKE THE RHODE ISLAND RED!
BENDER! WHERE DID YOU THROW THAT?
DON'T WORRY! I TOSSED IT SOMEWHERE THERE'S NEVER ANY PEOPLE. THE NEW NEW YORK PUBLIC LIBRARY. ALL THEY HAVE THERE IS EVERY BOOK EVER WRITTEN.
KRRRRRIP!
UH...GUYS! I THINK YOU OUGHTA SEE THIS!

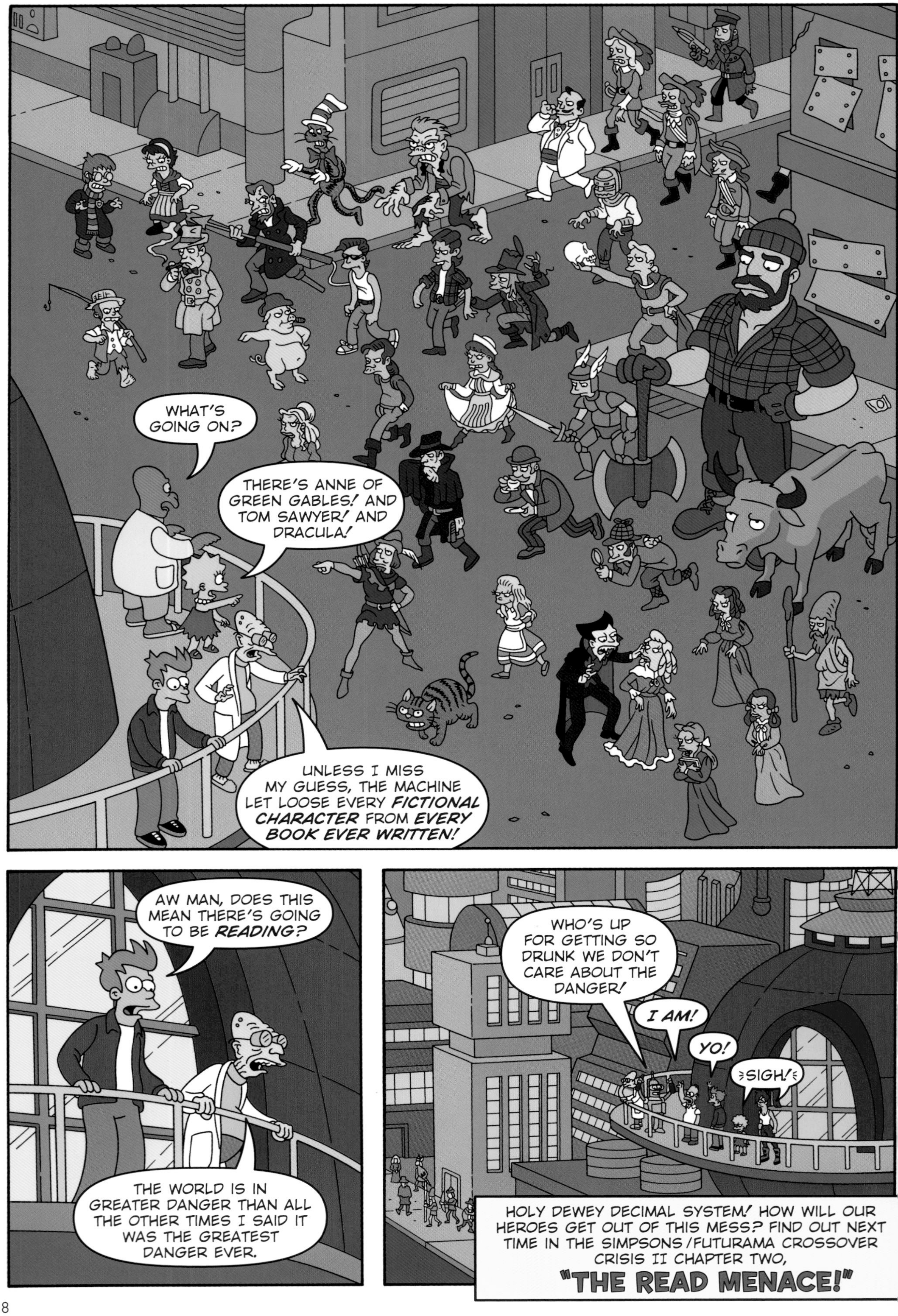
WHAT'S GOING ON?
THERE'S ANNE OF GREEN GABLES! AND TOM SAWYER! AND DRACULA!
UNLESS I MISS MY GUESS, THE MACHINE LET LOOSE EVERY *FICTIONAL CHARACTER* FROM *EVERY BOOK EVER WRITTEN!*
AW MAN, DOES THIS MEAN THERE'S GOING TO BE *READING*?
THE WORLD IS IN GREATER DANGER THAN ALL THE OTHER TIMES I SAID IT WAS THE GREATEST DANGER EVER.
WHO'S UP FOR GETTING SO DRUNK WE DON'T CARE ABOUT THE DANGER!
I AM!
YO!
SIGH!
HOLY DEWEY DECIMAL SYSTEM! HOW WILL OUR HEROES GET OUT OF THIS MESS? FIND OUT NEXT TIME IN THE SIMPSONS/FUTURAMA CROSSOVER CRISIS II CHAPTER TWO,
"THE READ MENACE!"

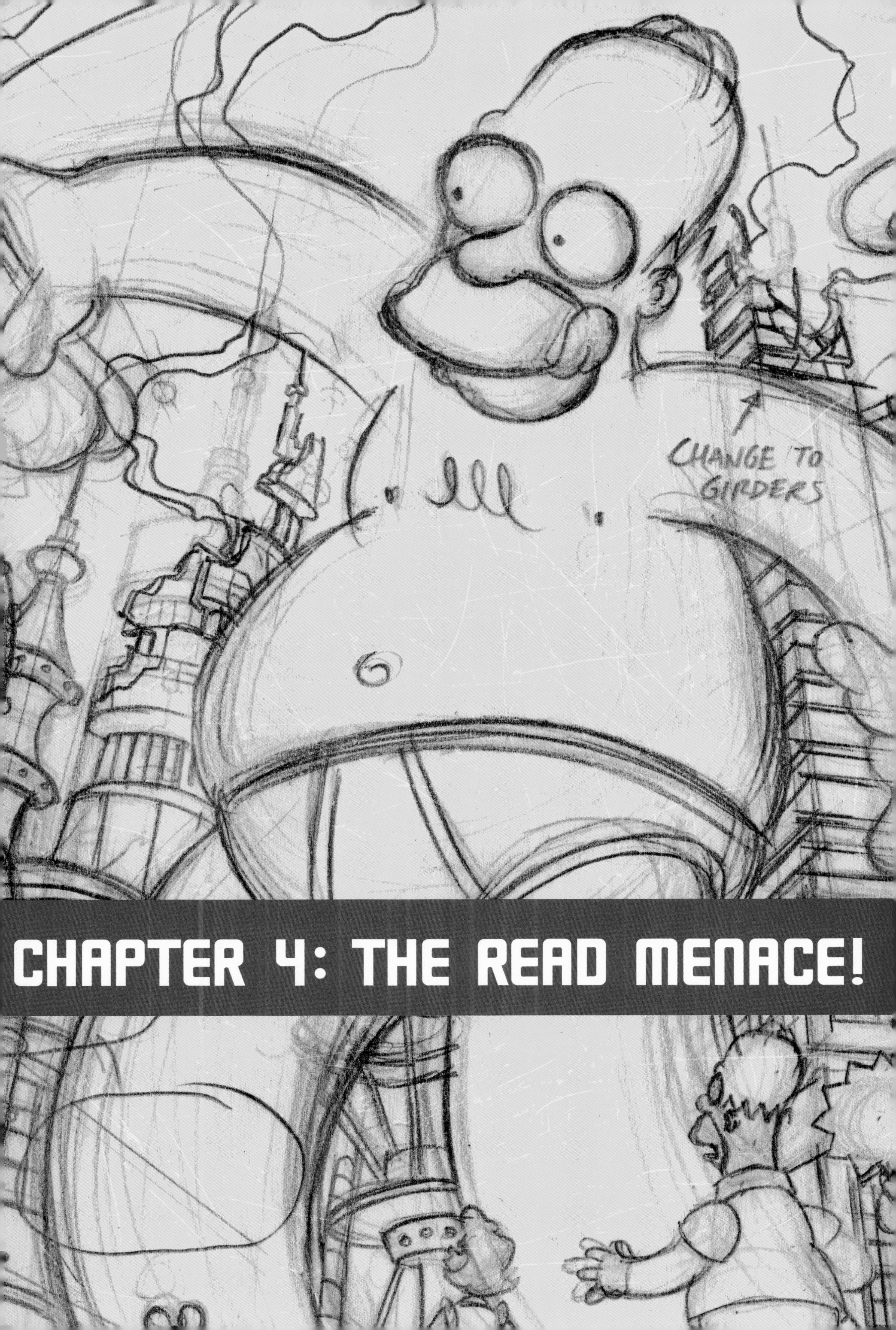
CHANGE TO GIRDERS

CHAPTER 4: THE READ MENACE!

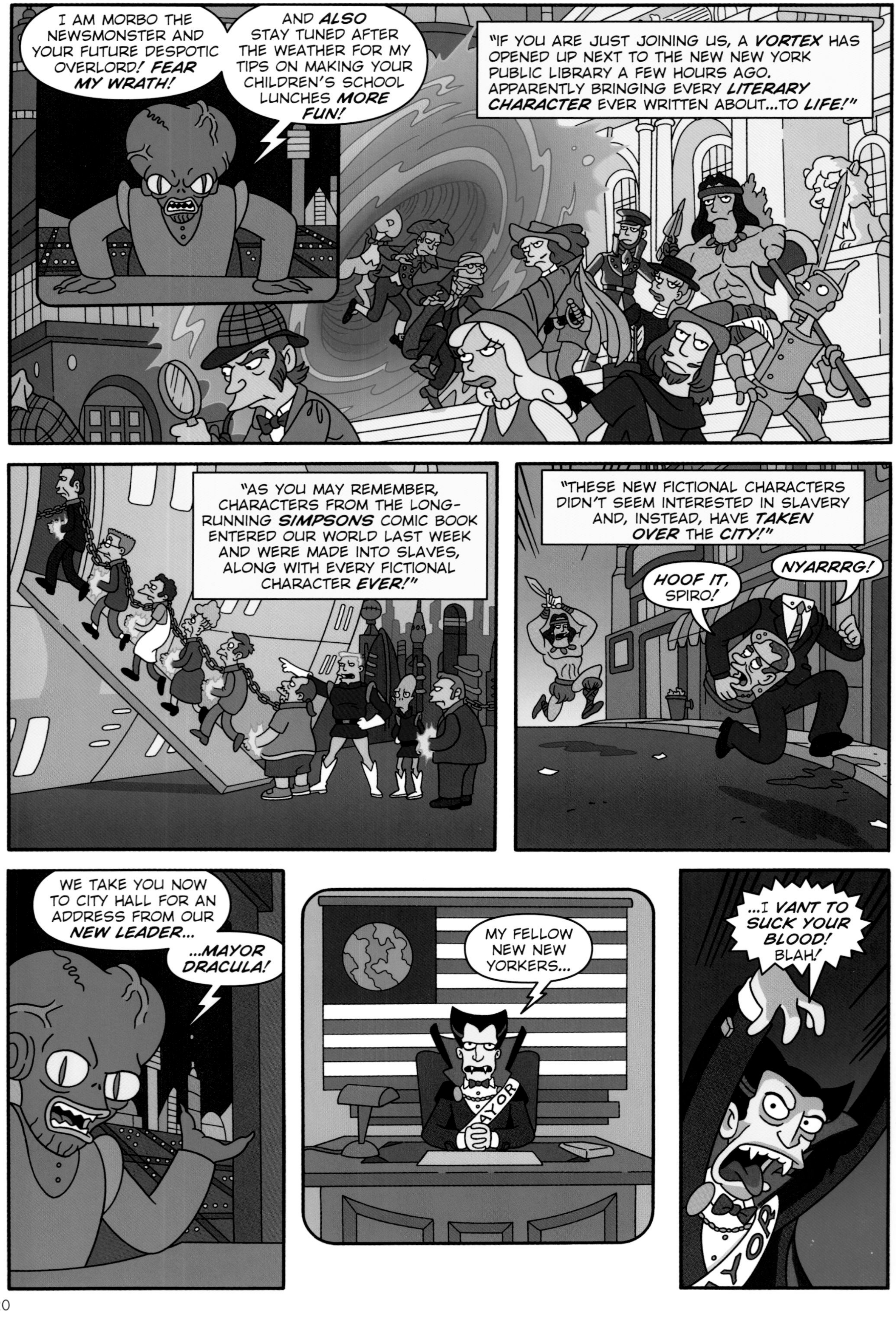
I AM MORBO THE NEWSMONSTER AND YOUR FUTURE DESPOTIC OVERLORD! FEAR MY WRATH!
AND ALSO STAY TUNED AFTER THE WEATHER FOR MY TIPS ON MAKING YOUR CHILDREN'S SCHOOL LUNCHES MORE FUN!
"IF YOU ARE JUST JOINING US, A VORTEX HAS OPENED UP NEXT TO THE NEW NEW YORK PUBLIC LIBRARY A FEW HOURS AGO. APPARENTLY BRINGING EVERY LITERARY CHARACTER EVER WRITTEN ABOUT...TO LIFE!"
"AS YOU MAY REMEMBER, CHARACTERS FROM THE LONG-RUNNING SIMPSONS COMIC BOOK ENTERED OUR WORLD LAST WEEK AND WERE MADE INTO SLAVES, ALONG WITH EVERY FICTIONAL CHARACTER EVER!"
"THESE NEW FICTIONAL CHARACTERS DIDN'T SEEM INTERESTED IN SLAVERY AND, INSTEAD, HAVE TAKEN OVER THE CITY!"
HOOF IT, SPIRO!
NYARRRG!
WE TAKE YOU NOW TO CITY HALL FOR AN ADDRESS FROM OUR NEW LEADER...
...MAYOR DRACULA!
MY FELLOW NEW NEW YORKERS...
MAYOR
...I VANT TO SUCK YOUR BLOOD! BLAH!

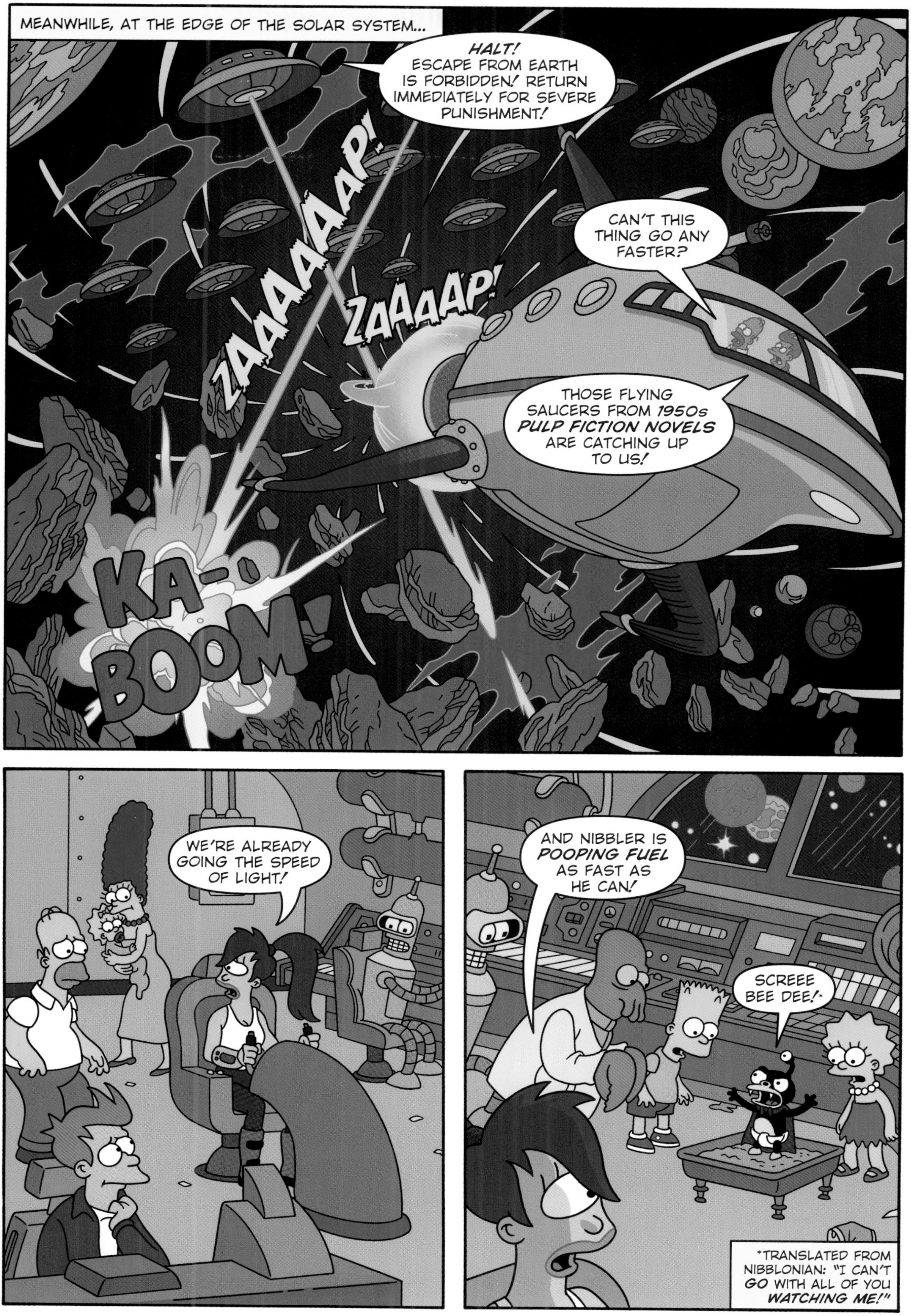
MEANWHILE, AT THE EDGE OF THE SOLAR SYSTEM...
HALT! ESCAPE FROM EARTH IS FORBIDDEN! RETURN IMMEDIATELY FOR SEVERE PUNISHMENT!
ZAAAAAAP!
ZAAAAP!
CAN'T THIS THING GO ANY FASTER?
THOSE FLYING SAUCERS FROM 1950s PULP FICTION NOVELS ARE CATCHING UP TO US!
KA-BOOM!
WE'RE ALREADY GOING THE SPEED OF LIGHT!
AND NIBBLER IS POOPING FUEL AS FAST AS HE CAN!
SCREEE BEE DEE!*
*TRANSLATED FROM NIBBLONIAN: "I CAN'T GO WITH ALL OF YOU WATCHING ME!"

ZAAAAP!
KA BLAM!
HOW ABOUT IF WE PUT RACING STRIPES ON THE SIDE?
I *LIKE* IT!
YOU ***WOULD***, YOU HALF WIT! IT MAKES NO ***SENSE!***
STILL, IT'S THE BEST PLAN WE'VE GOT.
MAKE IT SO!
LIGHTNING BOLTS? I THOUGHT WE WERE DOIN' ***FLAMES!***
WHY NOT BOTH?
YEAH, THEN THE SHIP'LL GO ***TWICE*** AS FAST!
MAN, ALL THIS WORK IS MAKING ME THIRSTY! HOW ABOUT A ***BEER?***
SURE, LET ME JUST GET THE ***HELMET*** OFF!
SOUNDS GOOD!
CATCH!
NO!

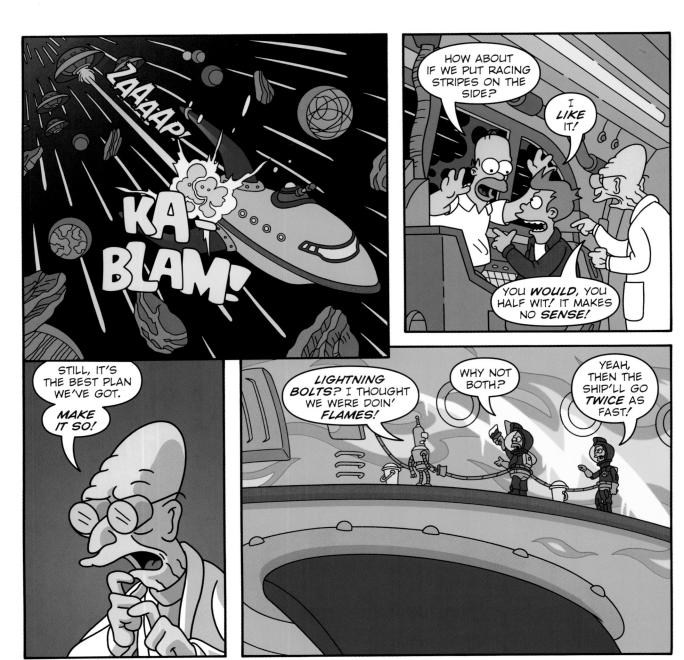

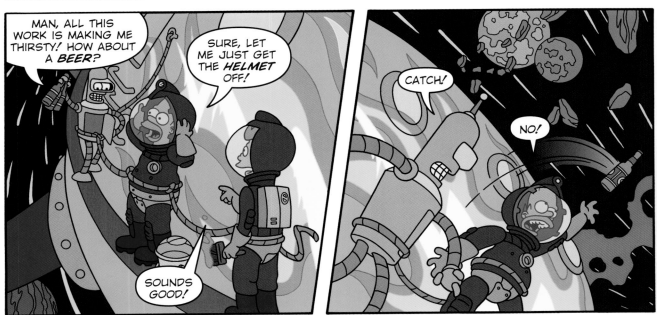

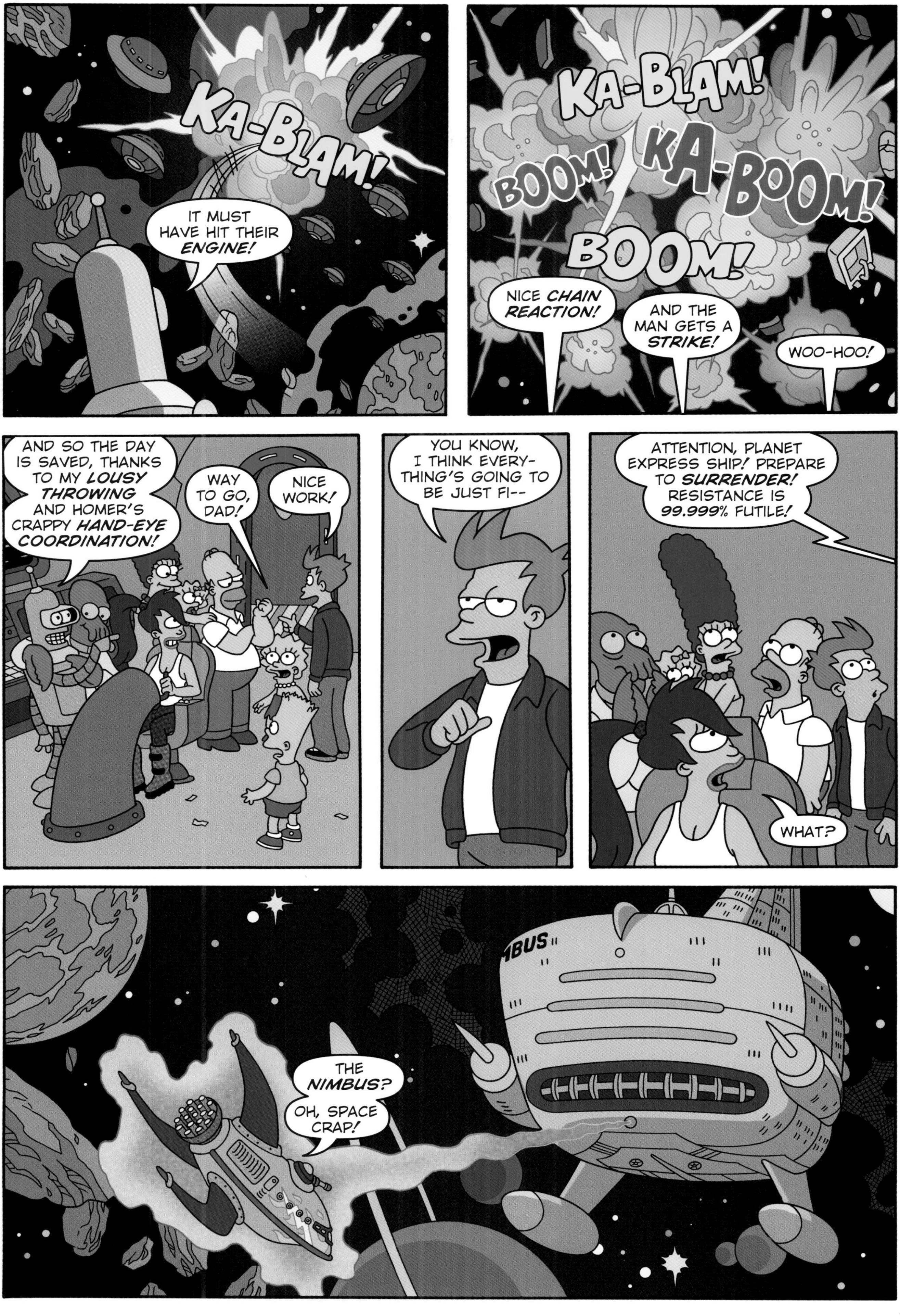
KA-BLAM!
IT MUST HAVE HIT THEIR *ENGINE!*
KA-BLAM!
BOOM!
KA-BOOM!
BOOM!
NICE *CHAIN REACTION!*
AND THE MAN GETS A *STRIKE!*
WOO-HOO!
AND SO THE DAY IS SAVED, THANKS TO MY *LOUSY THROWING* AND HOMER'S CRAPPY *HAND-EYE COORDINATION!*
WAY TO GO, DAD!
NICE WORK!
YOU KNOW, I THINK EVERY-THING'S GOING TO BE JUST FI--
ATTENTION, PLANET EXPRESS SHIP! PREPARE TO *SURRENDER!* RESISTANCE IS *99.999%* FUTILE!
WHAT?
MBUS
THE *NIMBUS?*
OH, SPACE CRAP!

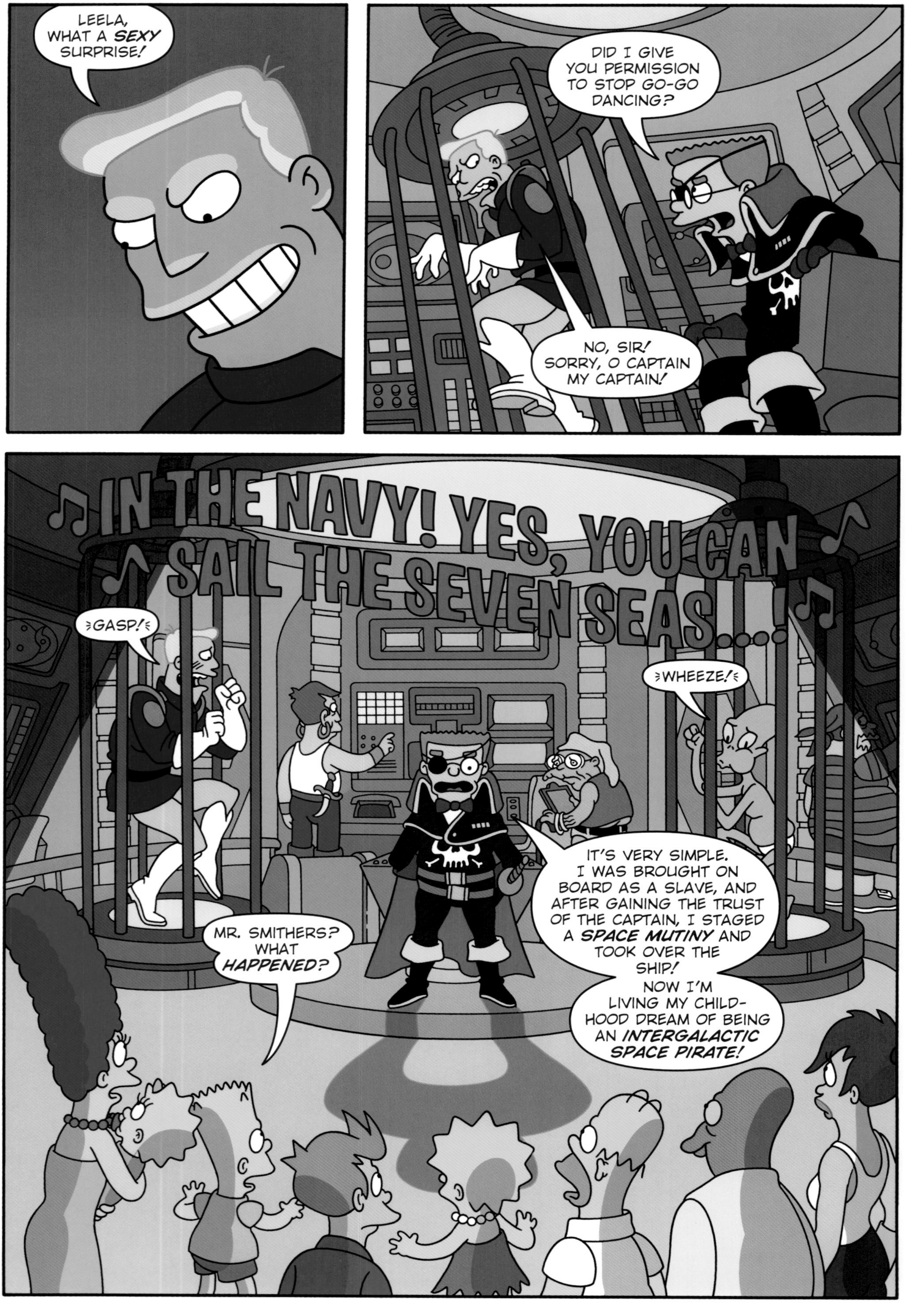
LEELA, WHAT A SEXY SURPRISE!
DID I GIVE YOU PERMISSION TO STOP GO-GO DANCING?
NO, SIR! SORRY, O CAPTAIN MY CAPTAIN!
IN THE NAVY! YES, YOU CAN SAIL THE SEVEN SEAS...!
GASP!
WHEEZE!
MR. SMITHERS? WHAT HAPPENED?
IT'S VERY SIMPLE. I WAS BROUGHT ON BOARD AS A SLAVE, AND AFTER GAINING THE TRUST OF THE CAPTAIN, I STAGED A SPACE MUTINY AND TOOK OVER THE SHIP!
NOW I'M LIVING MY CHILD-HOOD DREAM OF BEING AN INTERGALACTIC SPACE PIRATE!

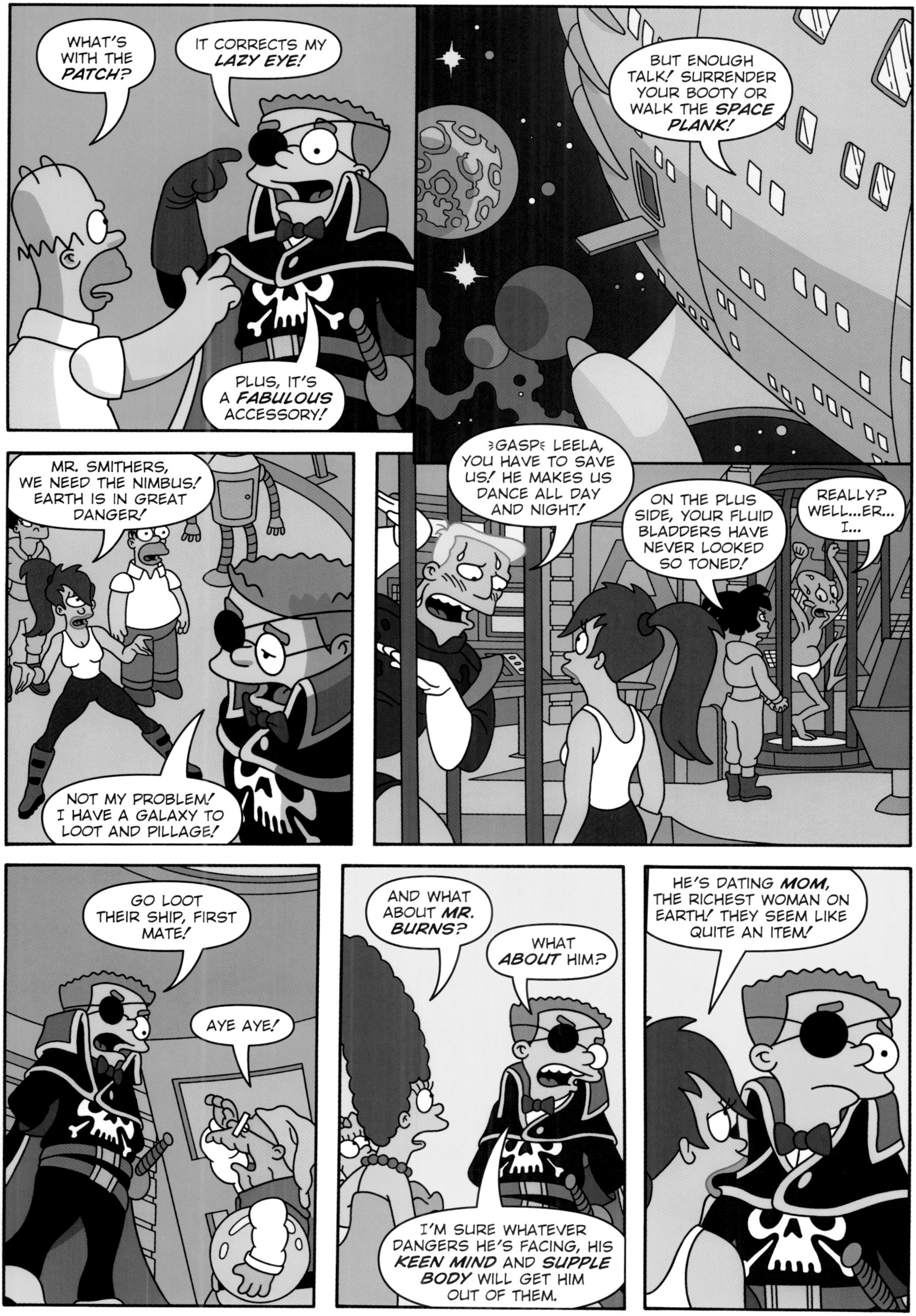
WHAT'S WITH THE PATCH?
IT CORRECTS MY LAZY EYE!
PLUS, IT'S A FABULOUS ACCESSORY!
BUT ENOUGH TALK! SURRENDER YOUR BOOTY OR WALK THE SPACE PLANK!
MR. SMITHERS, WE NEED THE NIMBUS! EARTH IS IN GREAT DANGER!
NOT MY PROBLEM! I HAVE A GALAXY TO LOOT AND PILLAGE!
GASP LEELA, YOU HAVE TO SAVE US! HE MAKES US DANCE ALL DAY AND NIGHT!
ON THE PLUS SIDE, YOUR FLUID BLADDERS HAVE NEVER LOOKED SO TONED!
REALLY? WELL...ER... I...
GO LOOT THEIR SHIP, FIRST MATE!
AYE AYE!
AND WHAT ABOUT MR. BURNS?
WHAT ABOUT HIM?
I'M SURE WHATEVER DANGERS HE'S FACING, HIS KEEN MIND AND SUPPLE BODY WILL GET HIM OUT OF THEM.
HE'S DATING MOM, THE RICHEST WOMAN ON EARTH! THEY SEEM LIKE QUITE AN ITEM!

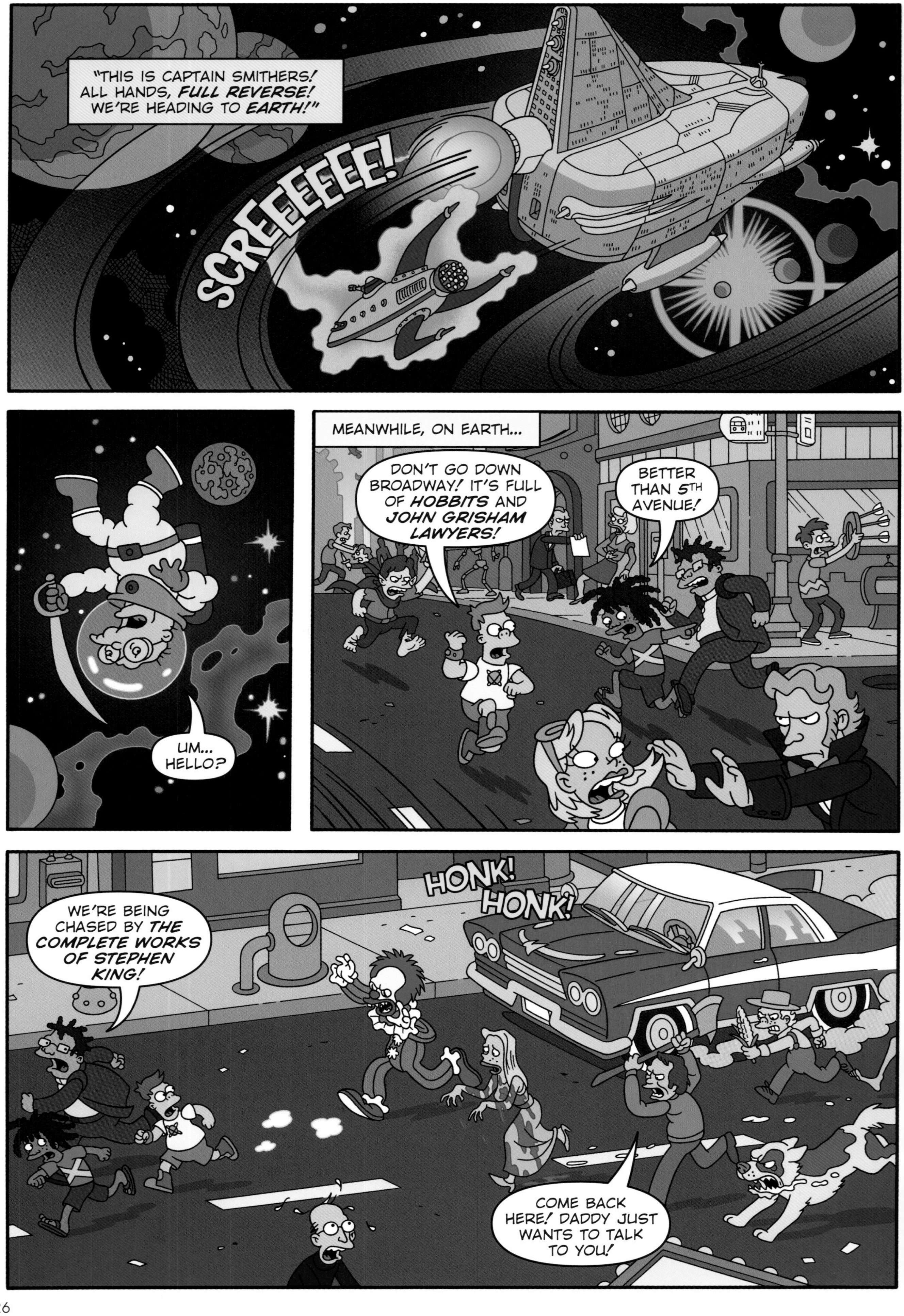
"THIS IS CAPTAIN SMITHERS! ALL HANDS, FULL REVERSE! WE'RE HEADING TO EARTH!"
SCREEEEEEE!
UM... HELLO?
MEANWHILE, ON EARTH...
DON'T GO DOWN BROADWAY! IT'S FULL OF HOBBITS AND JOHN GRISHAM LAWYERS!
BETTER THAN 5TH AVENUE!
WE'RE BEING CHASED BY THE COMPLETE WORKS OF STEPHEN KING!
HONK! HONK!
COME BACK HERE! DADDY JUST WANTS TO TALK TO YOU!

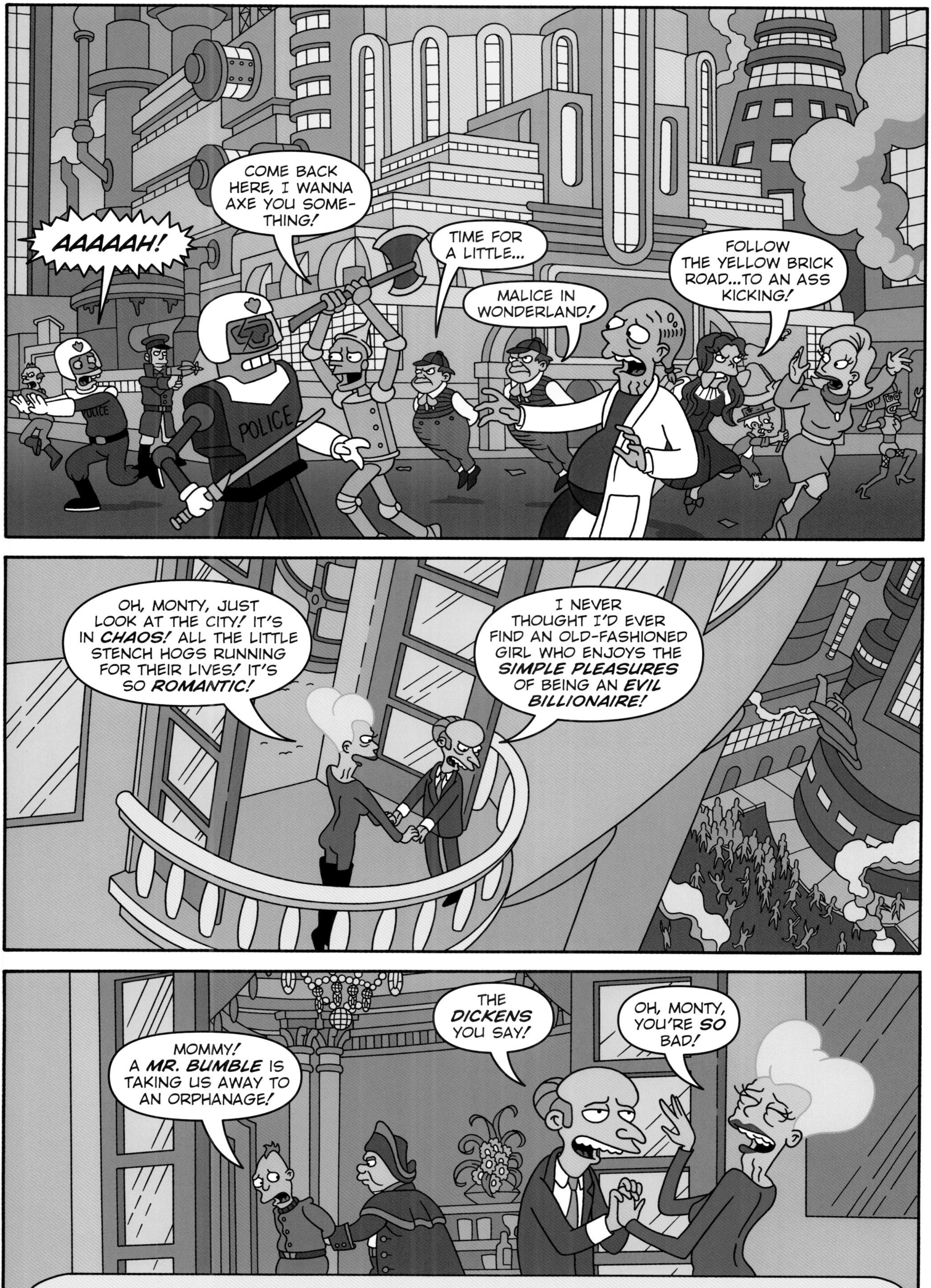
AAAAAH!
COME BACK HERE, I WANNA AXE YOU SOME-THING!
TIME FOR A LITTLE...
MALICE IN WONDERLAND!
FOLLOW THE YELLOW BRICK ROAD...TO AN ASS KICKING!
POLICE
POLICE
OH, MONTY, JUST LOOK AT THE CITY! IT'S IN CHAOS! ALL THE LITTLE STENCH HOGS RUNNING FOR THEIR LIVES! IT'S SO ROMANTIC!
I NEVER THOUGHT I'D EVER FIND AN OLD-FASHIONED GIRL WHO ENJOYS THE SIMPLE PLEASURES OF BEING AN EVIL BILLIONAIRE!
MOMMY! A MR. BUMBLE IS TAKING US AWAY TO AN ORPHANAGE!
THE DICKENS YOU SAY!
OH, MONTY, YOU'RE SO BAD!

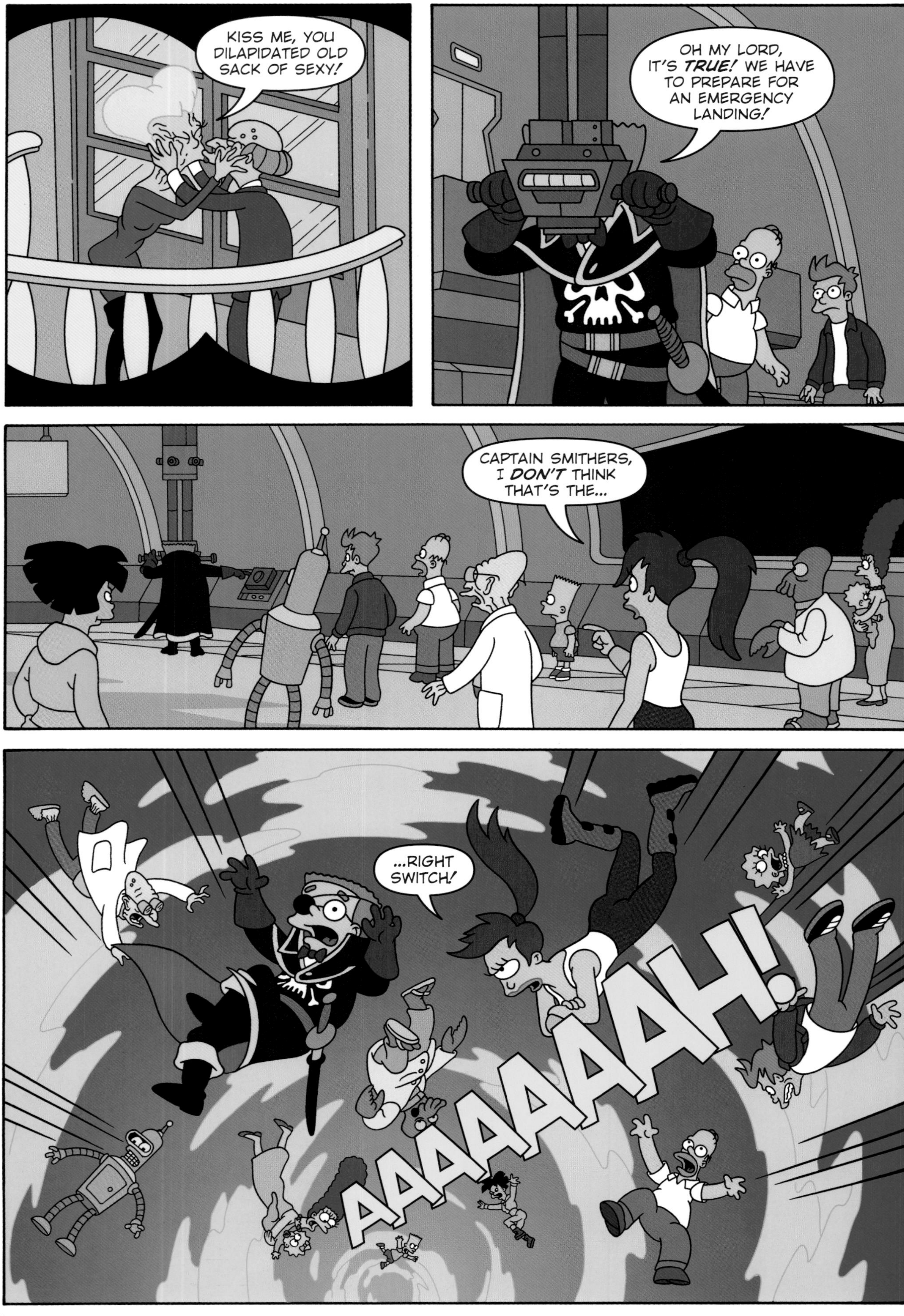
KISS ME, YOU DILAPIDATED OLD SACK OF SEXY!
OH MY LORD, IT'S **TRUE!** WE HAVE TO PREPARE FOR AN EMERGENCY LANDING!
CAPTAIN SMITHERS, I **DON'T** THINK THAT'S THE...
...RIGHT SWITCH!
AAAAAAAH!

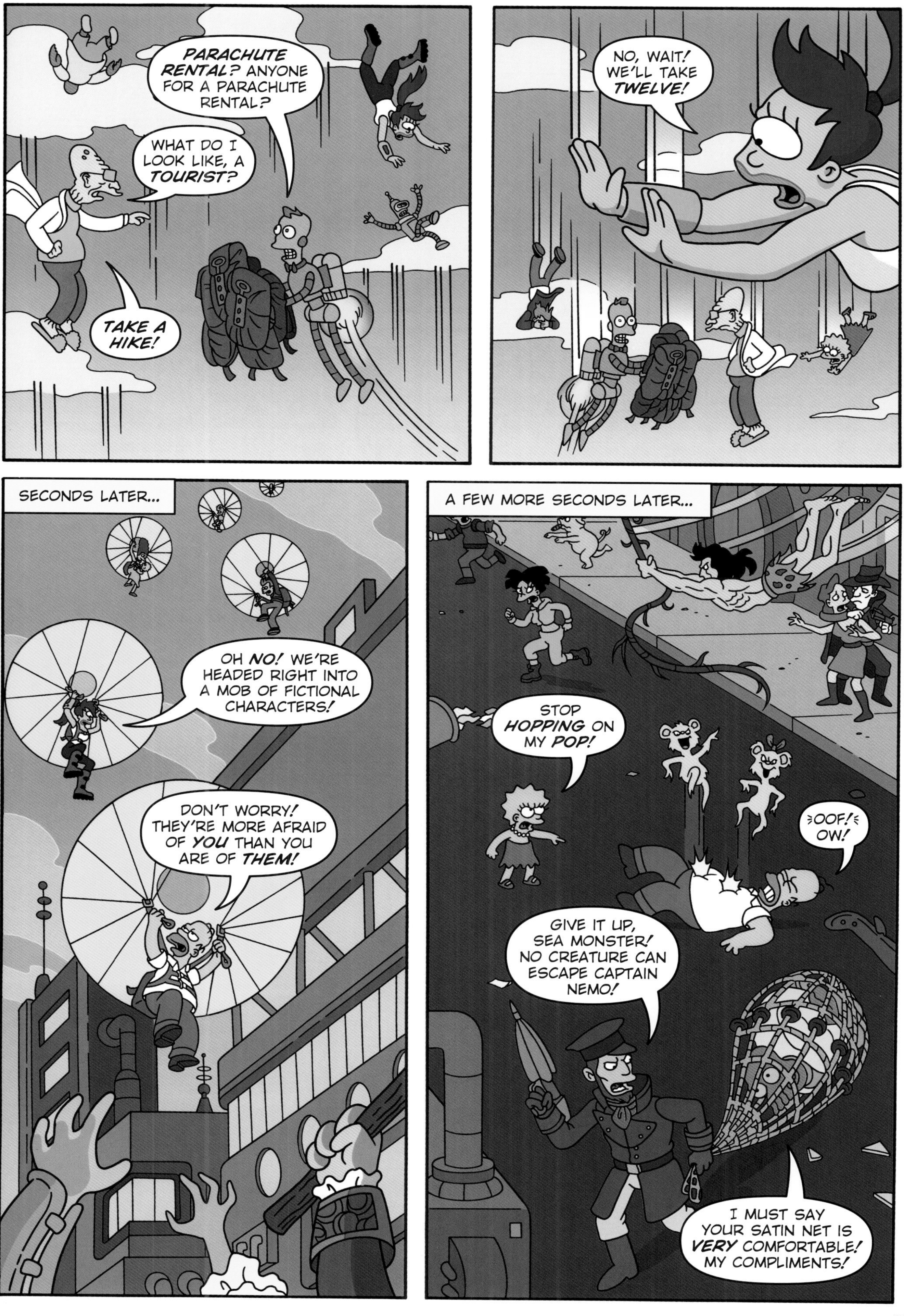

PARACHUTE RENTAL? ANYONE FOR A PARACHUTE RENTAL?
WHAT DO I LOOK LIKE, A TOURIST?
TAKE A HIKE!
NO, WAIT! WE'LL TAKE TWELVE!
SECONDS LATER...
OH NO! WE'RE HEADED RIGHT INTO A MOB OF FICTIONAL CHARACTERS!
DON'T WORRY! THEY'RE MORE AFRAID OF YOU THAN YOU ARE OF THEM!
A FEW MORE SECONDS LATER...
STOP HOPPING ON MY POP!
OOF! OW!
GIVE IT UP, SEA MONSTER! NO CREATURE CAN ESCAPE CAPTAIN NEMO!
I MUST SAY YOUR SATIN NET IS VERY COMFORTABLE! MY COMPLIMENTS!

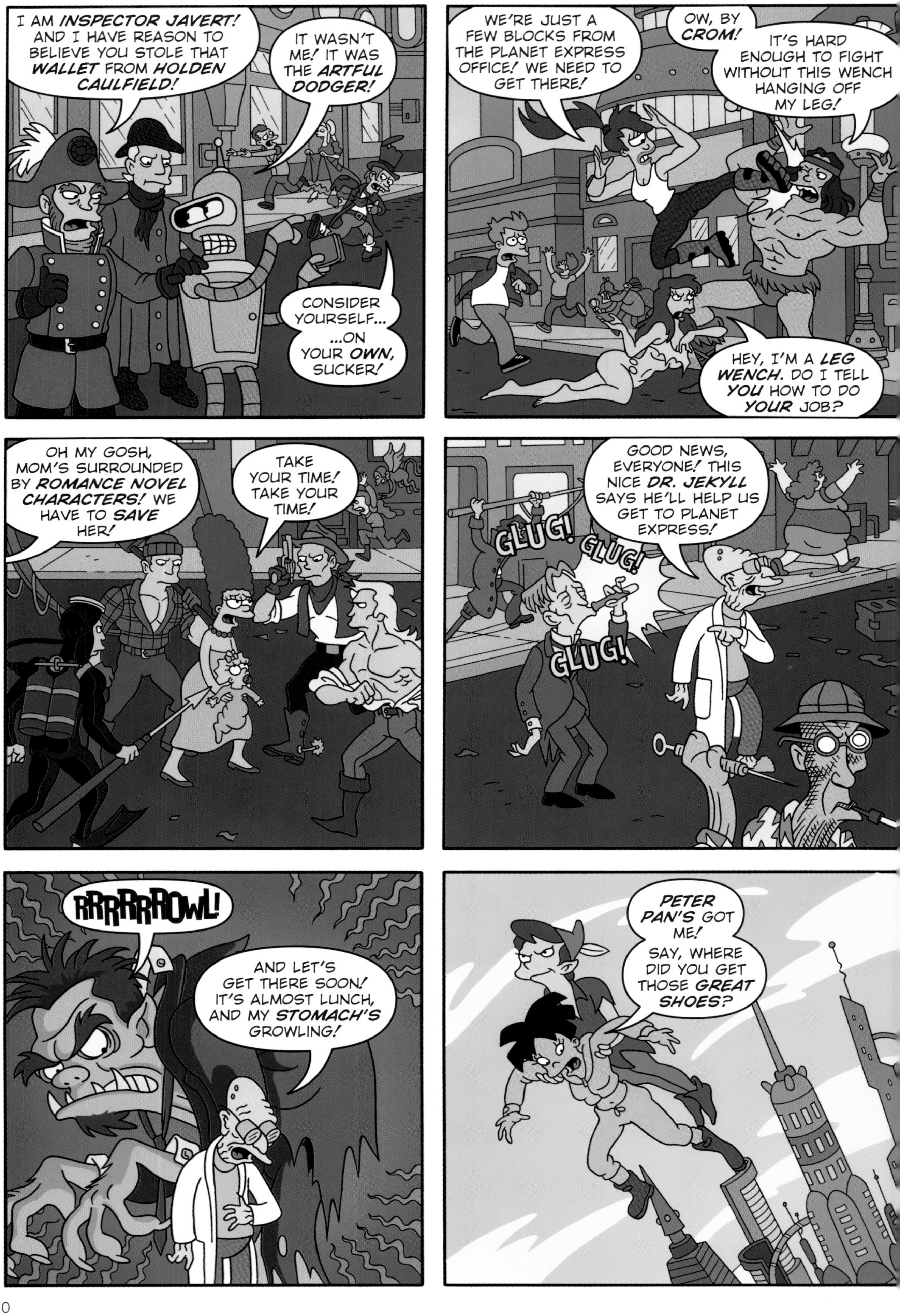
I AM ***INSPECTOR JAVERT!*** AND I HAVE REASON TO BELIEVE YOU STOLE THAT ***WALLET*** FROM ***HOLDEN CAULFIELD!***
IT WASN'T ME! IT WAS THE ***ARTFUL DODGER!***
CONSIDER YOURSELF... ...ON YOUR ***OWN,*** SUCKER!
WE'RE JUST A FEW BLOCKS FROM THE PLANET EXPRESS OFFICE! WE NEED TO GET THERE!
OW, BY ***CROM!***
IT'S HARD ENOUGH TO FIGHT WITHOUT THIS WENCH HANGING OFF MY LEG!
HEY, I'M A ***LEG WENCH.*** DO I TELL ***YOU*** HOW TO DO ***YOUR*** JOB?
OH MY GOSH, MOM'S SURROUNDED BY ***ROMANCE NOVEL CHARACTERS!*** WE HAVE TO ***SAVE*** HER!
TAKE YOUR TIME! TAKE YOUR TIME!
GOOD NEWS, EVERYONE! THIS NICE ***DR. JEKYLL*** SAYS HE'LL HELP US GET TO PLANET EXPRESS!
GLUG! GLUG! GLUG!
RRRRRROWL!
AND LET'S GET THERE SOON! IT'S ALMOST LUNCH, AND MY ***STOMACH'S*** GROWLING!
PETER PAN'S GOT ME! SAY, WHERE DID YOU GET THOSE ***GREAT SHOES?***

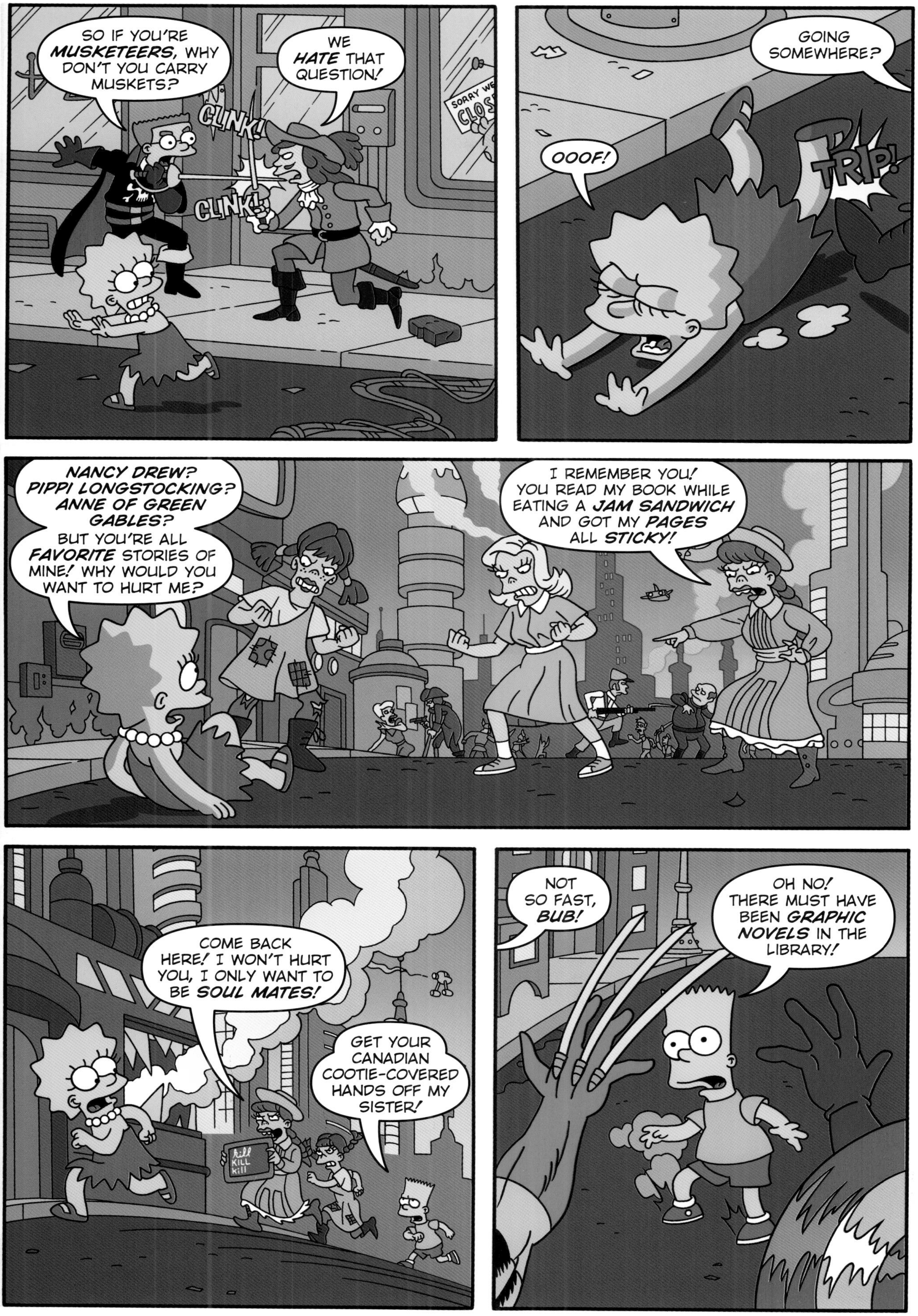
SO IF YOU'RE MUSKETEERS, WHY DON'T YOU CARRY MUSKETS?
WE HATE THAT QUESTION!
CLINK!
CLINK!
GOING SOMEWHERE?
OOOF!
TRIP!
NANCY DREW? PIPPI LONGSTOCKING? ANNE OF GREEN GABLES? BUT YOU'RE ALL FAVORITE STORIES OF MINE! WHY WOULD YOU WANT TO HURT ME?
I REMEMBER YOU! YOU READ MY BOOK WHILE EATING A JAM SANDWICH AND GOT MY PAGES ALL STICKY!
COME BACK HERE! I WON'T HURT YOU, I ONLY WANT TO BE SOUL MATES!
kill
KILL
kill
GET YOUR CANADIAN COOTIE-COVERED HANDS OFF MY SISTER!
NOT SO FAST, BUB!
OH NO! THERE MUST HAVE BEEN GRAPHIC NOVELS IN THE LIBRARY!

GRAPHIC NOVELS? *GREAT SCOTT!* I MEAN WHAT WAS WRONG WITH JUST CALLING THEM *COMICS BOOKS?*

WHY ARE YOU ALL STANDING IN SHADOW?

COPYRIGHT PROTECTION!

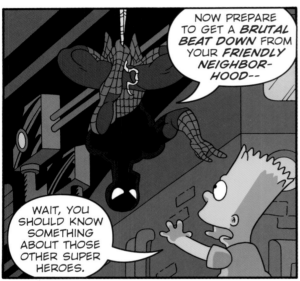

NOW PREPARE TO GET A *BRUTAL BEAT DOWN* FROM YOUR *FRIENDLY NEIGHBOR- HOOD--*

WAIT, YOU SHOULD KNOW SOMETHING ABOUT THOSE OTHER SUPER HEROES.

YEAH, WHAT?

THEY SAID EVERYONE FROM *YOUR* COMIC BOOK COMPANY IS A *SISSY!*

THEY *DID?!!*

GOOD WORK, BART! LUCKY YOU KNEW THAT COMIC BOOK HEROES'LL FIGHT EACH OTHER AT THE DROP OF A HAT!

POW!

BAM!

BIFF!

THOU HATH MADE ME *DROP* MY *HELMET!* HAVE *AT* THEE!

NOW LET'S GET TO PLANET EXPRESS!

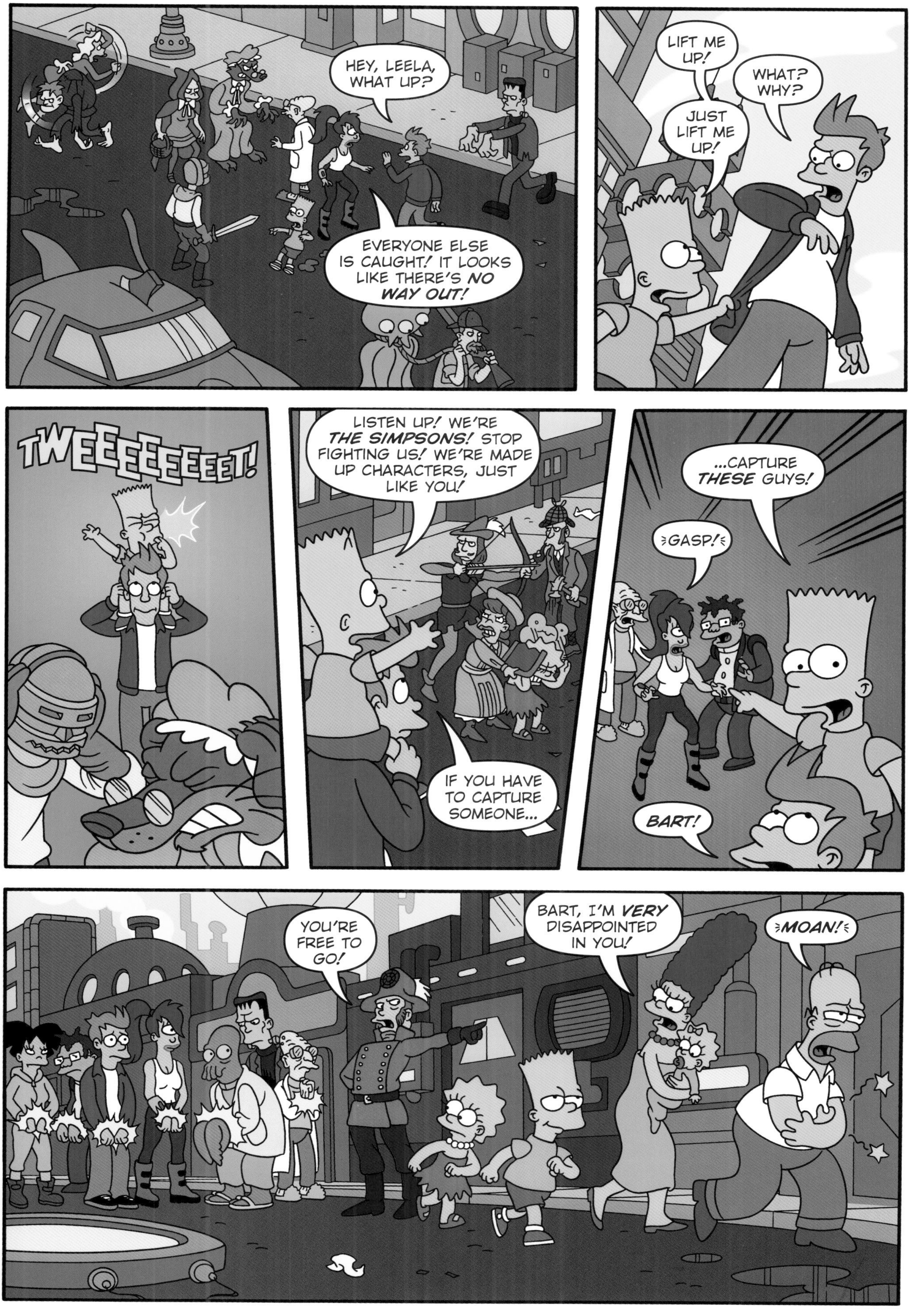
HEY, LEELA, WHAT UP?
EVERYONE ELSE IS CAUGHT! IT LOOKS LIKE THERE'S NO WAY OUT!
LIFT ME UP!
WHAT? WHY?
JUST LIFT ME UP!
TWEEEEEEEET!
LISTEN UP! WE'RE THE SIMPSONS! STOP FIGHTING US! WE'RE MADE UP CHARACTERS, JUST LIKE YOU!
IF YOU HAVE TO CAPTURE SOMEONE...
...CAPTURE THESE GUYS!
GASP!
BART!
YOU'RE FREE TO GO!
BART, I'M VERY DISAPPOINTED IN YOU!
MOAN!

UM...YEAH. THAT WAS THE *PLAN* ALL RIGHT!

NO, MOM! BART FREED US THE ONLY WAY POSSIBLE! AT LEAST WE NOW HAVE A *CHANCE* TO HELP EVERYONE ELSE!

GOOD *PLAN*, BART!

LOOK, THERE'S THE PLANET EXPRESS BUILDING!

HOOT! HOOT!

LOOK FOR *ANYTHING* WE CAN USE AS A WEAPON!

I FOUND AN M.C. ESCHER-SKETCH! BUT ALL I CAN DRAW ARE THINGS THAT HURT MY BRAIN!

HOW ABOUT THIS? THE LABEL SAYS IT'S THE *FINGLONGER*.

WHAT DOES IT DO?

DOOMSDAY MACHINES

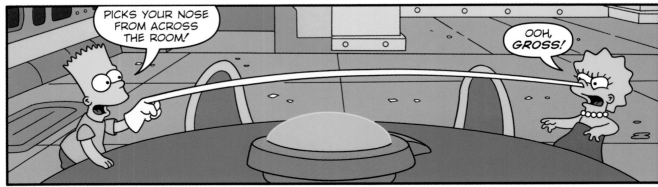

PICKS YOUR NOSE FROM ACROSS THE ROOM!

OOH, *GROSS!*

134

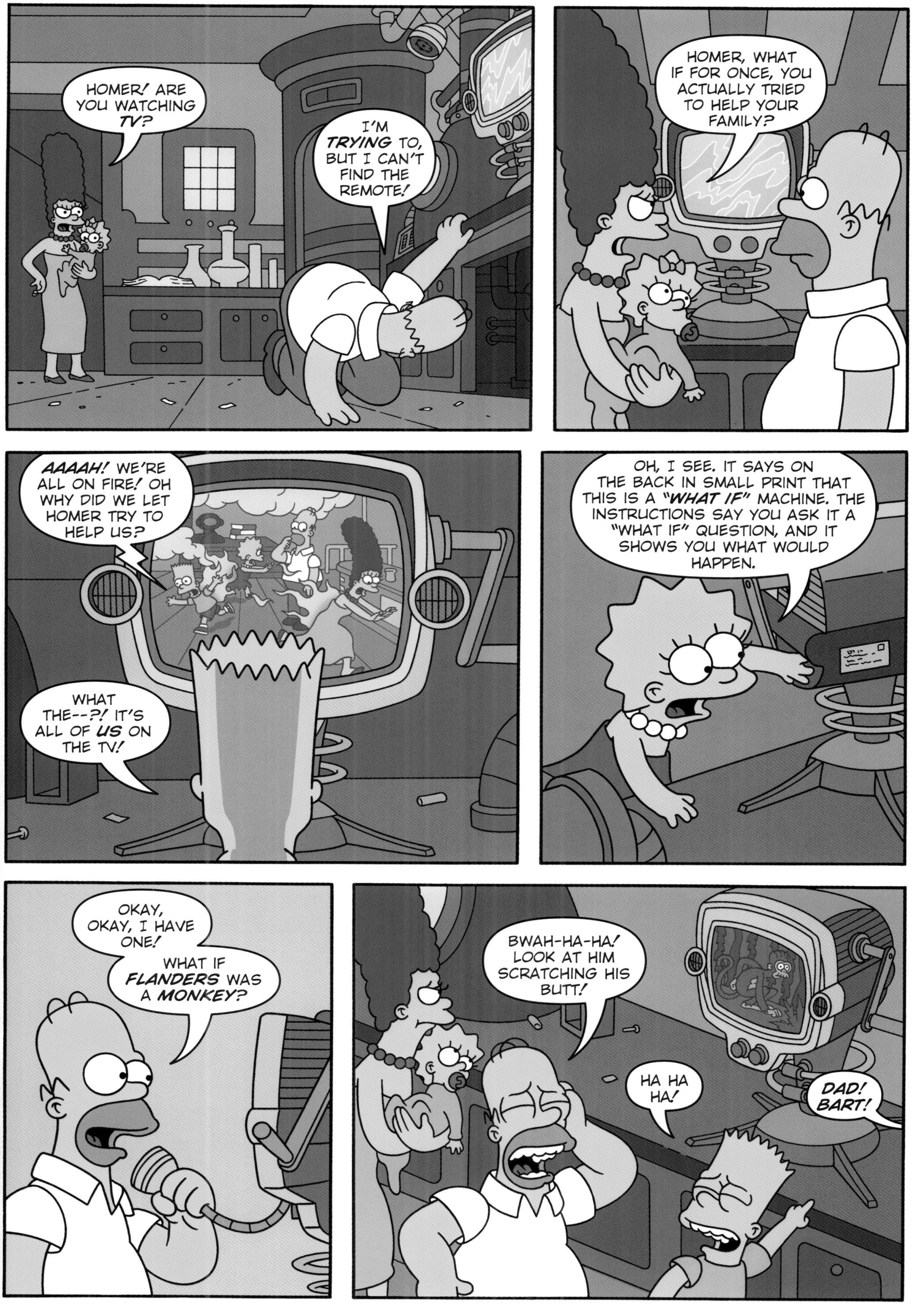
HOMER! ARE YOU WATCHING TV?
I'M TRYING TO, BUT I CAN'T FIND THE REMOTE!
HOMER, WHAT IF FOR ONCE, YOU ACTUALLY TRIED TO HELP YOUR FAMILY?
AAAAH! WE'RE ALL ON FIRE! OH WHY DID WE LET HOMER TRY TO HELP US?
WHAT THE--?! IT'S ALL OF US ON THE TV!
OH, I SEE. IT SAYS ON THE BACK IN SMALL PRINT THAT THIS IS A "WHAT IF" MACHINE. THE INSTRUCTIONS SAY YOU ASK IT A "WHAT IF" QUESTION, AND IT SHOWS YOU WHAT WOULD HAPPEN.
OKAY, OKAY, I HAVE ONE!
WHAT IF FLANDERS WAS A MONKEY?
BWAH-HA-HA! LOOK AT HIM SCRATCHING HIS BUTT!
HA HA HA!
DAD! BART!

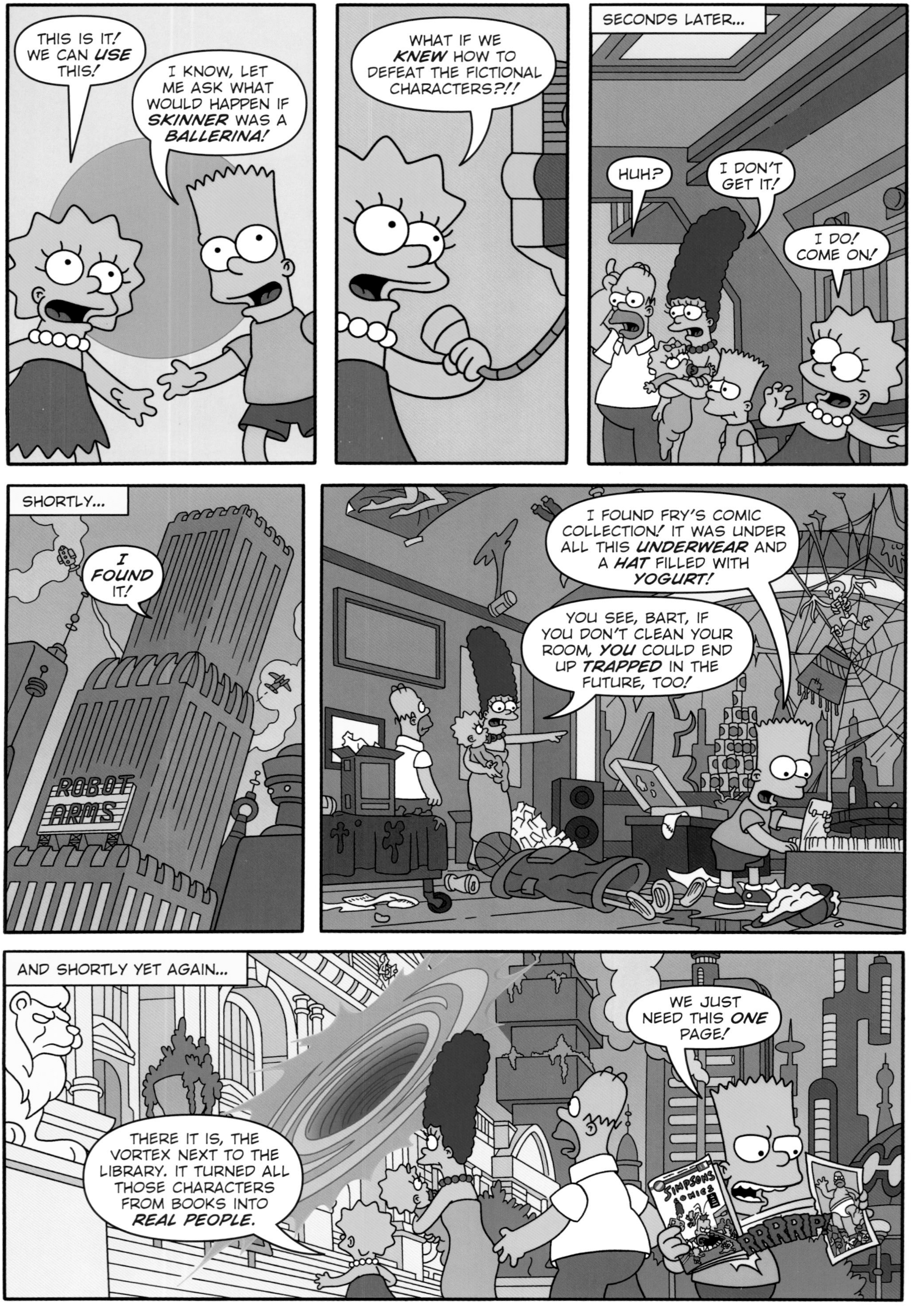
THIS IS IT! WE CAN *USE* THIS!
I KNOW, LET ME ASK WHAT WOULD HAPPEN IF *SKINNER* WAS A *BALLERINA!*
WHAT IF WE *KNEW* HOW TO DEFEAT THE FICTIONAL CHARACTERS?!!
SECONDS LATER...
HUH?
I DON'T GET IT!
I DO! COME ON!
SHORTLY...
I FOUND IT!
ROBOT ARMS
I FOUND FRY'S COMIC COLLECTION! IT WAS UNDER ALL THIS *UNDERWEAR* AND A *HAT* FILLED WITH *YOGURT!*
YOU SEE, BART, IF YOU DON'T CLEAN YOUR ROOM, *YOU* COULD END UP *TRAPPED* IN THE FUTURE, TOO!
AND SHORTLY YET AGAIN...
THERE IT IS, THE VORTEX NEXT TO THE LIBRARY. IT TURNED ALL THOSE CHARACTERS FROM BOOKS INTO *REAL PEOPLE*.
WE JUST NEED THIS *ONE* PAGE!
SIMPSONS COMICS
RRRRIP!

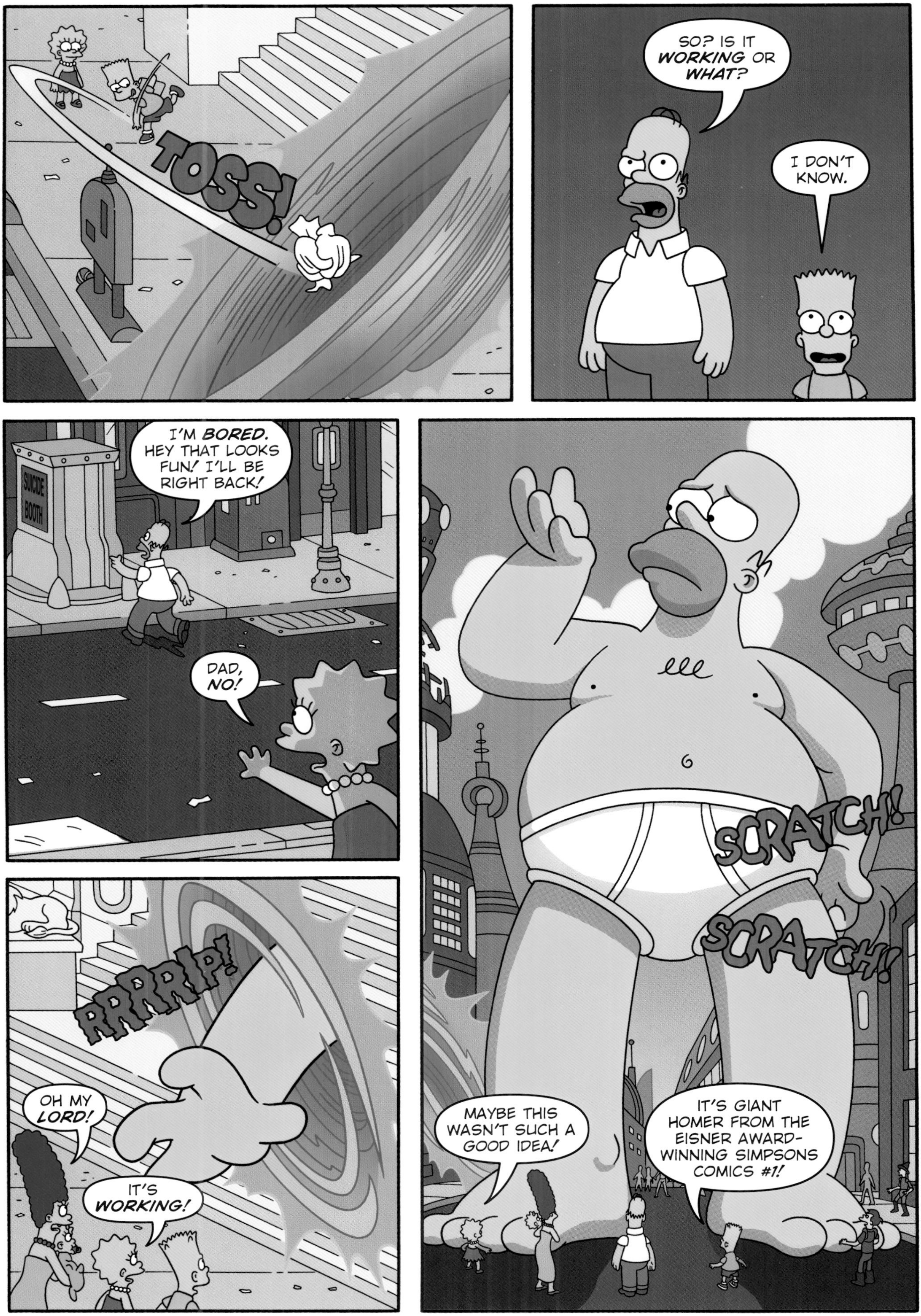
TOSS!
SO? IS IT WORKING OR WHAT?
I DON'T KNOW.
I'M BORED. HEY THAT LOOKS FUN! I'LL BE RIGHT BACK!
SUICIDE BOOTH
DAD, NO!
RRRRIP!
OH MY LORD!
IT'S WORKING!
SCRATCH!
SCRATCH!
MAYBE THIS WASN'T SUCH A GOOD IDEA!
IT'S GIANT HOMER FROM THE EISNER AWARD-WINNING SIMPSONS COMICS #1!

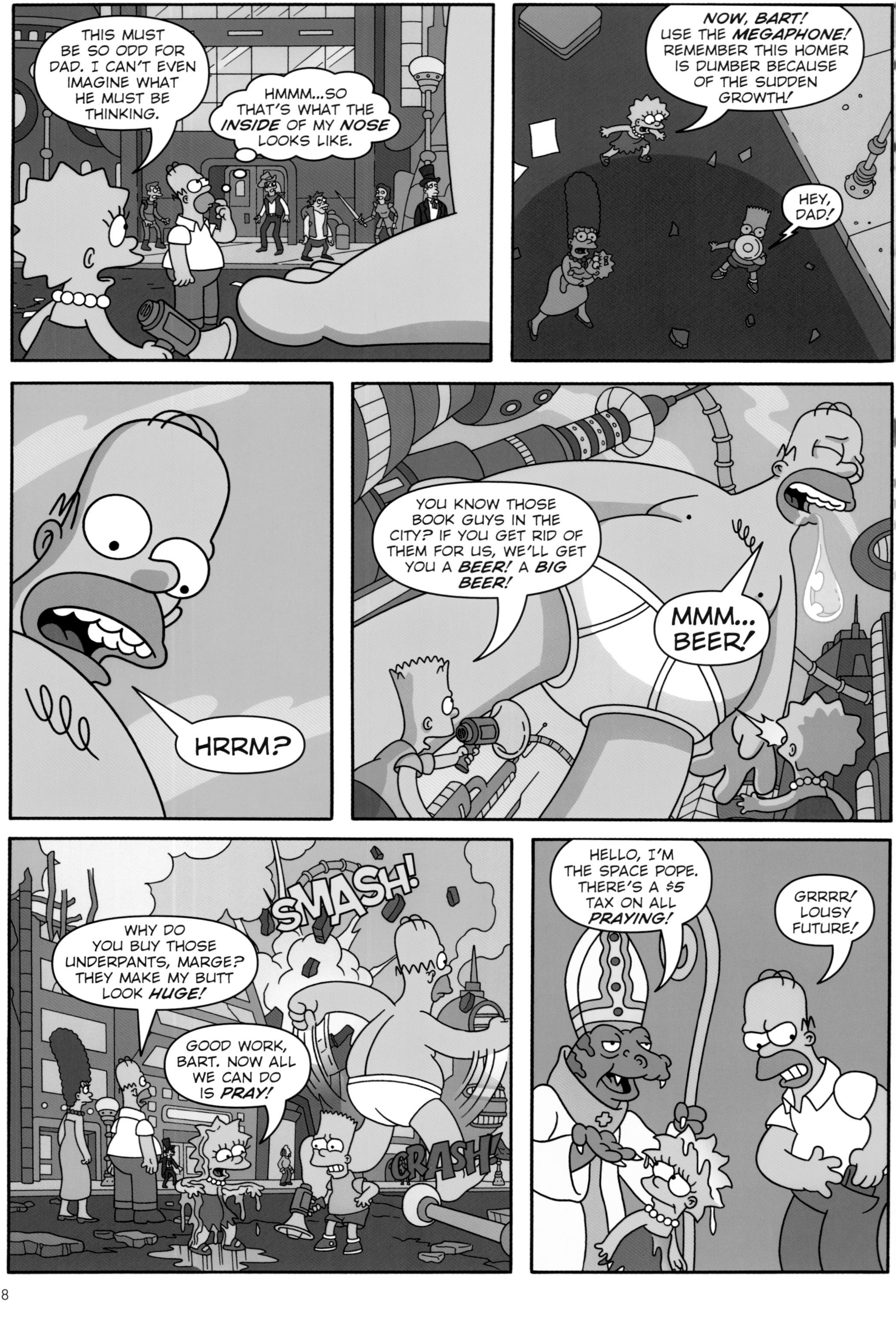
THIS MUST BE SO ODD FOR DAD. I CAN'T EVEN IMAGINE WHAT HE MUST BE THINKING.
HMMM...SO THAT'S WHAT THE INSIDE OF MY NOSE LOOKS LIKE.
NOW, BART! USE THE MEGAPHONE! REMEMBER THIS HOMER IS DUMBER BECAUSE OF THE SUDDEN GROWTH!
HEY, DAD!
HRRM?
YOU KNOW THOSE BOOK GUYS IN THE CITY? IF YOU GET RID OF THEM FOR US, WE'LL GET YOU A BEER! A BIG BEER!
MMM... BEER!
SMASH!
WHY DO YOU BUY THOSE UNDERPANTS, MARGE? THEY MAKE MY BUTT LOOK HUGE!
GOOD WORK, BART. NOW ALL WE CAN DO IS PRAY!
CRASH!
HELLO, I'M THE SPACE POPE. THERE'S A $5 TAX ON ALL PRAYING!
GRRRR! LOUSY FUTURE!

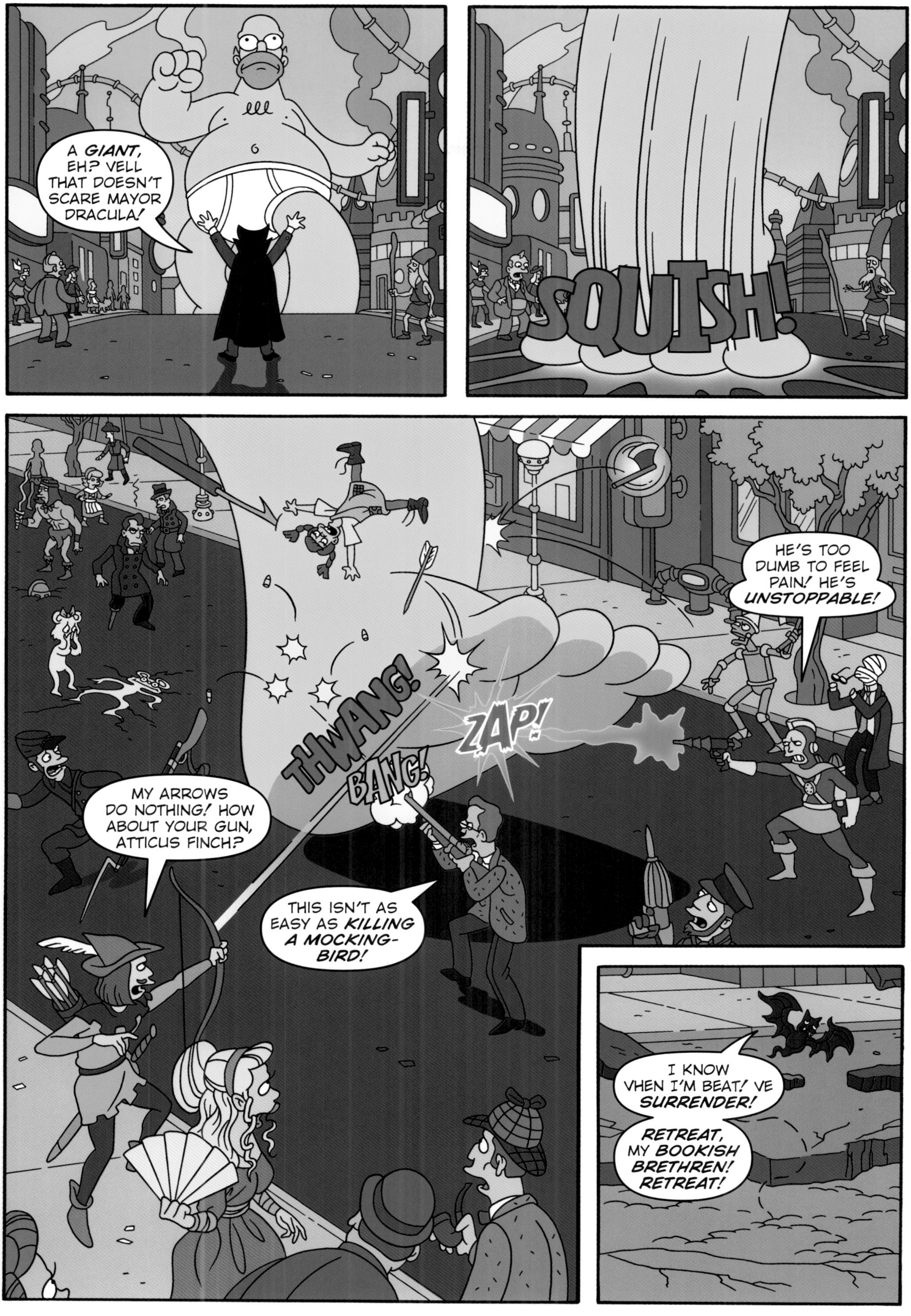
A *GIANT*, EH? VELL THAT DOESN'T SCARE MAYOR DRACULA!
SQUISH!
HE'S TOO DUMB TO FEEL PAIN! HE'S *UNSTOPPABLE!*
THWANG!
ZAP!
BANG!
MY ARROWS DO NOTHING! HOW ABOUT YOUR GUN, ATTICUS FINCH?
THIS ISN'T AS EASY AS *KILLING A MOCKING-BIRD!*
I KNOW VHEN I'M BEAT! VE *SURRENDER!*
RETREAT, MY *BOOKISH BRETHREN! RETREAT!*

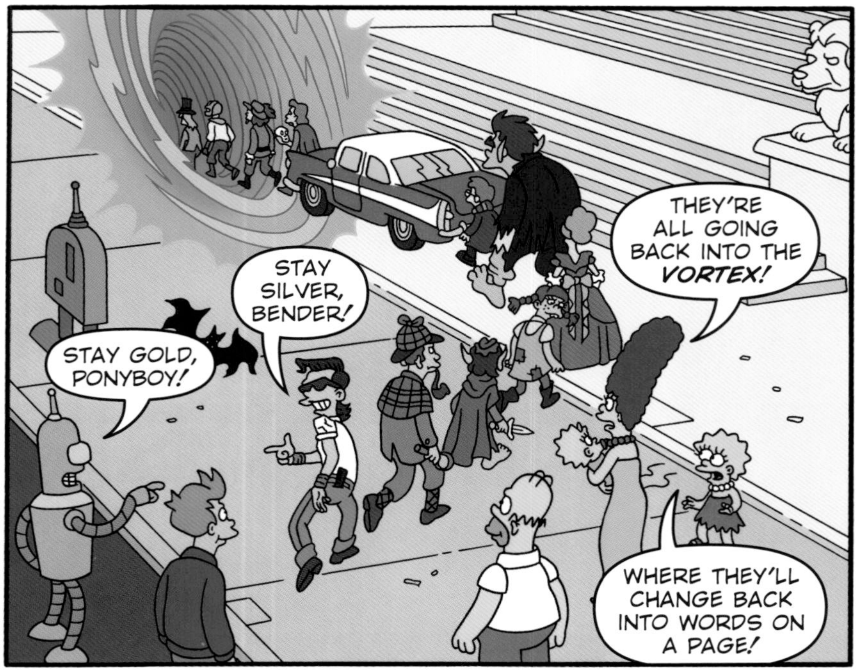
STAY GOLD, PONYBOY!
STAY SILVER, BENDER!
THEY'RE ALL GOING BACK INTO THE *VORTEX!*
WHERE THEY'LL CHANGE BACK INTO WORDS ON A PAGE!

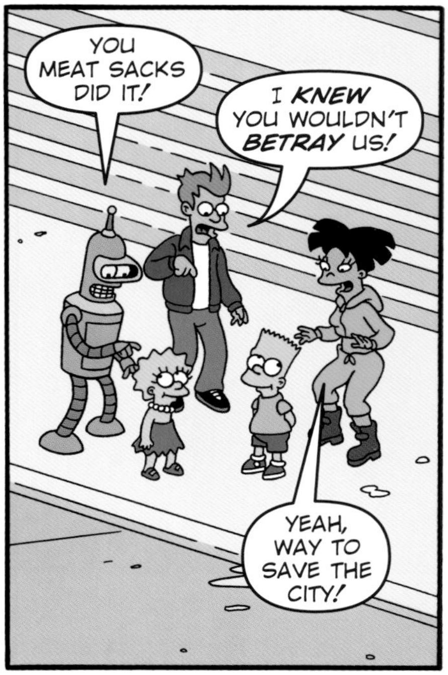
YOU MEAT SACKS DID IT!
I *KNEW* YOU WOULDN'T *BETRAY* US!
YEAH, WAY TO SAVE THE CITY!

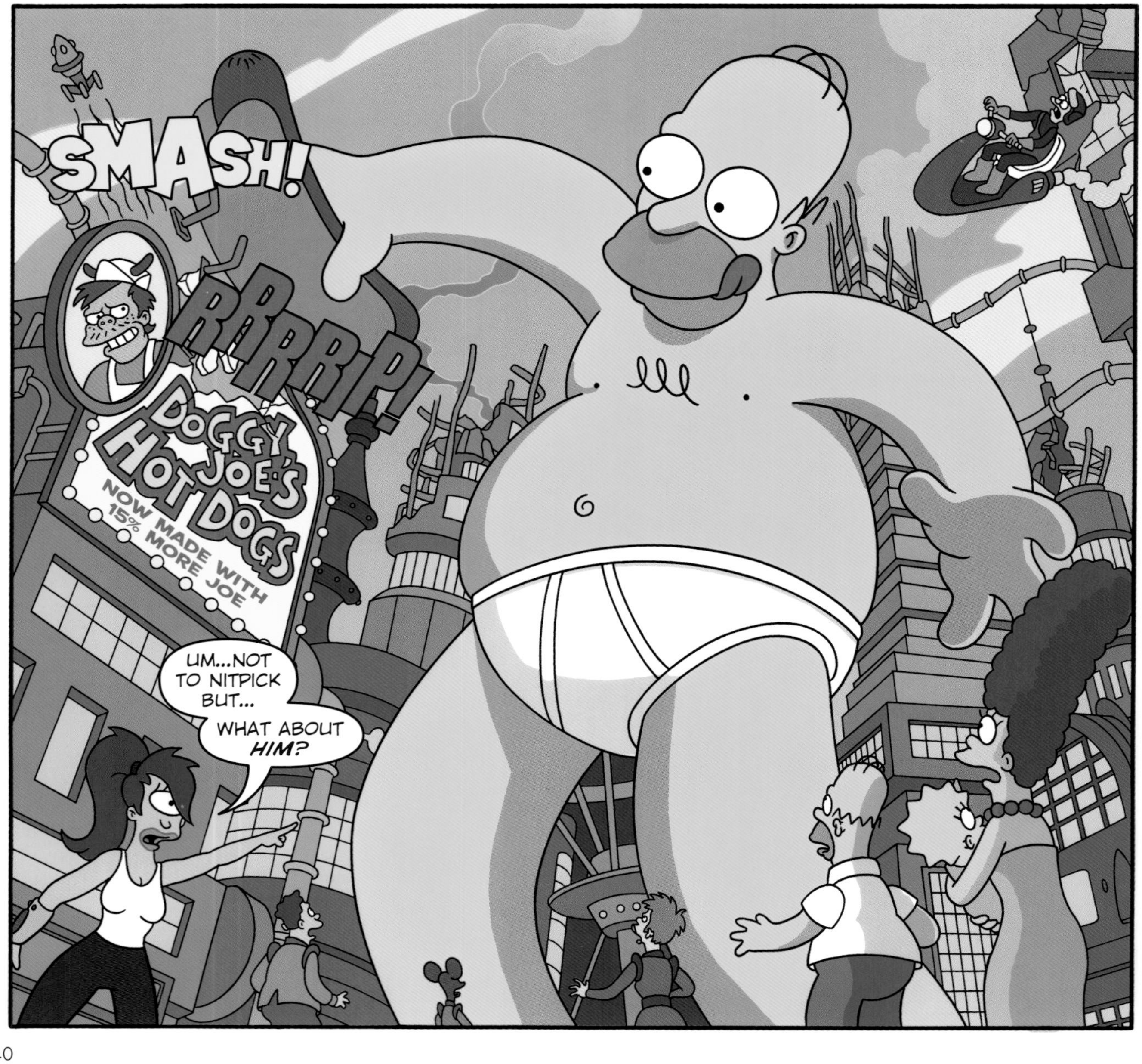
SMASH!
RRRRIP!
DOGGY JOE'S HOT DOGS
NOW MADE WITH 15% MORE JOE
UM...NOT TO NITPICK BUT...
WHAT ABOUT *HIM?*

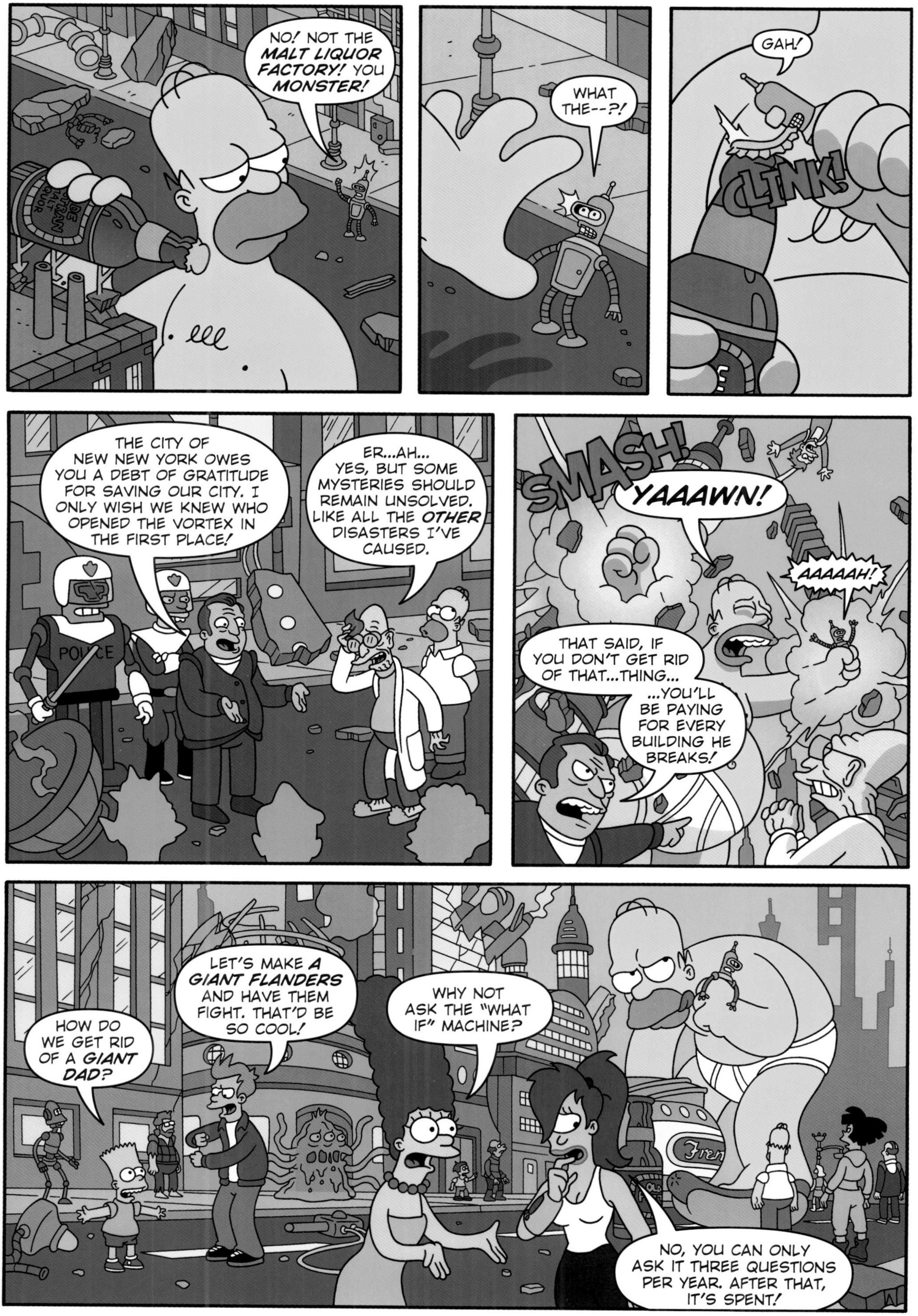

NO! NOT THE MALT LIQUOR FACTORY! YOU MONSTER!
WHAT THE--?!
GAH!
CLINK!
THE CITY OF NEW NEW YORK OWES YOU A DEBT OF GRATITUDE FOR SAVING OUR CITY. I ONLY WISH WE KNEW WHO OPENED THE VORTEX IN THE FIRST PLACE!
ER...AH... YES, BUT SOME MYSTERIES SHOULD REMAIN UNSOLVED. LIKE ALL THE OTHER DISASTERS I'VE CAUSED.
POLICE
SMASH!
YAAAWN!
AAAAAH!
THAT SAID, IF YOU DON'T GET RID OF THAT...THING...
...YOU'LL BE PAYING FOR EVERY BUILDING HE BREAKS!
HOW DO WE GET RID OF A GIANT DAD?
LET'S MAKE A GIANT FLANDERS AND HAVE THEM FIGHT. THAT'D BE SO COOL!
WHY NOT ASK THE "WHAT IF" MACHINE?
NO, YOU CAN ONLY ASK IT THREE QUESTIONS PER YEAR. AFTER THAT, IT'S SPENT!

MAYBE WE SHOULD *NUKE* HIM! *THAT'D* SHOW ME, I MEAN *HIM*, I MEAN...

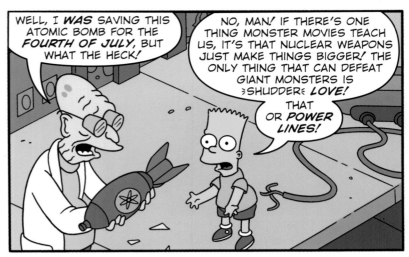

WELL, I *WAS* SAVING THIS ATOMIC BOMB FOR THE *FOURTH OF JULY*, BUT WHAT THE HECK!

NO, MAN! IF THERE'S ONE THING MONSTER MOVIES TEACH US, IT'S THAT NUCLEAR WEAPONS JUST MAKE THINGS BIGGER! THE ONLY THING THAT CAN DEFEAT GIANT MONSTERS IS ≶SHUDDER≶ *LOVE*!

THAT OR *POWER LINES*!

I HAVE AN IDEA, BUT WE NEED TO STOP HIM FROM MOVING AROUND. TELL ME, WHAT DOES HOMER SIMPSON *LOVE* MORE THAN *ANYTHING*?

MOM!

TV!

PORK CHOPS!

LATER, ON A GIANT TV IN NEW NEW YORK TIMES SQUARE...

IS THIS ON? GIANT-SIZED HOMIE? ARE YOU THERE?

HUH?

HEY!

KEEP IT DOWN, BENDER! WE'RE TRYING TO TRICK *GIANT HOMER*!

SMASH!

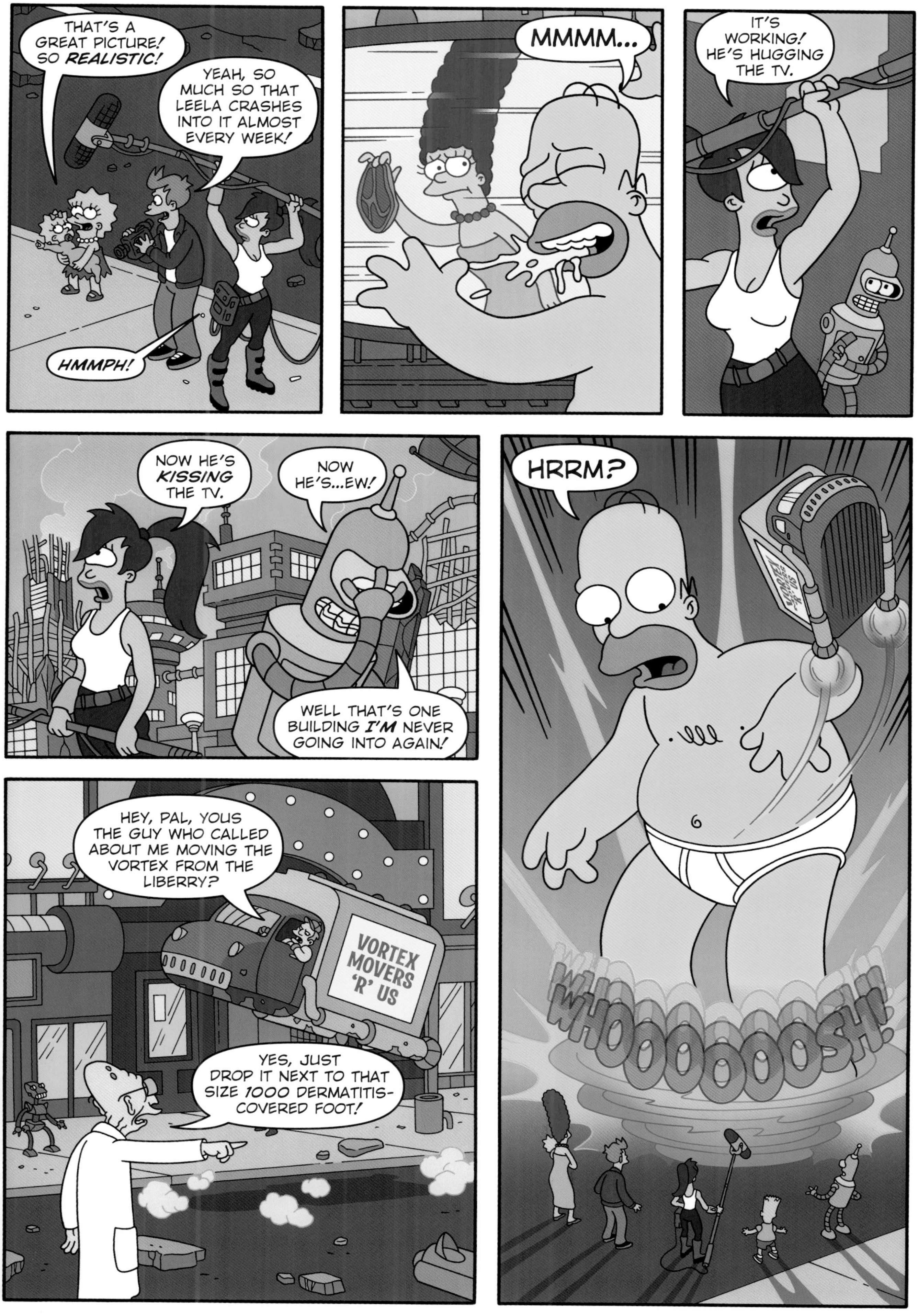
THAT'S A GREAT PICTURE! SO *REALISTIC!*
YEAH, SO MUCH SO THAT LEELA CRASHES INTO IT ALMOST EVERY WEEK!
HMMPH!
MMMM...
IT'S WORKING! HE'S HUGGING THE TV.
NOW HE'S *KISSING* THE TV.
NOW HE'S...EW!
WELL THAT'S ONE BUILDING *I'M* NEVER GOING INTO AGAIN!
HEY, PAL, YOUS THE GUY WHO CALLED ABOUT ME MOVING THE VORTEX FROM THE LIBERRY?
VORTEX MOVERS 'R' US
YES, JUST DROP IT NEXT TO THAT SIZE *1000* DERMATITIS-COVERED FOOT!
HRRM?
WHOOOOOOOSH!

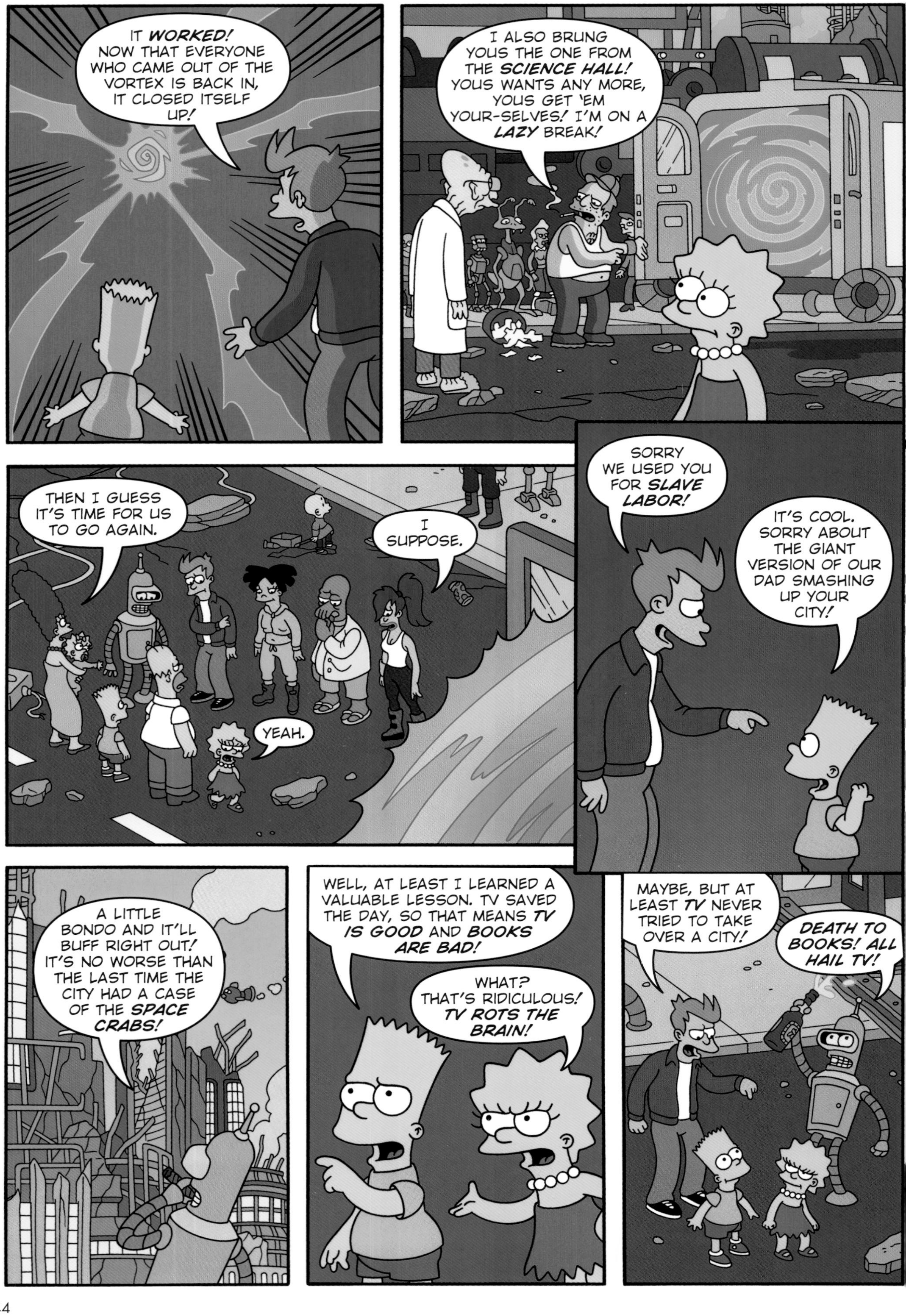
IT WORKED! NOW THAT EVERYONE WHO CAME OUT OF THE VORTEX IS BACK IN, IT CLOSED ITSELF UP!
I ALSO BRUNG YOUS THE ONE FROM THE SCIENCE HALL! YOUS WANTS ANY MORE, YOUS GET 'EM YOUR-SELVES! I'M ON A LAZY BREAK!
THEN I GUESS IT'S TIME FOR US TO GO AGAIN.
I SUPPOSE.
YEAH.
SORRY WE USED YOU FOR SLAVE LABOR!
IT'S COOL. SORRY ABOUT THE GIANT VERSION OF OUR DAD SMASHING UP YOUR CITY!
A LITTLE BONDO AND IT'LL BUFF RIGHT OUT! IT'S NO WORSE THAN THE LAST TIME THE CITY HAD A CASE OF THE SPACE CRABS!
WELL, AT LEAST I LEARNED A VALUABLE LESSON. TV SAVED THE DAY, SO THAT MEANS TV IS GOOD AND BOOKS ARE BAD!
WHAT? THAT'S RIDICULOUS! TV ROTS THE BRAIN!
MAYBE, BUT AT LEAST TV NEVER TRIED TO TAKE OVER A CITY!
DEATH TO BOOKS! ALL HAIL TV!

I WISH WE DIDN'T HAVE TO GO SO SOON.

WELL, WE *DO* HAVE TO ROUND UP THE REST OF THE SPRINGFIELDIANS. THEY GOT SHIPPED OUT ALL OVER THE PLACE.

IT'LL BE LIKE ONE LAST PICK-UP AND DELIVERY!

WHO'S UP FOR ONE MORE DAY OF *UNPAID LABOR?!*

HOORAY!

CAN I DRIVE THE SHIP?

I DON'T SEE WHY NOT!

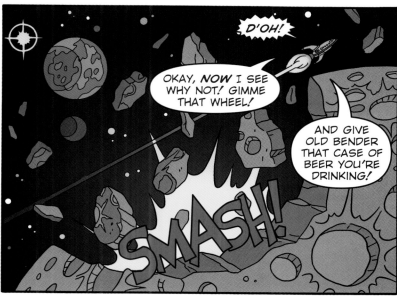

D'OH!

OKAY, *NOW* I SEE WHY NOT! GIMME THAT WHEEL!

AND GIVE OLD BENDER THAT CASE OF BEER YOU'RE DRINKING!

SMASH!

MEANWHILE, ON EARTH...

THAT'S *STRANGE!* IT SHOULD BE A *FULL* MOON TONIGHT!

I MISS OUR *DADDY!*

HE WAS NEVER OUR *FATHER!* HE WAS JUST A MAKE BELIEVE CHARACTER, AND NOW HE'S *GONE!*

STILL, IT WAS NICE HAVING BOTH A MOM *AND* A DAD SLAPPING US AROUND FOR A WHILE.

I WONDER IF MOMMY'S SAD. ALL SHE HAS LEFT OF HIM IS A *LOCK* OF HIS *HAIR!*

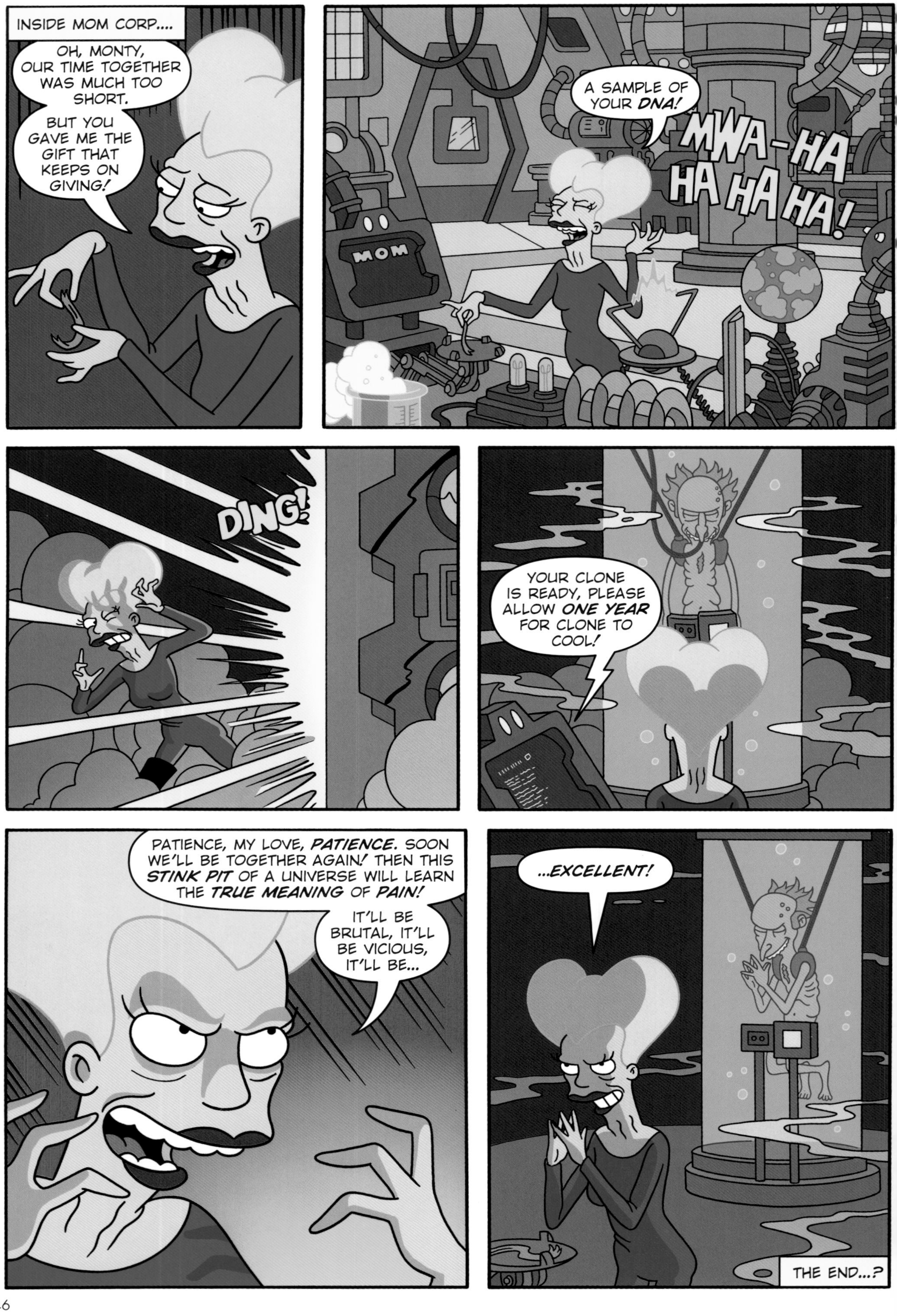

INSIDE MOM CORP....
OH, MONTY, OUR TIME TOGETHER WAS MUCH TOO SHORT.
BUT YOU GAVE ME THE GIFT THAT KEEPS ON GIVING!
A SAMPLE OF YOUR DNA!
MWA-HA HA HA HA!
DING!
YOUR CLONE IS READY, PLEASE ALLOW ONE YEAR FOR CLONE TO COOL!
PATIENCE, MY LOVE, PATIENCE. SOON WE'LL BE TOGETHER AGAIN! THEN THIS STINK PIT OF A UNIVERSE WILL LEARN THE TRUE MEANING OF PAIN!
IT'LL BE BRUTAL, IT'LL BE VICIOUS, IT'LL BE...
...EXCELLENT!
THE END...?

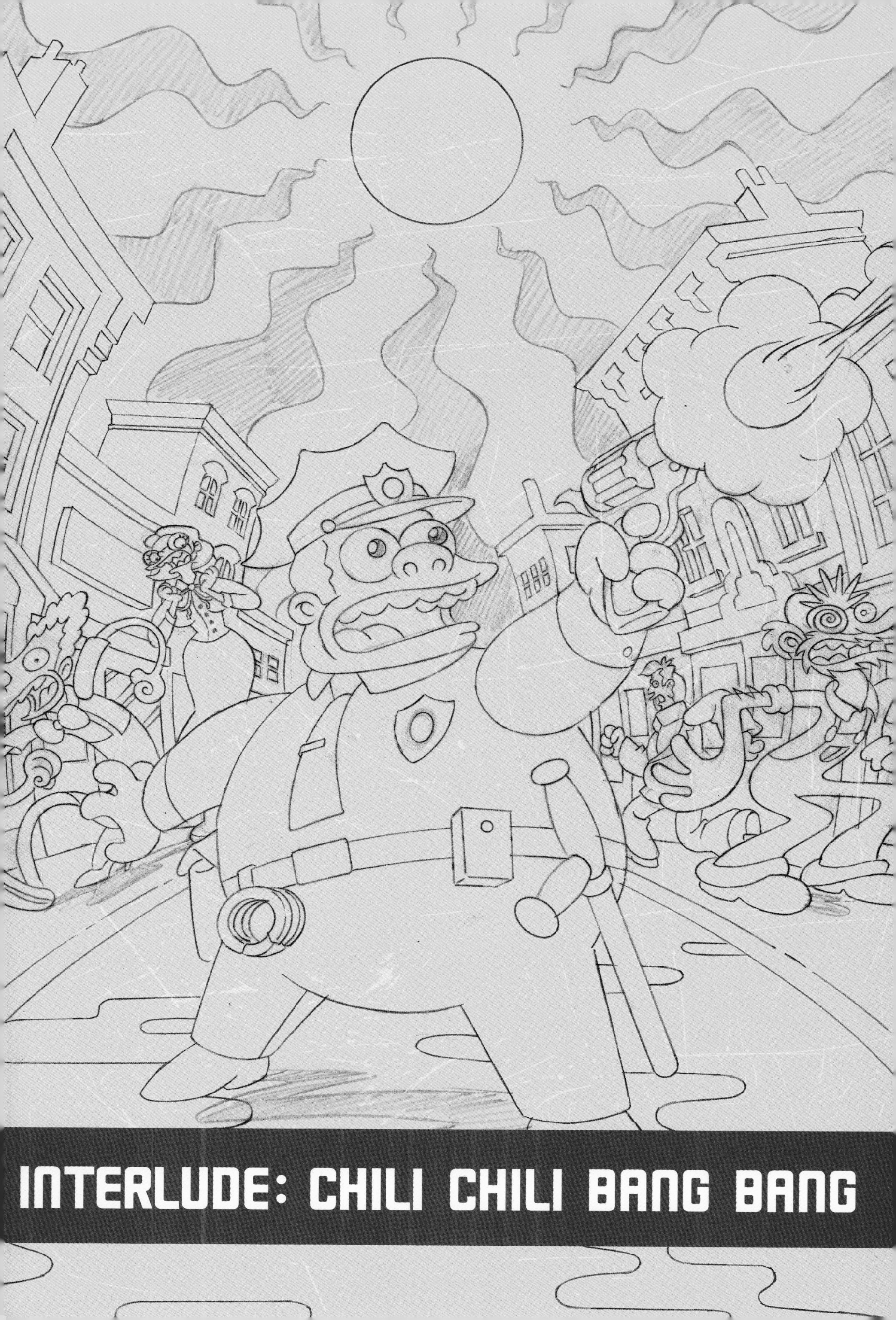

INTERLUDE: CHILI CHILI BANG BANG

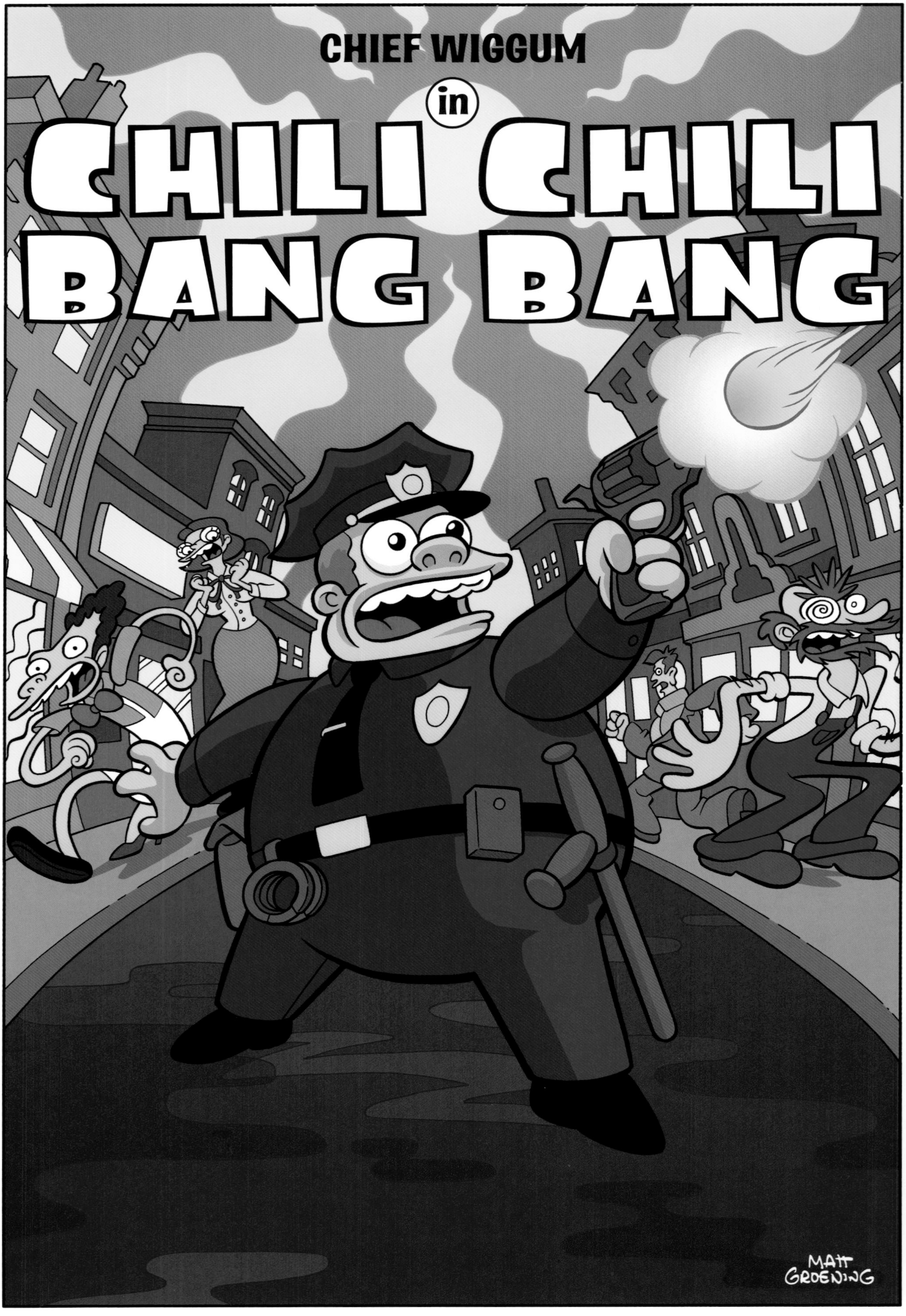
CHIEF WIGGUM
in
CHILI CHILI
BANG BANG
MATT GROENING

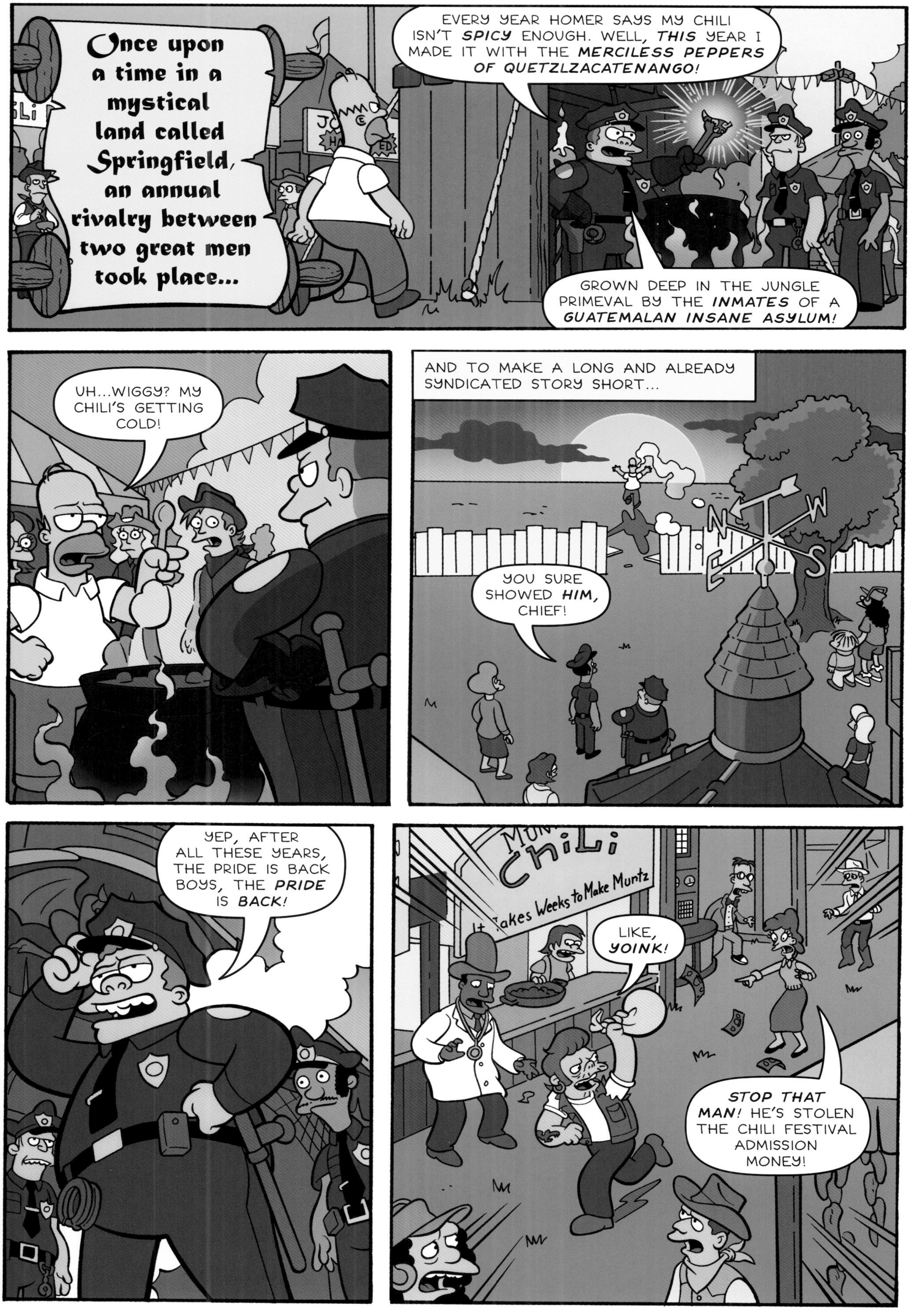

Once upon a time in a mystical land called Springfield, an annual rivalry between two great men took place...
EVERY YEAR HOMER SAYS MY CHILI ISN'T SPICY ENOUGH. WELL, THIS YEAR I MADE IT WITH THE MERCILESS PEPPERS OF QUETZLZACATENANGO!
GROWN DEEP IN THE JUNGLE PRIMEVAL BY THE INMATES OF A GUATEMALAN INSANE ASYLUM!
UH...WIGGY? MY CHILI'S GETTING COLD!
AND TO MAKE A LONG AND ALREADY SYNDICATED STORY SHORT...
N
W
E
S
YOU SURE SHOWED HIM, CHIEF!
YEP, AFTER ALL THESE YEARS, THE PRIDE IS BACK BOYS, THE PRIDE IS BACK!
ChiLi
It Takes Weeks to Make Muntz
LIKE, YOINK!
STOP THAT MAN! HE'S STOLEN THE CHILI FESTIVAL ADMISSION MONEY!

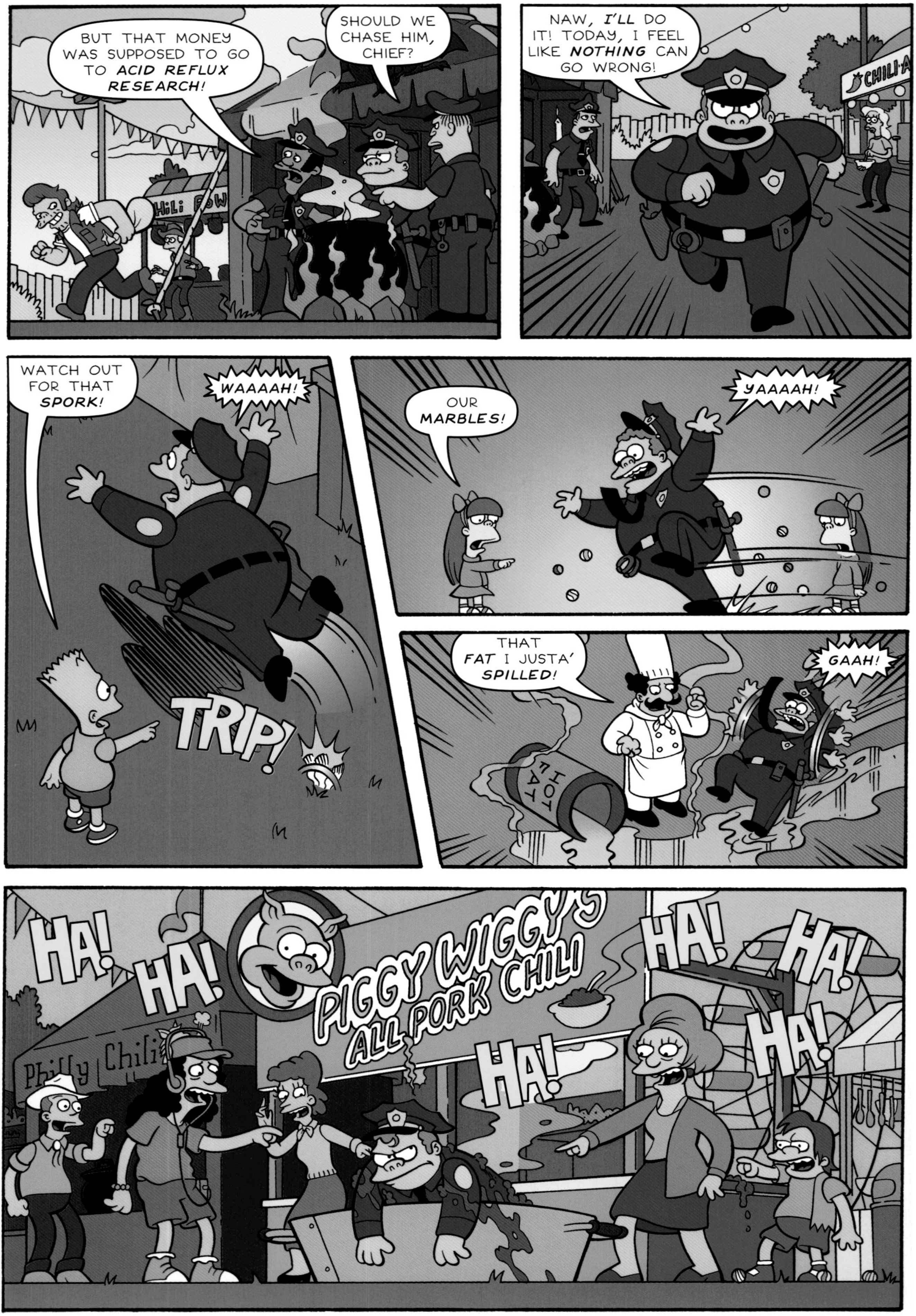
BUT THAT MONEY WAS SUPPOSED TO GO TO ACID REFLUX RESEARCH!
SHOULD WE CHASE HIM, CHIEF?
NAW, I'LL DO IT! TODAY, I FEEL LIKE NOTHING CAN GO WRONG!
WATCH OUT FOR THAT SPORK!
WAAAAH!
TRIP!
OUR MARBLES!
YAAAAH!
THAT FAT I JUSTA' SPILLED!
GAAH!
HOT FAT
HA!
HA!
PIGGY WIGGY'S ALL PORK CHILI
Philly Chili
HA!
HA!
HA!
HA!
HA!

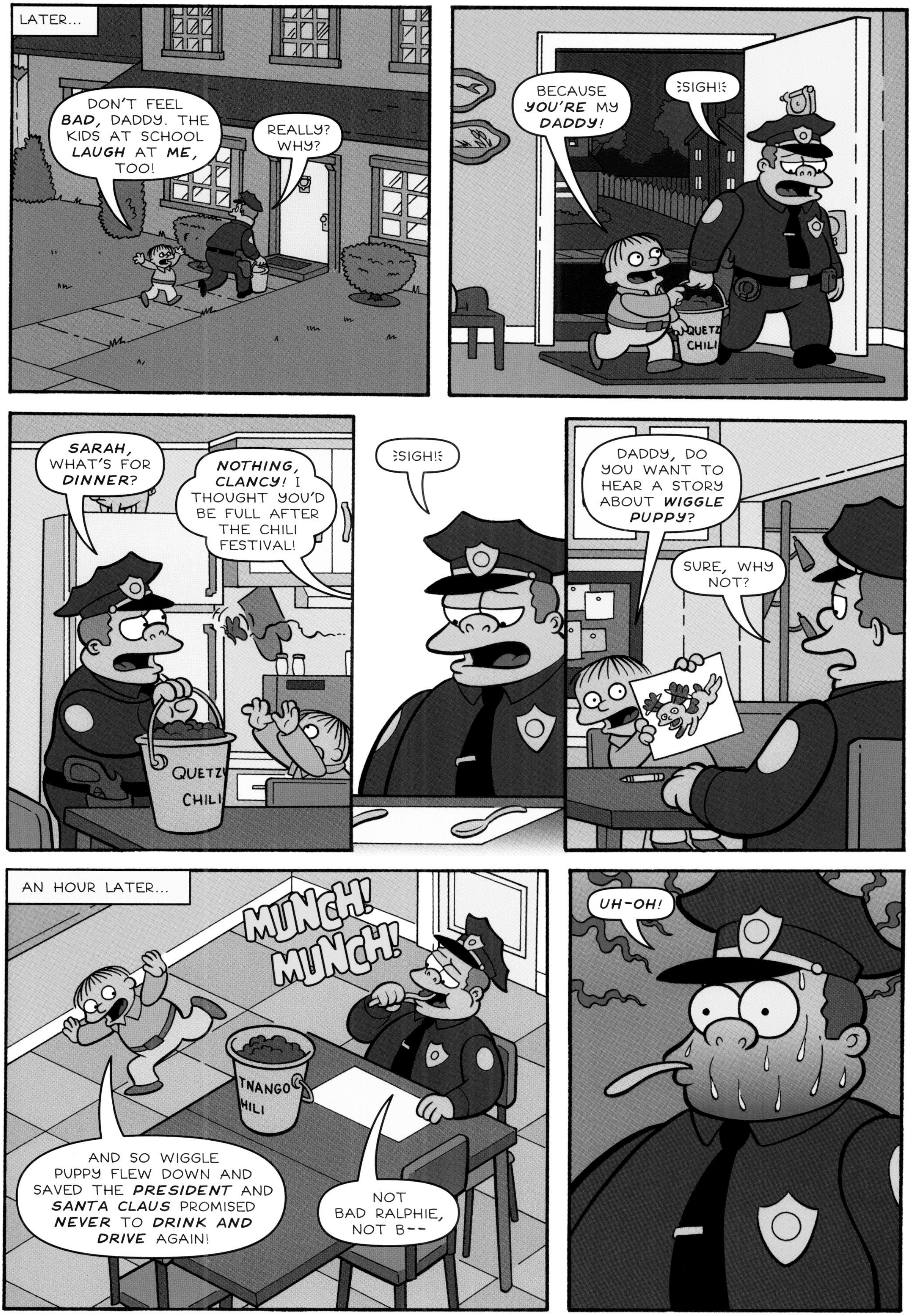
LATER...
DON'T FEEL BAD, DADDY. THE KIDS AT SCHOOL LAUGH AT ME, TOO!
REALLY? WHY?
BECAUSE YOU'RE MY DADDY!
SIGH!
QUETZ CHILI
SARAH, WHAT'S FOR DINNER?
NOTHING, CLANCY! I THOUGHT YOU'D BE FULL AFTER THE CHILI FESTIVAL!
QUETZ CHILI
SIGH!
DADDY, DO YOU WANT TO HEAR A STORY ABOUT WIGGLE PUPPY?
SURE, WHY NOT?
AN HOUR LATER...
MUNCH! MUNCH!
TNANGO HILI
AND SO WIGGLE PUPPY FLEW DOWN AND SAVED THE PRESIDENT AND SANTA CLAUS PROMISED NEVER TO DRINK AND DRIVE AGAIN!
NOT BAD RALPHIE, NOT B--
UH-OH!

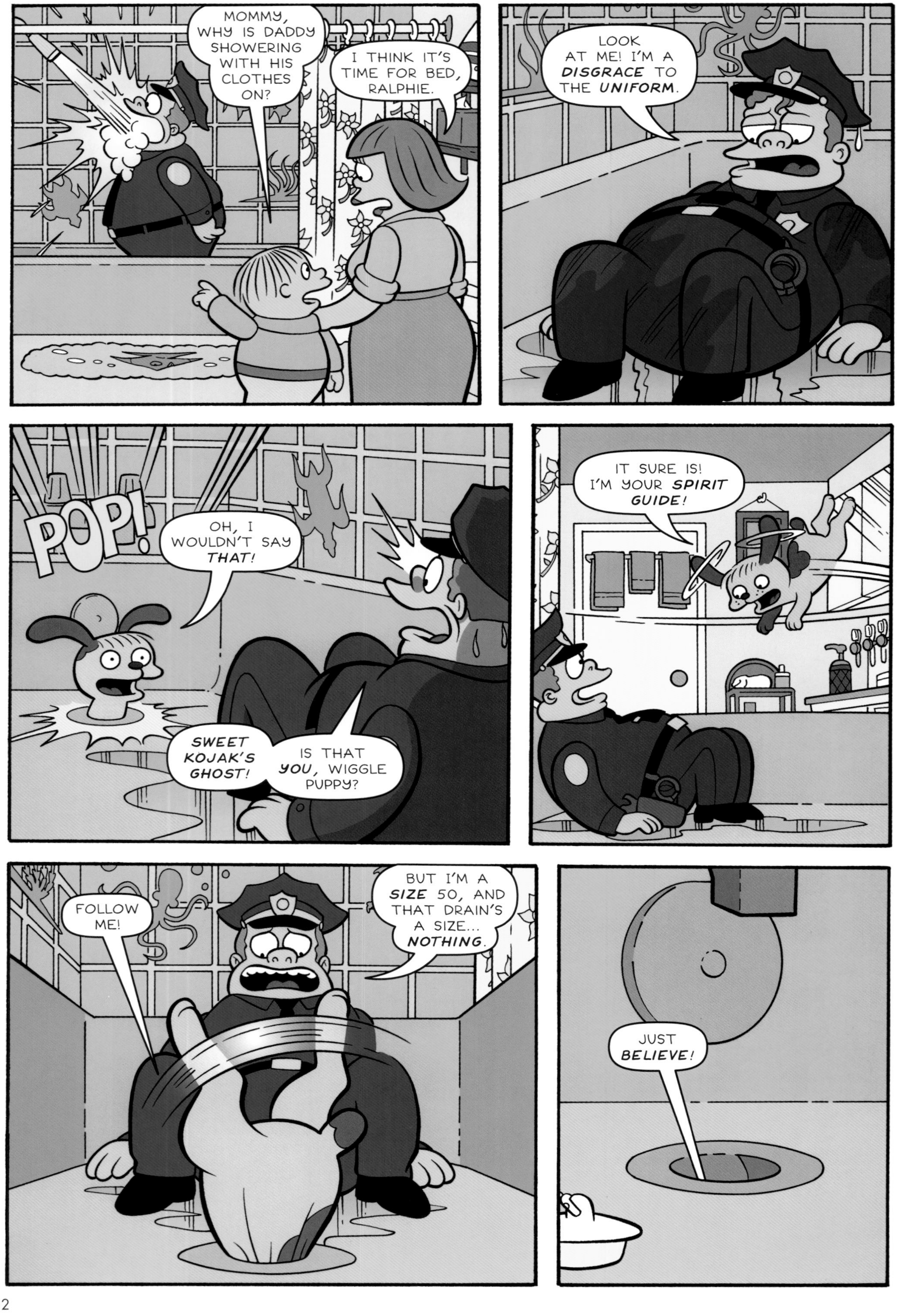
MOMMY, WHY IS DADDY SHOWERING WITH HIS CLOTHES ON?
I THINK IT'S TIME FOR BED, RALPHIE.
LOOK AT ME! I'M A **DISGRACE** TO THE **UNIFORM**.
POP!
OH, I WOULDN'T SAY **THAT!**
SWEET KOJAK'S GHOST!
IS THAT **YOU,** WIGGLE PUPPY?
IT SURE IS! I'M YOUR **SPIRIT GUIDE!**
FOLLOW ME!
BUT I'M A **SIZE** 50, AND THAT DRAIN'S A SIZE... **NOTHING**.
JUST **BELIEVE!**

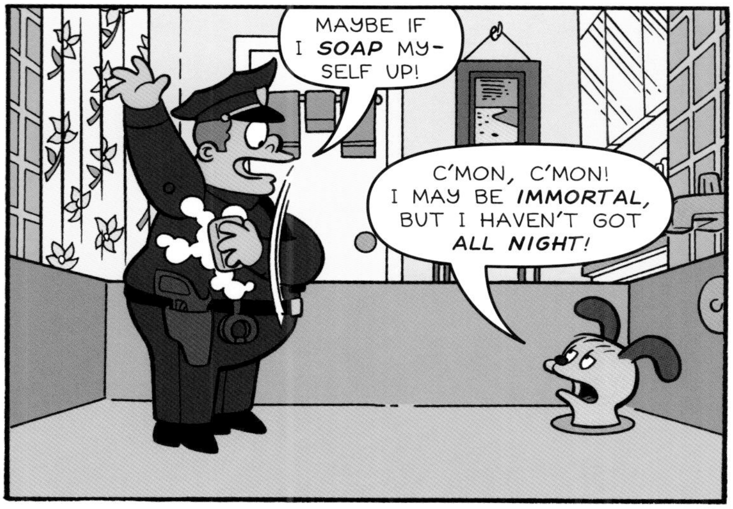
MAYBE IF I **SOAP** MY-SELF UP!
C'MON, C'MON! I MAY BE **IMMORTAL**, BUT I HAVEN'T GOT **ALL NIGHT**!

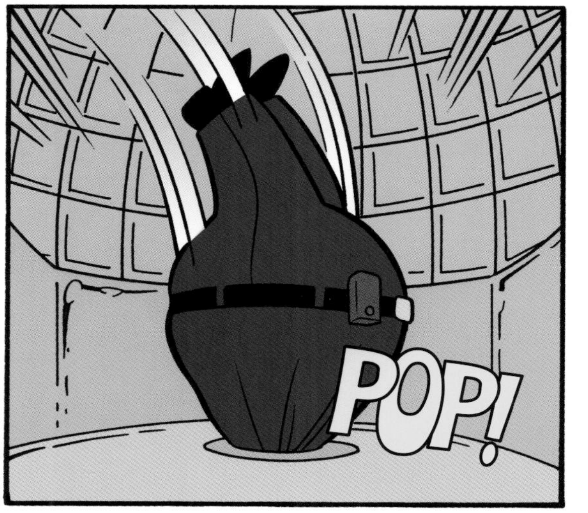
POP!

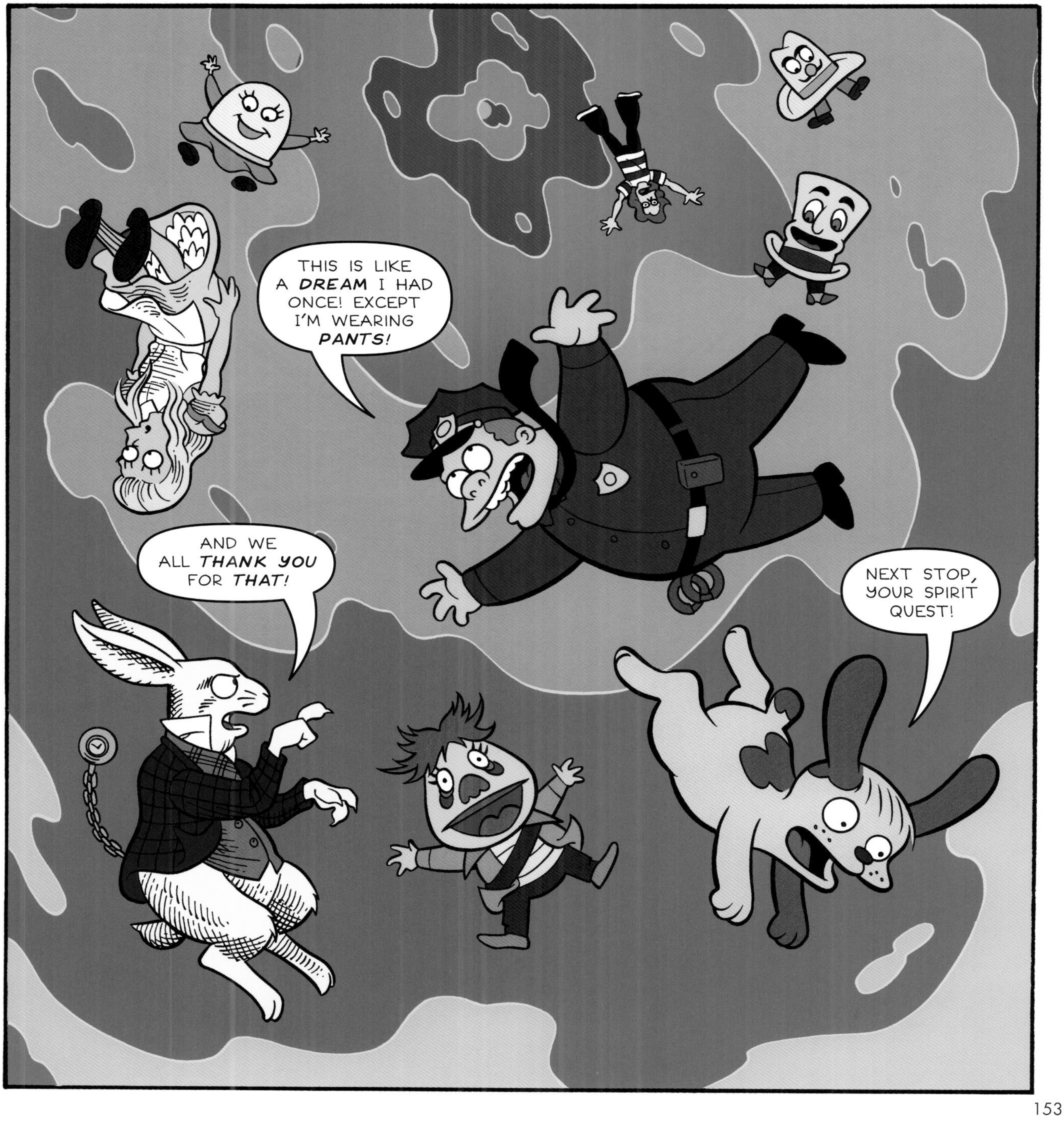
THIS IS LIKE A **DREAM** I HAD ONCE! EXCEPT I'M WEARING **PANTS**!
AND WE ALL **THANK YOU** FOR **THAT**!
NEXT STOP, YOUR SPIRIT QUEST!

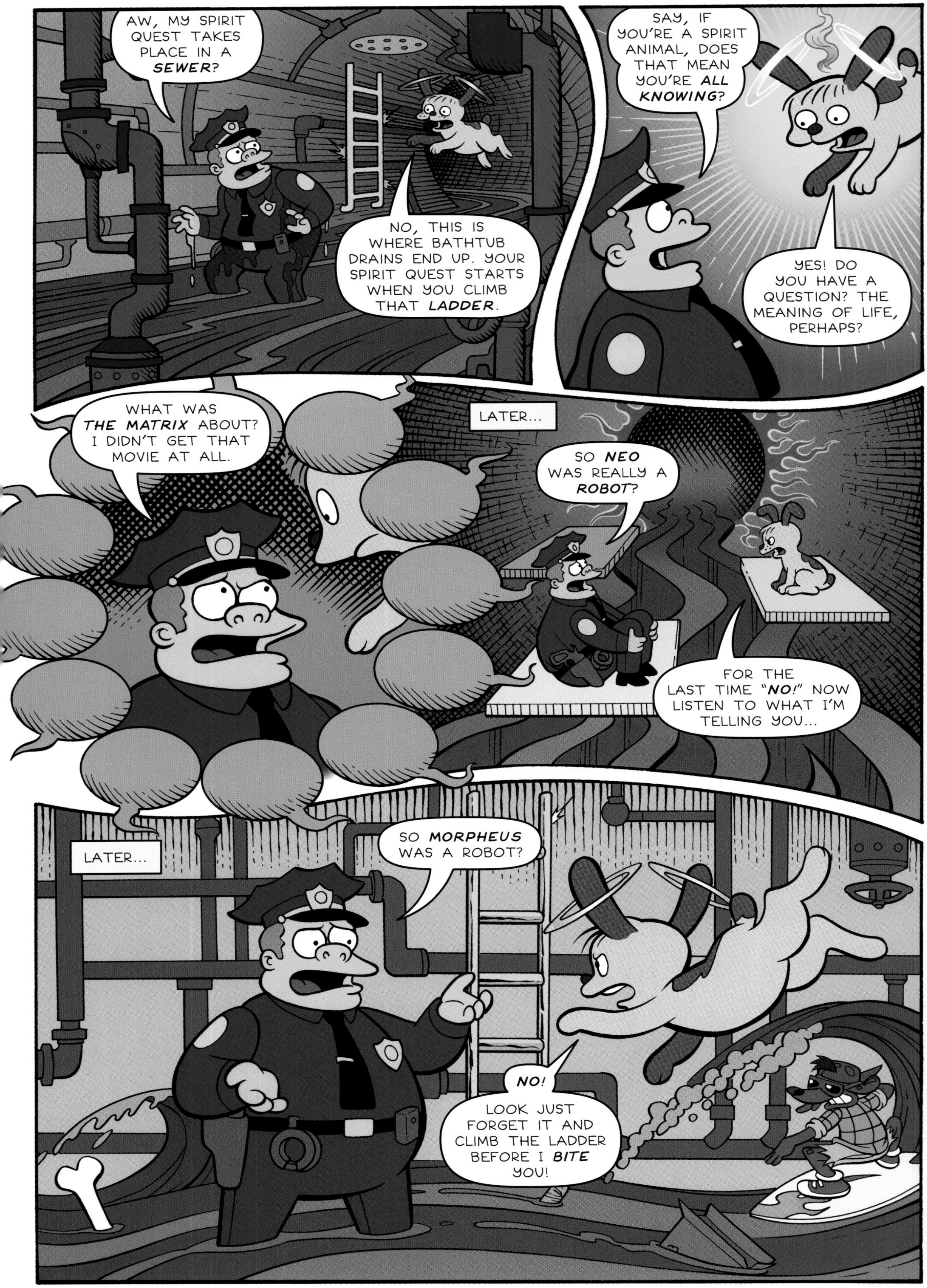
AW, MY SPIRIT QUEST TAKES PLACE IN A SEWER?
NO, THIS IS WHERE BATHTUB DRAINS END UP. YOUR SPIRIT QUEST STARTS WHEN YOU CLIMB THAT LADDER.
SAY, IF YOU'RE A SPIRIT ANIMAL, DOES THAT MEAN YOU'RE ALL KNOWING?
YES! DO YOU HAVE A QUESTION? THE MEANING OF LIFE, PERHAPS?
WHAT WAS THE MATRIX ABOUT? I DIDN'T GET THAT MOVIE AT ALL.
LATER...
SO NEO WAS REALLY A ROBOT?
FOR THE LAST TIME "NO!" NOW LISTEN TO WHAT I'M TELLING YOU...
LATER...
SO MORPHEUS WAS A ROBOT?
NO!
LOOK JUST FORGET IT AND CLIMB THE LADDER BEFORE I BITE YOU!

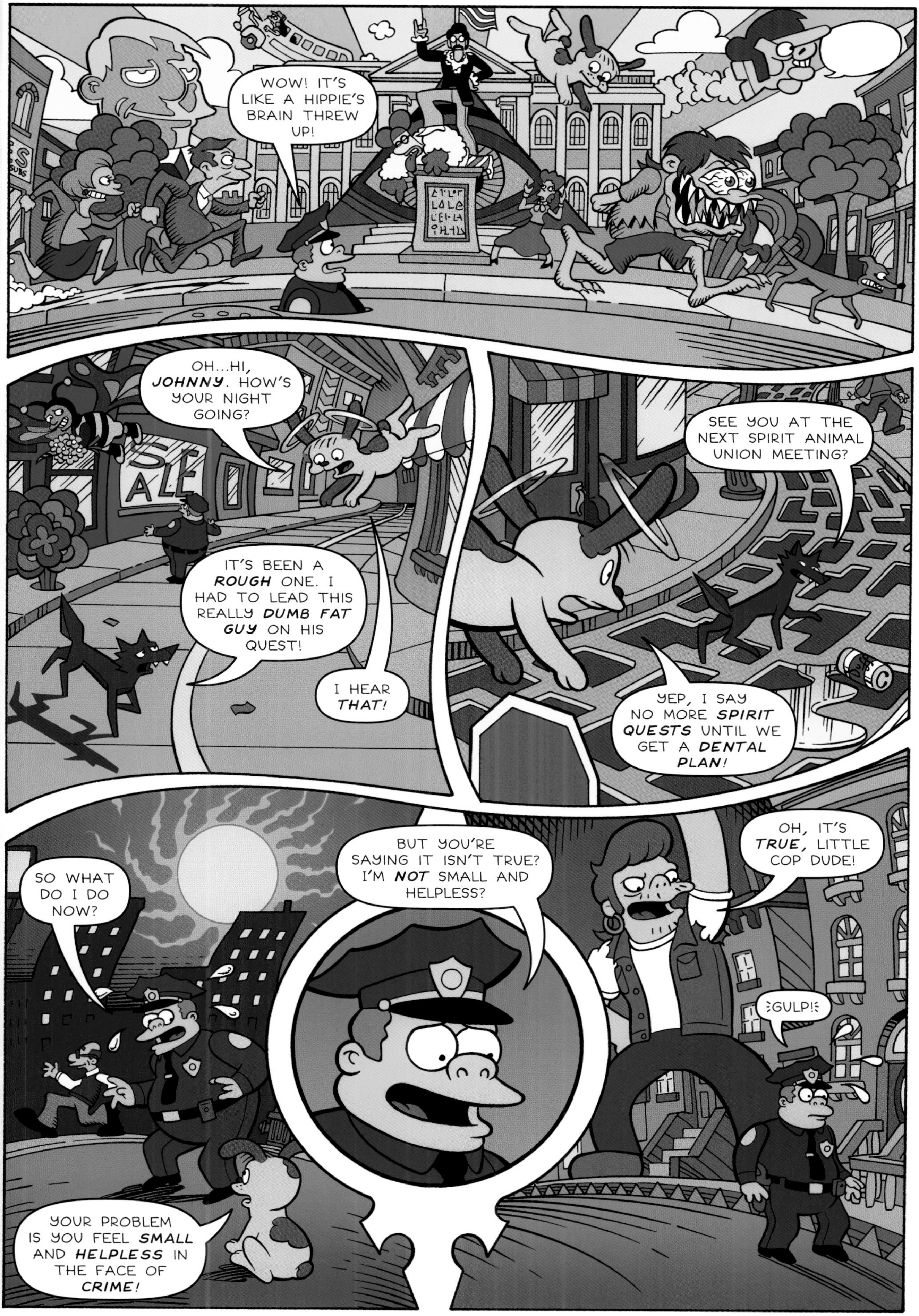

WOW! IT'S LIKE A HIPPIE'S BRAIN THREW UP!
OH...HI, JOHNNY. HOW'S YOUR NIGHT GOING?
IT'S BEEN A ROUGH ONE. I HAD TO LEAD THIS REALLY DUMB FAT GUY ON HIS QUEST!
I HEAR THAT!
SEE YOU AT THE NEXT SPIRIT ANIMAL UNION MEETING?
YEP, I SAY NO MORE SPIRIT QUESTS UNTIL WE GET A DENTAL PLAN!
SO WHAT DO I DO NOW?
YOUR PROBLEM IS YOU FEEL SMALL AND HELPLESS IN THE FACE OF CRIME!
BUT YOU'RE SAYING IT ISN'T TRUE? I'M NOT SMALL AND HELPLESS?
OH, IT'S TRUE, LITTLE COP DUDE!
GULP!

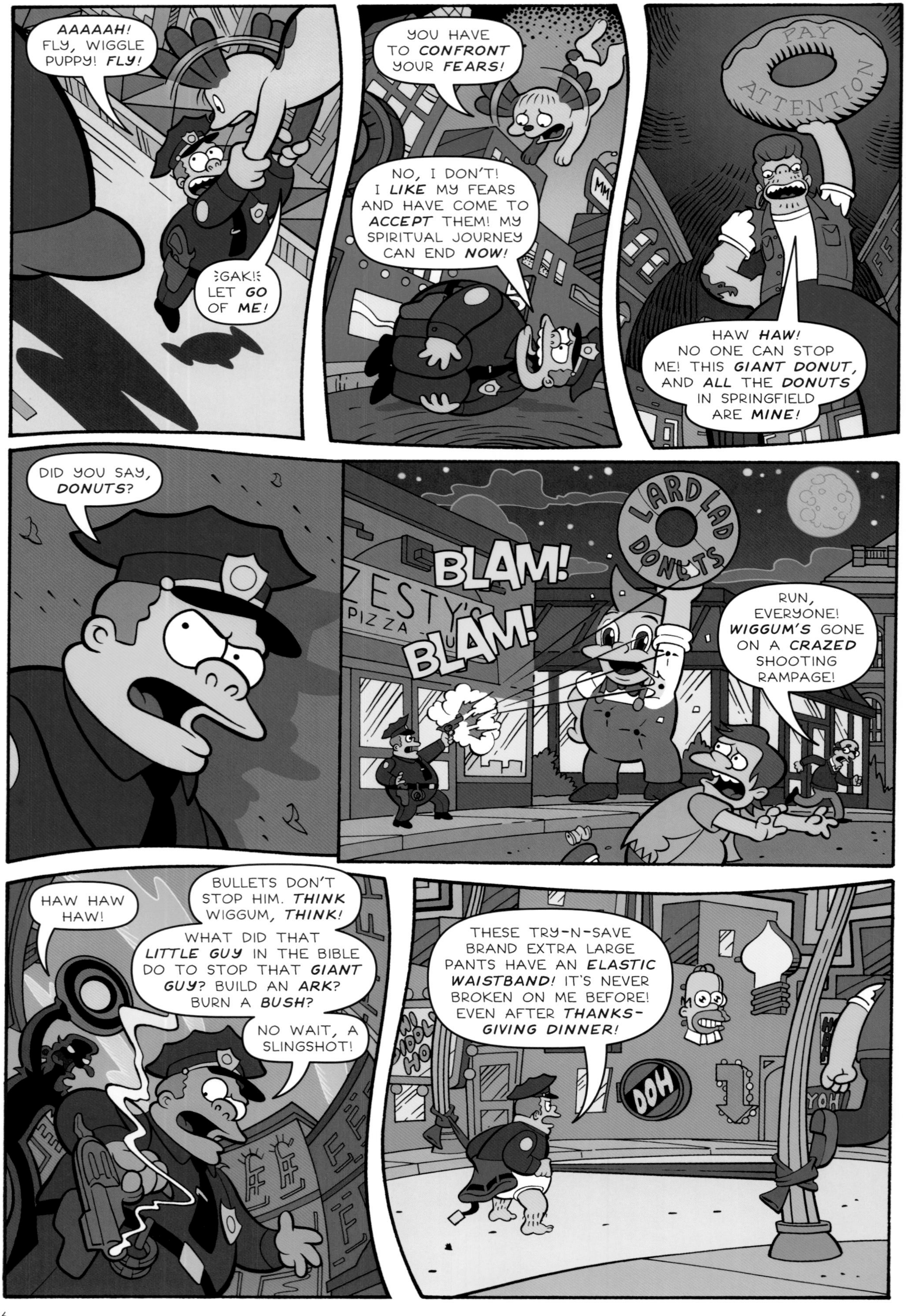
AAAAAH! FLY, WIGGLE PUPPY! FLY!
¡GAK!¡ LET GO OF ME!
YOU HAVE TO CONFRONT YOUR FEARS!
NO, I DON'T! I LIKE MY FEARS AND HAVE COME TO ACCEPT THEM! MY SPIRITUAL JOURNEY CAN END NOW!
PAY ATTENTION
HAW HAW! NO ONE CAN STOP ME! THIS GIANT DONUT, AND ALL THE DONUTS IN SPRINGFIELD ARE MINE!
DID YOU SAY, DONUTS?
LARD LAD DONUTS
ZESTY'S PIZZA
BLAM!
BLAM!
RUN, EVERYONE! WIGGUM'S GONE ON A CRAZED SHOOTING RAMPAGE!
HAW HAW HAW!
BULLETS DON'T STOP HIM. THINK WIGGUM, THINK!
WHAT DID THAT LITTLE GUY IN THE BIBLE DO TO STOP THAT GIANT GUY? BUILD AN ARK? BURN A BUSH?
NO WAIT, A SLINGSHOT!
THESE TRY-N-SAVE BRAND EXTRA LARGE PANTS HAVE AN ELASTIC WAISTBAND! IT'S NEVER BROKEN ON ME BEFORE! EVEN AFTER THANKSGIVING DINNER!
DOH

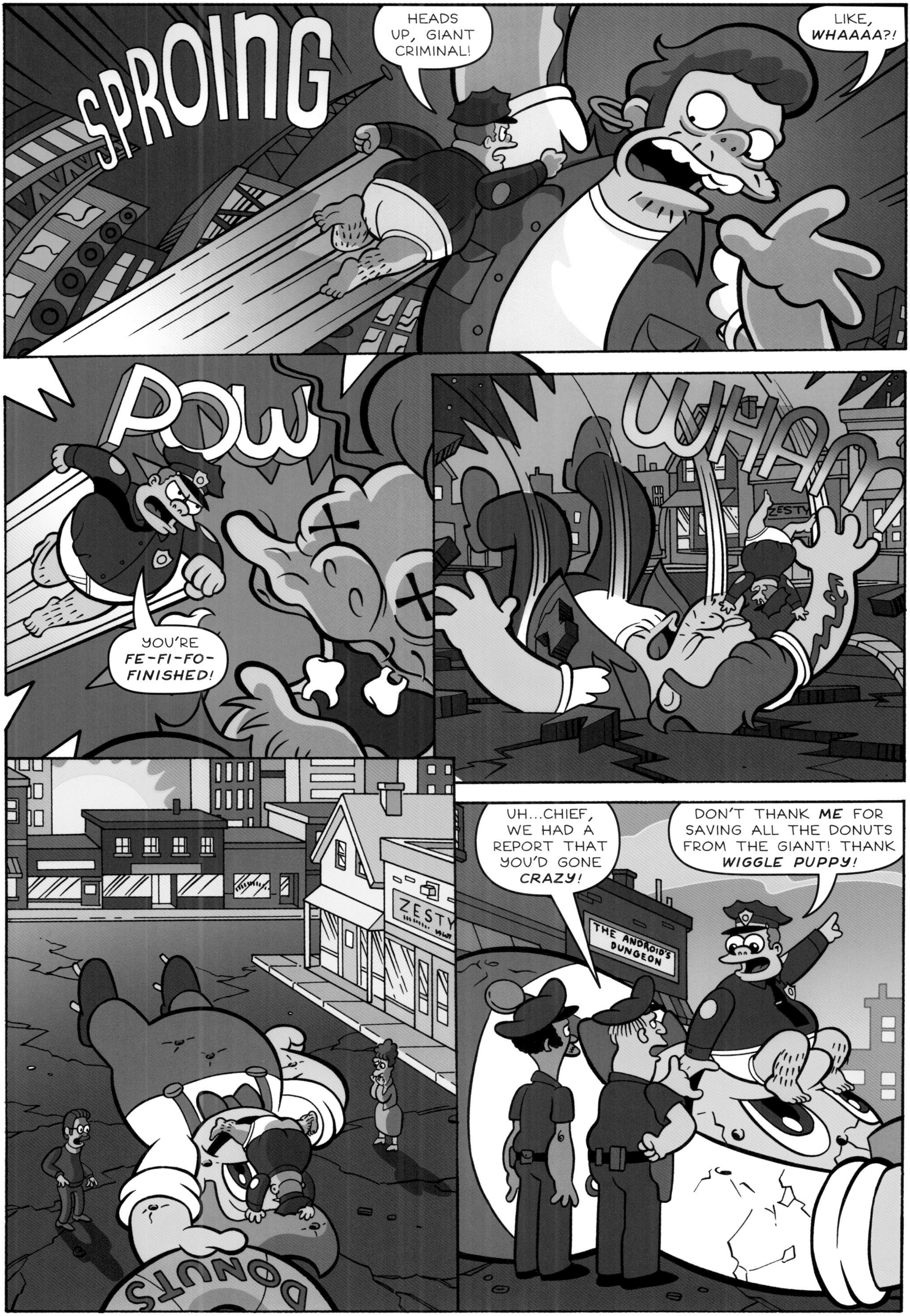
SPROING
HEADS UP, GIANT CRIMINAL!
LIKE, WHAAAA?!
POW
YOU'RE FE-FI-FO-FINISHED!
WHAM
ZESTY
ZESTY
DONUTS
UH...CHIEF, WE HAD A REPORT THAT YOU'D GONE CRAZY!
DON'T THANK ME FOR SAVING ALL THE DONUTS FROM THE GIANT! THANK WIGGLE PUPPY!
THE ANDROID'S DUNGEON

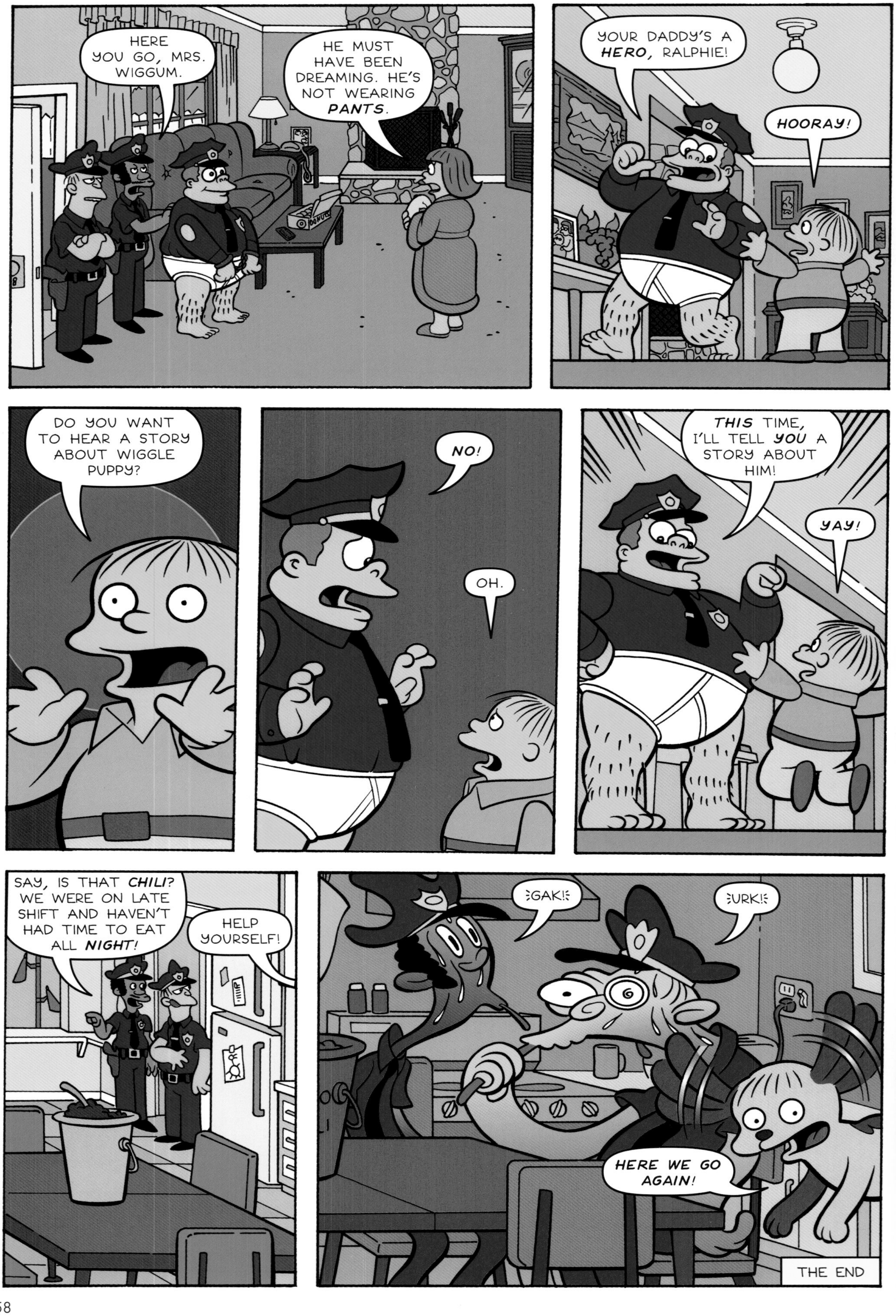
HERE YOU GO, MRS. WIGGUM.
HE MUST HAVE BEEN DREAMING. HE'S NOT WEARING PANTS.
DONUTS
YOUR DADDY'S A HERO, RALPHIE!
HOORAY!
DO YOU WANT TO HEAR A STORY ABOUT WIGGLE PUPPY?
NO!
OH.
THIS TIME, I'LL TELL YOU A STORY ABOUT HIM!
YAY!
SAY, IS THAT CHILI? WE WERE ON LATE SHIFT AND HAVEN'T HAD TIME TO EAT ALL NIGHT!
HELP YOURSELF!
GAK!
URK!
HERE WE GO AGAIN!
THE END

COVER GALLERY

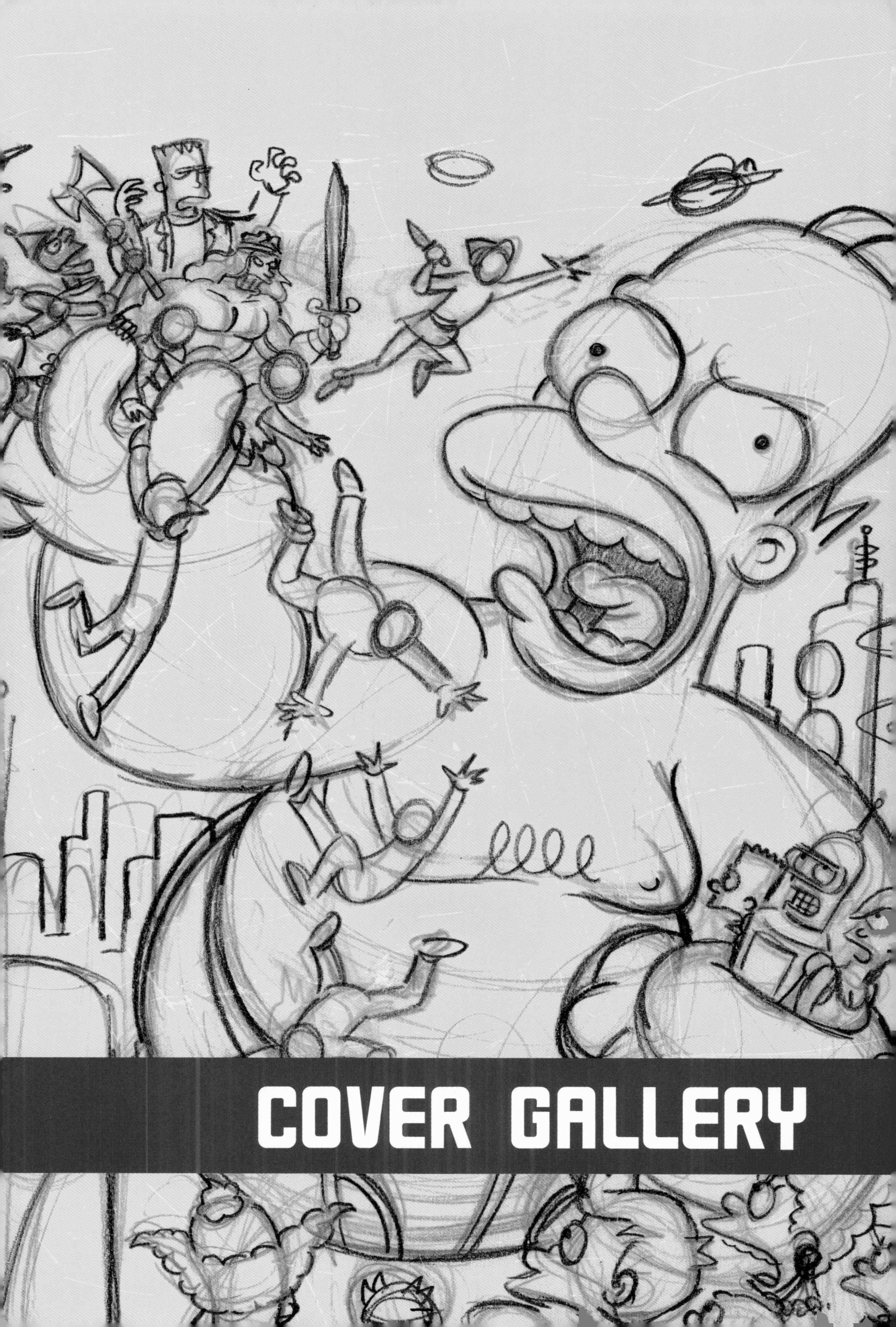

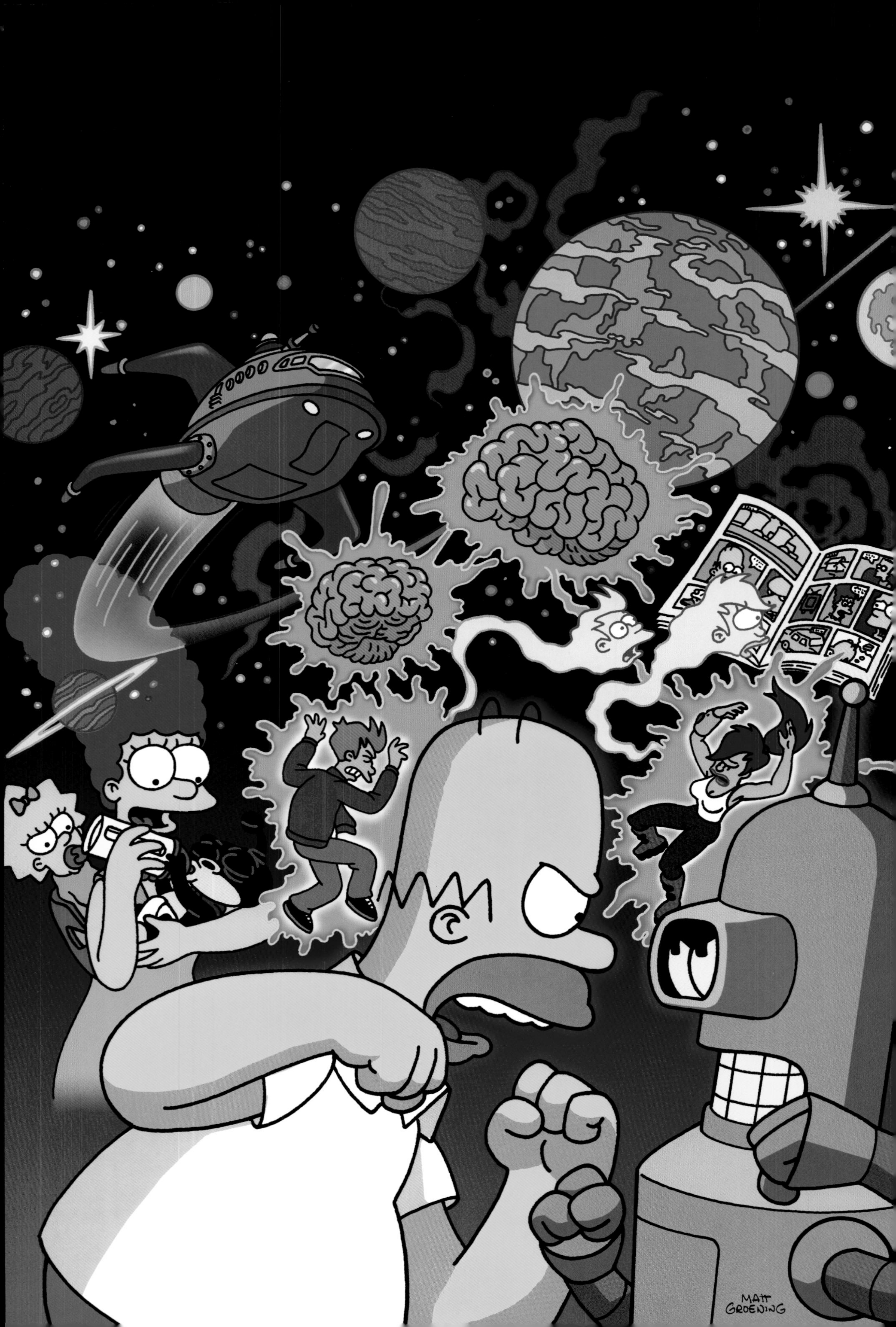
MATT GROENING

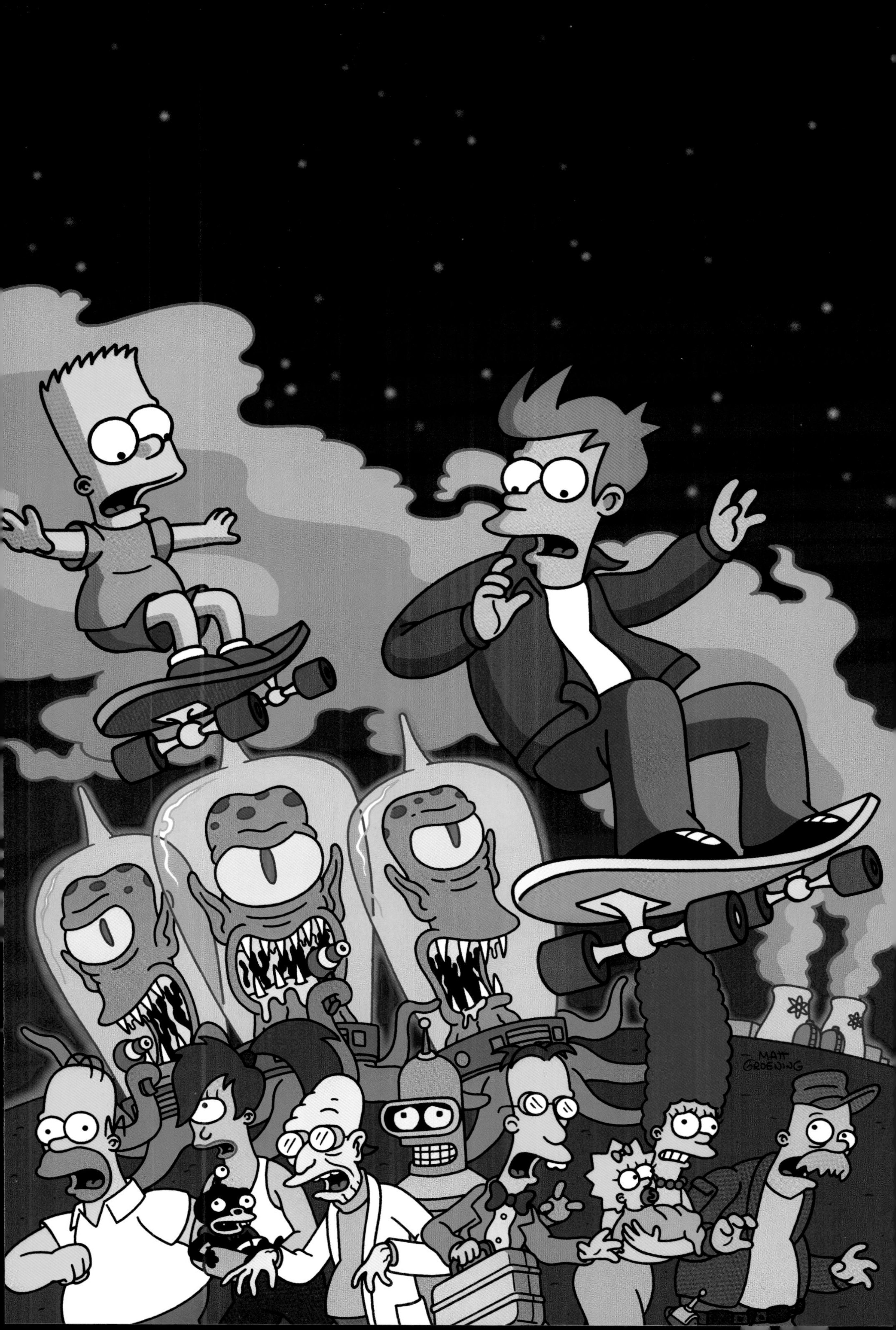

— MATT GROENING

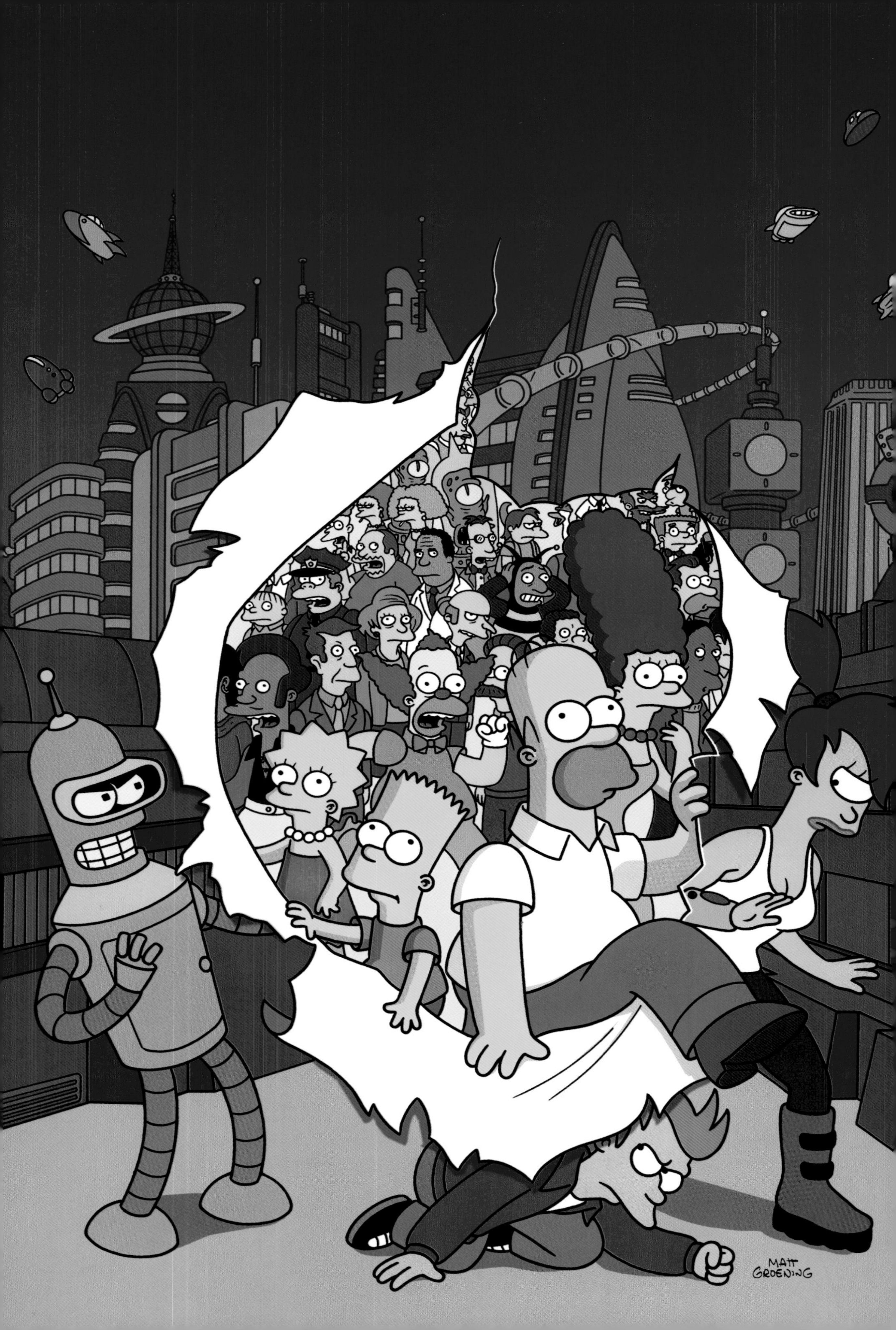
MATT
GROENING

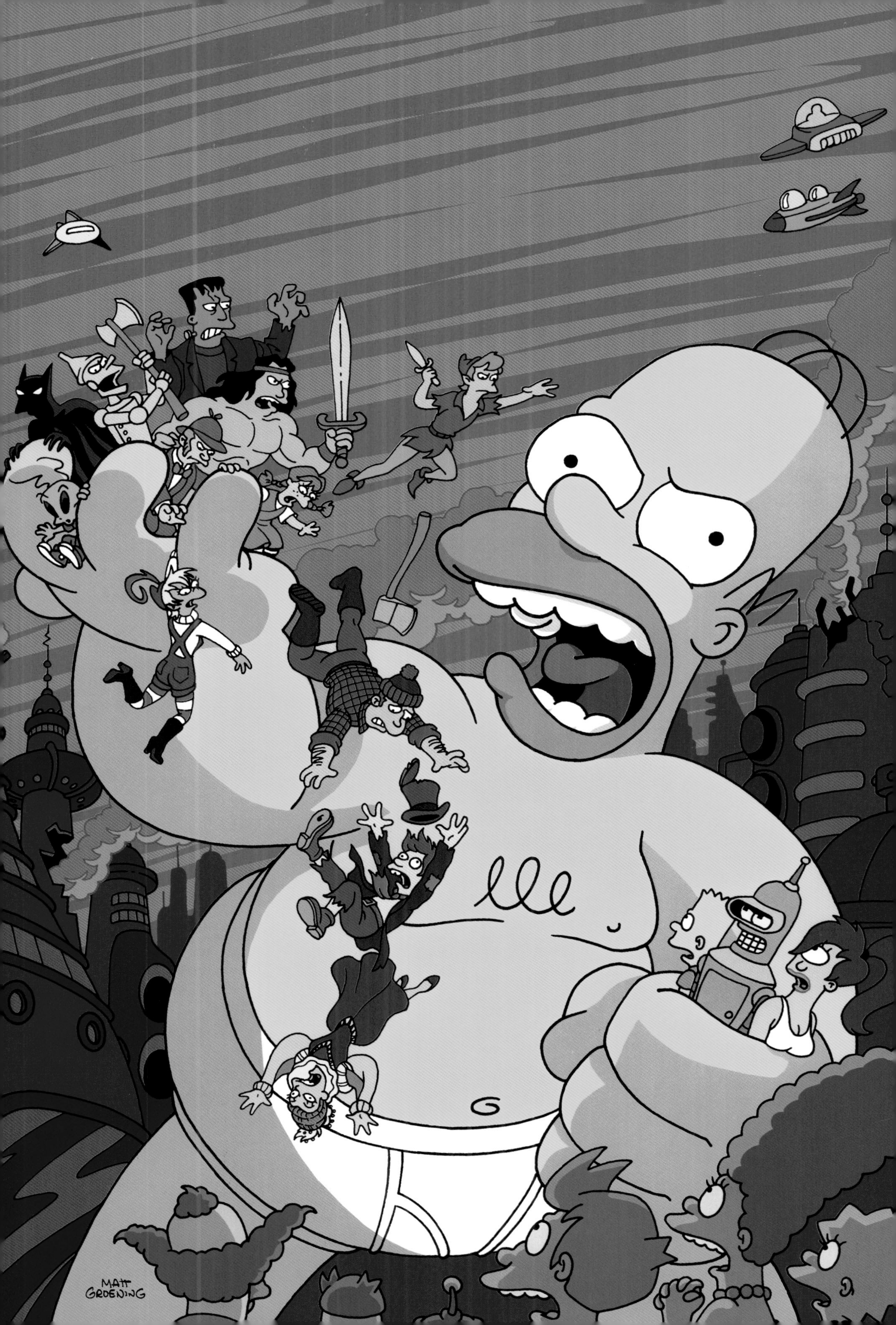
MATT GROENING

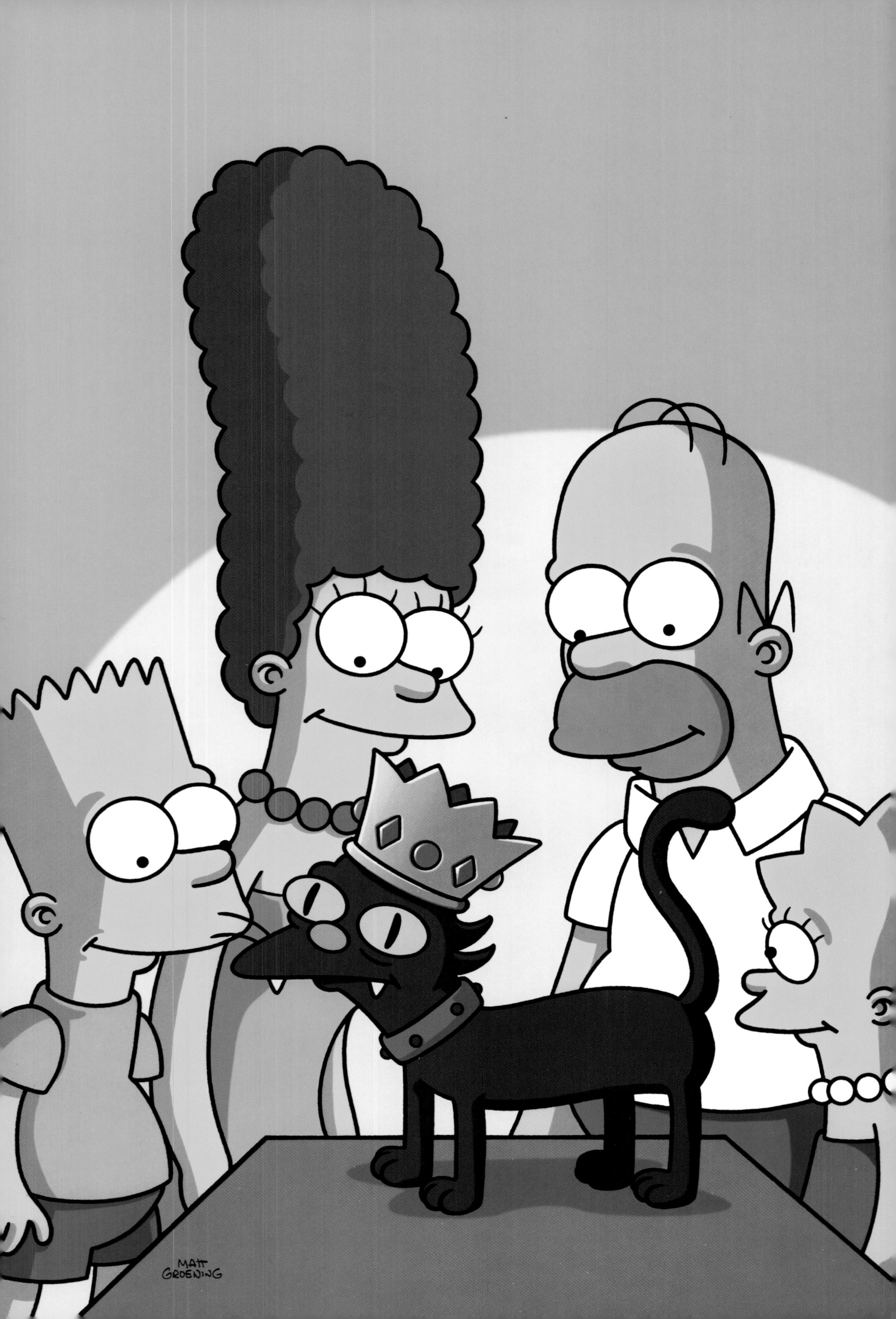
MATT
GROENING

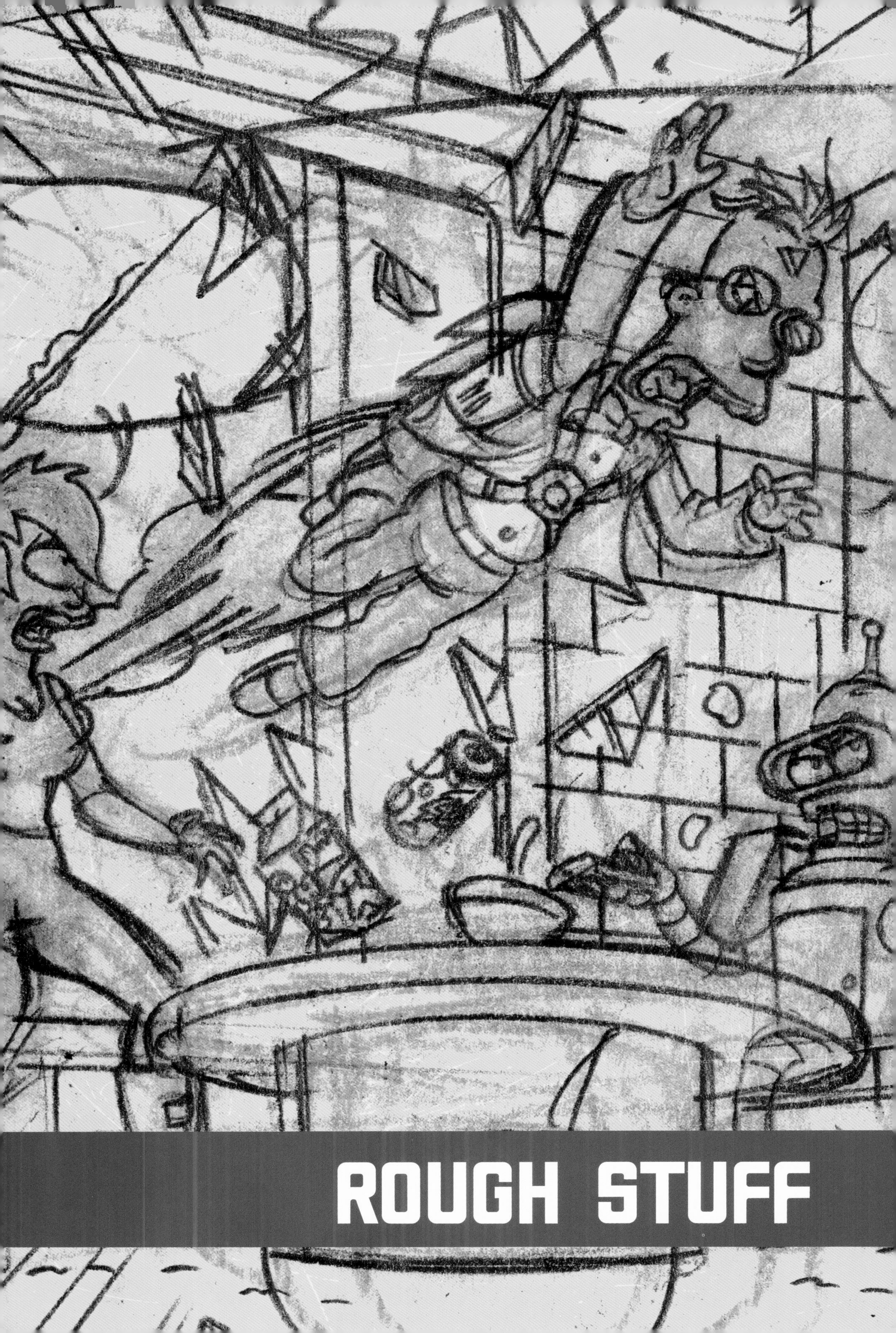

ROUGH STUFF

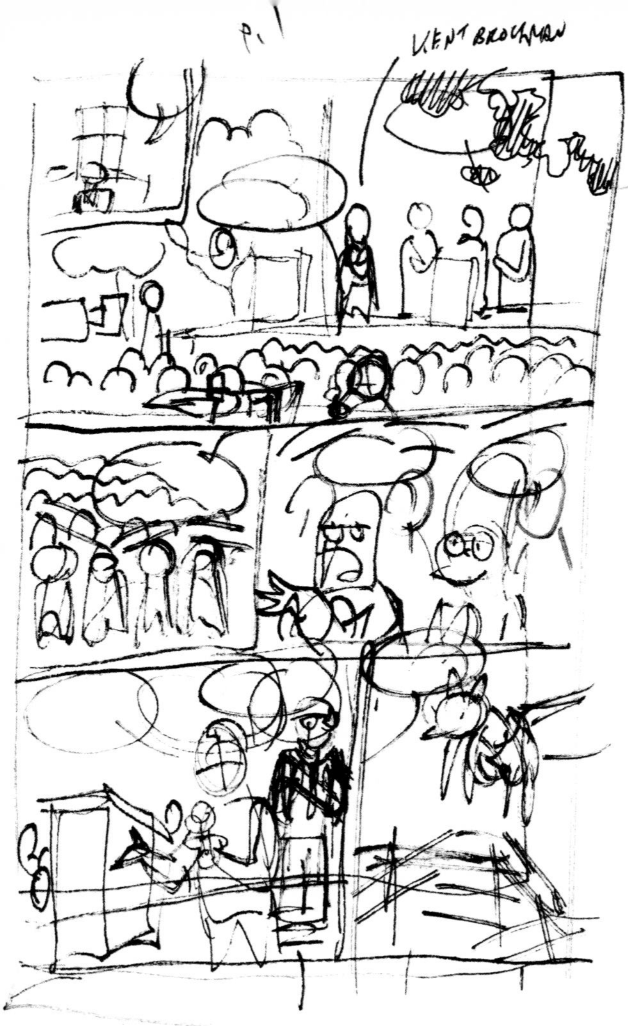
p. 1
KENT BROCKMAN

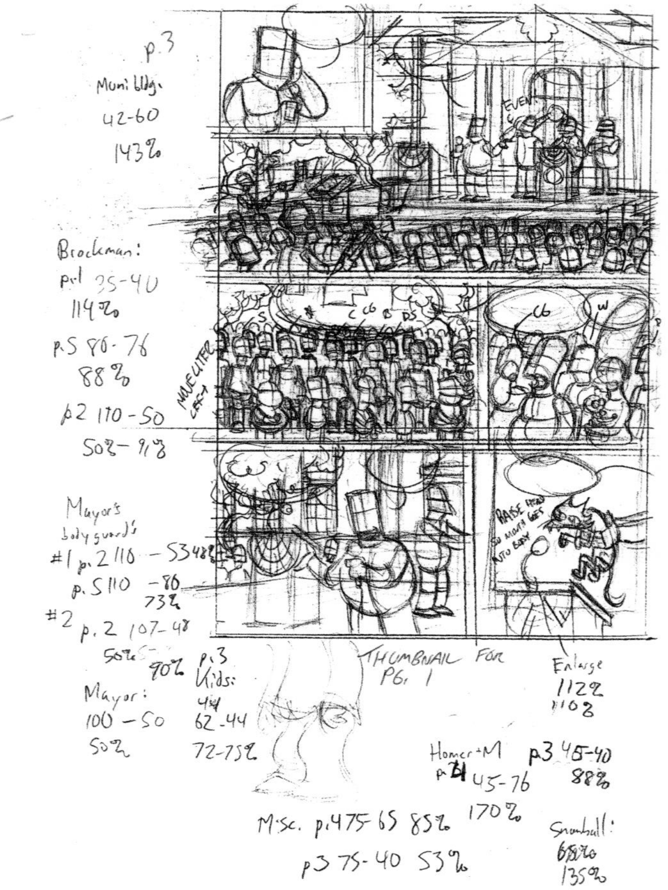
p.3
Muni Bldg.
42-60
143%
Brockman:
p.1 35-40
114%
p.5 80-76
88%
p2 110-50
50%-91%
Mayor's
bodyguards
Mayor:
100-50
50%
p.3
Kids:
44
62-44
72-75%
THUMBNAIL FOR
PG. 1
Enlarge
112%
110%
Homer+M
p3 45-40
88%
170%
Misc. p.4 75-65 85%
p3 75-40 53%
Snowball:
135%

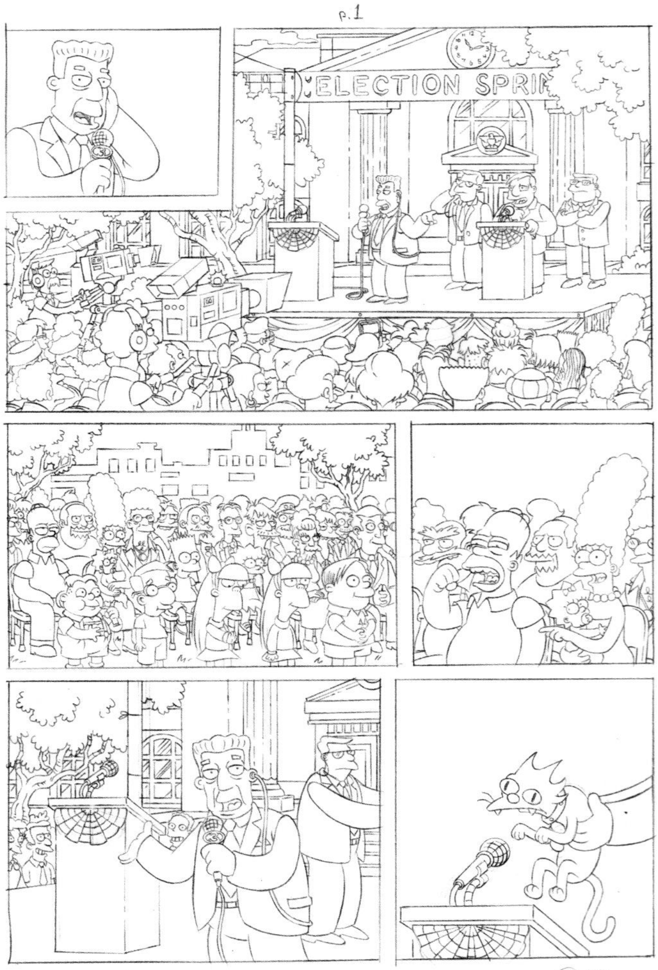
p. 1
ELECTION SPRI

GOOD NEWS, EVERYONE!

We have two dozen, or so, extra pages, so we thought you might enjoy a rare glimpse of the creative process behind this epic saga!

The Matt Groening style may look simple and easy to replicate, but the following thumbnail layouts, rough pencils, and character designs illustrate how brilliant composition, careful storytelling, beautiful design, and lots of precise drawing all come into play when bringing Matt's characters to the comic book page!

Here is a beautiful example of the process from loose thumbnail design, to rough layout, to finished tight pencil drawing. The final inked, colored, and lettered version of this page can be seen on page 72 of this book.

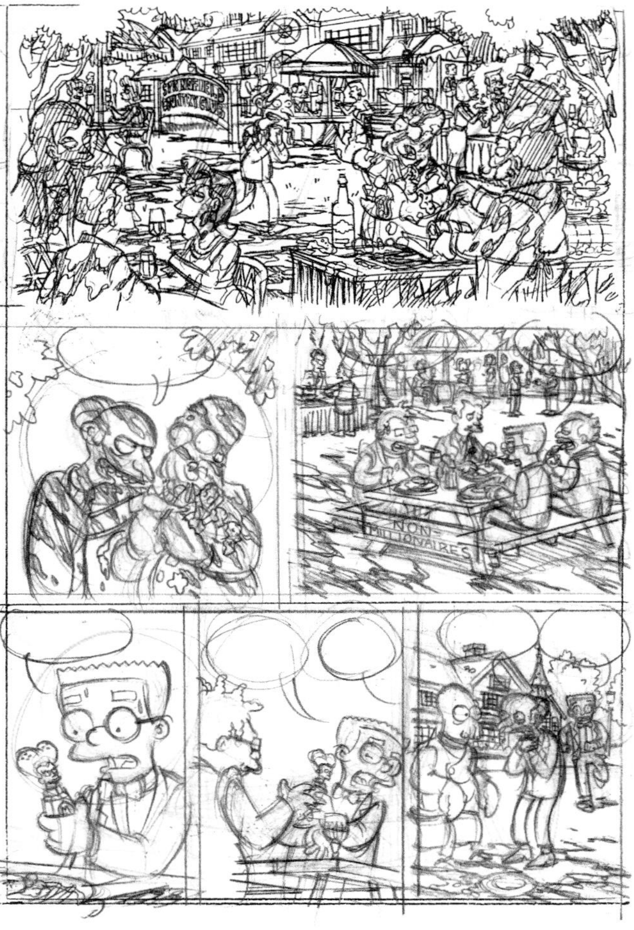
SPRINGFIELD COUNTRY CLUB
NON-MILLIONAIRES

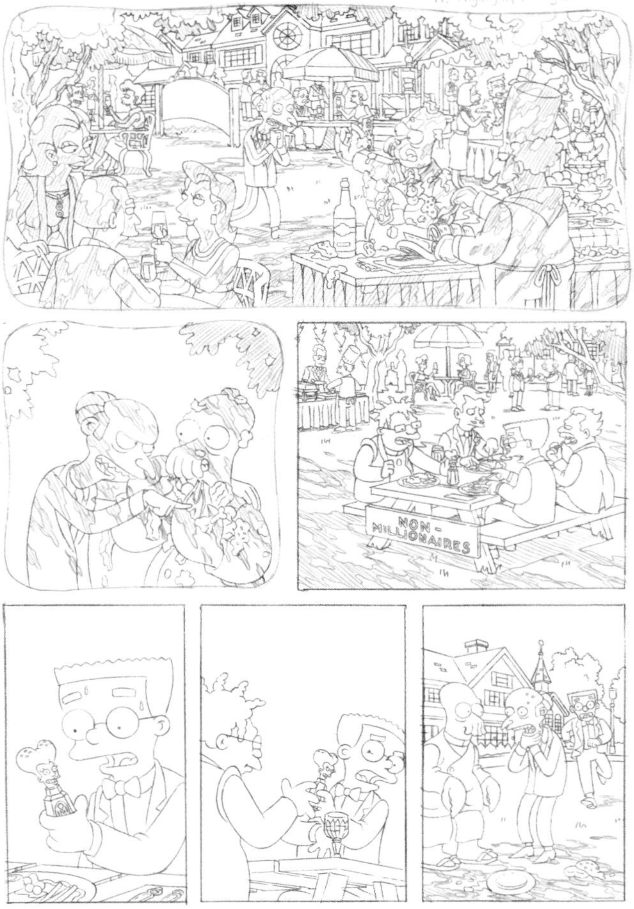
NON-MILLIONAIRES

Raise table

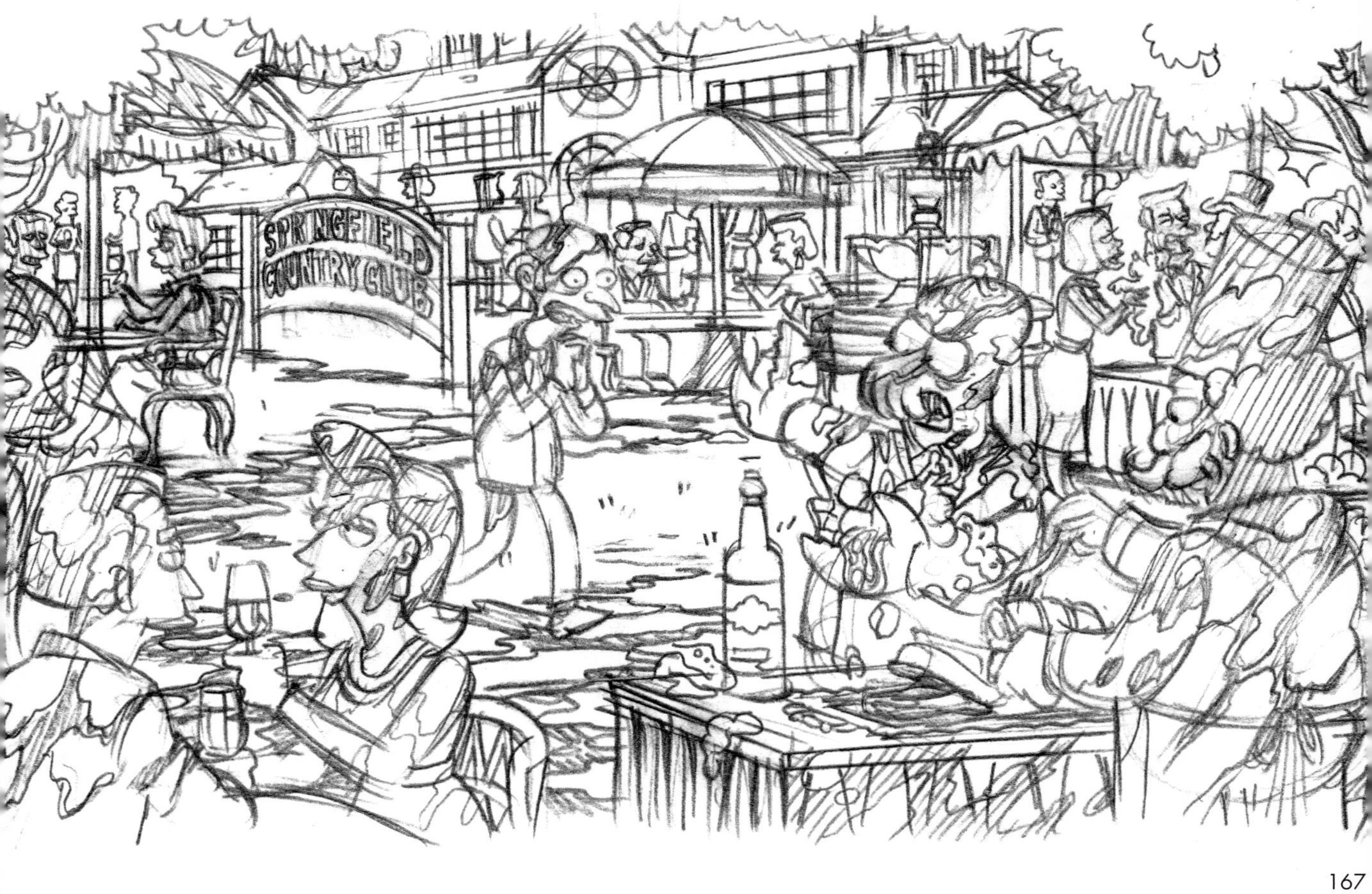
SPRINGFIELD COUNTRY CLUB

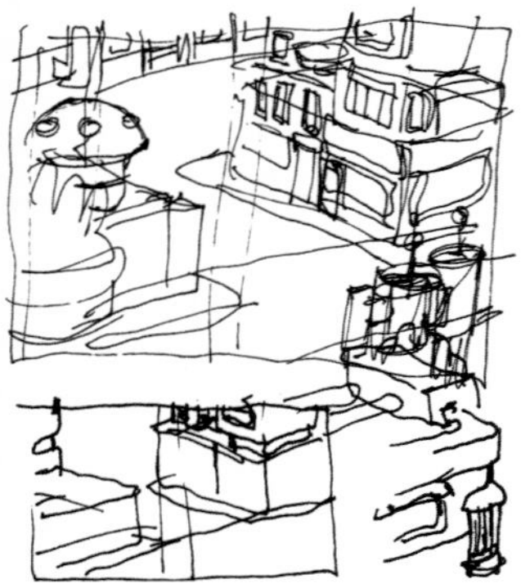

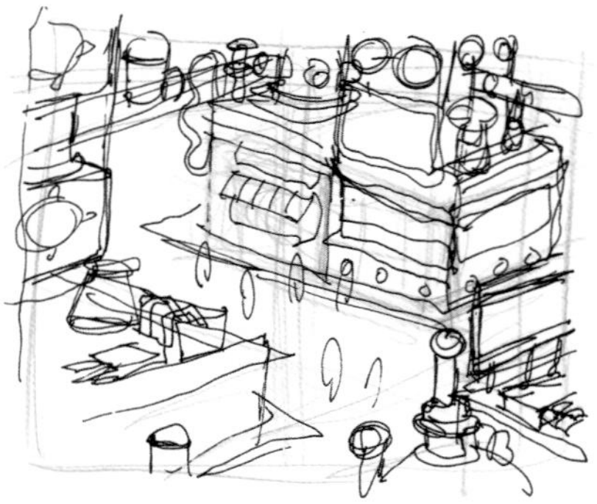

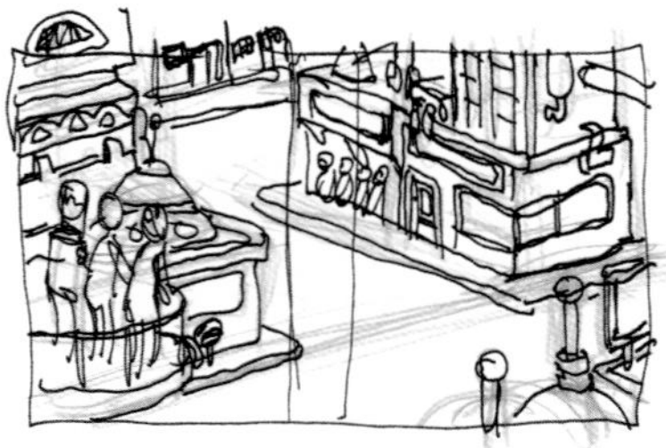

Here is the complete evolution, from very loose thumbnail sketches to tight finished pencils, of a fantastically complicated spread! The final version of these pages is located on pages 58 and 59.

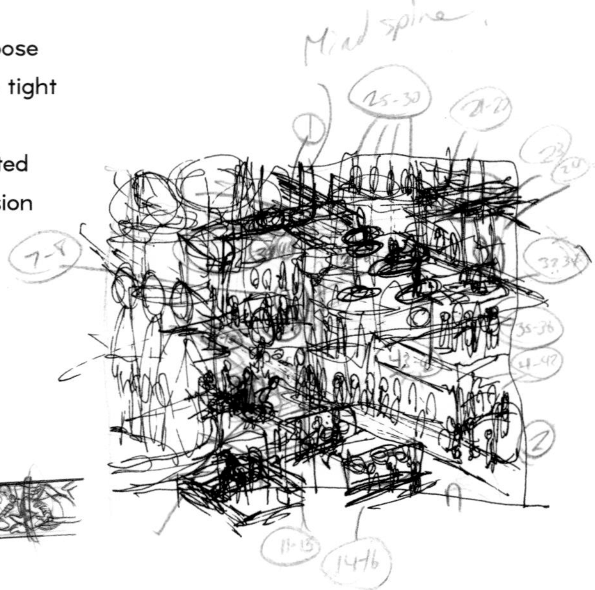
Mind spine!

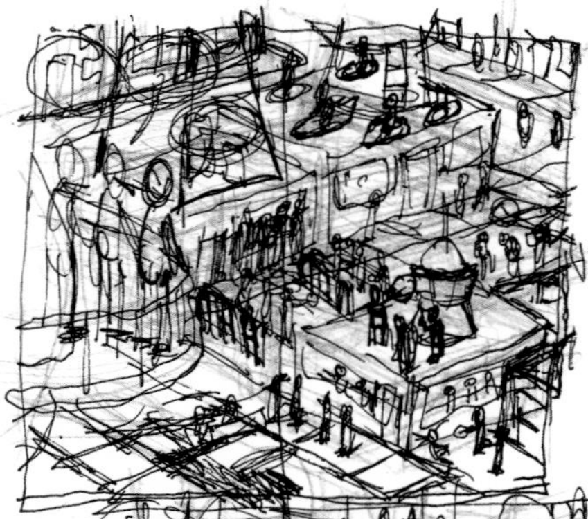

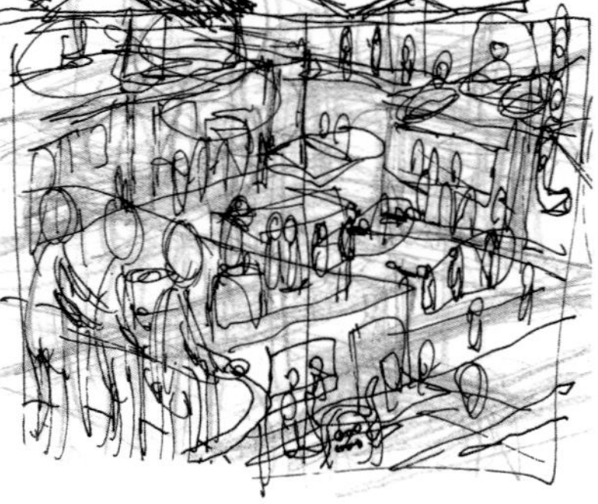

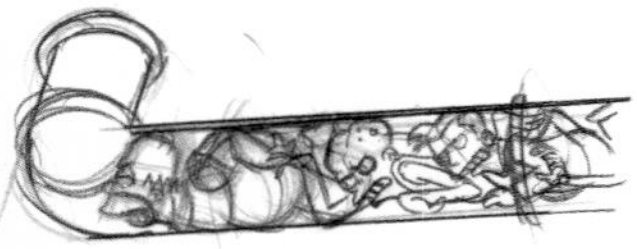

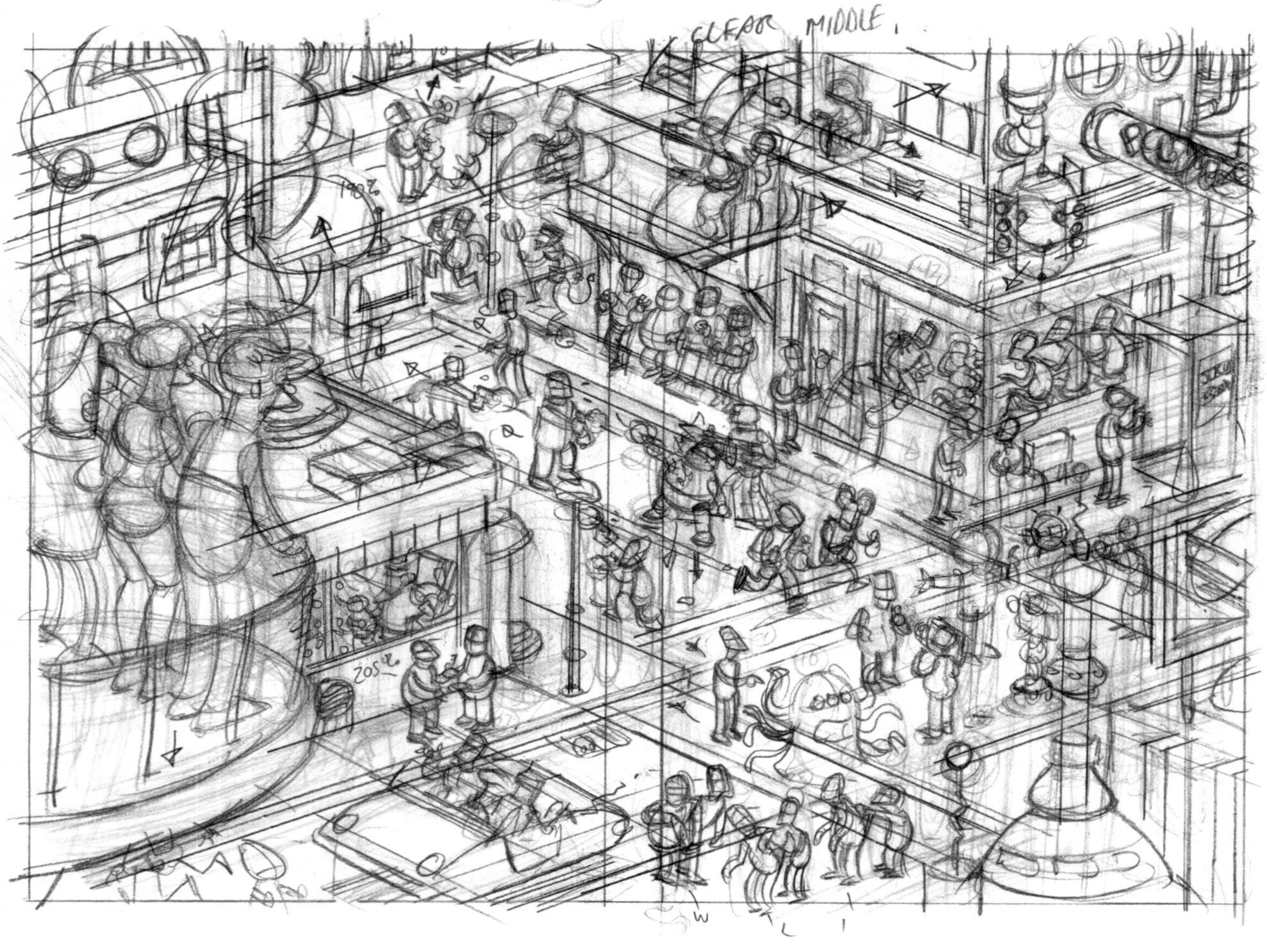
CLEAR MIDDLE

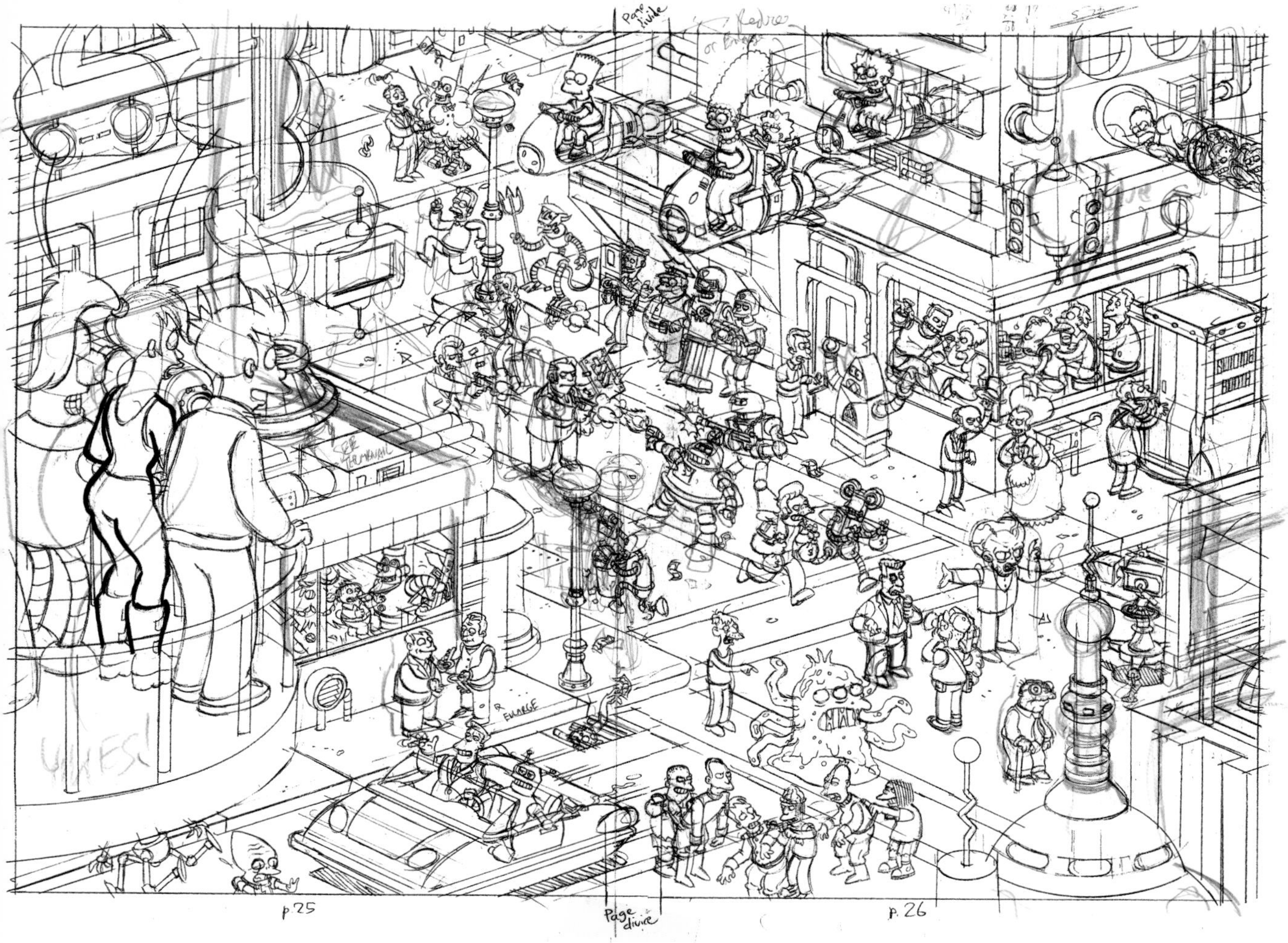

SUICIDE BOOTH
p.25
Page divide
p.26

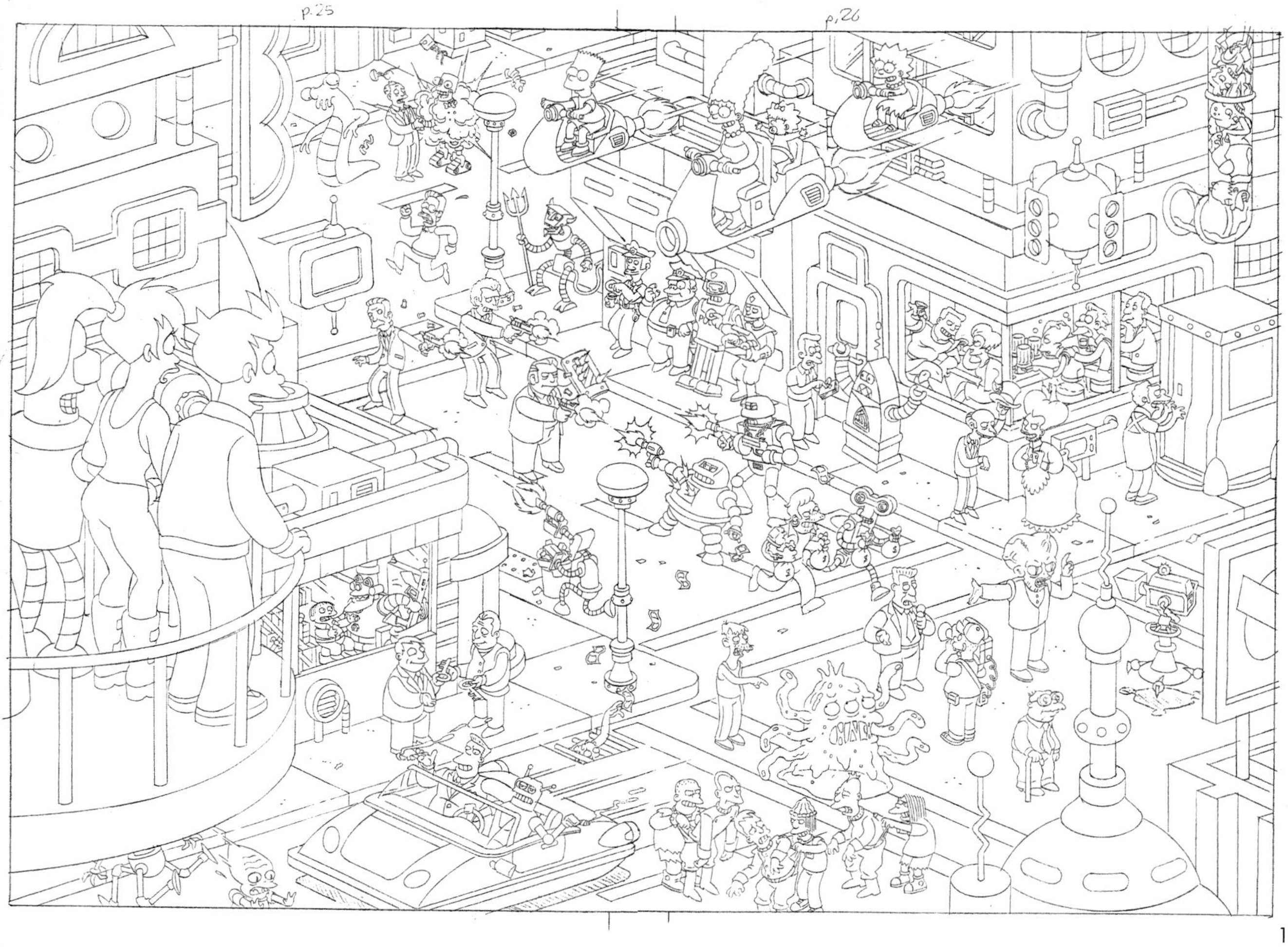

p.25
p.26

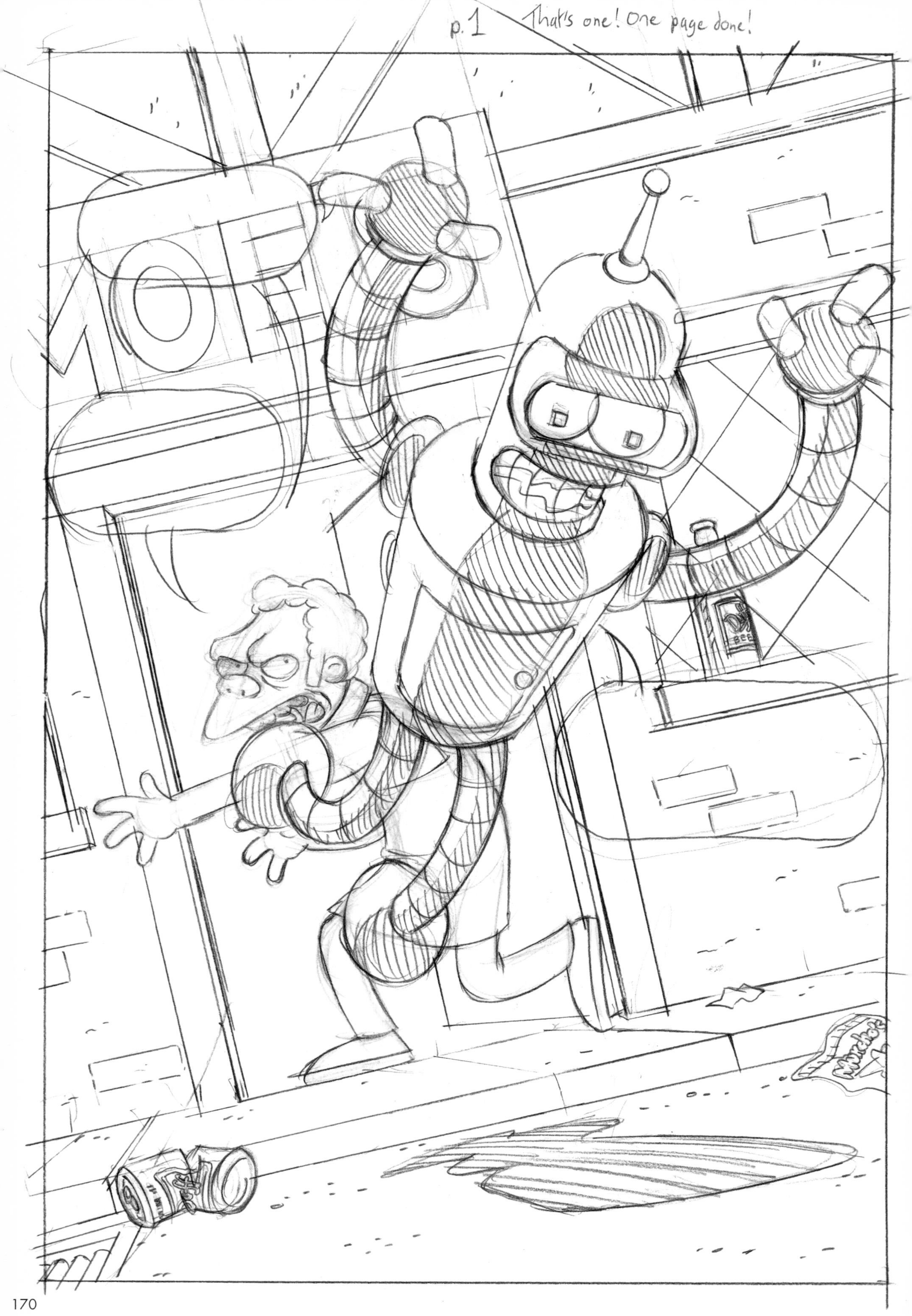
p. 1
That's one! One page done!

p.3

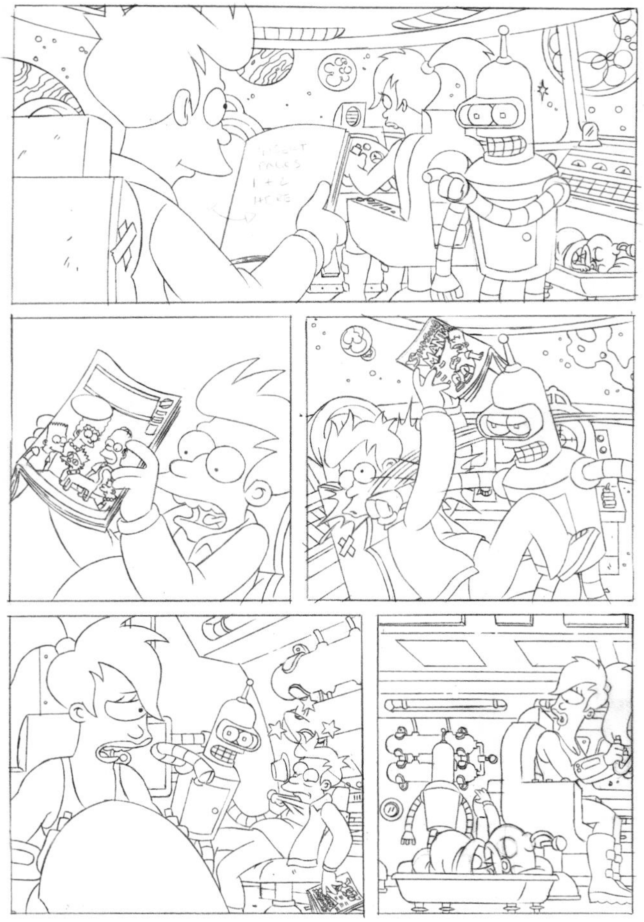

INSERT PAGES 1 + 2 HERE

p.10

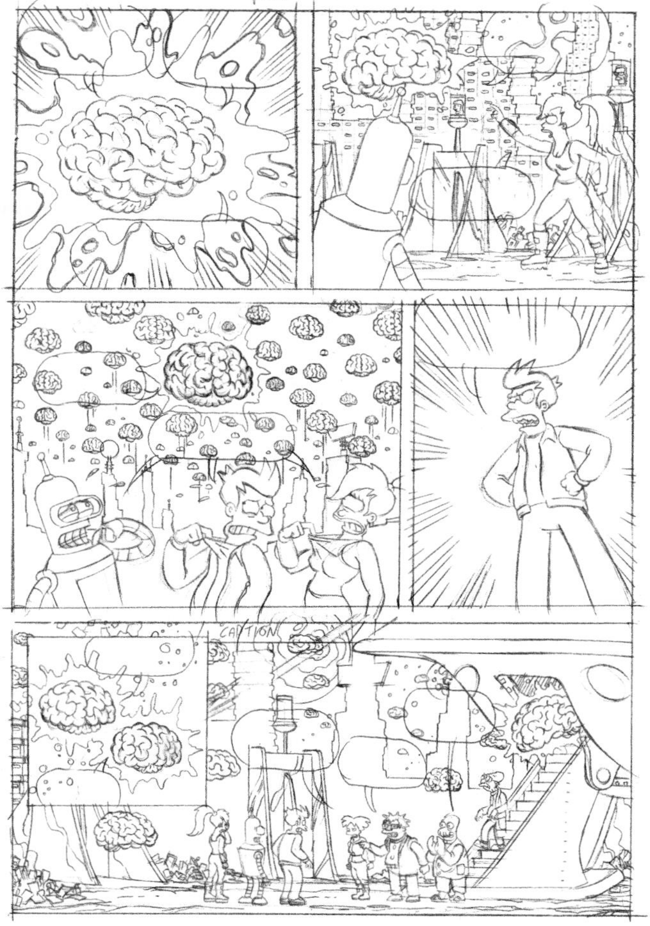

CAPTION

p.11

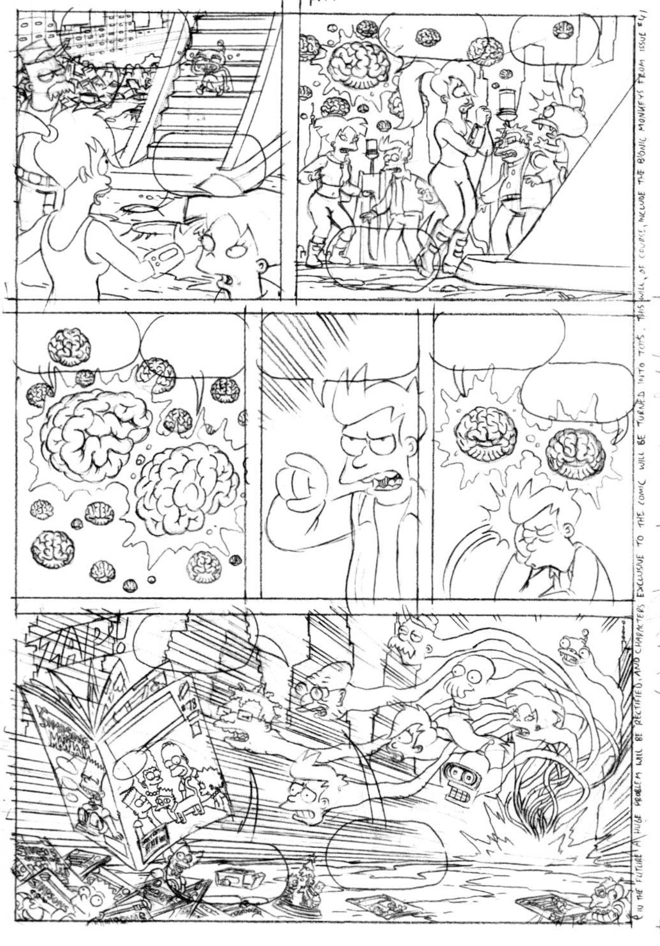

ZAP!
IN THE FUTURE A HUGE PROBLEM WILL BE RECTIFIED, AND CHARACTERS EXCLUSIVE TO THE COMIC WILL BE TURNED INTO TOYS. THIS WILL, OF COURSE, INCLUDE THE BIONIC MONKEYS FROM ISSUE #41

p.20

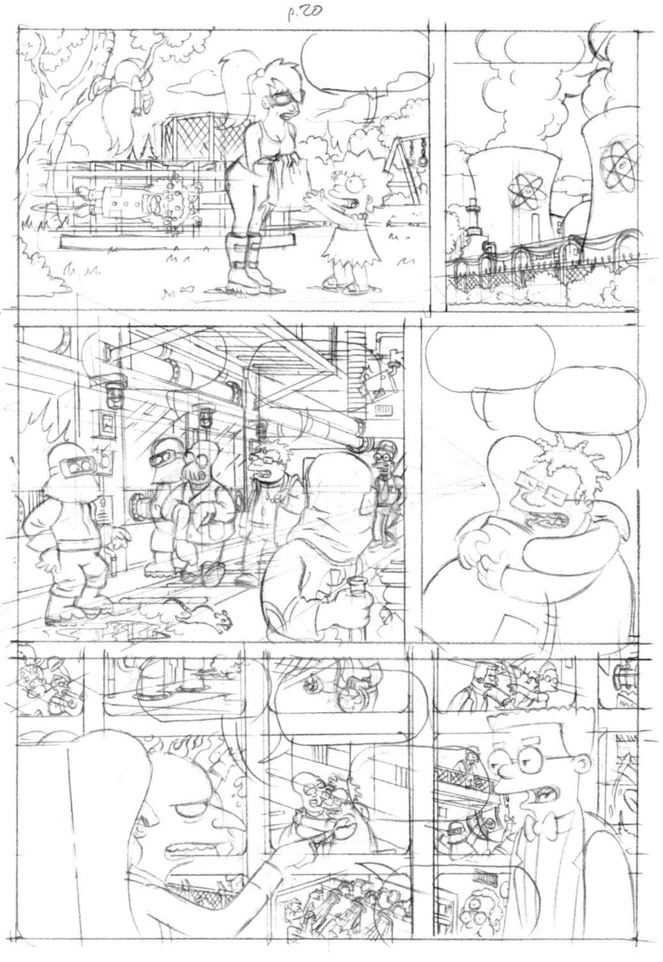

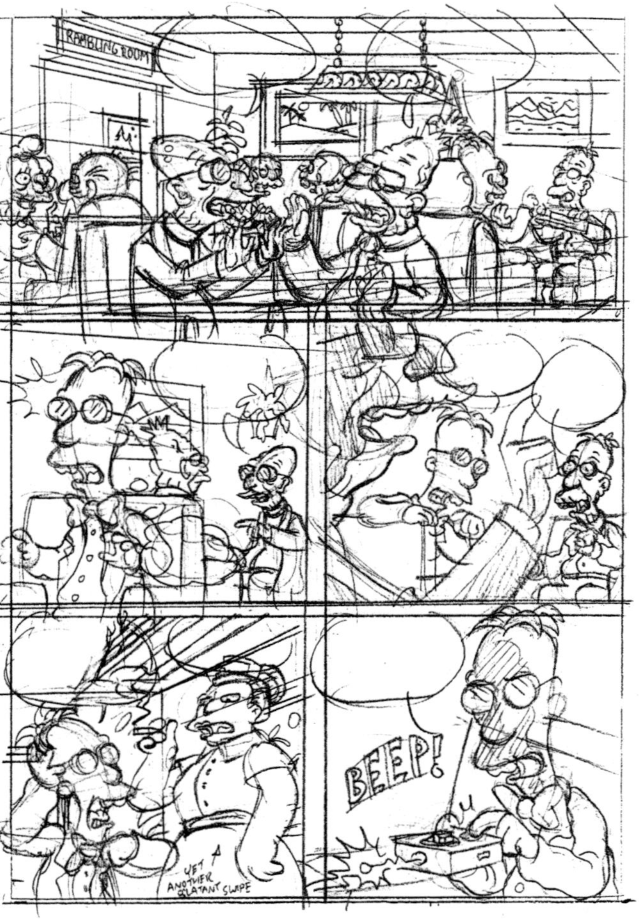
RAMBLING ROOM
BEEP!
YET ANOTHER BLATANT SWIPE

p.8

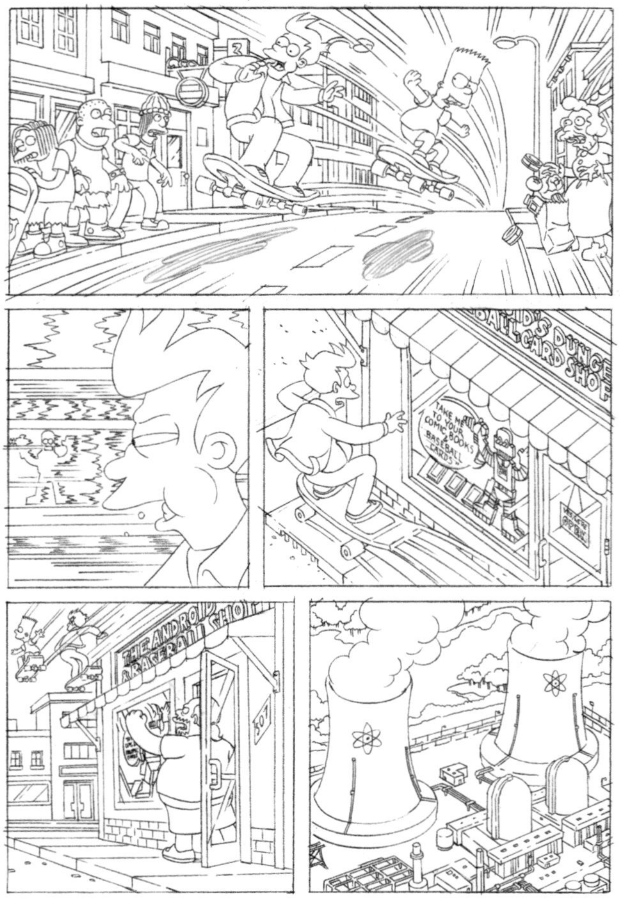
TAKE ME TO YOUR COMIC BOOKS & BASEBALL CARDS

p.14

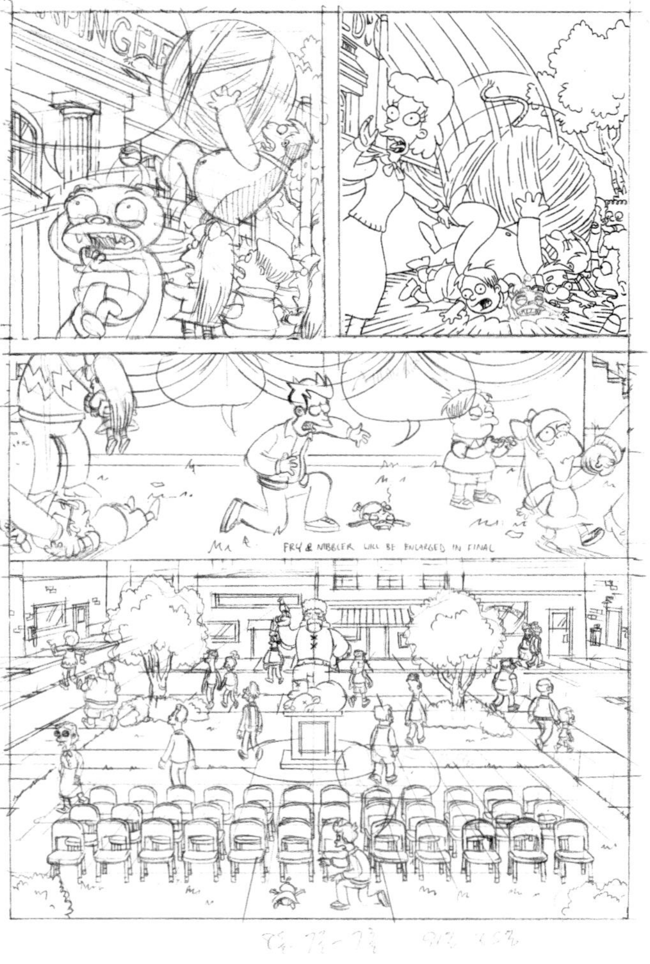
FRY & NIBBLER WILL BE ENLARGED IN FINAL

p.15

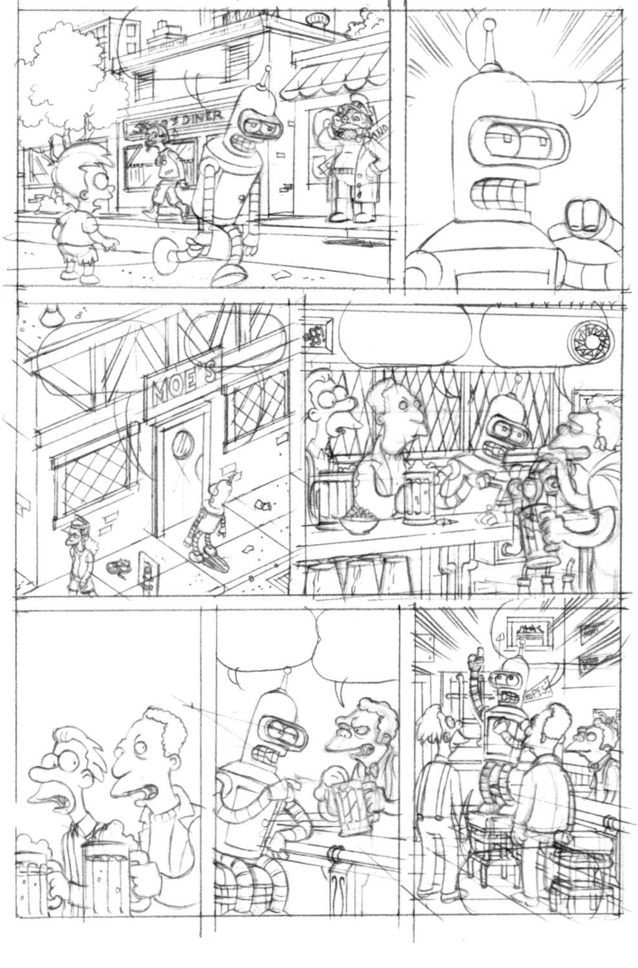
DINER
MOE'S

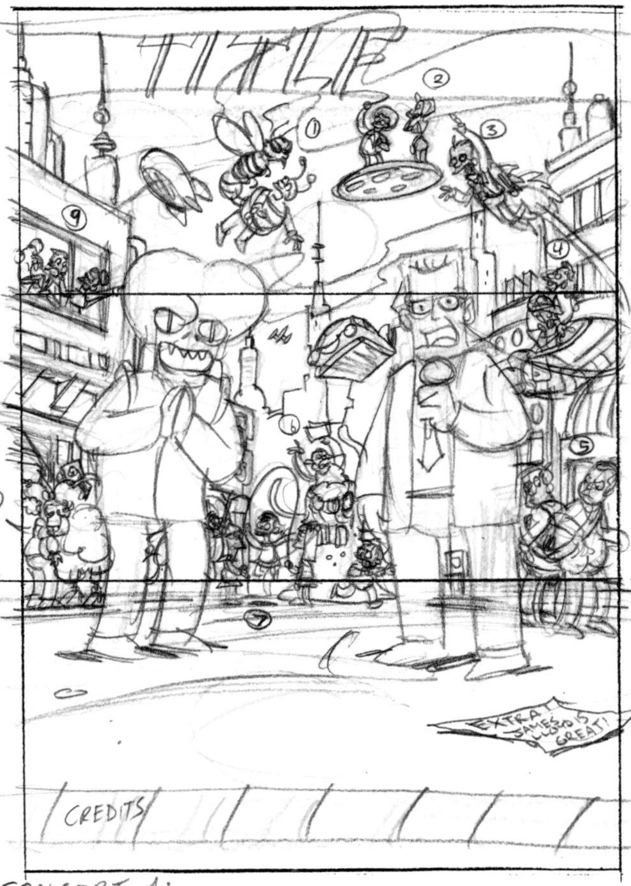

TITLE
CREDITS

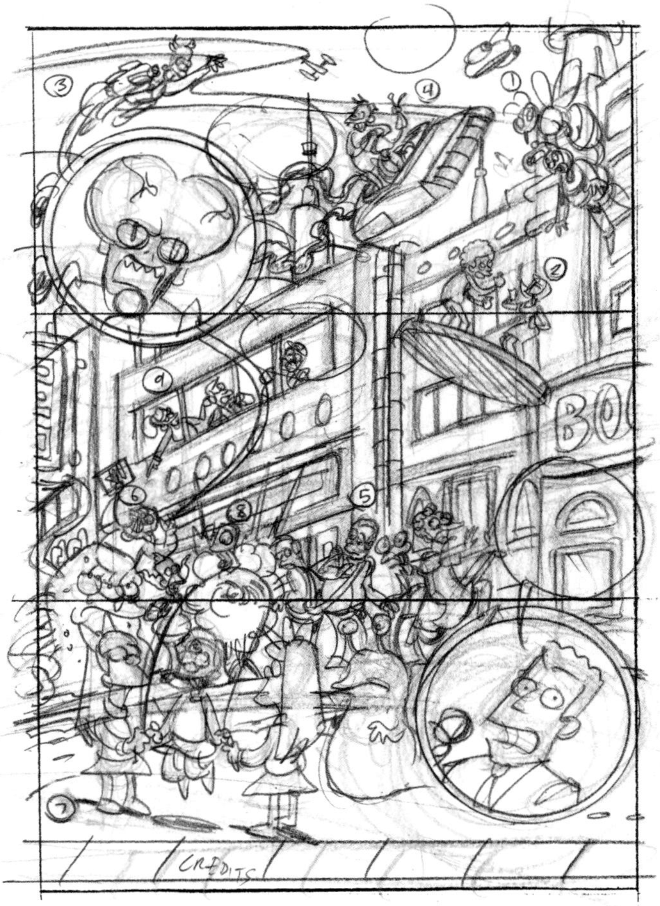

CREDITS

CONCEPT 1:

CONCEPT 2

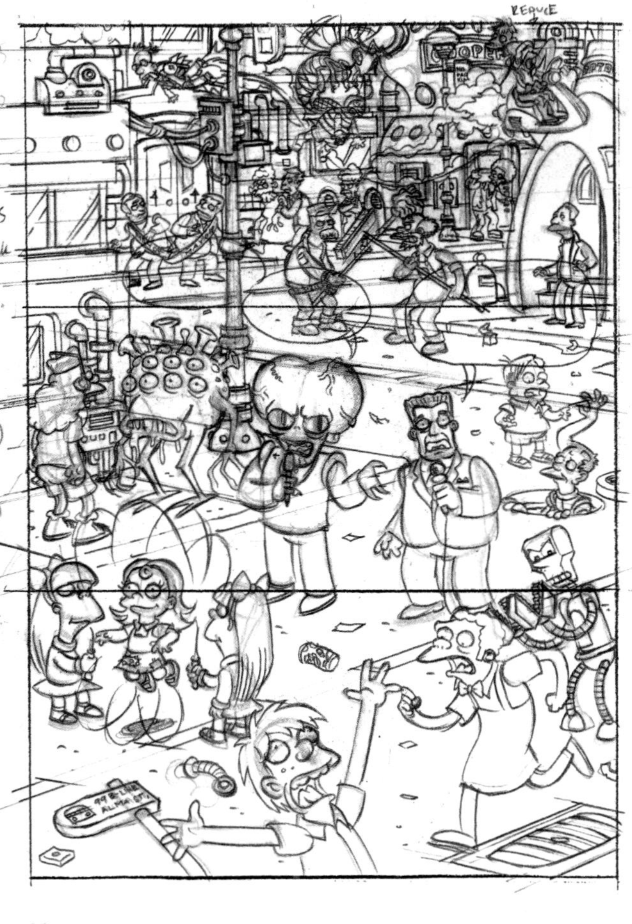

REDUCE
OPER
99 B-LINE ALMA ST.

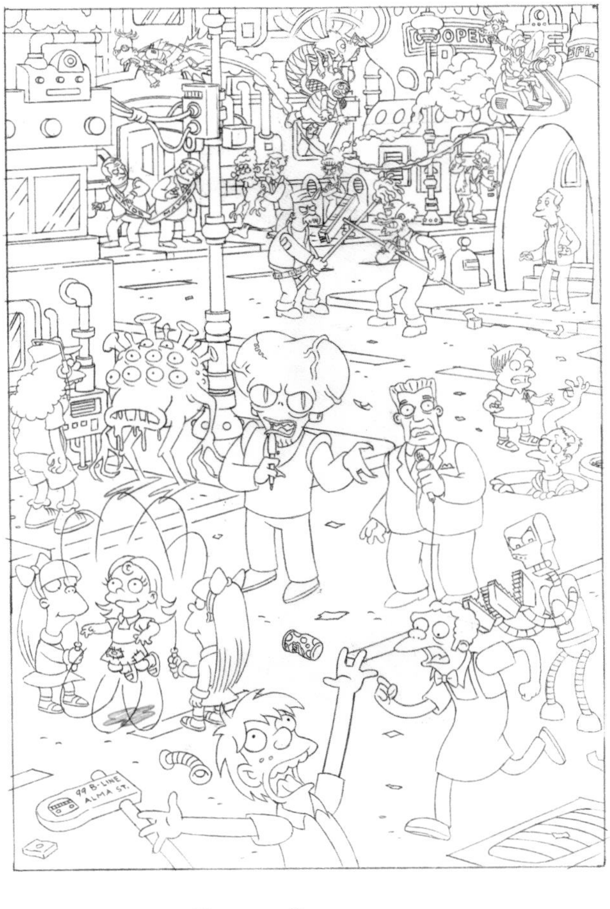

OPER
99 B-LINE ALMA ST.

Here are two very involved attempts at laying out the opening splash page of Chapter 3, followed by both the rough and tight versions of the one that worked best. The finished version of this drawing is on page 90.

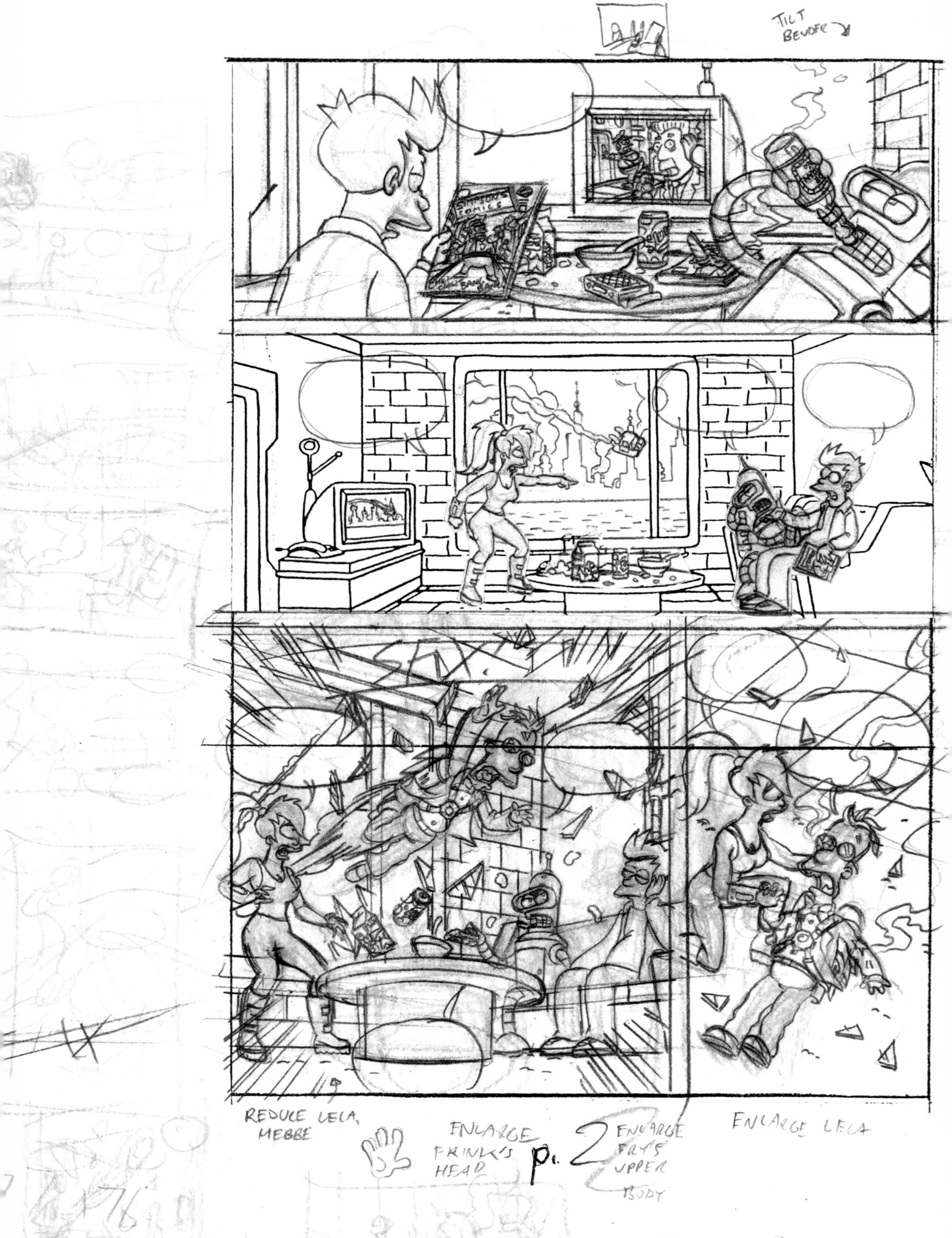
TILT BENDER
REDUCE LELA, MEBBE
ENLARGE FRINK'S HEAD
p. 2
ENLARGE FRY'S UPPER BODY
ENLARGE LELA
180-190-200
160-150

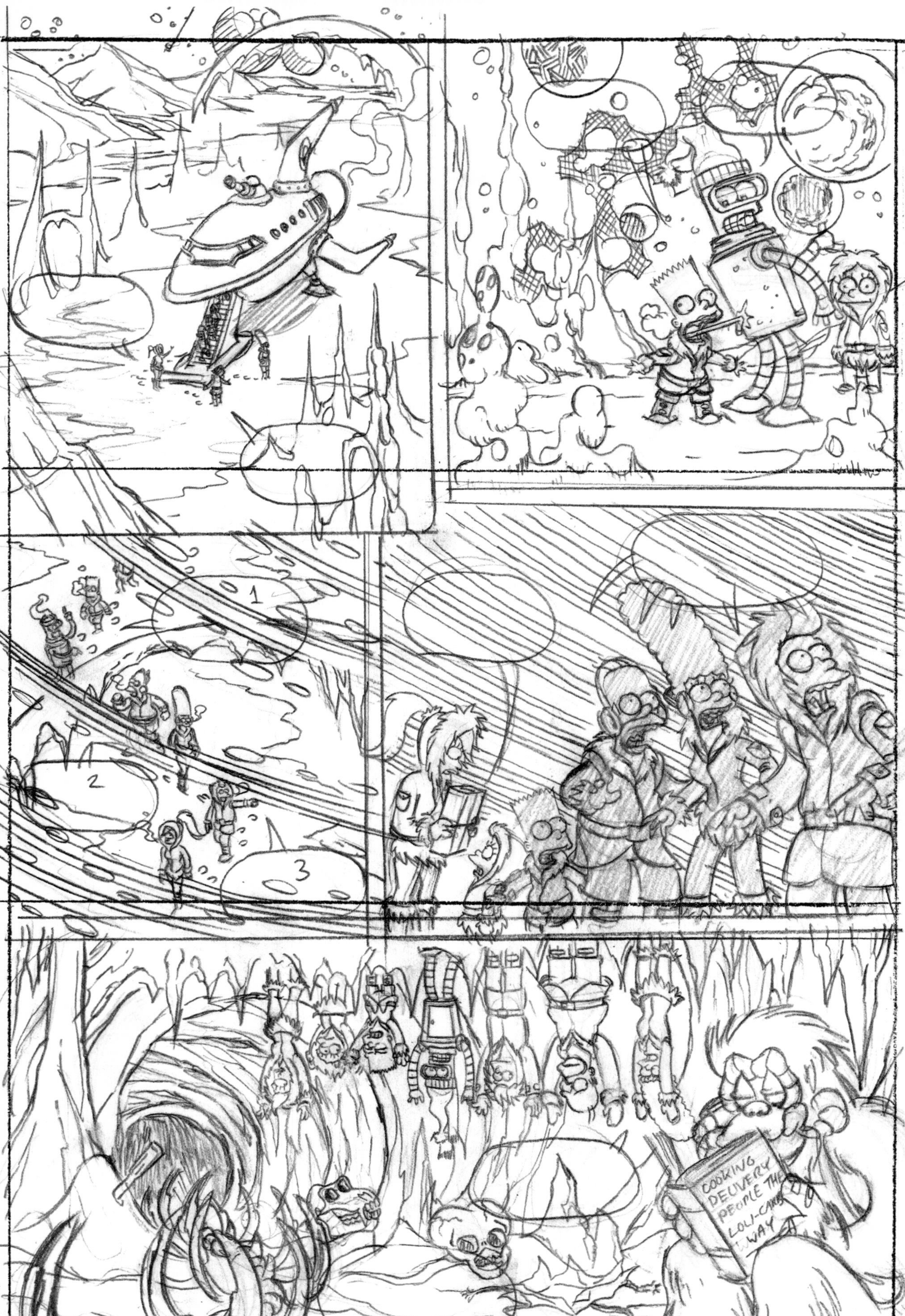
COOKING DELIVERY PEOPLE THE LOLI-CAR WAY

p. 18

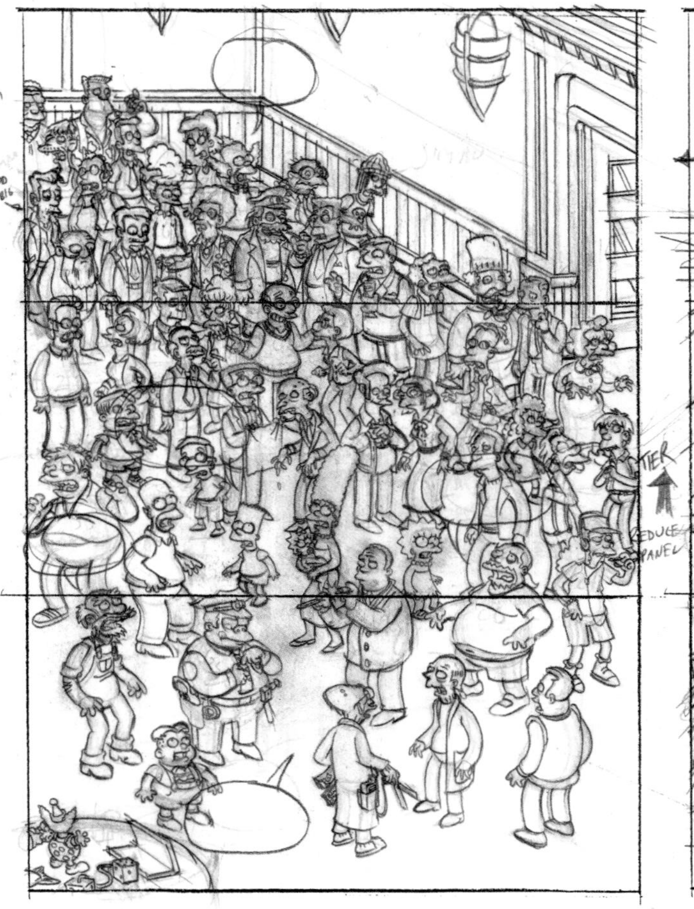
HEAD TOO BIG
TIER
REDUCE PANEL

p. 7

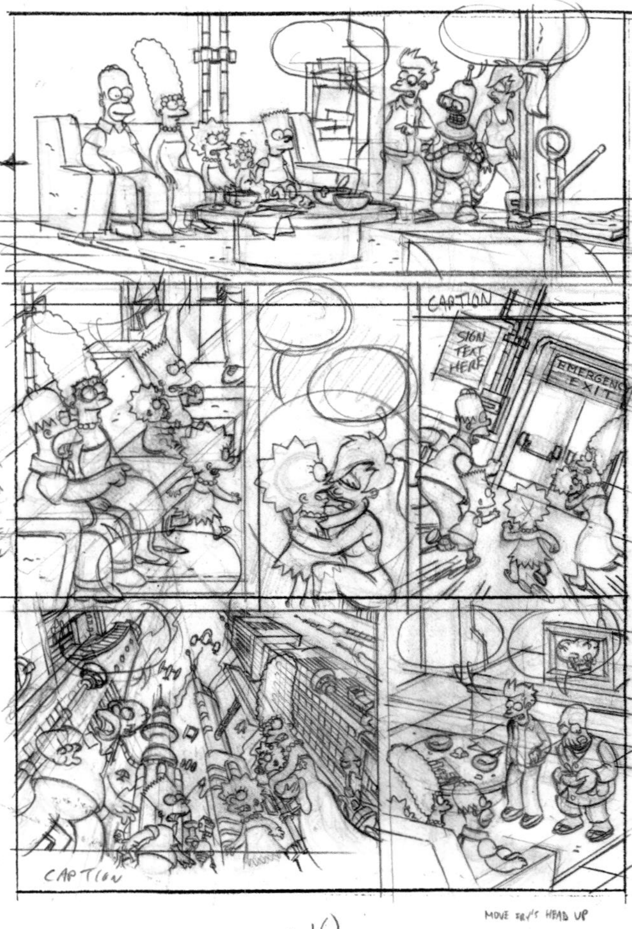
CAPTION
SIGN TEXT HERE
EMERGENCY EXIT
CAPTION
MOVE FRY'S HEAD UP

p. 10

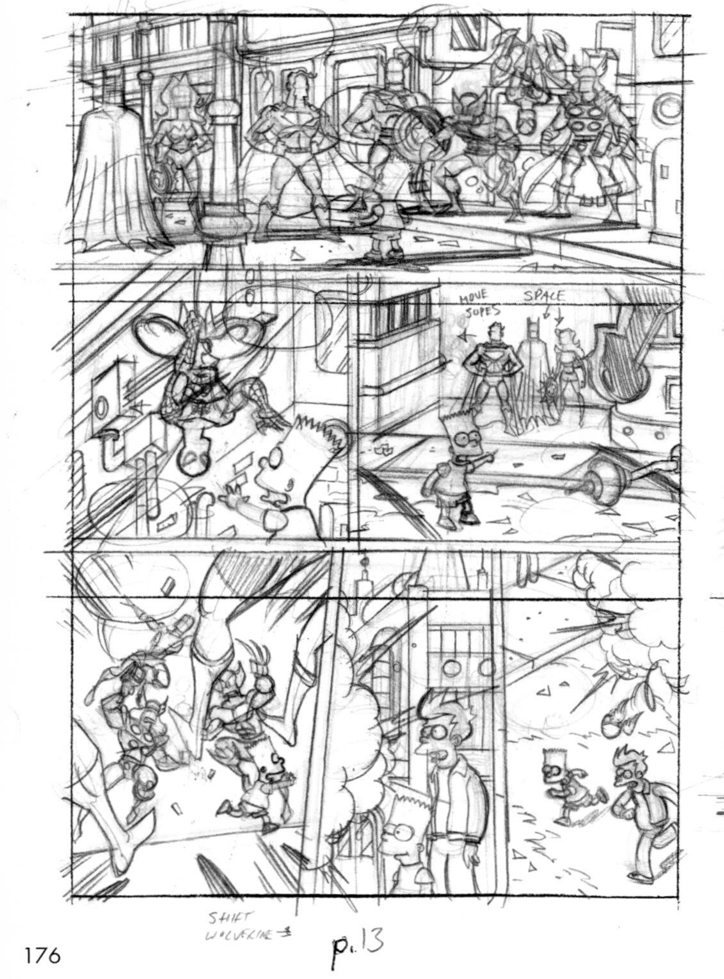
MOVE SUPES
SPACE
SHIFT WOLVERINE

p. 13

HEY, DO WE NEED A CAPTION? THIS THING'S GOT PUNCH!

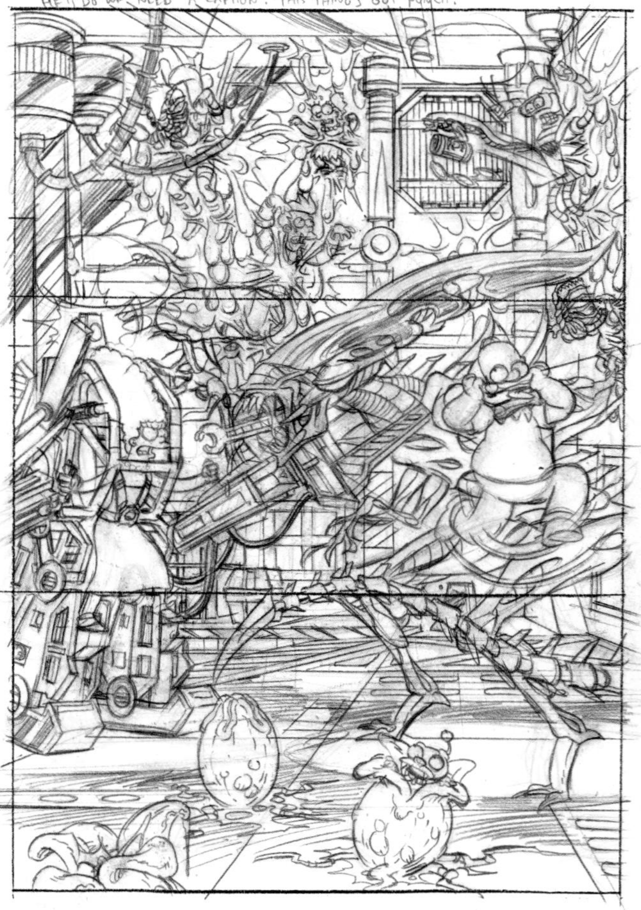

p. 20

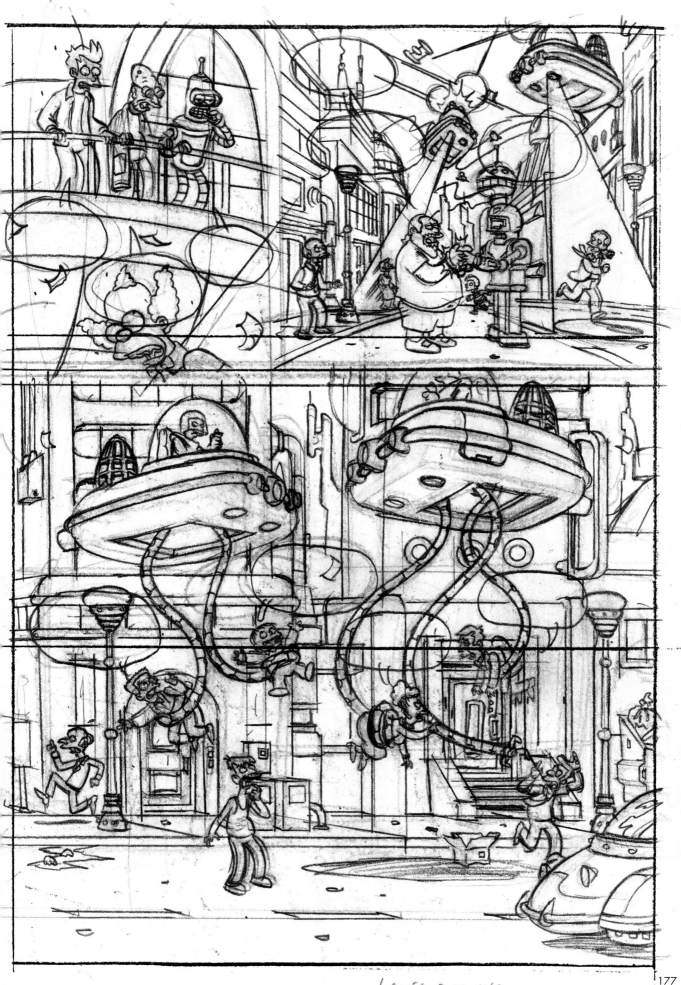

LOWER DOORWAYS

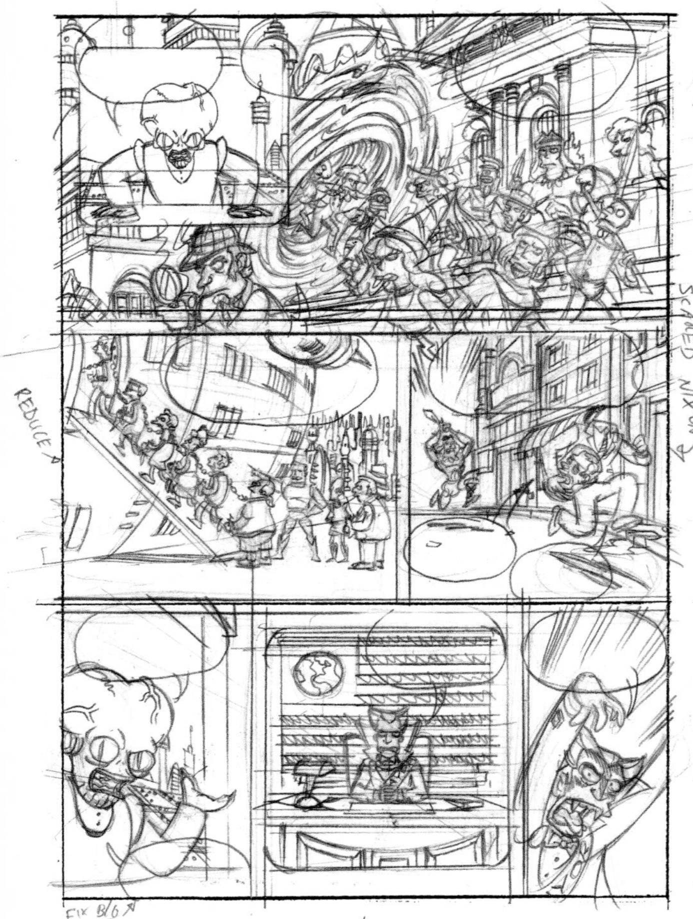
REDUCE
SCARED NIXON
FIX BG

p. 1

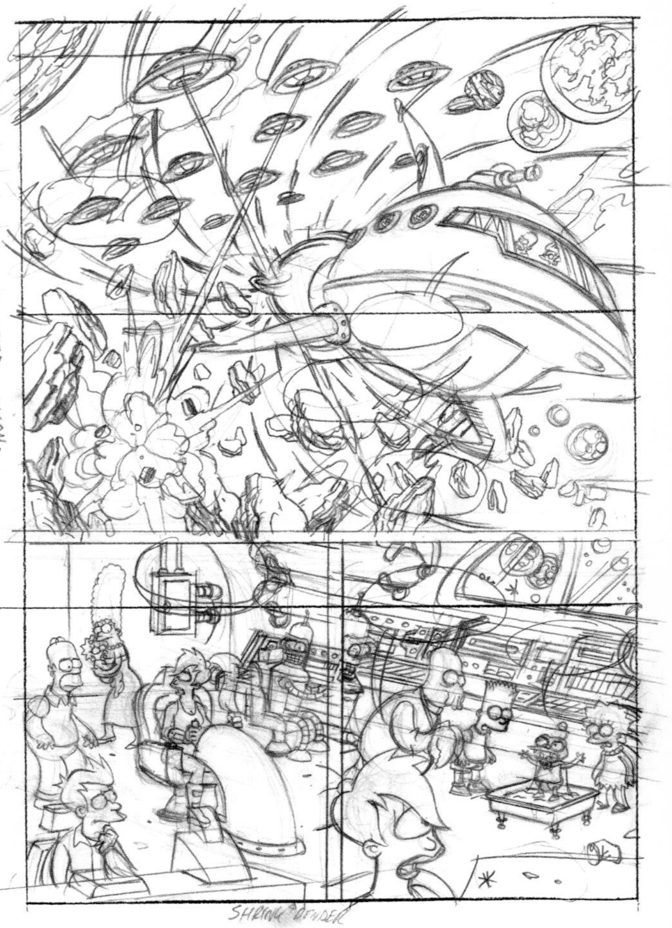
SHRINK BENDER

p. 2

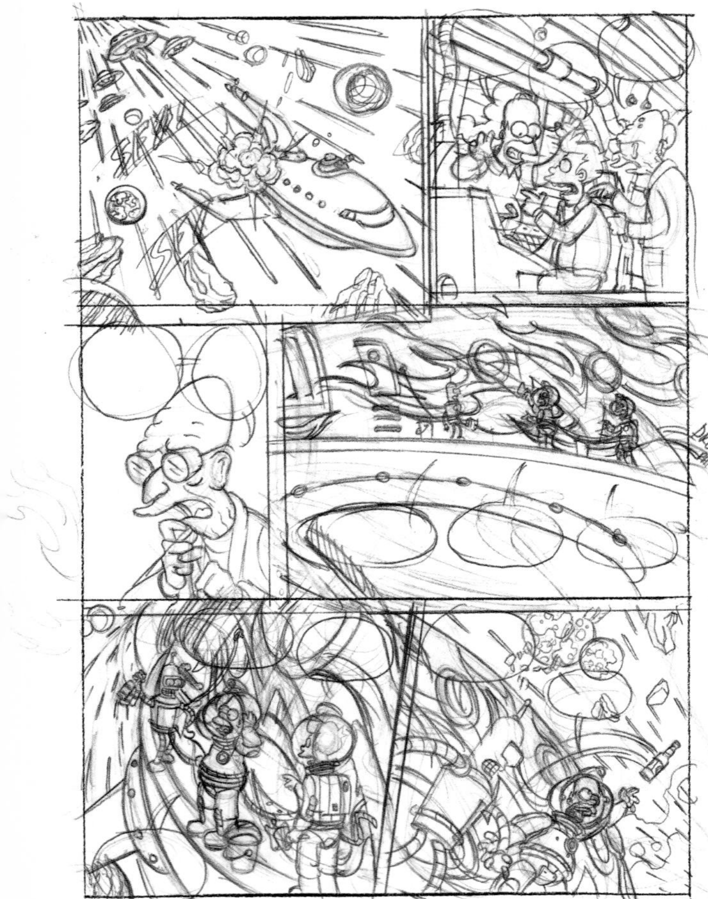
RAISE HOMER'S HEAD

p. 3

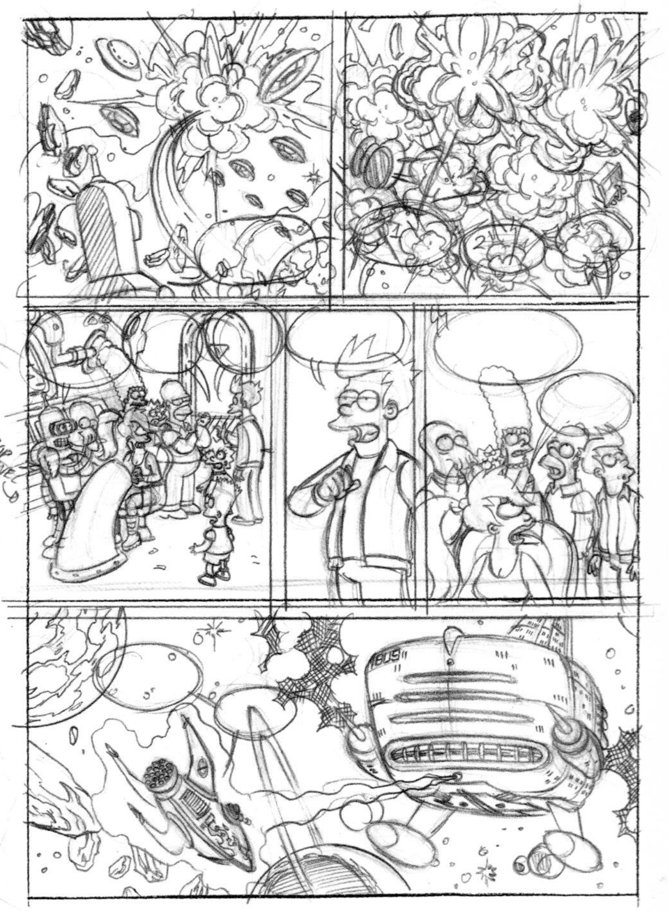

p. 4

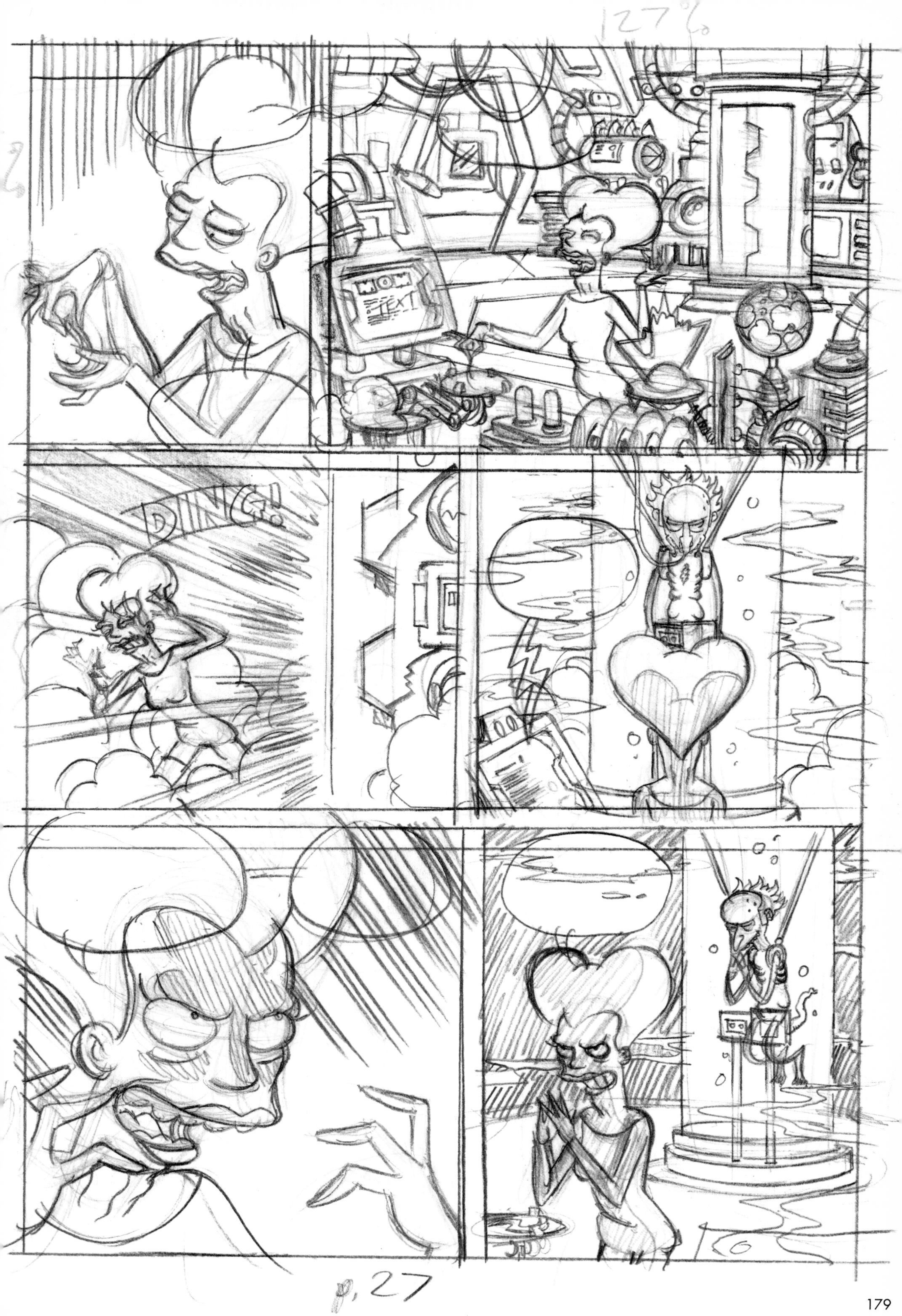
127%
MOM
TEXT
DING!
p. 27

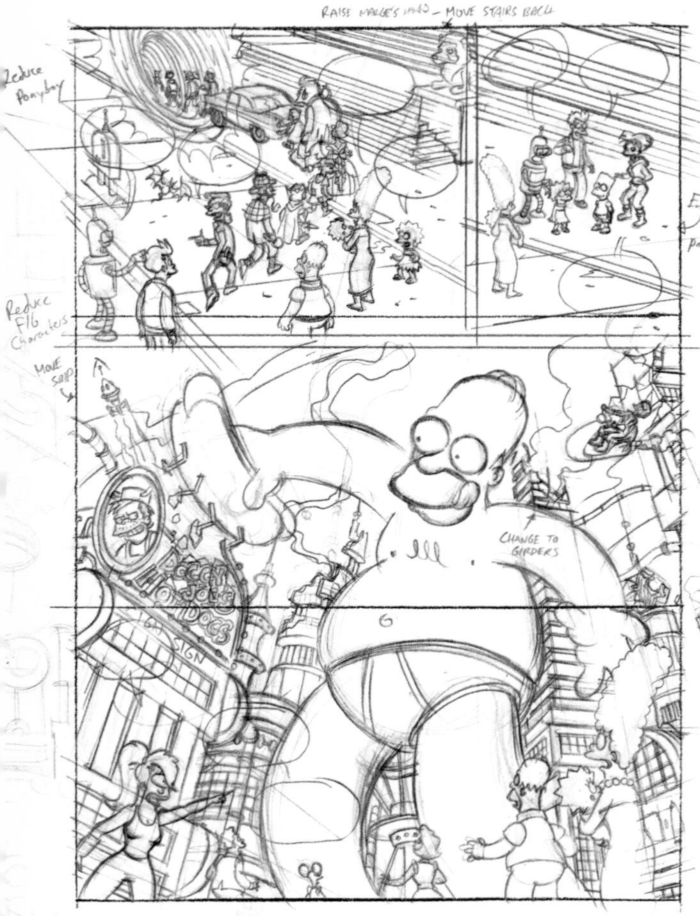
RAISE MARGE'S HAND — MOVE STAIRS BACK
Reduce Ponyboy
Enlarge panel
Reduce F/G Characters
MOVE SHIP
CHANGE TO GIRDERS
REDUCE G.H.'s HEAD
p.21

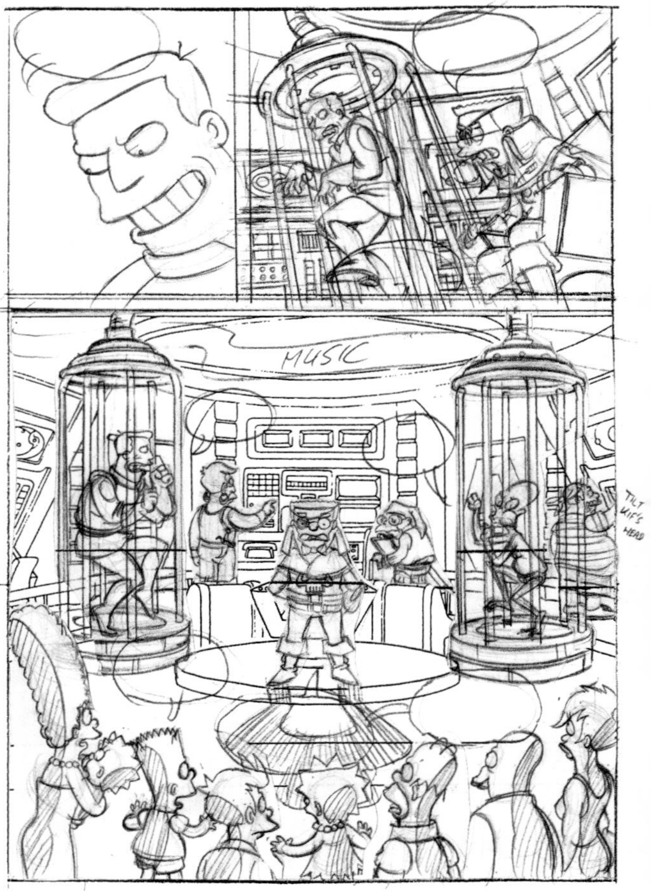
MUSIC
TILT KIF'S HEAD
p.5

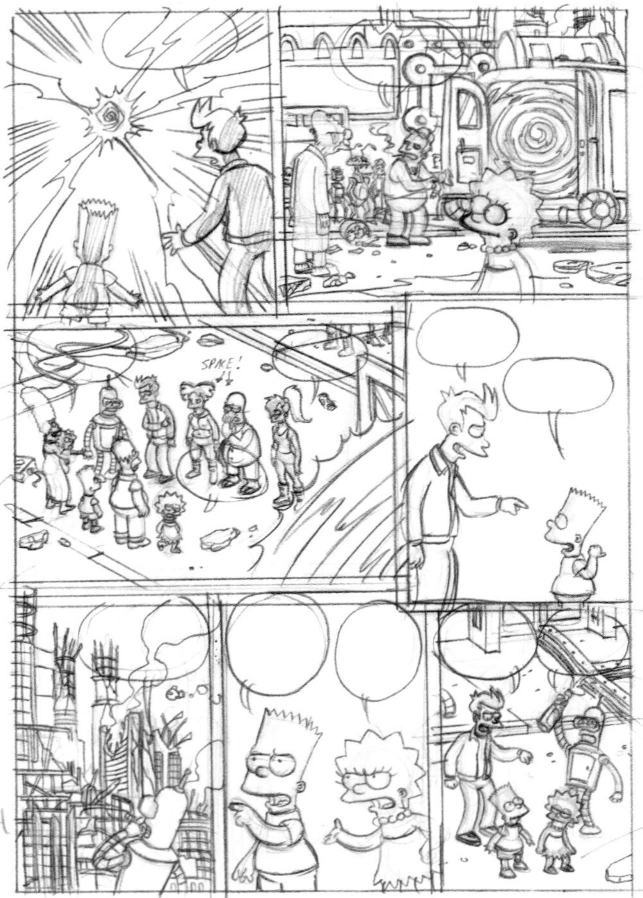
SPAKE!
p.25

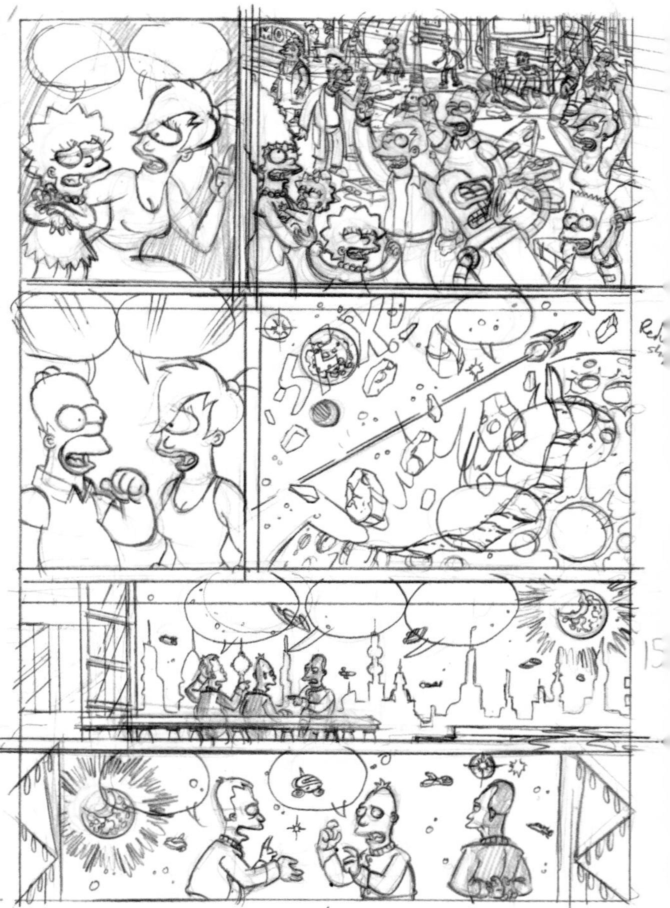
p.26

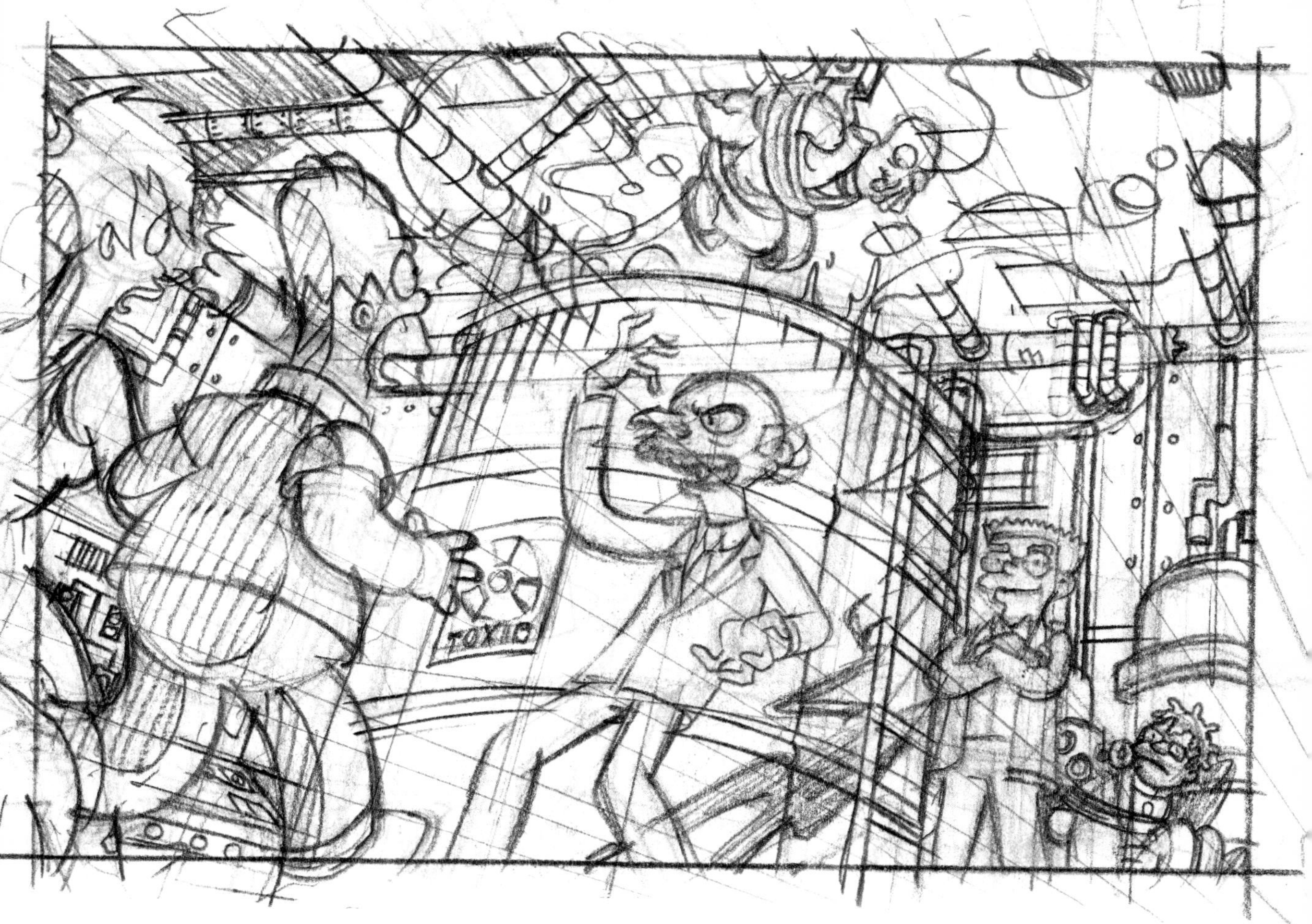
TOXIC

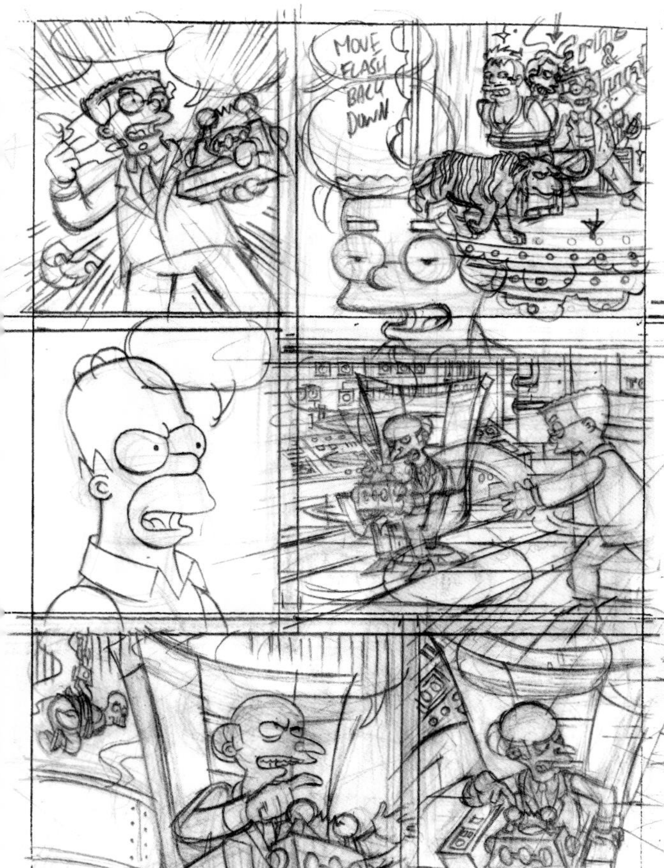
MOVE FLASH BACK DOWN

p.20

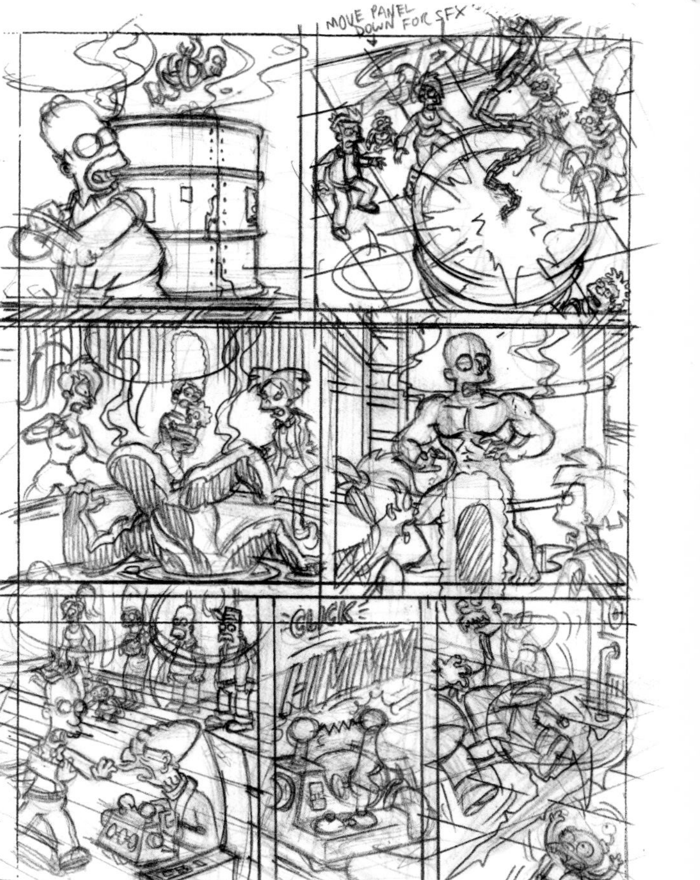
MOVE PANEL DOWN FOR SFX
CLICK
HMMM

p.22

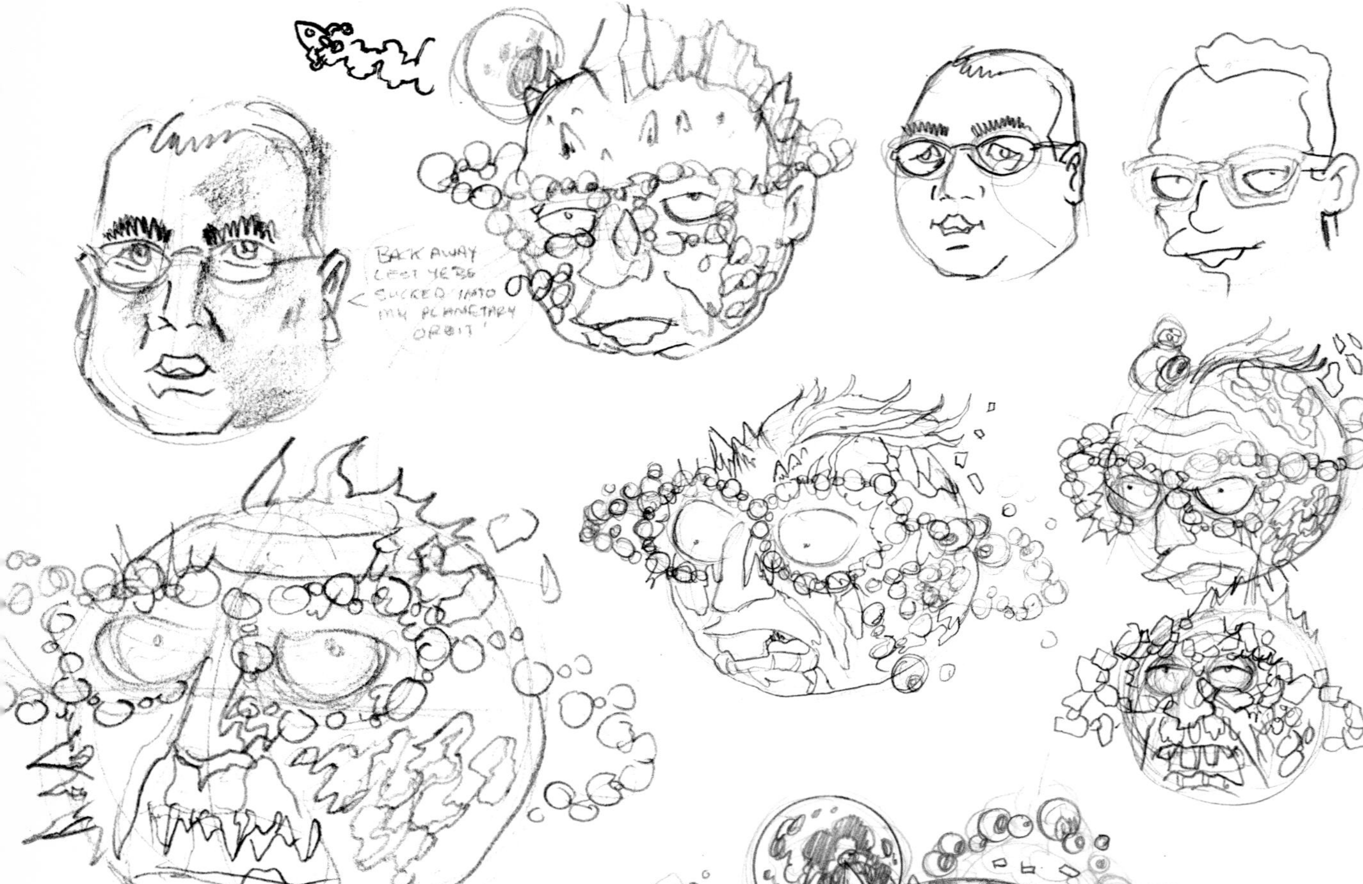
BACK AWAY LEST YE BE SUCKED INTO MY PLANETARY ORBIT!

Ian Boothby's fantastic script called for a plethora of new character designs.

For the first of these, James Lloyd began with a sketch of one of his close friends and transmogrified it into Nerdanus XII The Living Planet!

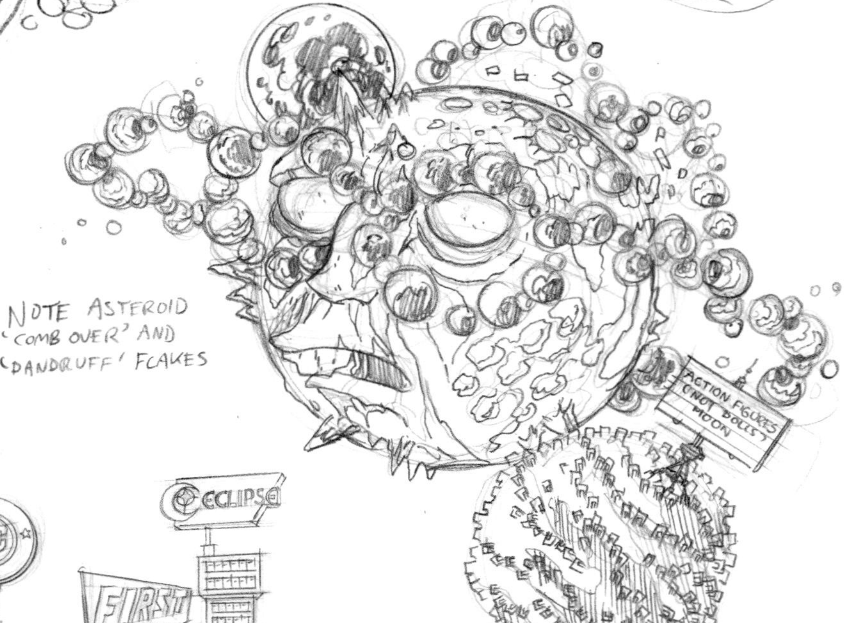
NOTE ASTEROID 'COMB OVER' AND 'DANDRUFF' FLAKES
ACTION FIGURES (NOT DOLLS!) MOON

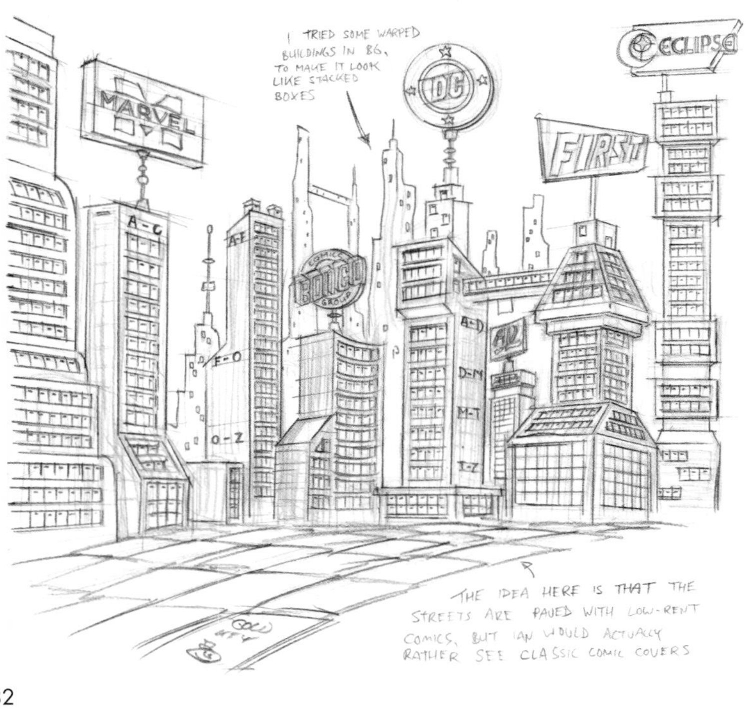
I TRIED SOME WARPED BUILDINGS IN BG, TO MAKE IT LOOK LIKE STACKED BOXES
MARVEL
DC
ECLIPSE
FIRST
THE IDEA HERE IS THAT THE STREETS ARE PAVED WITH LOW-RENT COMICS, BUT IAN WOULD ACTUALLY RATHER SEE CLASSIC COMIC COVERS

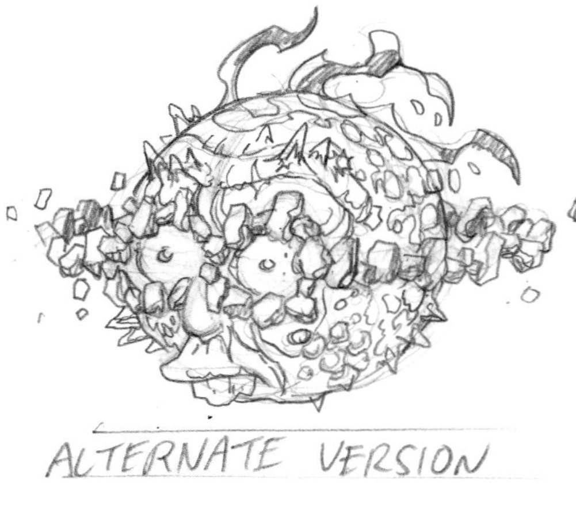
ALTERNATE VERSION

HEROES-

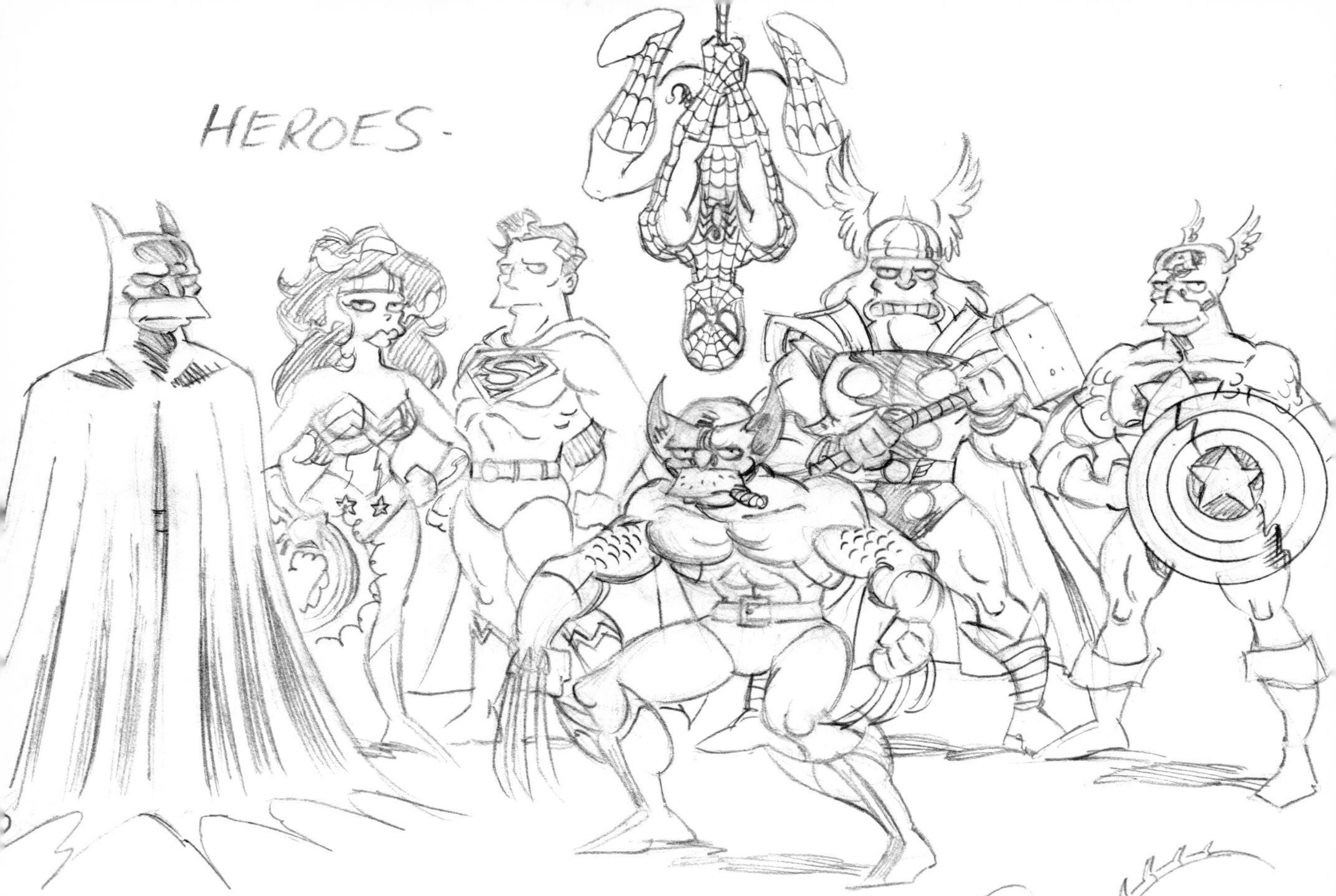

MARGE IN POWERLOADER

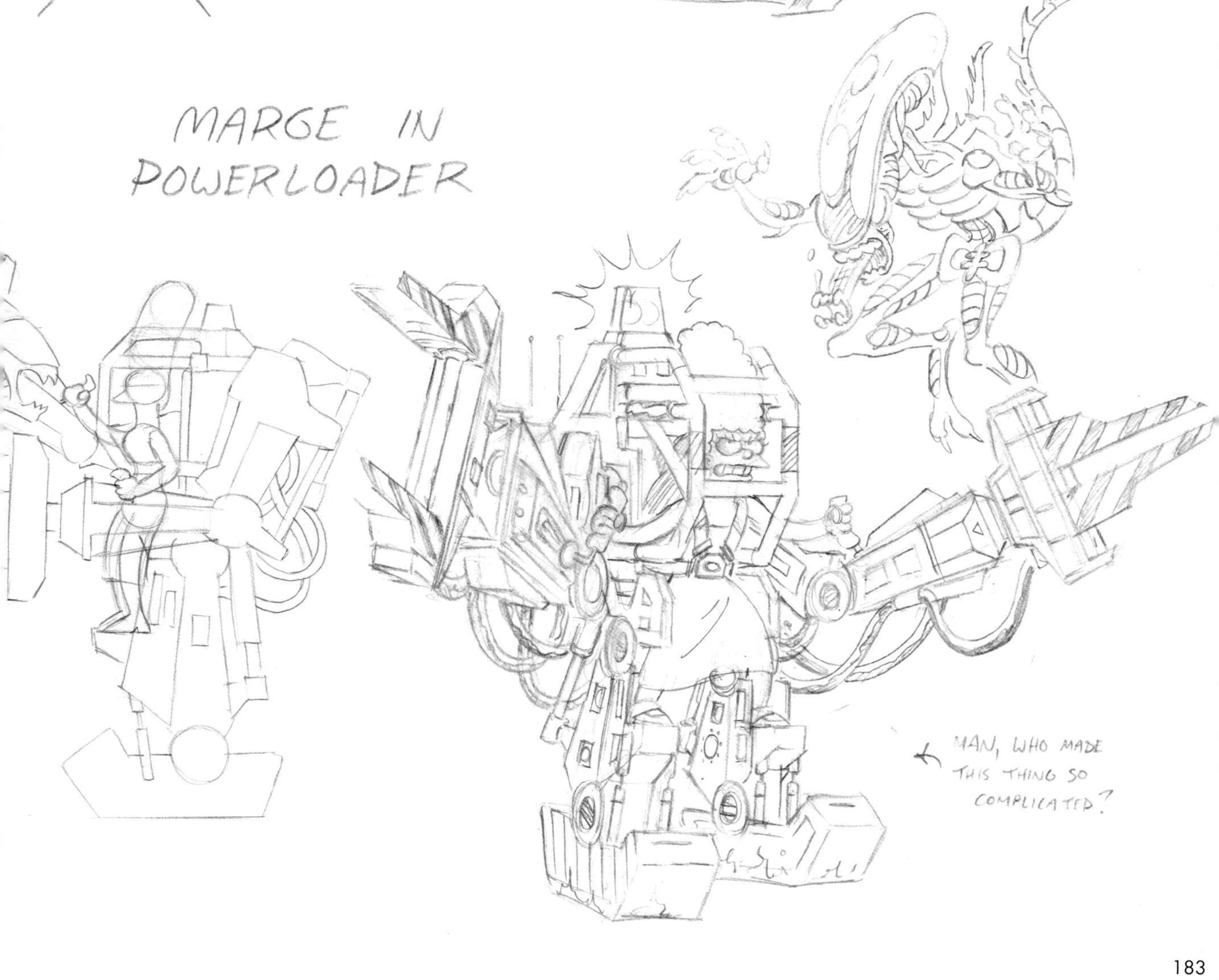
MAN, WHO MADE THIS THING SO COMPLICATED?

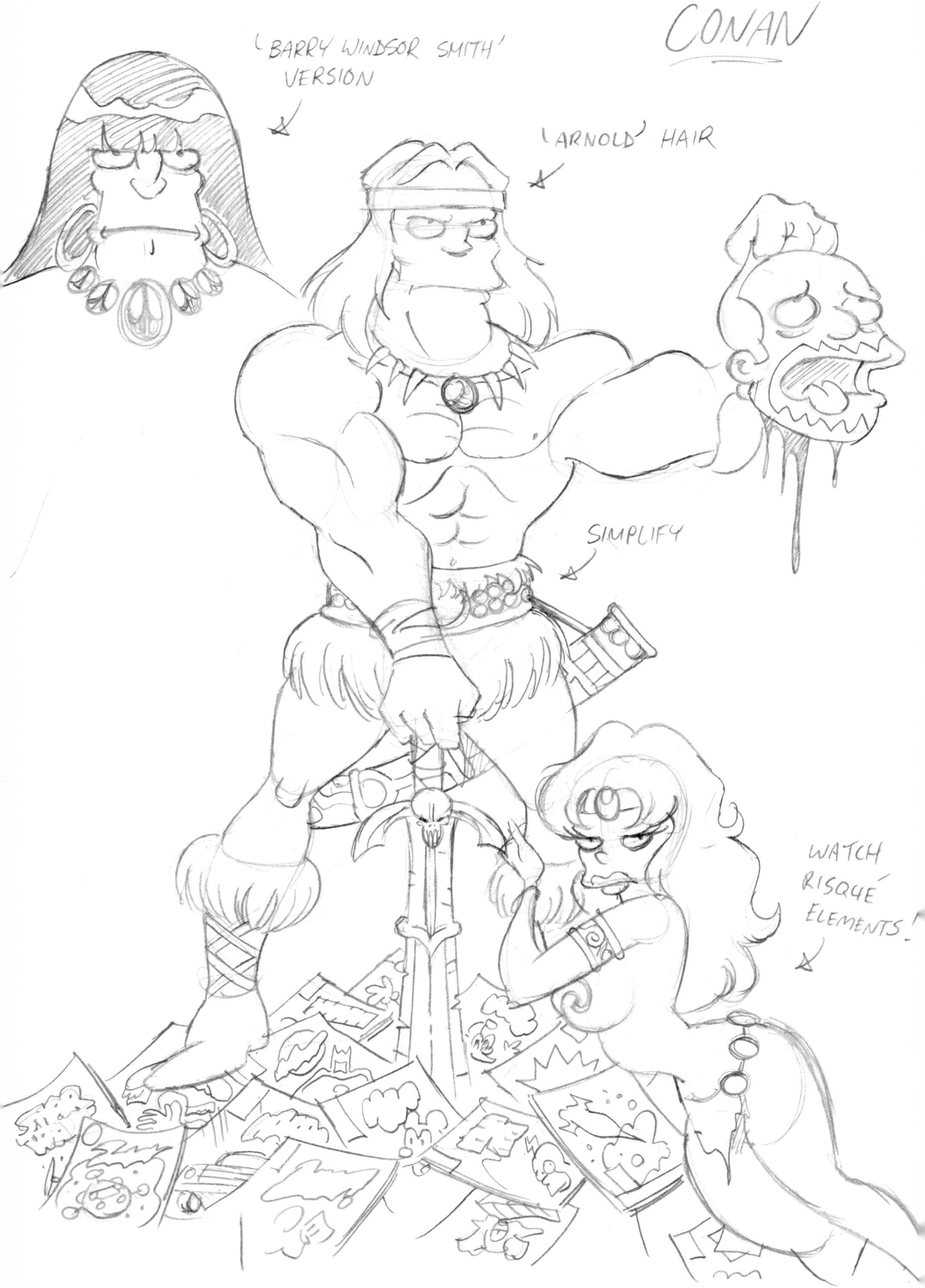
CONAN
'BARRY WINDSOR SMITH' VERSION
'ARNOLD' HAIR
SIMPLIFY
WATCH RISQUÉ ELEMENTS!

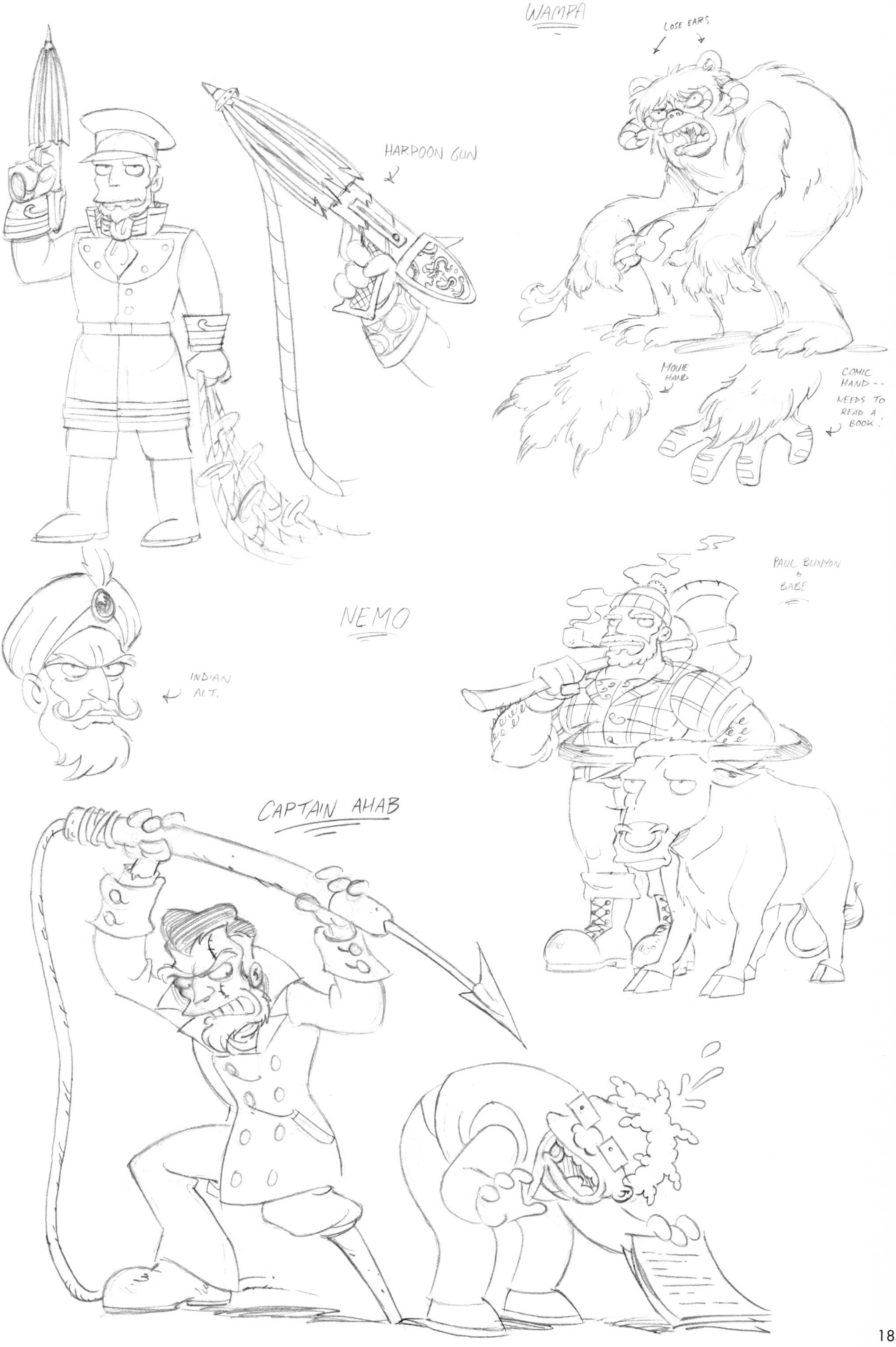

WAMPA
LOSE EARS
HARPOON GUN
MOVIE HAND
COMIC HAND -- NEEDS TO READ A BOOK!
NEMO
INDIAN ALT.
PAUL BUNYON & BABE
CAPTAIN AHAB

SHERLOCK HOLMES

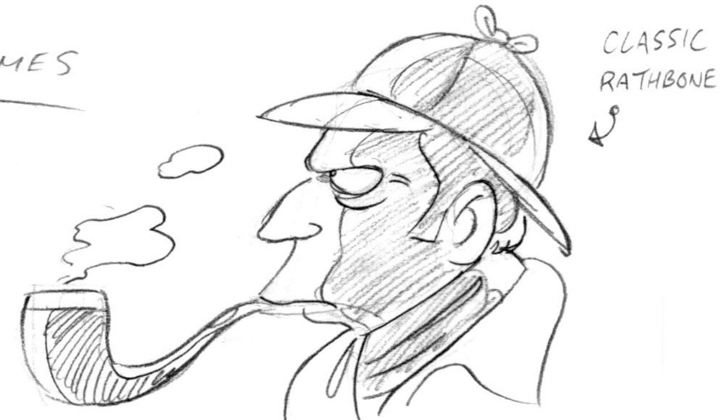
CLASSIC RATHBONE

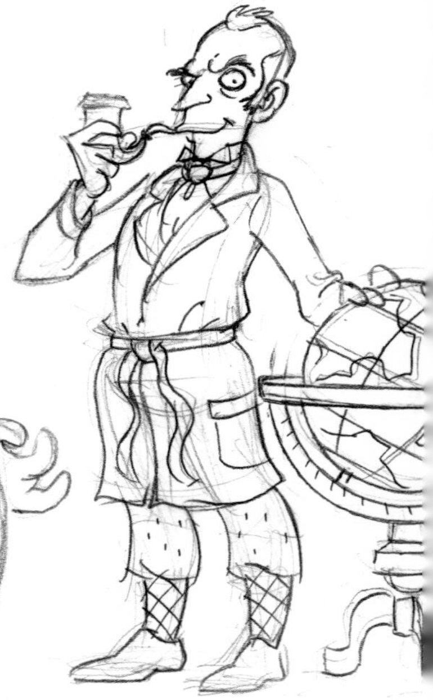

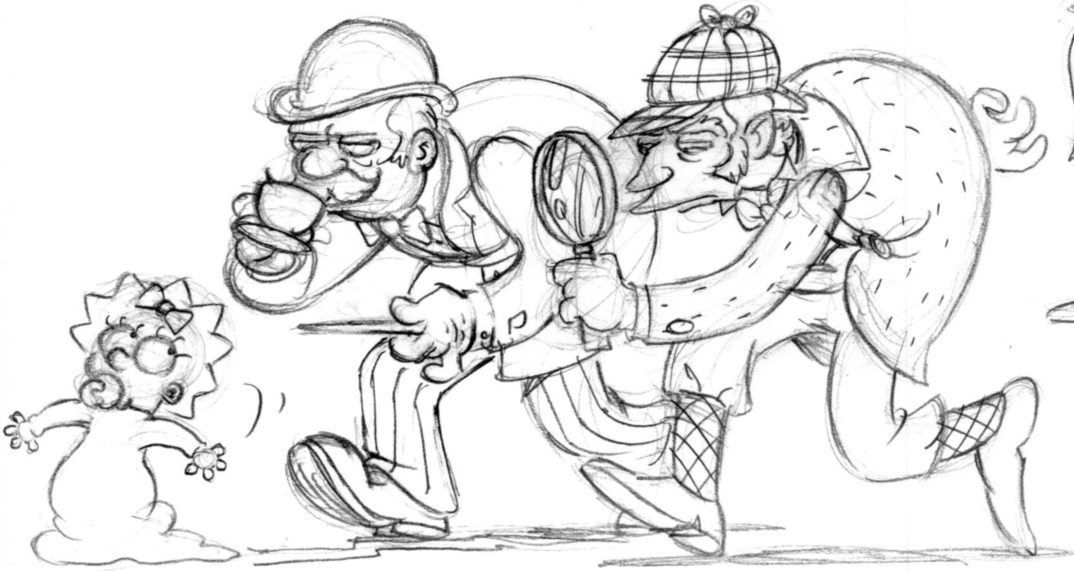

DR. JEKYLL + MR. HYDE

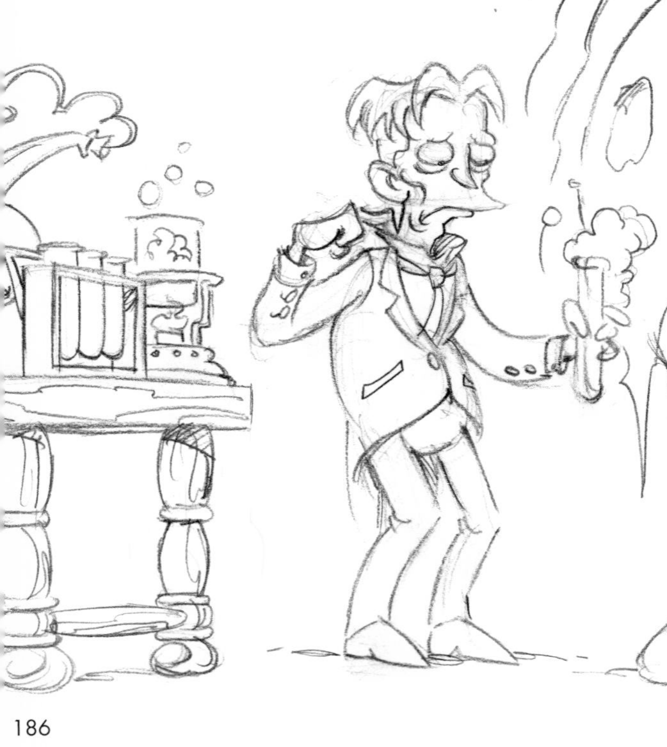

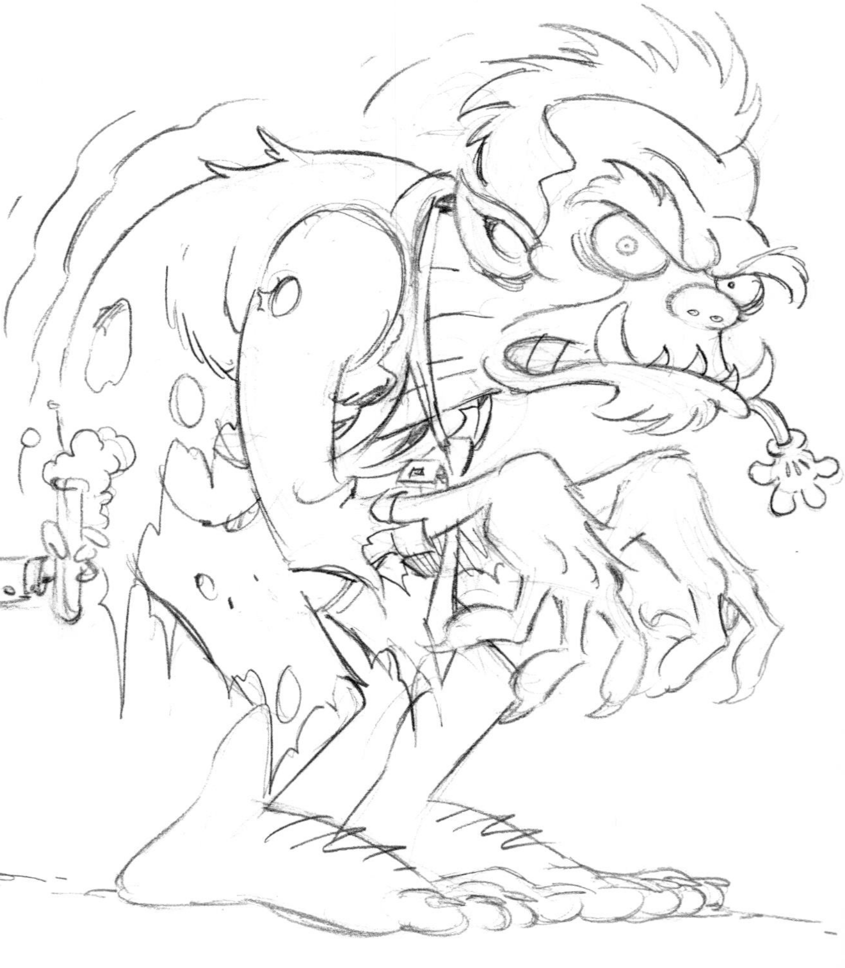

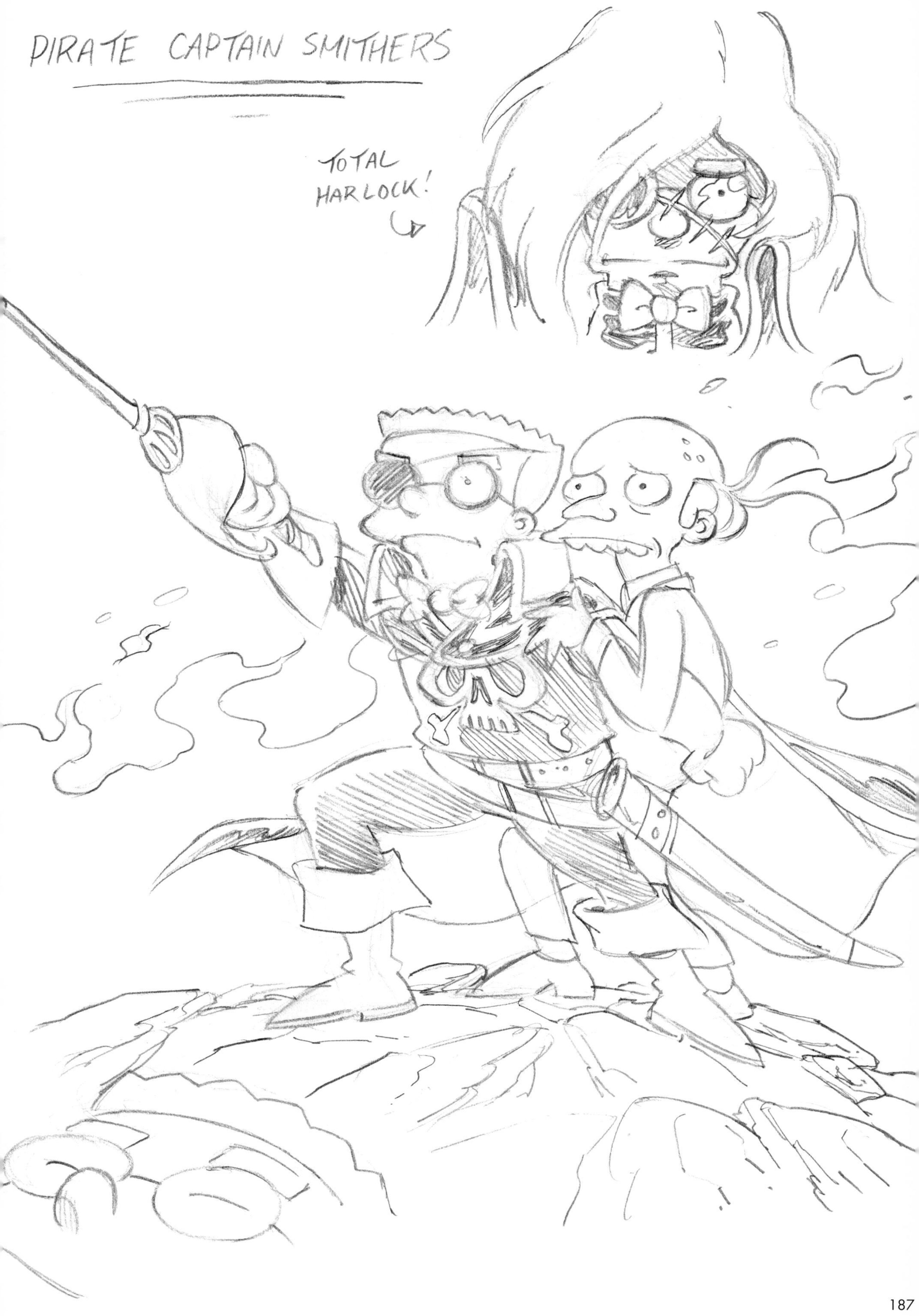
PIRATE CAPTAIN SMITHERS
TOTAL HARLOCK!

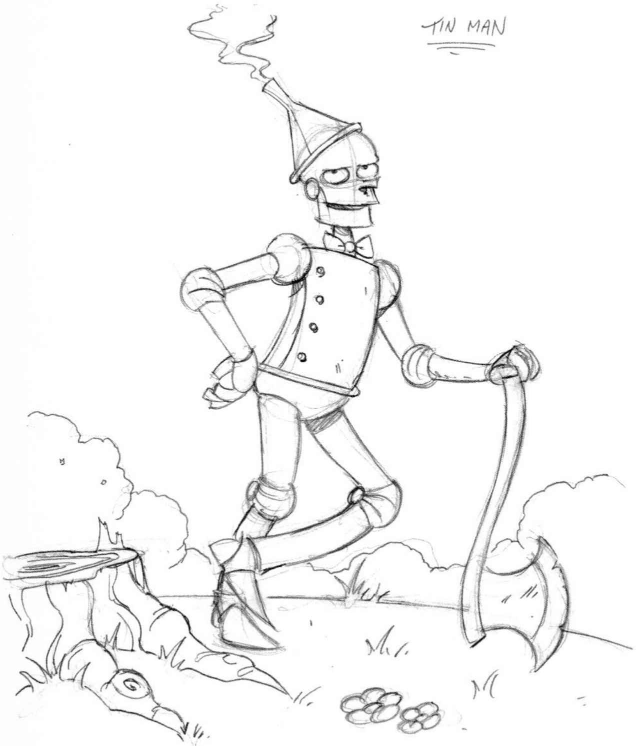
TIN MAN

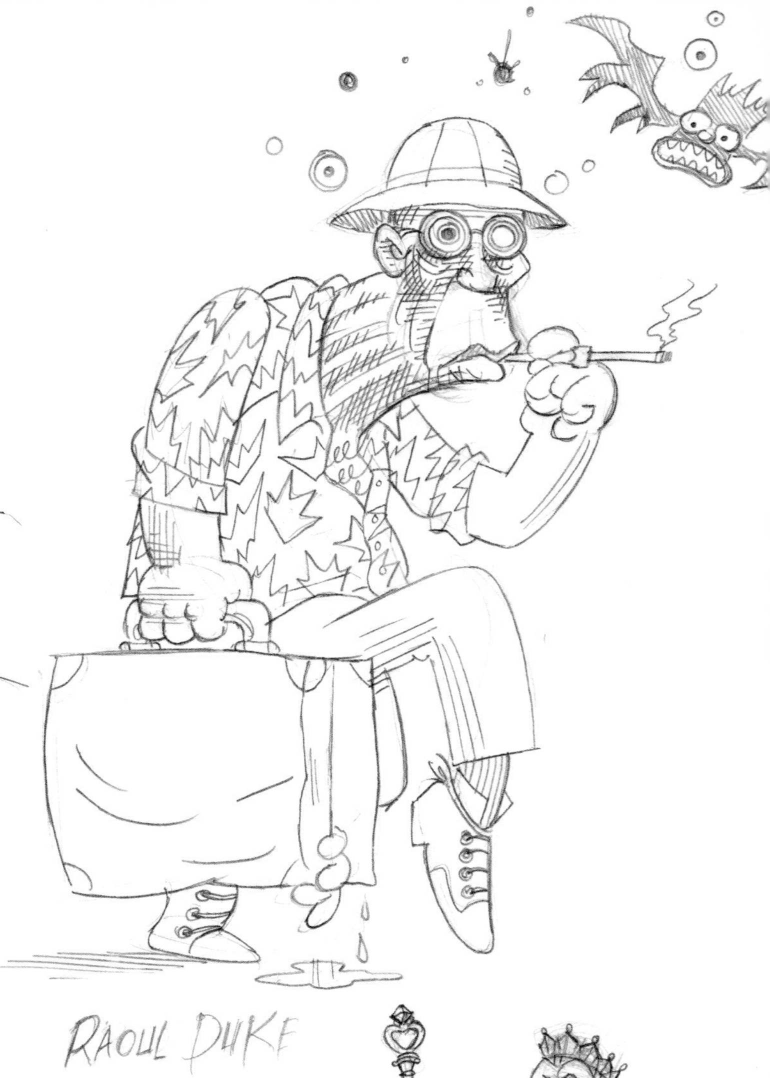
RAOUL DUKE

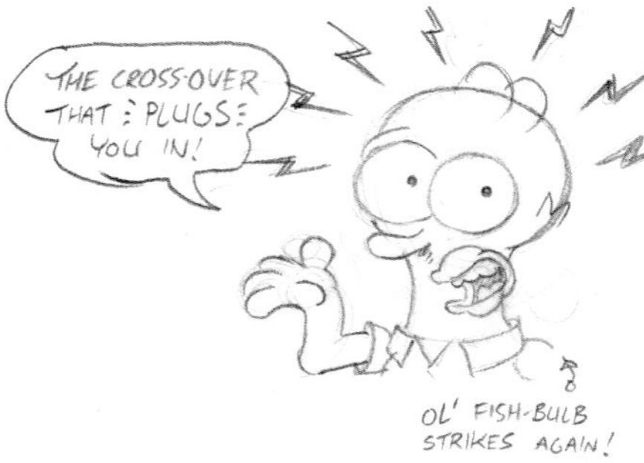
THE CROSS-OVER THAT PLUGS YOU IN!
OL' FISH-BULB STRIKES AGAIN!

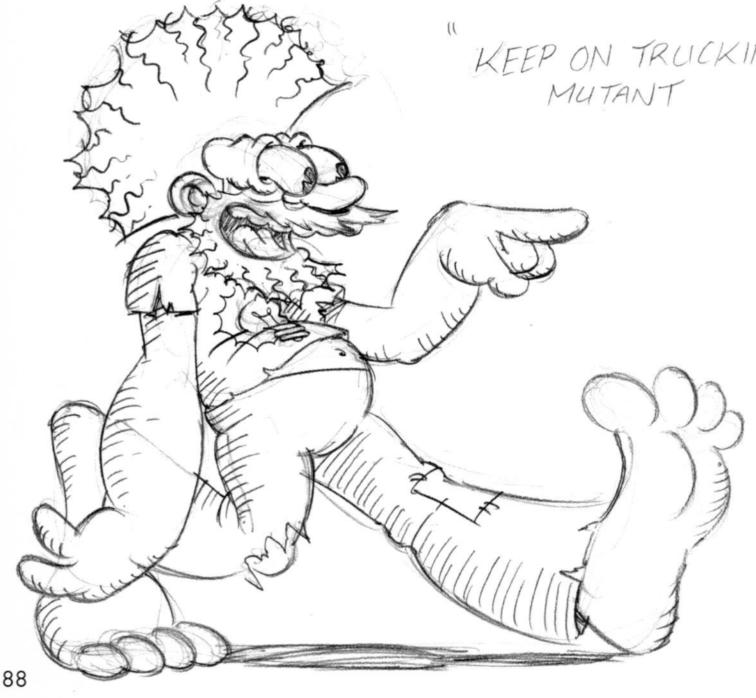
"KEEP ON TRUCKIN'" MUTANT

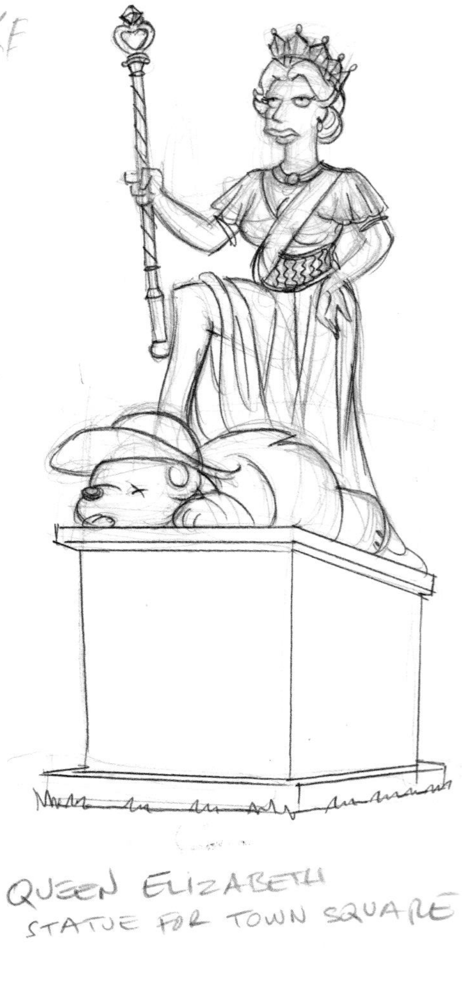
QUEEN ELIZABETH
STATUE FOR TOWN SQUARE

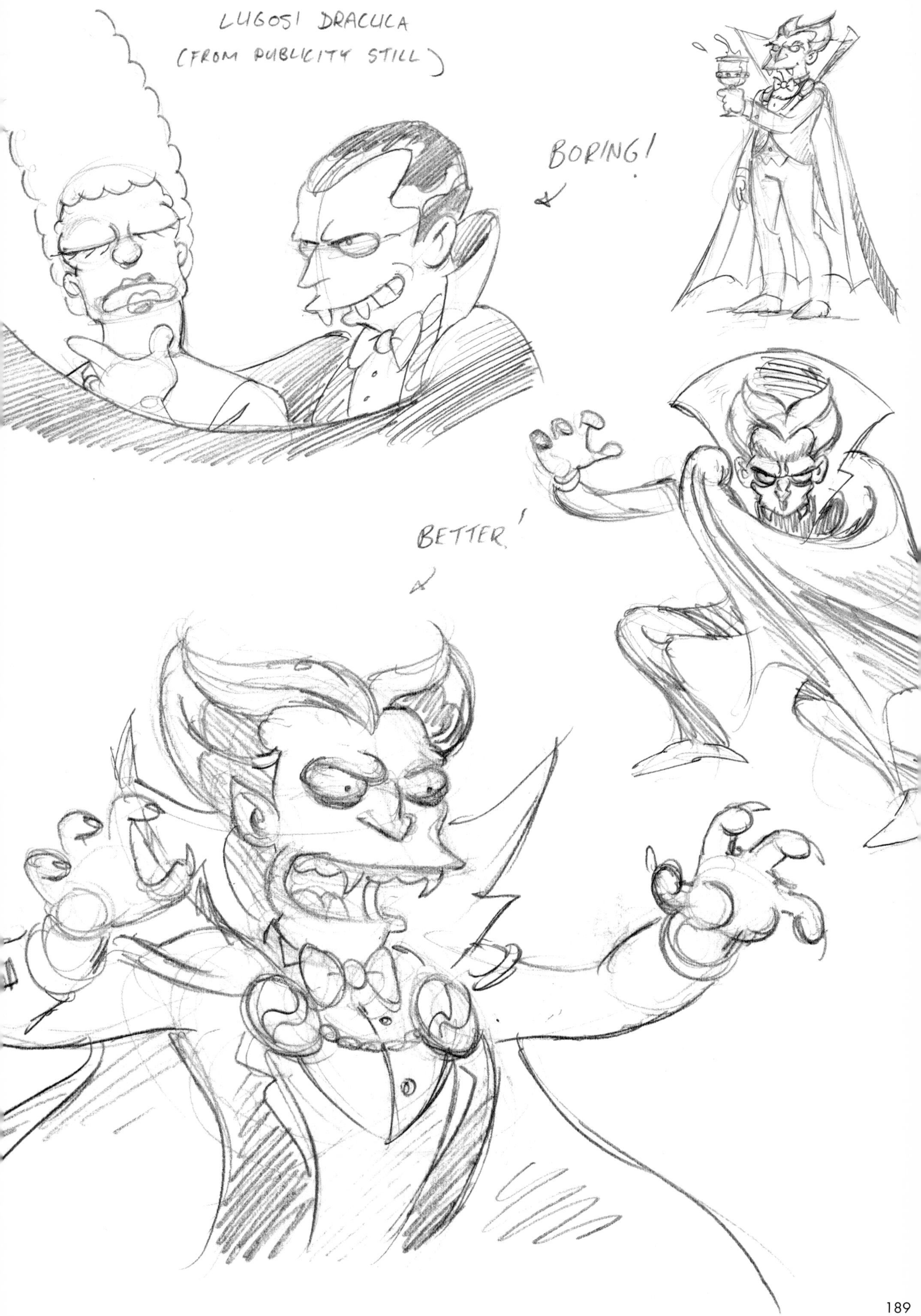
LUGOSI DRACULA
(FROM PUBLICITY STILL)
BORING!
BETTER!

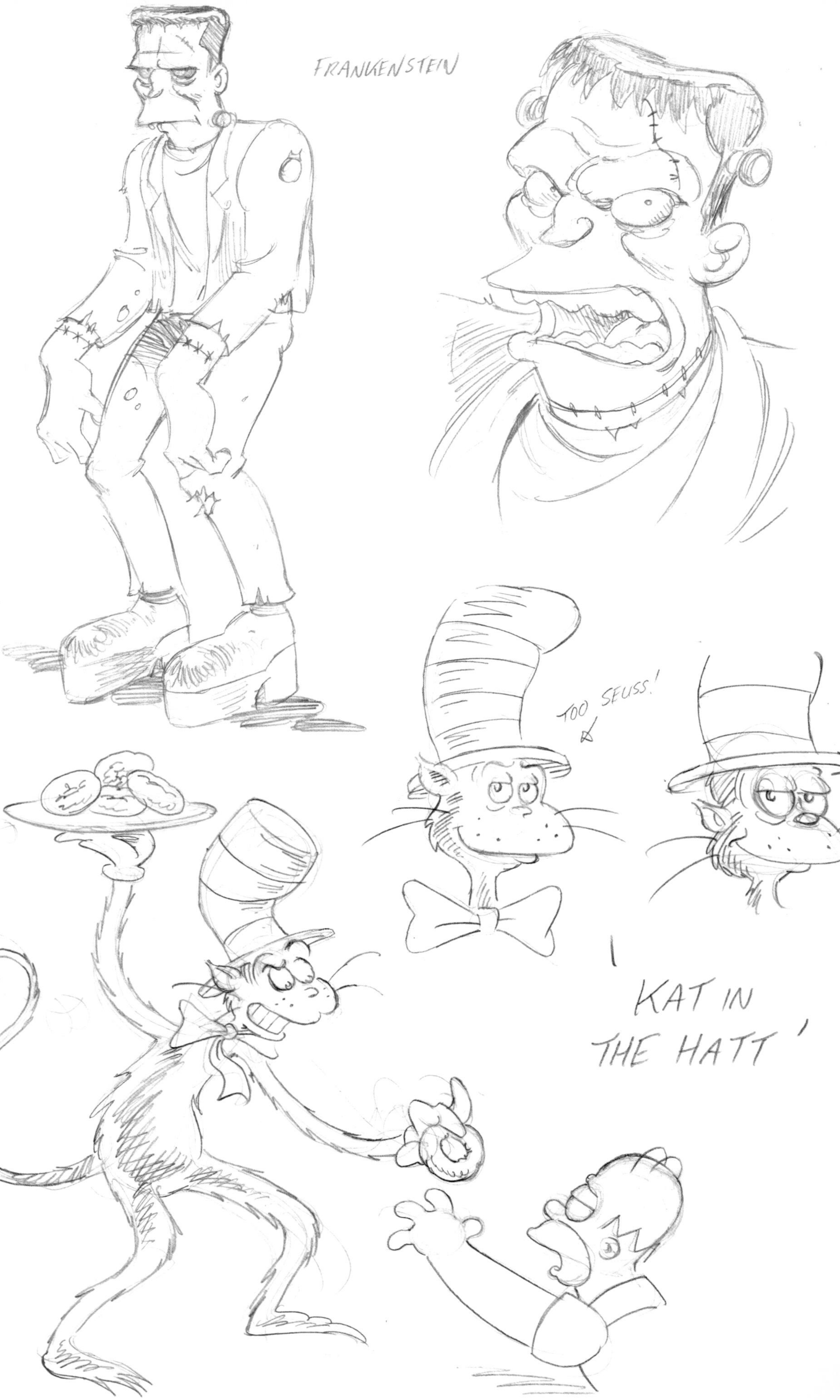
FRANKENSTEIN
TOO SEUSS!
KAT IN THE HATT'

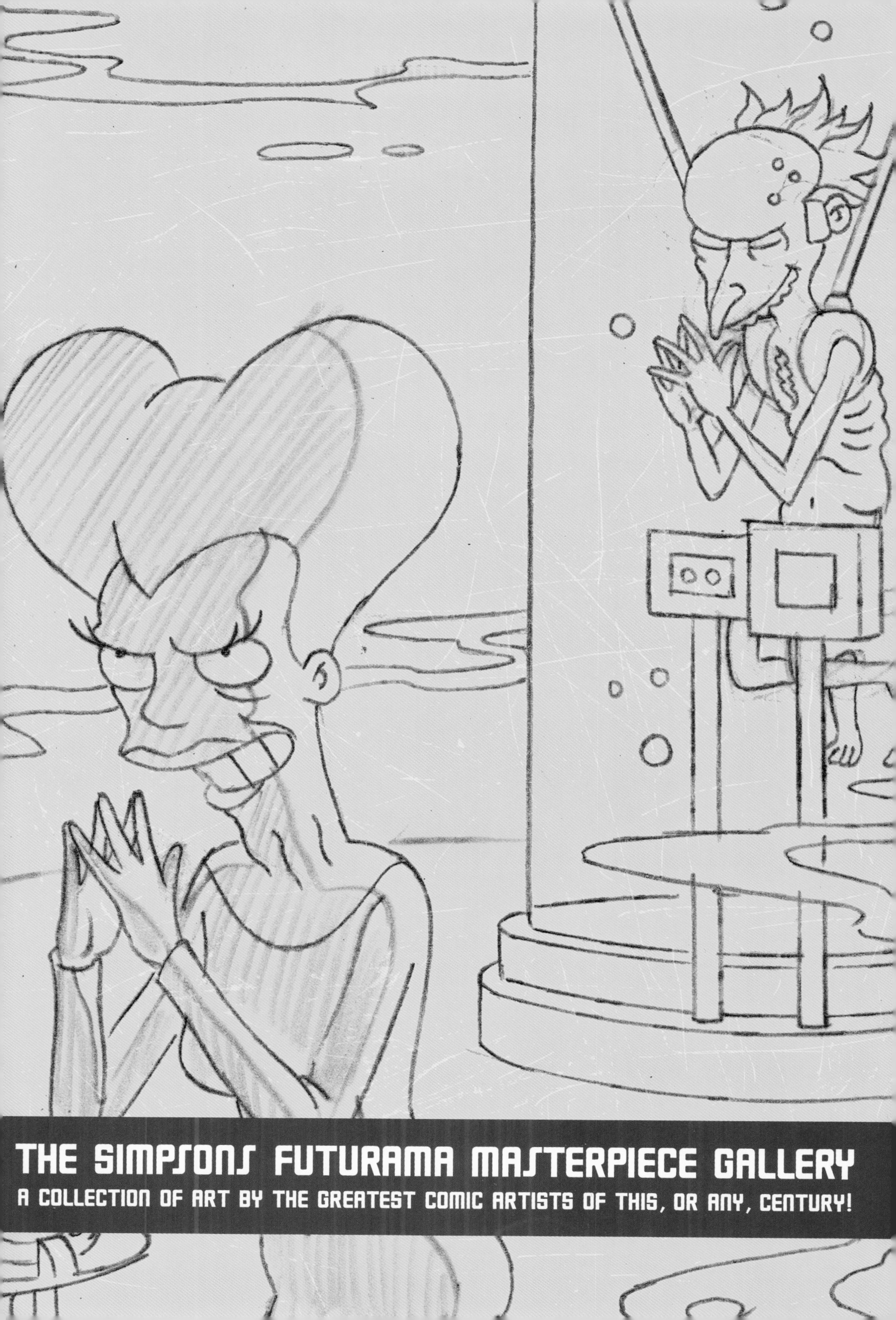

THE SIMPSONS FUTURAMA MASTERPIECE GALLERY

A COLLECTION OF ART BY THE GREATEST COMIC ARTISTS OF THIS, OR ANY, CENTURY!

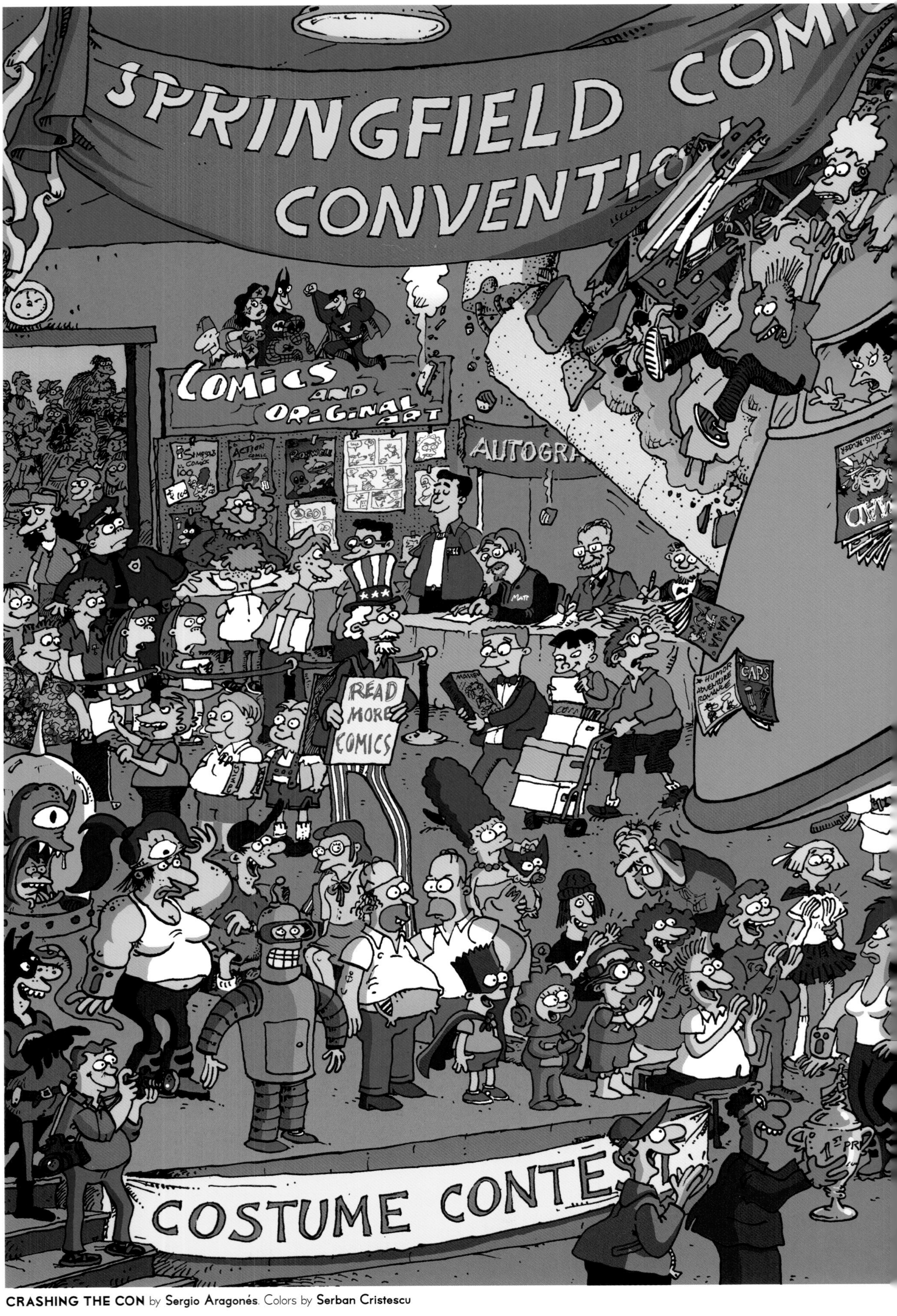
SPRINGFIELD COMI
CONVENTIO
COMICS AND ORIGINAL ART
AUTOGRA
READ MORE COMICS
HUMOR ADVENTURE ROMANCE
CAPS
COSTUME CONTES

CRASHING THE CON by **Sergio Aragonés**. Colors by **Serban Cristescu**

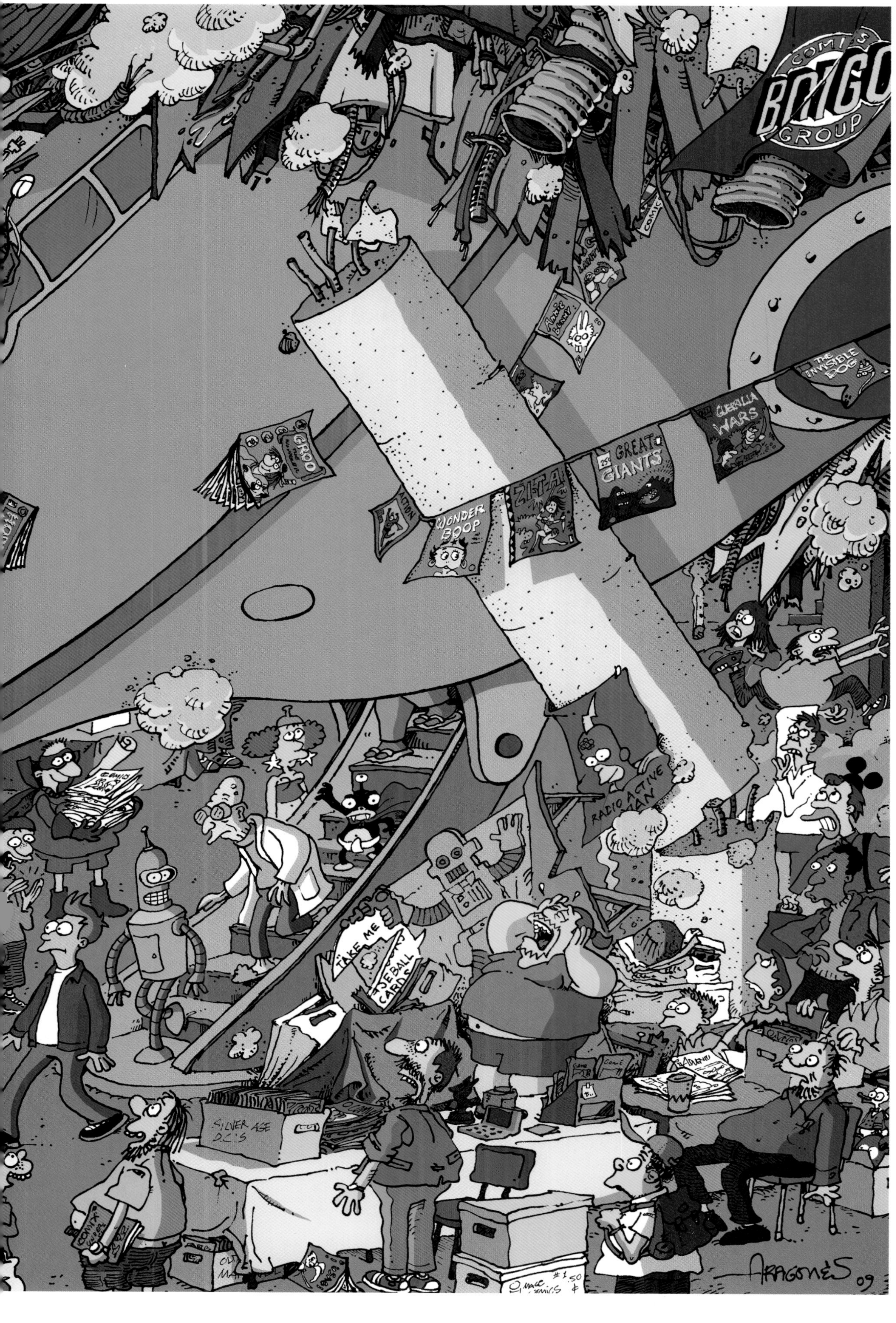

COMICS
BONGO
GROUP
THE INVISIBLE DOG
GUERRILLA WARS
25¢ GREAT GIANTS
ZITA
WONDER BOOP
ACTION
GROO
RADIO ACTIVE MAN
TAKE ME
SILVER AGE D.C.'S
ARAGONES 09

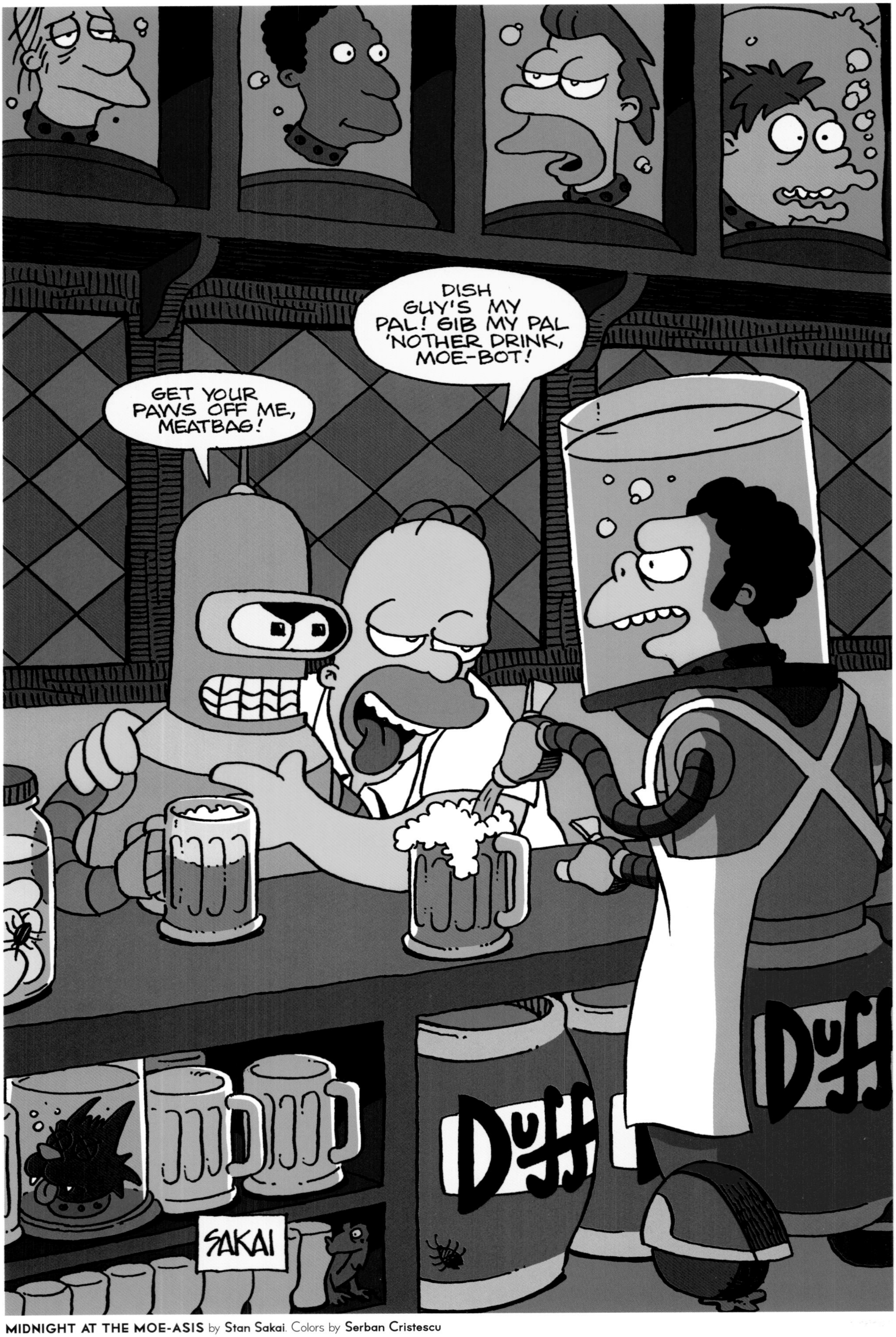
GET YOUR PAWS OFF ME, MEATBAG!
DISH GUY'S MY PAL! GIB MY PAL 'NOTHER DRINK, MOE-BOT!
Duff
Duff
SAKAI

MIDNIGHT AT THE MOE-ASIS by **Stan Sakai**. Colors by **Serban Cristescu**

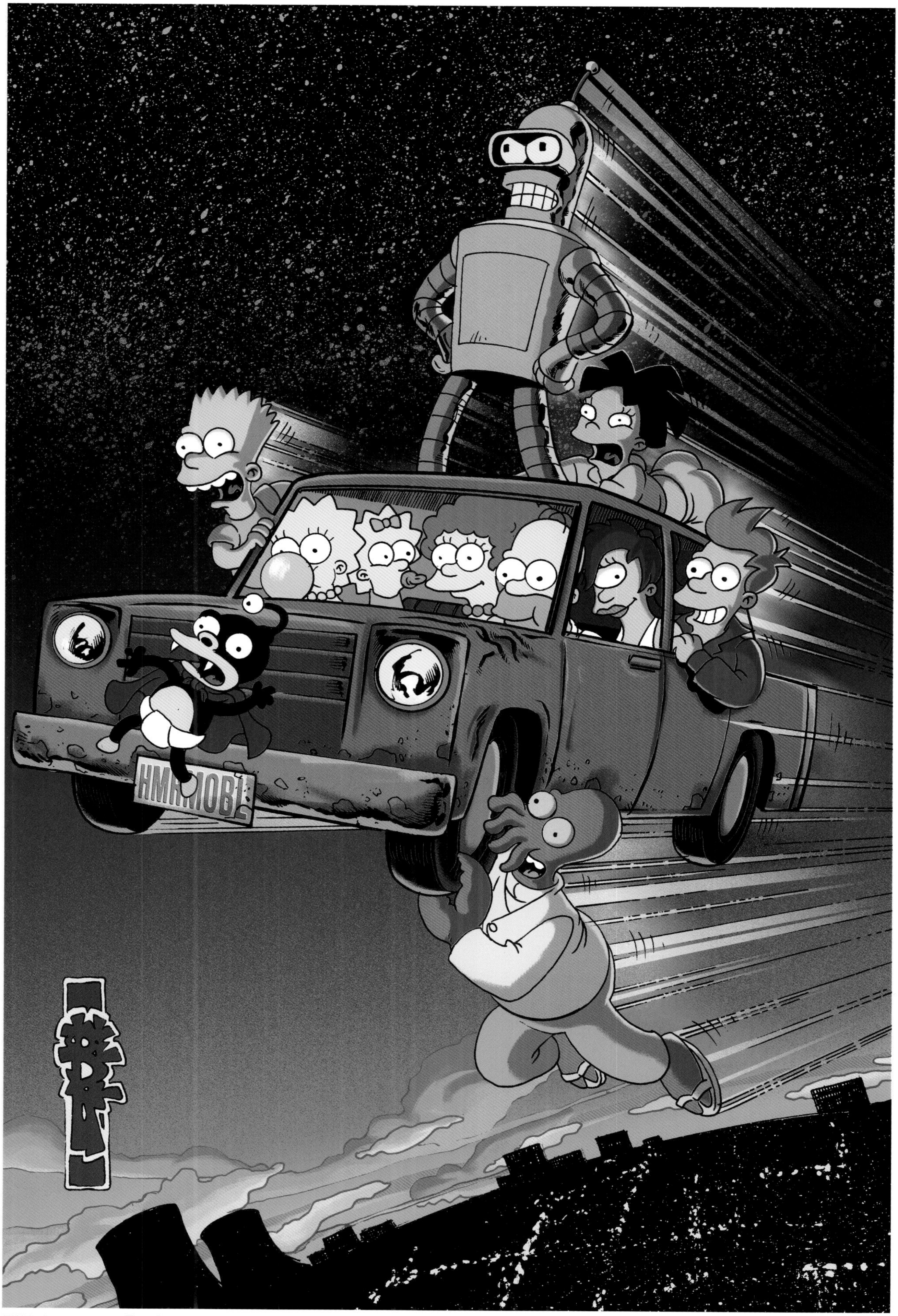
HMRMOBL

FLYING UNITED by **Tone Rodriguez**. Colors by **Serban Cristescu**

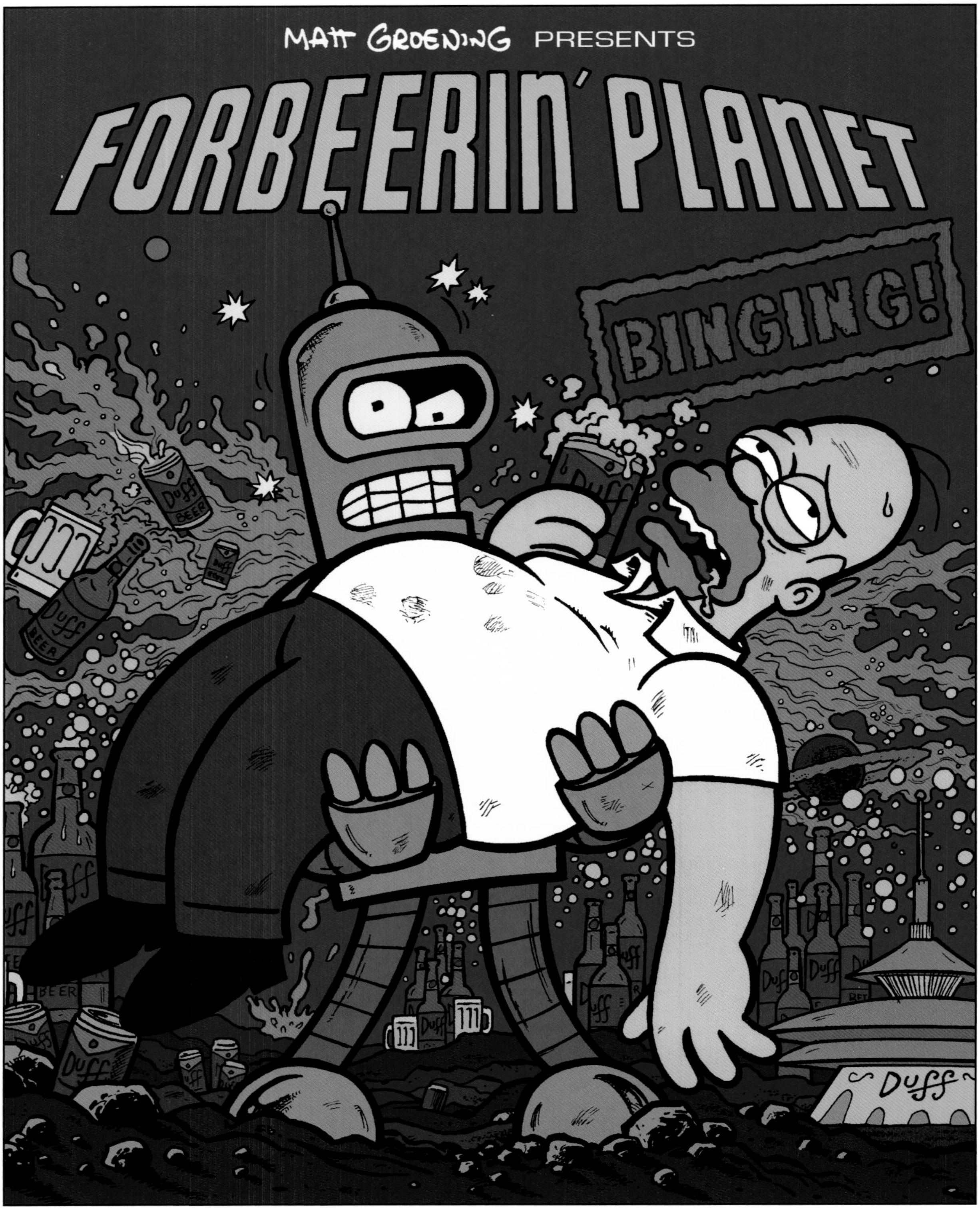
MATT GROENING PRESENTS
FORBEERIN' PLANET
BINGING!
Duff
BEER

STARRING HOMER SIMPSON . MARGE SIMPSON . DUFFMAN

WITH VIC TAYBACK AND INTRODUCING BENDER, THE ROBOT DRUNK

BASED ON A HALLUCINATION BY BARNEY GUMBLE

SCANNED ON A COMPUTER

PRODUCED BY DIXON TICONDEROGA IN COMICBOOKSCOPE AND COLOR

A GROENING-DORKIN-DYER PICTURE

FORBEERIN' PLANET by **Evan Dorkin**. Colors by **Sarah Dyer**

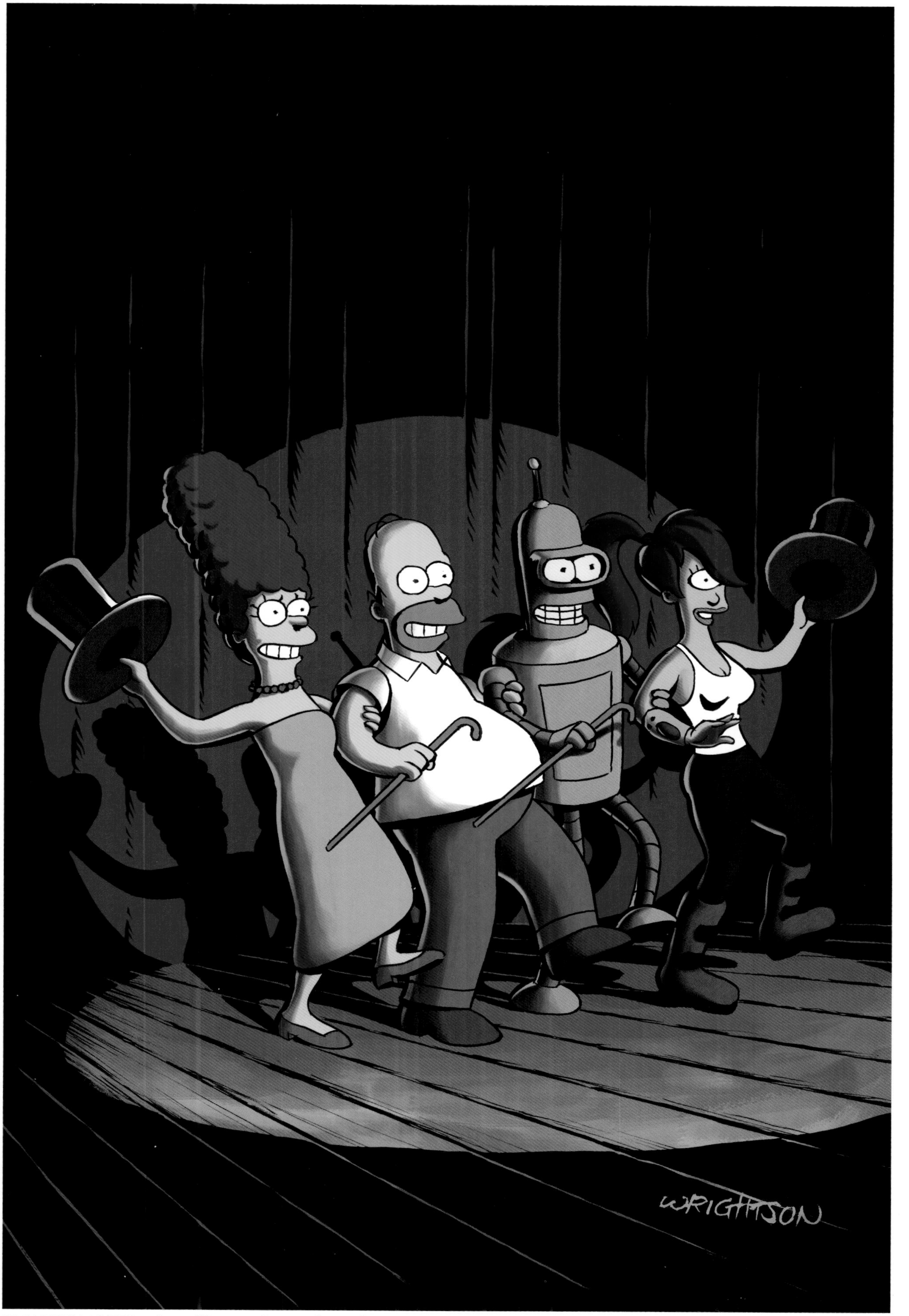
WRIGHTSON

BROADWAY MAYBES by **Bernie Wrightson**. Colors by **Serban Cristescu**

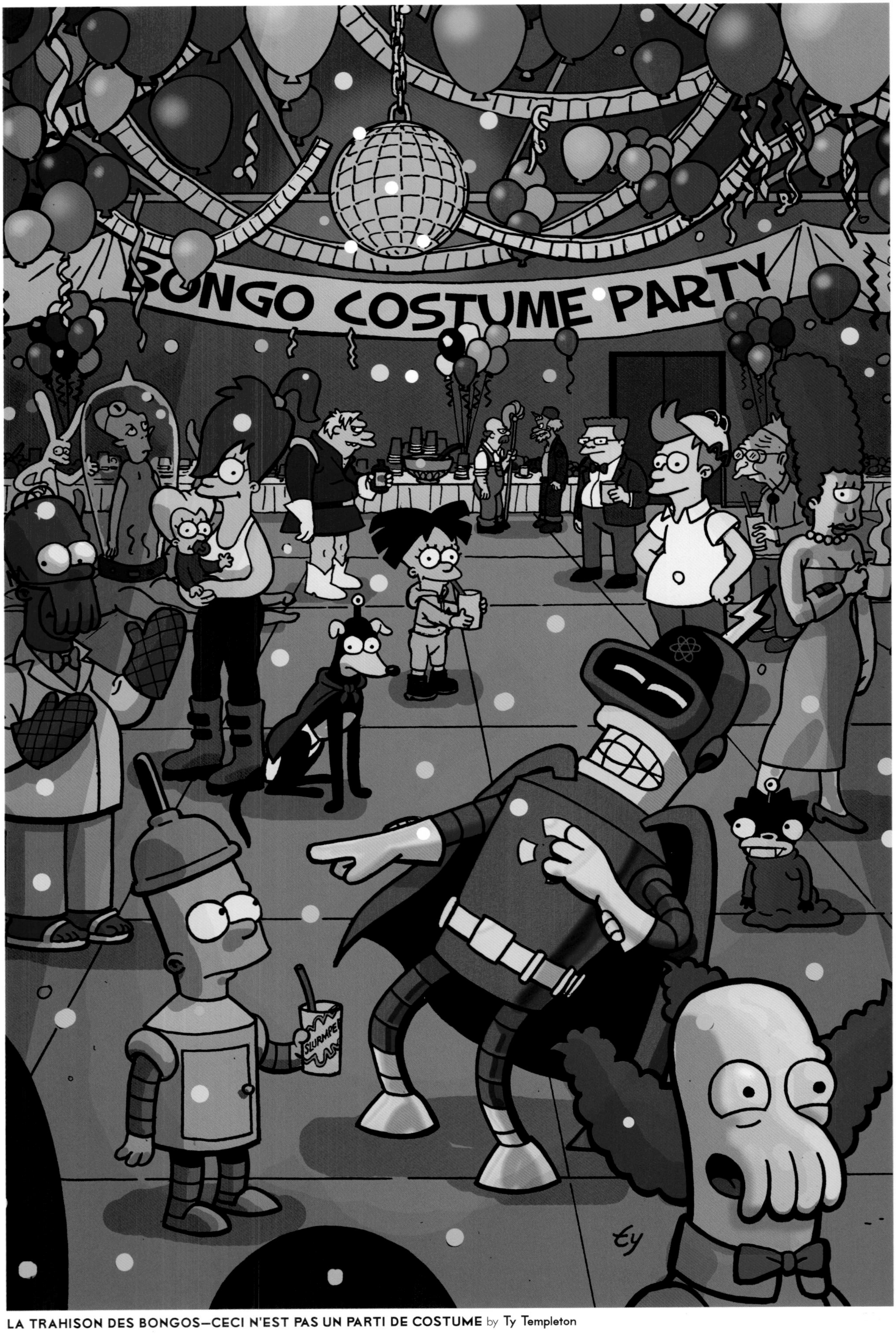
BONGO COSTUME PARTY
SLURMPE!

LA TRAHISON DES BONGOS—CECI N'EST PAS UN PARTI DE COSTUME by Ty Templeton

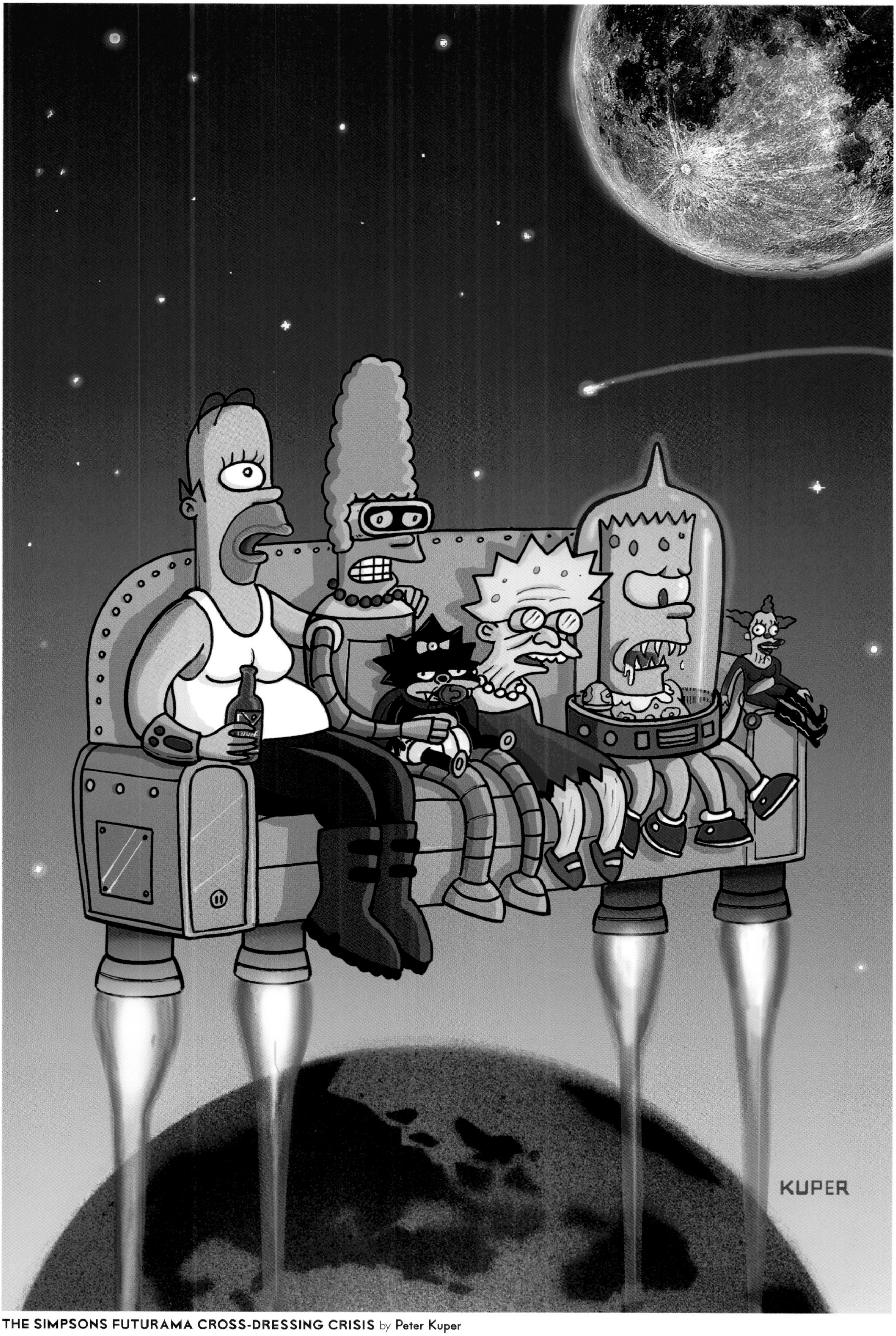
KUPER

THE SIMPSONS FUTURAMA CROSS-DRESSING CRISIS by Peter Kuper

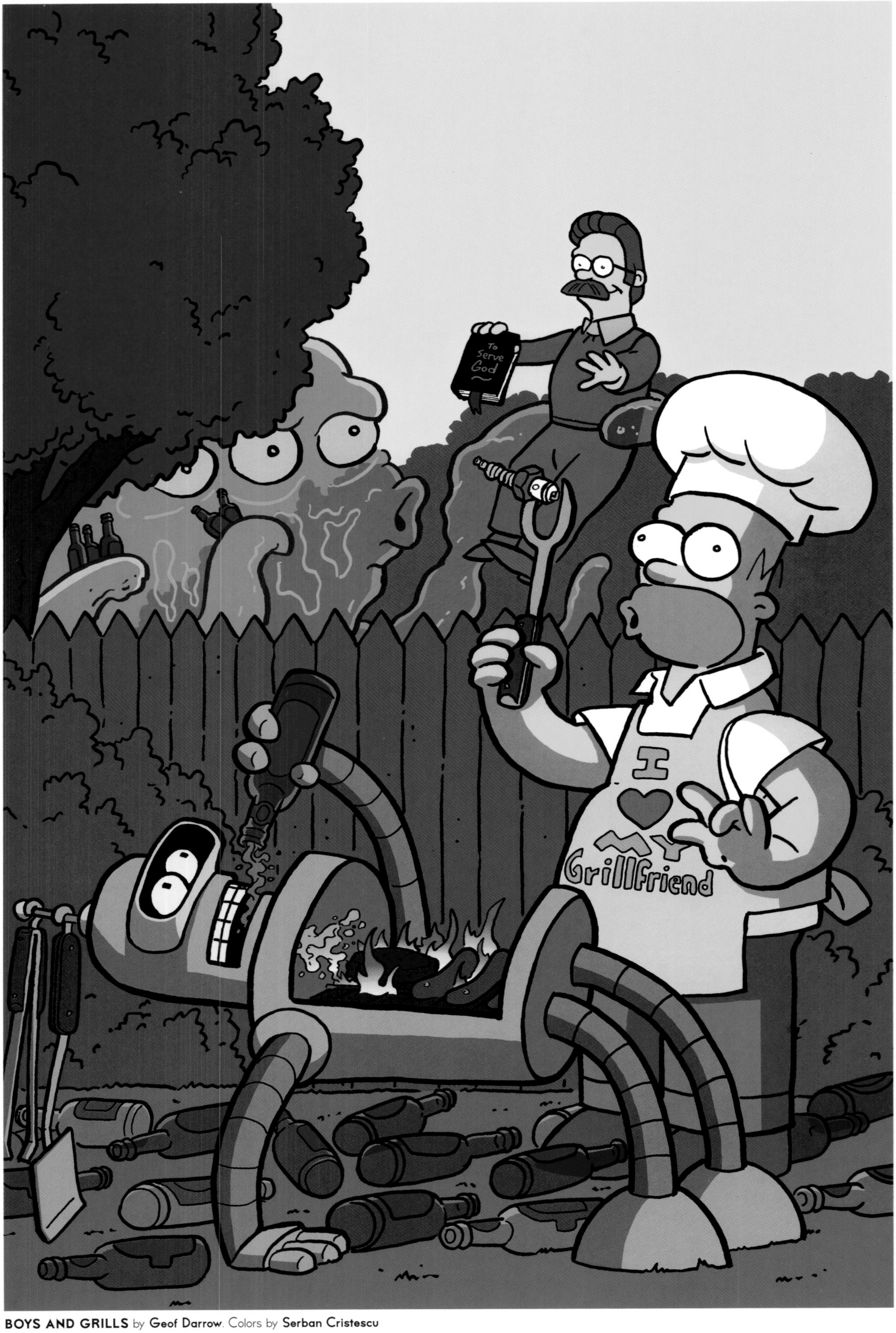
To Serve God
I ♥ MY Grillfriend

BOYS AND GRILLS by **Geof Darrow**. Colors by **Serban Cristescu**

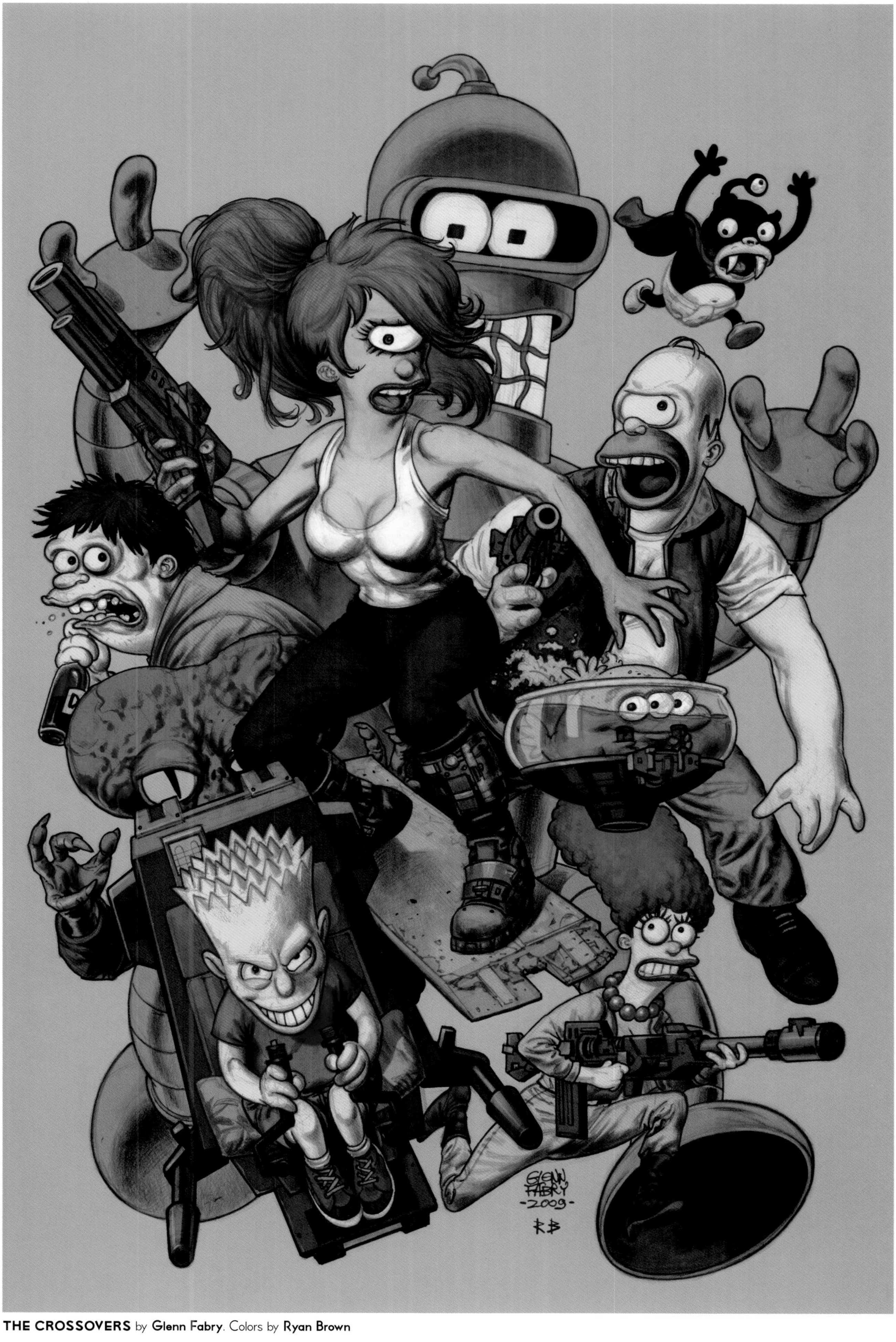
GLENN FABRY -2009-
RB

THE CROSSOVERS by **Glenn Fabry**. Colors by **Ryan Brown**

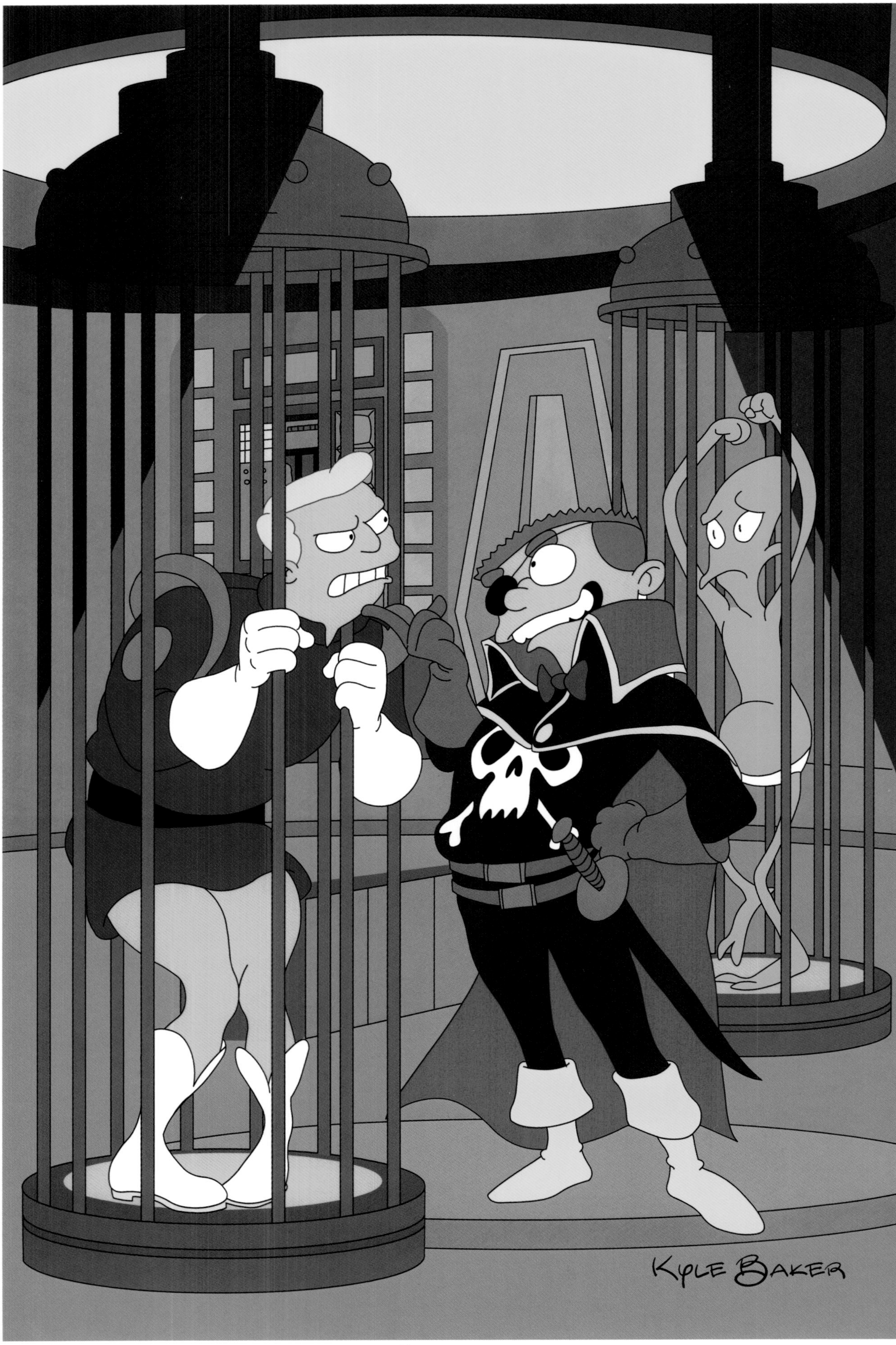
KYLE BAKER

THAT'S NOT THE KIND OF CROSSOVER I HAD IN MIND by Kyle Baker

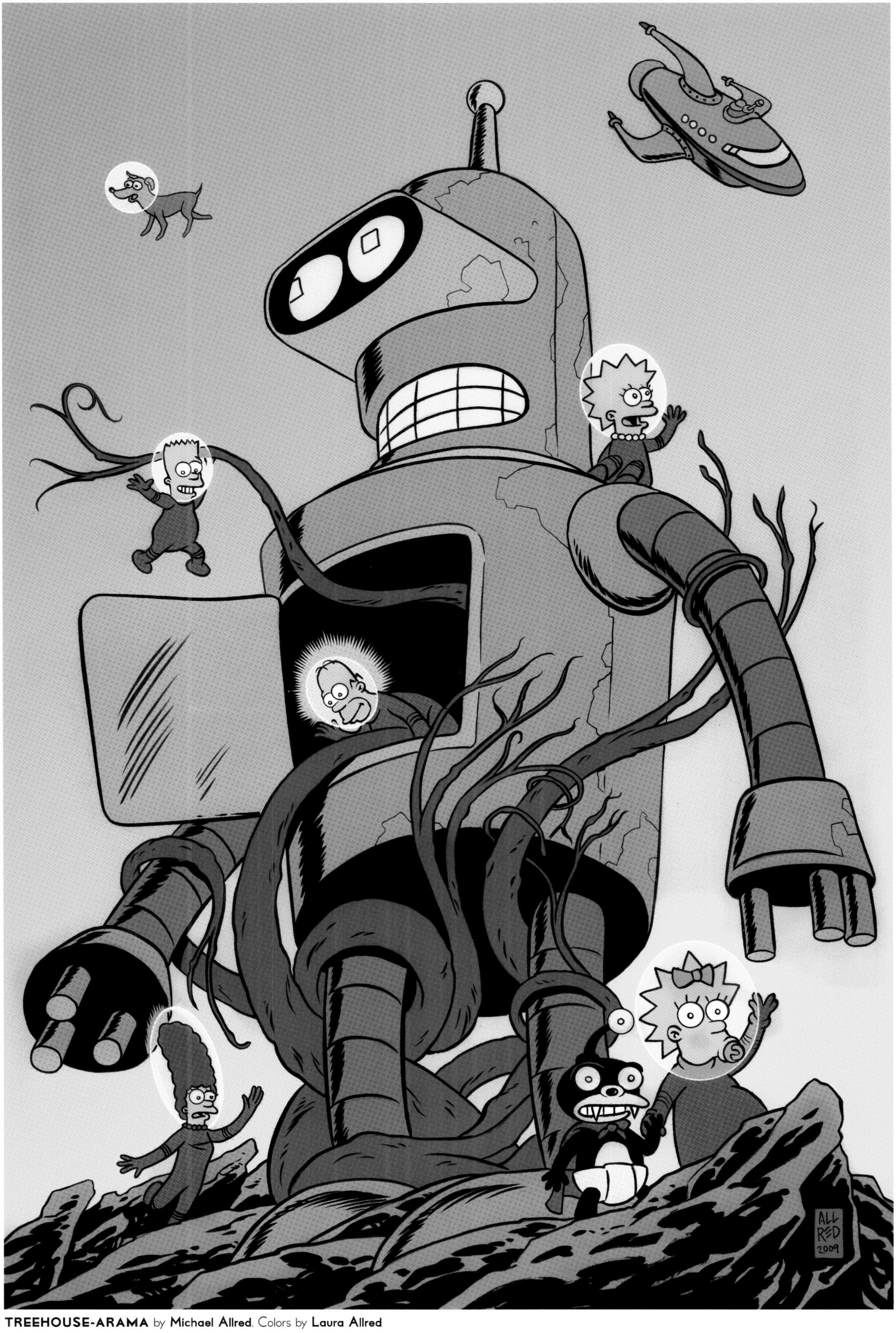
ALL
RED
2009

TREEHOUSE-ARAMA by **Michael Allred**. Colors by **Laura Allred**

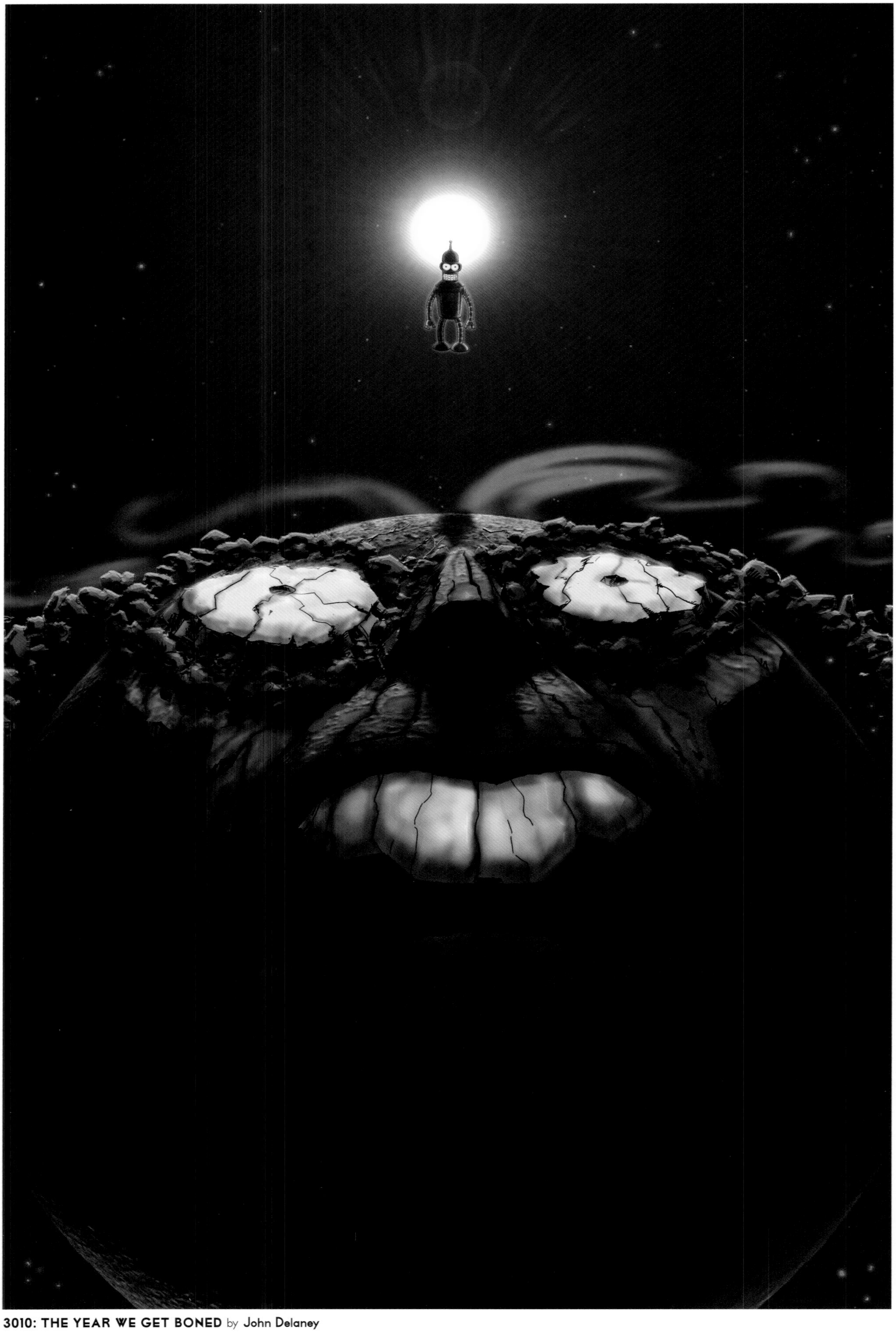

3010: THE YEAR WE GET BONED by John Delaney

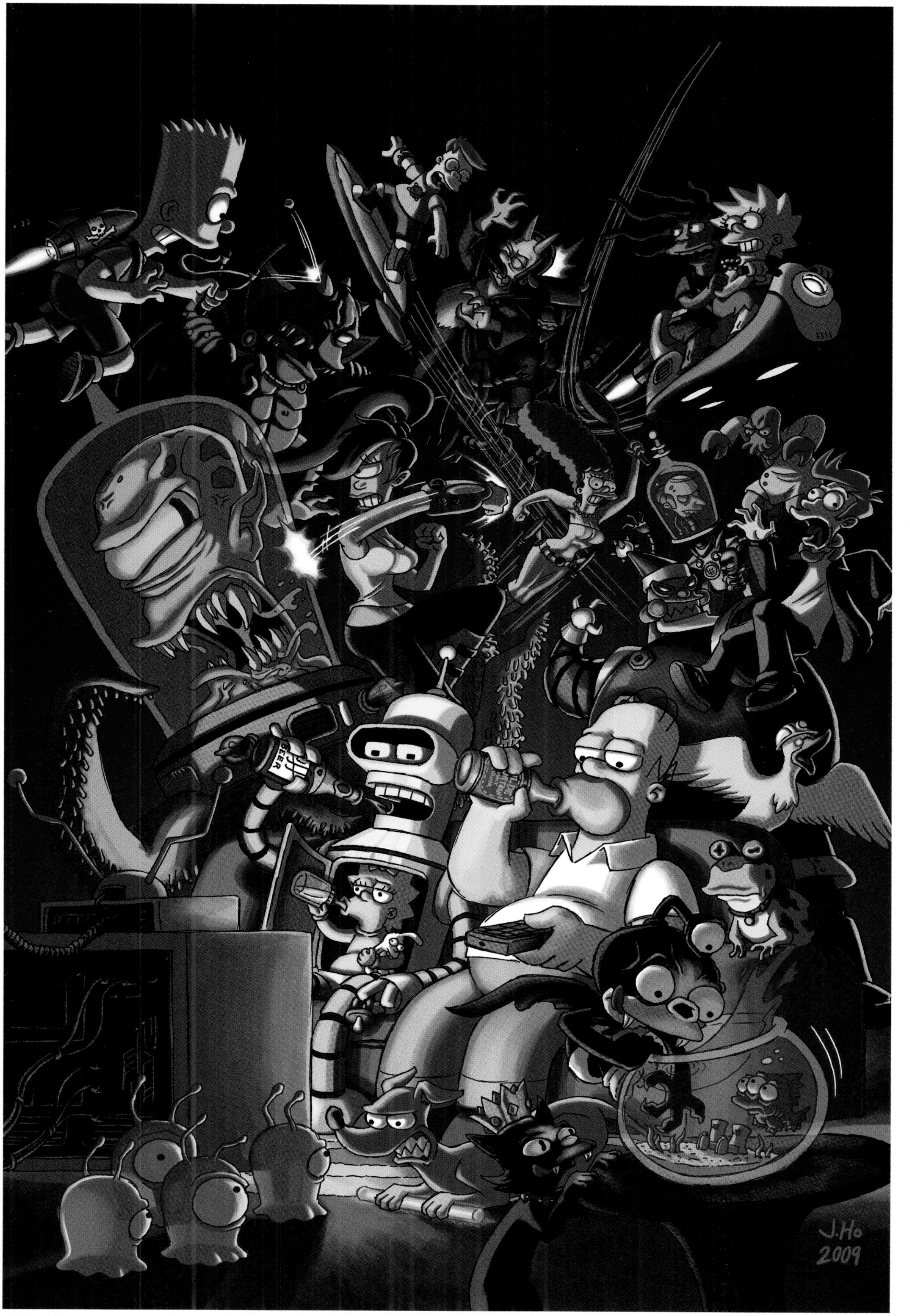
J.Ho
2009

COSMIC BROUHAHA by Jason Ho

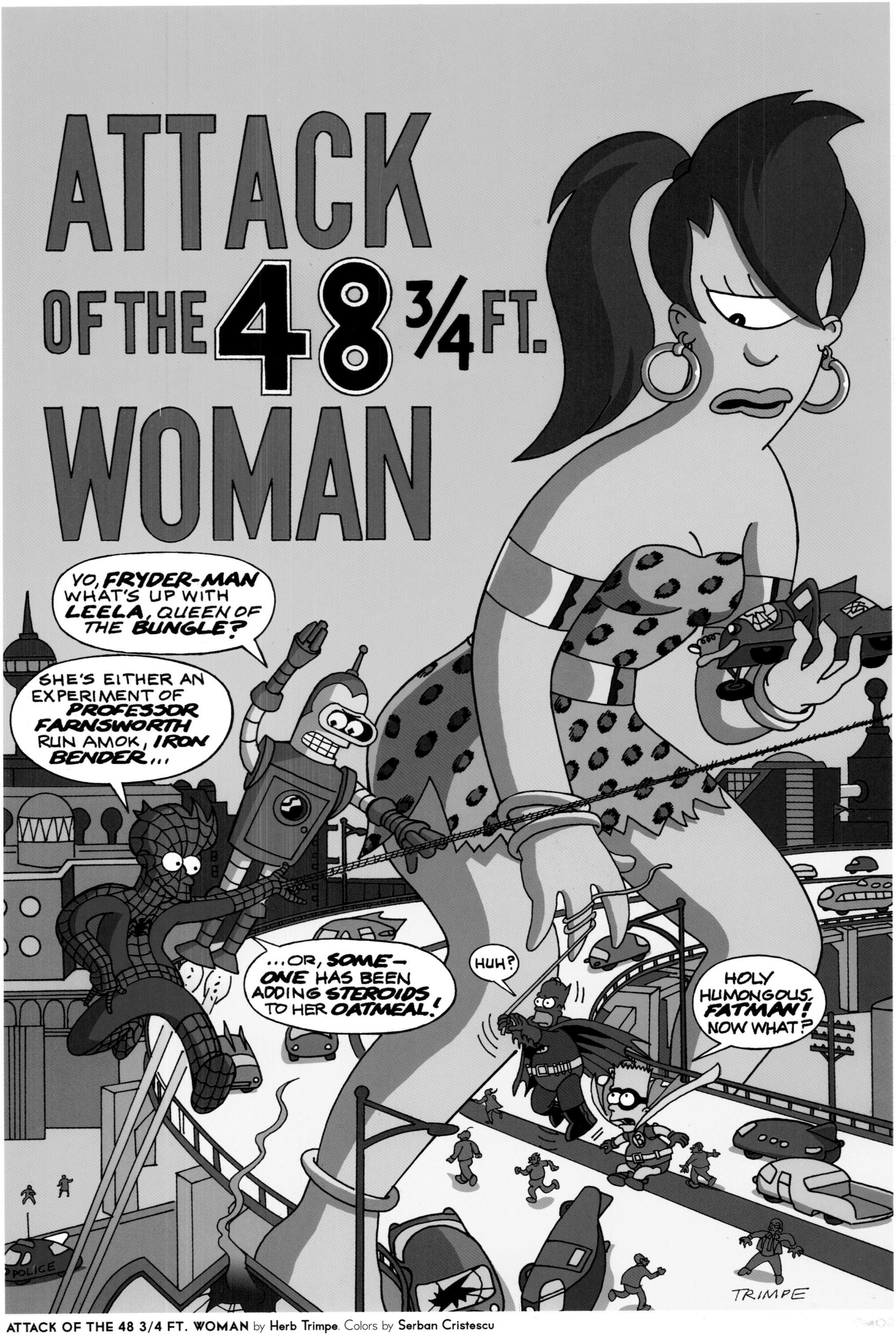
ATTACK OF THE 48 3/4 FT. WOMAN
YO, FRYDER-MAN WHAT'S UP WITH LEELA, QUEEN OF THE BUNGLE?
SHE'S EITHER AN EXPERIMENT OF PROFESSOR FARNSWORTH RUN AMOK, IRON BENDER...
...OR, SOME-ONE HAS BEEN ADDING STEROIDS, TO HER OATMEAL!
HUH?
HOLY HUMONGOUS, FATMAN! NOW WHAT?
POLICE
TRIMPE

ATTACK OF THE 48 3/4 FT. WOMAN by **Herb Trimpe**. Colors by **Serban Cristescu**

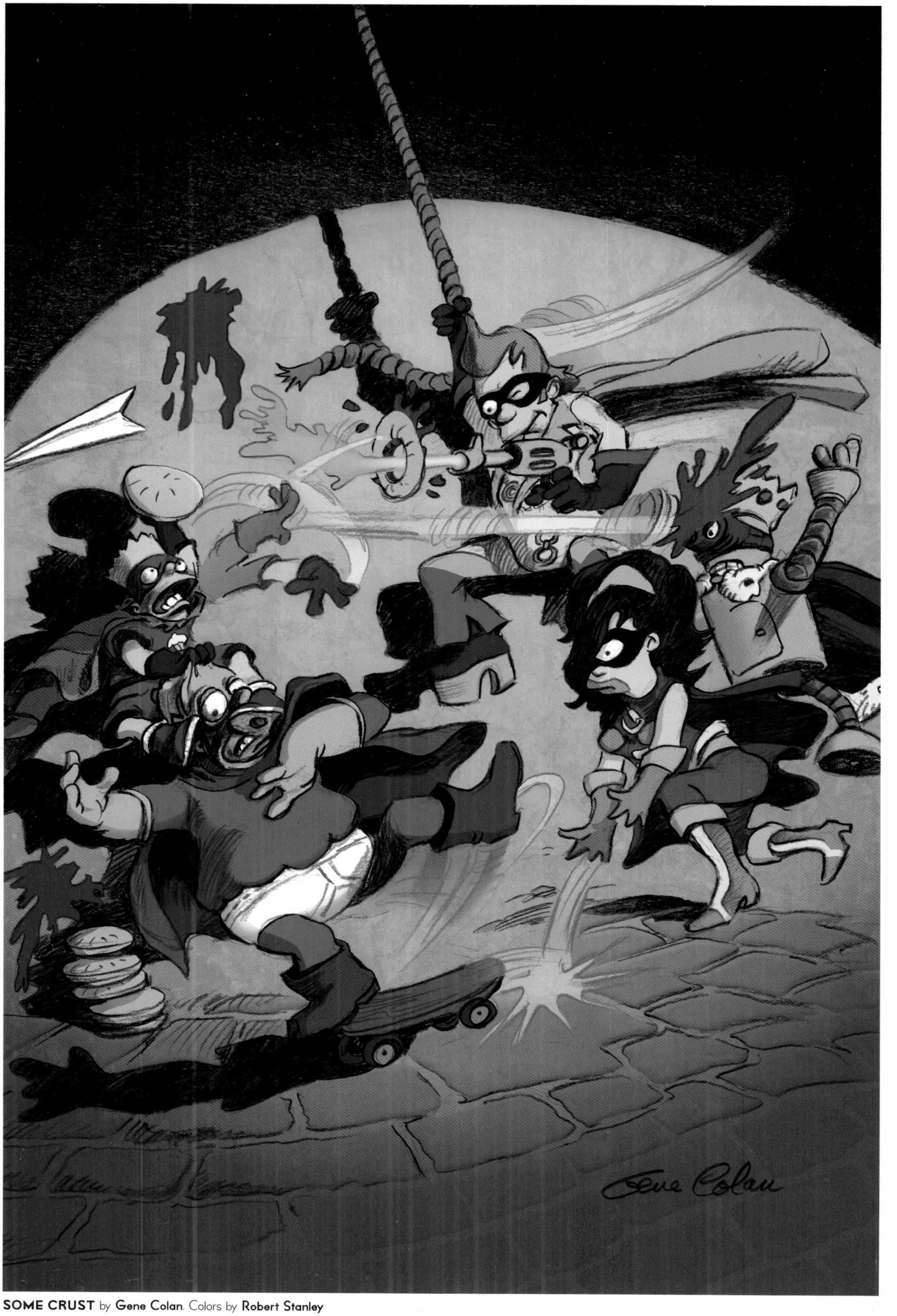
Gene Colan

SOME CRUST by **Gene Colan**. Colors by **Robert Stanley**

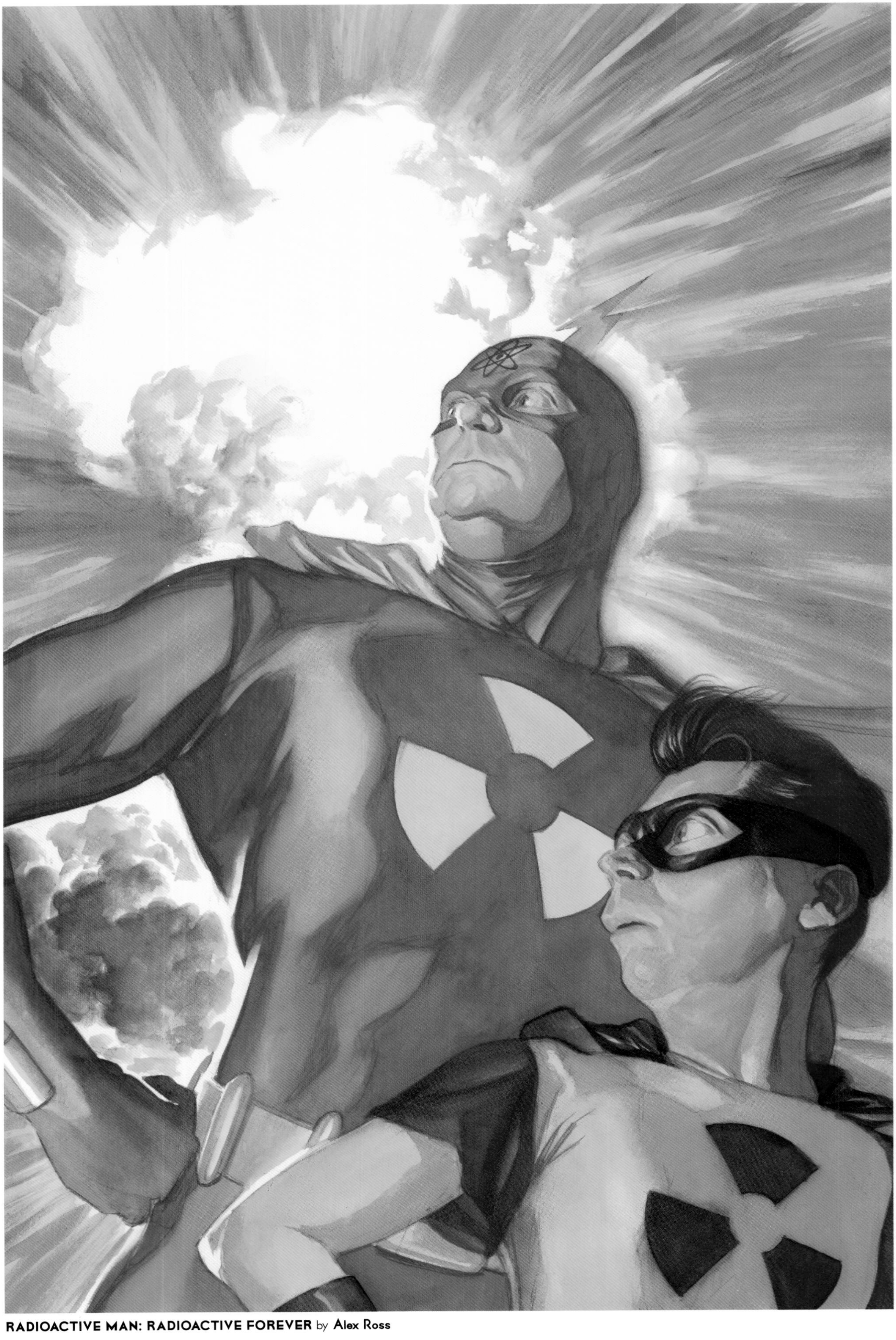

RADIOACTIVE MAN: RADIOACTIVE FOREVER by Alex Ross